ASPECTS OF TOURISM 16
Series Editors: Chris Cooper (*University of Queensland, Australia*),
C. Michael Hall (*University of Otago, New Zealand*)
and Dallen Timothy (*Arizona State University, USA*)

Strategic Management for Tourism Communities
Bridging the Gaps

Peter E. Murphy and Ann E. Murphy

D0914551

CHANNEL VIEW PUBLICATIONS
Clevedon • Buffalo • Toronto

We wish to dedicate this book to
Susan and Margaret Murphy,
the two family members
working hard behind the scenes

Library of Congress Cataloging in Publication Data
Murphy, Peter E.
Strategic Management for Tourism Communities: Bridging the Gaps
Peter E. Murphy and Ann E. Murphy.
Aspects of Tourism: 16
Includes bibliographical references
1. Tourism–Management. 2. Strategic planning. I. Murphy, Ann E. II. Title. III. Series.
G155.A1M859 2004
910'.68'4–dc22   2004002644

British Library Cataloguing in Publication Data
A catalogue entry for this book is available from the British Library.

ISBN 1-873150-84-9 (hbk)
ISBN 1-873150-83-0 (pbk)

Channel View Publications
An imprint of Multilingual Matters Ltd

UK: Frankfurt Lodge, Clevedon Hall, Victoria Road, Clevedon BS21 7HH.
USA: 2250 Military Road, Tonawanda, NY 14150, USA.
Canada: 5201 Dufferin Street, North York, Ontario, Canada M3H 5T8.

Typeset by Archetype-IT Ltd (http://www.archetype-it.com).
Printed and bound in Great Britain by the Cromwell Press.

Strategic Management
for Tourism Communities

ASPECTS OF TOURISM
Series Editors: Professor Chris Cooper, *University of Queensland, Australia*
Dr C. Michael Hall, *University of Otago, Dunedin, New Zealand*
Dr Dallen Timothy, *Arizona State University, Tempe, USA*

Aspects of Tourism is an innovative, multifaceted series which will comprise
authoritative reference handbooks on global tourism regions, research volumes, texts
and monographs. It is designed to provide readers with the latest thinking on tourism
world-wide and in so doing will push back the frontiers of tourism knowledge. The
series will also introduce a new generation of international tourism authors, writing
on leading edge topics. The volumes will be readable and user-friendly, providing
accessible sources for further research. The list will be underpinned by an annual
authoritative tourism research volume. Books in the series will be commissioned that
probe the relationship between tourism and cognate subject areas such as strategy,
development, retailing, sport and environmental studies. The publisher and series
editors welcome proposals from writers with projects on these topics.

Other Books in the Series
Classic Reviews in Tourism
   Chris Cooper (ed.)
Progressing Tourism Research
   Bill Faulkner, edited by Liz Fredline, Leo Jago and Chris Cooper
Managing Educational Tourism
   Brent W. Ritchie
Recreational Tourism: Demand and Impacts
   Chris Ryan
Coastal Mass Tourism: Diversification and Sustainable Development in Southern
Europe
   Bill Bramwell (ed.)
Sport Tourism Development
   Thomas Hinch and James Higham
Sport Tourism: Interrelationships, Impact and Issues
   Brent Ritchie and Daryl Adair (eds)
Tourism, Mobility and Second Homes
   C. Michael Hall and Dieter Müller
Strategic Management for Tourism Communities: Bridging the Gaps
   Peter E. Murphy and Ann E. Murphy
Oceania: A Tourism Handbook
   Chris Cooper and C. Michael Hall (eds)
Tourism Marketing: A Collaborative Approach
   Alan Fyall and Brian Garrod
Music and Tourism: On the Road Again
   Chris Gibson and John Connell
Tourism Development: Issues for a Vulnerable Industry
   Julio Aramberri and Richard Butler (eds)
Nature-Based Tourism in Peripheral Areas: Development or Disaster?
   C. Michael Hall and Stephen Boyd (eds)
Tourism, Recreation and Climate Change
   C. Michael Hall and James Higham (eds)

For more details of these or any other of our publications, please contact:
Channel View Publications, Frankfurt Lodge, Clevedon Hall,
Victoria Road, Clevedon, BS21 7HH, England
http://www.channelviewpublications.com

Contents

Acknowledgements

This book has taken several years to come to fruition and along the way there has been a collection of special people who have helped us put our facts and ideas together. We would like to acknowledge the growing and thoughtful literature provided by our peers in a variety of disciplines and the assistance of Ms Yan Zhang in accessing that material. We would like to thank our partners in the development of the four cases – Paul Miller, Wayne Kayler-Thomson, Theresa Szymanis and Robin Saunders. Their contributions have provided the real examples to flesh out our skeleton of ideas and observations.

In our various travels and work experiences we have been fortunate to come across many industry and government contributors committed to making tourism work for the industry and the host community. Among those who have been particularly helpful and inspirational are Rick Lemon, John Parker, Melissa McLean and Lorne Whyte in British Columbia. On the Florida Keys, particular thanks are due to the Monroe County Marathon City Council, Frank Greenman, the Board of County Commissioners, Shirley Freeman, and dedicated community advocates, especially Betty Vale. In Victoria, Australia, the helpful ideas and comments from Nicholas Hunt, Kathryn MacKenzie, David Riley and Tom O'Toole are appreciated.

Last, and by no means least, we wish to thank Glennis Derrick and the reviewers of the draft text. Glennis has been a wonderful person to work with in the preparation of this manuscript, transforming our scrawl and continuous changes into the document it is today. The two reviewers of the original draft provided much encouragement and some invaluable references. Plus we would like to thank the authors who have allowed us to reproduce their work and illustrations as cited individually.

With this significant academic and practitioner input it is hoped we have created a thoughtful and useful work. If there are any mistakes of fact or misinterpretations they remain the responsibility of the authors alone.

Part 1

Prologue

Setting the Scene

Many communities are entering the global tourism market in a naive and dangerous manner. One danger is to misread the market and the community's true competitive position within that market, leading to disappointing development results and financial losses. Another danger occurs when communities are successful with their development plans, and become a recognised destination but fail to appreciate the changes that tourism can bring. These changes can result in a form of community that may not have been foreseen or even wanted by local residents. While much has been made of tourism problems, little has been written about practical and widely applicable techniques that communities can use to develop tourism offerings that meet the needs of both tourists and residents.

This book takes a business and community approach to assessing and offering guidance on strategic tourism management. This dual approach is based on assessing the economic feasibility of pursuing tourism options that further community goals and objectives. Tourism is a business that requires extensive planning, marketing and investment in products and services. At the same time tourism relies on the host communities in which it occurs. The attitudes of local people, the quality of the environment and the availability of desired products and services are all factors in whether tourism will be a success. Without a solid understanding of the business and community aspects of tourism, resources can be squandered on inappropriate tourism developments that fail to meet the expectations of either the host community or the tourists.

Background

'Those who ignore history are doomed to repeat it,' is the message from researchers who warn of the negative impacts of tourism. In his book *Devil's Bargains* Rothman (1998) relates the disappointment experienced by many small and rural communities in the western reaches of the United States during the twentieth century. He notes that tourism often turned into a 'devil's bargain' for many of the regions and communities that embraced the industry as an economic boon. The tourism problems arose from the 'irrevocable changes' that occurred in 'unanticipated and uncontrollable ways' (Rothman, 1998: 10). He notes that 'community leaders make

3

imperfect choices based on insufficient information without recognising the consequences . . . The economist's fallacious dream of rational choice based on perfect information collapses as unanticipated consequences overwhelm expectations in tourist communities' (Rothman, 1998: 17). Like many before him Rothman finds tourism lacking, especially with regard to its promise of economic salvation, yet offers no solutions.

Tourism development 'solutions' in terms of practical advice derived from real world situations are what can help communities to decide what type of development works best for them. Tourism, like other resource industries, alters the landscape and social fabric of destination areas, while much of its development pace and direction are guided by broader global forces. Tourism, with its high visibility, is often seen as the primary cause of change rather than as one of many agents. However, the tourism industry is just a small part of larger global forces that are transforming the world's economic, environmental and societal relations. The combined impacts of the growth in the influence of international economic unions and multimedia organisations, changes in population patterns, environmental degradation, shifting political allegiances, terrorism and evolving cultural practices are all agents of profound global change.

As Brown (1998: 49) observes, 'unless we are prepared to sit back and literally do nothing, we have to expect that everything we do will have some effect on the environment'. The ability to guide the development of tourism in a manner that meets communities' needs is dependent upon understanding the factors intrinsically tied to this industry and then directing tourism development in a manner that promotes desired end-states, while mitigating less desirable impacts. Communities that are prepared to learn from the history and experiences of the tourism industry are better suited to adopt management plans that meet their needs.

On the whole tourism has been a successful growth industry since the end of World War II and holds much promise for the future. The key to successful and sustainable tourism development is to engage in this activity with as much careful analysis and planning as possible. Due diligence is also required in terms of monitoring industry progress and making appropriate adjustments to ensure that it is managed in a manner that meets stakeholder requirements.

Tourism Expectations

So much has been expected of tourism that it has often fallen short of the mark. Part of the problem has been its exaggerated role as an economic and social panacea with associated unrealistic expectations in many communities. Community enthusiasm or desperation can override economic realities when considering an area's tourism potential. Business issues relating to tourism supply and demand, accessibility and financing options all need to be considered in combination with community needs and available resources.

Another factor is that tourism is a more complex industry than many appreciate, since it crosses the traditional divisions of primary through to quaternary industries. Tourism's natural attractions can be equated with other primary industries in that they all are dependant on natural resources. Tourism's resort development and associated infrastructure are developed along the manufacturing lines of secondary industries. As a major service industry, tourism depends on varied customer segments each with their specific experience expectations. Tourism's global scale and need for detailed destination and travel information has resulted in its gaining a prominent place on the Internet and in other quaternary information businesses.

Part of the problem in developing realistic tourism expectations has been the limited focus of past research. Tourism researchers have restricted themselves in the main to engaging in critical analysis of the industry and its impacts rather than taking the next progressive step to prescriptive recommendations. In this regard the comments of Buck (1977) and Brown (1998) are very germane. Buck, an anthropologist, was critical of fellow social scientists for simply criticising the industry's efforts to represent culture rather than showing it how to produce more authentic and educational experiences. Brown, the past editor of *Tourism Management*, rightly states that, 'the proponents of alternative tourism have been better at highlighting the negative side of tourism than at providing cures' (Brown, 1998: 100).

Purpose

The purpose of this book is to provide strategic management guidance from a wide range of researchers and practitioners to assist communities in meeting their tourism expectations. Source material is drawn from the fields of social science, planning, business studies and environmental management. The book should be viewed as a sequel to Peter Murphy's book, *Tourism: A Community Approach*. That first book, which was published in 1985, has been described by some as a seminal work (Wheeler, 1994). This book builds on the multi-dimensional aspects promoted in the first book, while providing more of a business-oriented framework. It also builds on the community involvement principles that were presented in the first book. Collaborative decision-making processes are presented as an integral and practical way to ensure that stakeholders guide and evaluate the tourism plans and strategies to ensure their goals and objectives as well as those of the larger community are met. This new focus reflects the experiences of the authors since the original book was published. We believe that communities are better positioned to take the prescribed 'community approach' to tourism if they allow their actions to be guided by key business management principles and adopt a strategic management focus.

Professor Peter Murphy has over 25 years' experience as a tourism researcher, professor and consultant. He has served on several tourism boards, including Tourism Victoria in BC, Canada and Bendigo Tourism in Victoria, Australia, and been involved in a range of practical tourism studies, most notably the Visitor Surveys conducted via Tourism Victoria from 1989 to 1997. Professor Murphy has received many distinguished awards including the following: Association of American Geographers; Roy Wolfe Award for contributions to Tourism Research (1992); elected to the International Academy for the Study of Tourism (1995); and granted the Rino and Diana Grollo Endowed Chair on Tourism and Hospitality at La Trobe University (1997) in Melbourne.

In 1990, Professor Peter Murphy transferred from his long-standing association with Geography to a Faculty of Business to continue his research and teaching in tourism management. There he found many business principles and techniques relevant to resident and social science aspirations for community participation in tourism. As a result of his increased work with business entrepreneurs and tourism organisations he has found a willingness by these groups to work with the broader community, to achieve the type of community and quality of life that can be enjoyed by all.

In addition to representing an extension of academic thought, this book benefits from the views and experiences of an additional author – Ann Murphy, AICP. During Ann's career as a professional planner, she has worked for public and private firms in Canada, the US and Australia. Most of her tourism planning work has been conducted in British Columbia, Canada and the Florida Keys, in the United States. While working in the Florida Keys she initiated and oversaw the first ever Keys-wide survey of resident attitudes towards tourism. She is currently working on a PhD in Law at the University of Melbourne that explores ways in which Alternative Dispute Resolution techniques can be used to create solutions for community land use planning issues. She is committed to finding ways in which communities can survive and prosper as social units while engaging in a range of commercial endeavours, such as tourism, that enable them to meet their goals and objectives.

In this book, tourism is viewed from a business perspective and within that framework advocates a community development and strategic management approach. To achieve this objective it examines the multidimensional nature of tourism and its significant economic, social and environmental impacts, while emphasising certain features over others. These features start from the premise that tourism is a business, and to properly understand a community's tourism prospects, impacts and responsibilities the whole activity must be analysed in a business context.

To do this we will examine how broad business principles can be, and in some cases have been, applied to the development and management of tourism. The ways that modern business science overlaps with the social science's interest in tourism and its development issues will be demonstrated in the process.

To make the best of the situation where more communities are becoming involved with tourism, either willingly or unwillingly, requires a particular type of tourism development and planning. With respect to the emerging tourism community, it reflects a strong sense of belonging together and wanting to preserve and enhance the home territory. Such feelings are synonymous with smaller sized communities and could be equated with localised destination areas. The tourism within these communities is likely to include a combination of international tourists, domestic tourists and excursionists. Ideally an area's tourism industry is a mixture of direct, indirect and induced businesses, with the actual combination determined by the size, resources and aspirations of the host community and its travel markets.

Hence this book defines strategic tourism management at the community level as follows:

> Tourism activity that engages local community interests in a meaningful partnership with the tourism industry to construct a destination product that is appropriate from a local business, societal and environmental perspective.

This definition recognises that if a community is to become a successful destination within the competitive global marketplace it needs to enter a business partnership with the industry. Therefore each party brings to the table their own assets and priorities to see if there is a mutual and sustainable business opportunity. If it is felt that such an opportunity exists then the community and local industry could proceed together along established business lines muted with societal and environmental awareness and obligations. Community tourism is moving toward the positions of mutually beneficial partnerships and balanced tourism development. The outlook for these positions is shown to be promising in emerging research and practices. However, these sources also reveal that it will take a great deal of understanding, resources and cooperative efforts to build and sustain robust community tourism initiatives. To assist in this process the book starts with an assessment of present-day community tourism analysis and its relationship to general business management principles.

The primary audience for this book is serious students of tourism strategic planning. This would include senior undergraduate and postgraduate students taking topics related to strategic tourism management and community tourism. It is anticipated that professionals working in tourism planning, government agencies and community activists will also find this book a useful reference tool for understanding and managing tourism impacts.

Structure

Part 1

The opening part of the book sets the scene for the later more prescriptive emphasis found in subsequent sections. The Prologue introduces the concept of community tourism and the need to develop and adhere to prescriptive management strategies to realise its potential. Chapter 1 examines key definitions and theories used in community tourism and illustrates their relevance to developing broad-based tourism development. The second chapter of this part, Chapter 2, outlines the four basic functions of business management and their relevance to the study and development of strategic tourism management in host communities.

Part 2

The second part is structured around the four functions of business management: planning, organising, leadership and controlling. Chapter 3 examines the need for planning and how communities can benefit from adopting a business and community approach to developing mutual goals and objectives for their development aspirations. Such a process will encourage community residents to come together and express their particular interests and should provide an early indication as to whether local tourism development can be a part of such objectives. Chapter 4 describes how business sets about organising its resources to produce its product and suggests similar techniques are needed in strategic tourism planning. Strategic community tourism will need to consider organising multiple interests, resources and factions to deliver products that are acceptable to markets and residents alike.

Chapter 5 examines the important element of leadership in business management and tourism development. Business research has found leadership to be a vital catalyst to success and describes the qualities and context that encourage its formation. Leadership has become a major issue in community tourism, given the need to coordinate different stakeholder aspirations within a fragmented and complex industry. As with business in general, many tourism success stories can be attributed to the presence of a local leader and often exhibit themselves in the concept of entrepreneurship. So this chapter goes on to examine the qualities of entrepreneurship and how they can assist in moving from ideas to realities. Chapter 6, completes the review of business principles with an examination of the need to control business processes and outputs in order to meet organisational goals. For strategic community tourism management this requires a blending of business control principles with the administrative responsibilities regarding the management of public resources, so the two are mutually supportive.

Part 3

The third part examines how major stakeholder groups can be expected to play their roles with respect to the four business functions. The term 'stakeholders' refers to individuals, groups or organisations with a shared interest in an issue or problem. Few communities are homogeneous in their membership or aspirations, so a key feature of strategic community tourism management is how to access and integrate these varying perspectives into a community plan. The traditional division of community stakeholder groups is supply driven, in that it includes the host community's constituents of residents, industry and government. The principal focus from a business perspective is meeting the expectations and demands of the customer. To realise the tourism potential and development appropriate for a community it is essential to look at both the demand and supply side of the equation in terms of affected parties and developmental practices. Hence this book offers information and observations on the following four stakeholder groups: customers, industry, residents and government.

Chapter 7 examines customers' perspective on community tourism based on the four business functions. The choice of the title 'customer' rather than 'tourist' is deliberate in that it involves an analysis of both tourist and resident demands. This involves reviewing traditional marketing mix information and the evolving post-modernism research implications of increased market segmentation and micromarketing. Chapter 8 turns the spotlight on the industry and starts by examining the general relevance of a select number of business strategies and techniques to community tourism. As small and medium-sized businesses make up 80–90% of the industry, attention is focused on small business development and the crucial role of the entrepreneur in this process.

Chapter 9 investigates the roles of residents and the contributions they can make to this community industry. It examines what is meant by 'meaningful participation', the type of person who is willing and able to participate in joint ventures and how such participation can be facilitated. Chapter 10 describes how government and non-government organisations (NGOs) influence and are influenced by the previously identified business principles. It discusses the growing roles of partnership and facilitation.

Part 4

The final part proposes a community tourism strategic management framework that combines business principles with the needs and views of the four stakeholder groups. Chapter 11 examines aspects of group decision-making from a conflict resolution perspective. This chapter details issues of conflict, challenges with traditional decision-making processes and ways that Alternative Dispute Resolution methods, including collaborative decision making, can be used in a tourism planning context. Chapter 12 examines the applicability of gap analysis methods to tourism planning and pulls together the concepts and practices discussed earlier in the book to present a new model – bridging community tourism gaps.

Summary

The contribution of this book to the field of tourism study is the integration of established business practices and principles with current community tourism needs and processes. To date much of the research on tourism has focused on highlighting shortcomings and problems with the industry, with a handful of best practice cases. This book offers widely applicable prescriptive measures for managing tourism within its primary setting, the destination community. It is intended as a tool to empower people to make the strategic tourism management decisions that are right for them and their communities.

Chapter 1

Definitions, Theory and Practice

Tourism Definitions and Data

Tourism as the world's largest business is a complex system of integrated parts, and each dimension receives attention at different times and locations, depending on the specific purpose and interest of the study at hand. In a recent review of tourism development in Australia, Richardson (1999: 144) states 'somewhere along the way travel and tourism (have) become the world's biggest business'. He cites a World Tourism Organisation publication as an authority on the subject:

> Tourism is now the largest industry in the world by virtually any economic measure, including gross output, value added, employment, capital investment and tax contributions. (Wheatcroft, 1994)

Others have made increasing reference to the calculations and estimates emerging from the World Travel and Tourism Council (WTTC). This influential body came into existence in 1990 with membership open to chief executive officers of companies from all sectors of tourism and tourism related businesses. Its chief goal is to demonstrate the overall significance of this disparate collection of businesses to national and world economic development. Consequently it has hired consulting companies and researchers to develop estimates of the 'industry's' overall size and contribution. It estimated that 'in 2000 travel and tourism would generate, directly and indirectly, across the global economy US$4.2 trillion of economic activity and 7.8% of total employment' (World Travel and Tourism Council, 2002).

To collect the data to make estimates of tourism's impacts requires a definition of terms that have universal application. While considerable progress has been made in this direction over the past 10 years or so the situation is still clouded by inconsistencies. Reviews of these definitional problems can be encountered in good introductory texts such as French *et al.* (1999) and Goeldner *et al.* (2000). Therefore, this book focuses on the issues involved with using tourism definitions and data for the purpose of community analysis and planning. The structure suggested by Smith (1995) in his excellent survey of tourism data analysis is adapted. Namely, we need to define the principal customer (tourist), describe that person,

11

define their trip, define the tourism businesses that serve the tourist and help to make the trips successful, and finally describe the principal components of the resulting 'tourist industry'.

The tourist

As with all sound business practice, community strategic tourism management should start with the definition of its principal customer – the tourist, but as will be discussed at a later stage another important customer is the local clientele. According to the World Tourism Organisation a tourist is a visitor who travels either internationally, by crossing an international border, or domestically by travelling within her/his own country. In both cases the visitor travels to a place other than her/his usual (home) environment, is away from home for at least one night and the purpose of the visit is not paid for by the place visited. Tourists that stay for a few hours but not overnight are called excursionists (World Tourism Organisation, 1991).

Distances travelled

Even this most recent definition of a tourist is not completely satisfactory, especially from an analytical and planning perspective. For example, there is no consistency regarding what area constitutes a usual (home) environment, because different countries and jurisdictional levels possess different scale needs. Therefore, to provide a technical-spatial description of the distance a person must travel from home before they become classified as a tourist varies from one country to another. In the United States the distance is 160 kms (100 miles), in Canada 80 kms (50 miles), and in Australia 40 kms (25 miles). Within these national classifications there is nothing to prevent state and local jurisdictions from further revising the actual cut-off distances to suit local scale conditions, so it is not uncommon to find a range of values from 30–50 kms being used to classify a traveller as a tourist. Furthermore, the remuneration clause can cause difficulties for occasions like Australia's recent and successful Olympic Games. In some cases the athletes and officials had their expenses covered by the Sydney Organising Committee of the Olympic Games, yet most would classify them as tourists to Sydney and Australia.

Masberg (1998) has explored the definition of a tourist from an interesting perspective – that of a user. She notes how the various official definitions of a tourist vary around the world and from publication to publication, so she asked managers of convention and visitors bureaux how they defined their customers. Most selected to do it by distance, a distance that 'fluctuates between 20 and 150 miles', but a considerable proportion also used 'purpose of trip', 'residence of the traveller' and 'length of stay' (Masberg, 1998: 68).

The trip

Having defined the tourist, it is also important to define the trip, which is the essence of the tourist experience. A trip can be considered to occur each time an individual or group leave their place of residence, travel a specified distance, and return home. It can involve one or more destinations, or be a circuit with no single destination. As such a trip is so intertwined with the tourist that the British Tourist Authority has long preferred to use tourist trips rather than tourist numbers as its guide to industry size and growth.

The tourism business

If there are still some difficulties associated with the definition of a tourist there is even more difficulty in defining the range of industries that serve and supply the tourist. Since the *tourism business* has grown into such a broad range of activities and penetrated every corner of the globe everyone is agreed that defining the business is a major and complex undertaking. Leiper (1979: 400) considers '(t)he tourist industry consists of all those firms, organizations, and facilities which are intended to serve the specific needs and wants of tourists'. Goeldner *et al.* (2000: 26) have developed an integrated systems model to capture the essential elements of what they call 'the tourism phenomenon'. In addition to the regular industry sectors of tourism, such as transport and accommodation, they included government and quasi-government agencies, the built environment, the natural environment and its resources, as well as activities such as research and stewardship.

As Smith (1995: 34–9) has indicated, such definitions of tourism businesses have two common features. They are supply-side oriented in that they focus on the production or supply of commodities for the tourist and not the demand for such products. These definitions also have a common weakness in terms of defining the tourism industry, in that they are so comprehensive they include ubiquitous businesses that serve local residents as well as tourists. This latter point is a major challenge to the World Travel and Tourism Council (WTTC) and any others who wish to differentiate the tourism component of businesses such as bakeries, petrol stations and restaurants that are used by both tourists and locals.

Tourism tiers of business

To solve the problem of over-counting tourism's share from such businesses and to indicate some businesses are core to the tourism industry while others are peripheral requires a more accurate and systematic description of the tourism industry and its component parts. A solution proffered to tackle this problem by the (Canadian) National Task Force on Tourism Data (1985) divides the tourist industry into two tiers of businesses, as detailed below.

- *Tier 1* tourism businesses are those that cannot exist if there were no tourism activity. Examples of these include airlines, travel agents and hotels.
- *Tier 2* tourism businesses are those that exist even in the absence of tourism, though at a lower capacity. Examples of such businesses include restaurants, taxis, and most shops. The actual division will be influenced by local conditions, with some shops and taxi businesses in small resort destinations being more reliant on the tourist trade than local customers, and hence in danger of closing if the tourist business disappeared.

To operate such a division of tourist businesses requires a classification system, so the (Canadian) National Task Force on Tourism Data based their division on the percentage of revenue expected to be generated from tourism. Utilising past empirical evidence they determined that businesses earning 91–100% of their revenue from tourists should be considered as Tier 1 tourism businesses. Those earning 10–90% of their revenue from tourists would be classed as Tier 2 tourism businesses. Like all classification systems of social activity there can be some discussion over the true break-points, but the task force attempted to act in a conservative manner to avoid any suggestion of inflating the industry's significance.

Smith (1995) considers that this system offers several important advantages. First, it is consistent with other industry definitions, in that it emphasises the commodities they produce. Second, it permits relatively easy measurement of the magnitude of the tourism activity, based on established Standard Industrial Classification (SIC) codes from industrial census studies and empirical surveys of individual firms. Third, the description recognises the WTO's distinction between tourists and excursionists. Tourists travelling long distance and staying overnight are served by Tier 1 businesses almost exclusively, while Tier 2 businesses serve both the tourists and excursionists. However, some would say there is a need for a still more elaborate classification system in order to reflect the total impact of this large and diverse industry.

One possibility is to emulate the economists' distinctions in their economic multiplier. For the direct expenditure, we could offer the task force's Tier 1 classification of tourist related facilities. For the indirect expenditure, we could offer the Tier 2 industries, but with a more conservative revenue generation classification of 25–90%. For the induced expenditure, we could include those professional firms which have become more involved in the operation of tourism businesses, yet have generally not been associated with tourism in past assessments. These include the growing number of service providers, such as lawyers, accountants, consultants and financial institutions. For such firms 10–24% would probably be a sufficient magnitude score, but some sectors, such as the consultants, can often exceed such levels of tourism-related business. One of the key areas where this type of classification is becoming important is with satellite accounting.

Satellite accounts

In several countries governments have developed tourism satellite accounts to obtain a clearer picture of tourism's size and contribution to the economy. As Campbell and Lapierre (1991: 7) state 'because tourism does not fit into the traditional industry structure established in most countries to measure economic activity, it has not enjoyed an acceptable level of "credibility" amongst other economic measures'. Consequently, Canada and other OECD countries have created statistics on the industry by 'mining' existing data sources and encouraging more standardised categorisation and survey definitions. An important part of this process has been to determine those industries that can be declared tourism industries or support activities, and to provide more rigour to the current tourist definition that includes the phrase 'away from the home environment'. Such accounting practices have helped to rationalise tourism definitions and data collection, but the cynics amongst us also realise they contributed to the development of the Goods and Service Tax (GST) and the Value Added Tax (VAT) taxes on the industry.

Meis (2001: 18–19) in a summary of Canada's experience with tourism satellite accounts (TSA) and a comparison with four other national TSA systems (Mexico, New Zealand, Norway and USA) finds the results 'from five very different and diverse countries indicate that tourism translates into significant and amazingly consistent levels of output, value added and employment'. For example, in terms of tourism's total output as a portion of the national Gross Domestic Product (GDP) for a year, Mexico's tourism was 6.5%, Canada 5%, Norway 4.3%, New Zealand 3.4% and the USA 2%. The slight difference between these figures is explained by the relative strength and diversity of the various national economies.

Community Definitions

The ability of community members to pull together and improve their quality of life is an oft-repeated story in religion, philosophy, history and everyday events. The following quote from Matthew Fox, a theologian cited by Anita Roddick, sums up some of the grandeur and promise of communities:

> Community comes from the word communion, to share a common task together. And it's in the sharing of that task that people do bigger things than they knew they were capable of. Then there is really something to celebrate. (Roddick, 2000: 55)

Two of the most remarkable aspects of communities can be their strength and their ability to get things done. The following paragraphs try to bring some structure and clarity as to what is meant by the term 'community'.

Paraphrasing Barkham's (1973: 218) description of carrying capacity the term 'community' is 'delightful in its simplicity, complex in its meaning, and difficult to define'. The simplicity of community lies in a word that has common usage, so everyone has a general idea as to what it refers. But its complexity starts to emerge when one turns to a dictionary, and finds a multiple definition. A good example of this is found in the *Macquarie Dictionary* (Delbridge & Bernard, 1988: 185) which defines community as 'a social group of any size whose members reside in a specific locality, share government and have a cultural and historical heritage'. Such multiple function definitions lead to a discussion of which aspects are more important, a question that is generally settled by the focus and intent of the inquirer.

A more recent discussion of community in terms of tourism supports many of these earlier notions and adds some new considerations. Joppe (1996: 475) claims that community is a self-defining term 'based on a sense of shared purpose and common goals'. Community can grow from mutual interests, such as caring for the environment. A community can also reflect geographic features and spatial relationships, such as natural boundaries that define a tourist region. However, a review of its definitions and uses would indicate that community has three general dimensions: social functions, spatial area and external recognition.

Social functions

The social function of people working together to create a place of their own, such as a neighbourhood, is a continuous feature of community research and planning. These social functions can be described as follows:

> Interest in community is based on the practical grounds that people increasingly are coming together to identify their needs and through co-operative action improve their social and physical environment. (Dalton & Dalton, 1975: Introduction)

This 'coming together' is viewed as a process of community building, whereby previously independent individuals or household units find they have common interests and choose to take some responsibility for what is happening to their lives. This social cohesion can take on a community development approach 'which encourages citizen participation, with or without government assistance, in efforts to improve the economic, social and cultural conditions of the locality, with emphasis on self-help' (Dalton & Dalton, 1975 : 1).

Gill (1997) feels one sociological definition of community is particularly relevant to community tourism. She focuses on Warren's definition of 'community' as:

> . . . an aggregation of people competing for space. The shape of the community, as well as its activities are characterized by differential use of space and by various processes according to which one type of people and/or type of social function succeeds another in the ebb and flow of structural change in a competitive situation. (Warren, 1977: 208)

The relevance of this definition to community tourism is derived from its being based on 'ecological principles that conceptualise change as an outcome of competition' (Gill, 1997: 56).

Gill has studied mountain resort communities and feels there are two crucial steps to understanding community tourism in those settings. The first is to recognise that residents have to compete with tourists for basic community resources such as space (on the road, on the ski slopes and in the restaurants) and facilities (such as decent and affordable housing, community centres, and public transit). The second is to recognise the number of stakeholder sub-groups that can exist within the usual classifications, resulting in very different views on what makes a good community. For example, in ski resort communities residents' views can be distinctively different along the lines of whether they are permanent residents, transient residents or second-home owners. A key discriminator between temporary residents, who are often the casual employees of the industry, and permanent residents would be the importance of property values. Temporary residents in the rental market would like to see property values kept low, whereas permanent residents would prefer to see them increase. The importance of stakeholder differences and the search for common ground will be discussed at length in Part 3 of this book.

Growth machine perspective

The link between community and development has been applied most strongly in the areas of social planning and economic development. In social planning communities can be viewed as locations of political and economic change (Gilbert, 1982). With the emphasis on change this often overlaps into struggles regarding the impact and direction of community development. Within this framework Molotch and others have developed a 'growth machine perspective' that suggests communities can become self-defined on the basis of their attitude to resource competition and future land use decisions (Logan & Molotch, 1987; Molotch, 1976).

Molotch found that three groups often emerge within a community over land development issues and that the future of the community often depends on the outcome of their power struggle. These *interest groups* can be divided into three categories.

- *Advocates* of change: Stand to benefit directly from economic and land development (e.g. land owners, speculators and investors).
- *Statesman* of the growth   Facilitators of change (e.g. Realtors machine: and bankers).
- *Local residents*:   React to the development proposals, often creating local (nested) communities of interest.

In their examination of tourism development on the Hawaiian island of Molokai, Canan and Hennessy (1989) find the growth machine hypothesis explains much about the community tensions and development patterns that had occurred there. They point out that the growth machine perspective fits the political and economic competition over Molokai's land. Over a 15-year period its tourism development primarily benefited a small exploitative coalition (of advocates and statesmen). An anti-growth coalition of primarily native Hawaiians and environmental groups appeared because of the narrow spread of tourism's benefits and its perceived negative impact on the general population's quality of life.

Although tourism development has been successful in many areas, due to its highly visible nature it is often the negative experiences that receive most exposure. In both the media and academia it is the bad news and problems that have received the majority of attention. This is only natural since bad news sells papers and research is drawn to problem areas by funding priorities and an interest in helping to ameliorate problems. But these negative inclinations can provide a distorted picture of tourism's true record.

Tourism trepidations

Anti-growth sentiments can become focused on tourism due to its highly visible nature within communities (Mormont, 1987). 'It is easy to exaggerate impacts arising from tourism' according to Jenkins (1997: 58), because it is concentrated in a few areas and it emphasises conspicuous consumption. Anti-tourism sentiments of residents can be expressed in relatively benign ways, such as taunting bumper stickers, T-shirts (Figure 1.1) and critical letters in editorial pages. Such sentiments can inspire local residents to new endeavours, as in the case of one Floridian news columnist – Carl Hiaasen. His wonderfully humorous novels, starting with *Tourist Season* (Hiaasen, 1986), often draw upon irresponsible tourism practices and development in Florida as source material. More direct action against tourists includes vandalising and removing local access and tourism promotion signs, or confronting tourists to inform them that they are not welcome.

Figure 1.1 Anti-tourism sentiment on a holiday destination T-shirt

As an emerging service based industry, the range and magnitude of tourism's positive impacts, including the opportunities associated with tourism employment are not widely known. Tourism has helped to restore the cultural vitality of many indigenous groups and helped to justify the preservation of the natural, cultural and historical heritage in many countries. Tourism's labour intensive character and array of entry level positions make it an ideal long-term employer of the typically under-employed and unemployed sectors of the labour force, including women, youth, recent immigrants and Aboriginals (Gershuny & Miles, 1983). However, by employing those who do not typically have a strong economic or political voice, many of the voices of those who benefit most directly from tourism opportunities are not heard.

Benefits that Aboriginal groups can gain from tourism have been shown to go beyond job creation and income generation, to bringing new meaning to their cultural identity and a resurgence of traditional values and practices (Grinder, 1992). Tourism's potential benefits to Aboriginal people were summed at a recent Aboriginal achievement awards presentation in Canada by the following comments. 'Thanks to the visitors' high regard for traditional First Nations' culture, young Anishinable have become conscious of their own values, which is the greatest achievement of this project' (Mann, 2000: 29).

One of the few to address this bias issue against tourism is Brown, who notes the increasingly negative tone of research into tourism impacts, yet finds few critics have taken into account the context in which tourism takes place. 'Tourism impacts are difficult to isolate, invariably interrelated and conditioned also by phenomena external to tourism' (Brown, 1998: 91). The spread of Western culture, technological advances, the growth of multinational companies and the encroachment of development into previously remote areas are evident in many of the same areas as tourism growth (Mann, 2000). However, the spread of people from foreign lands can make more of an immediate and tangible impression than the spread of ideas.

Spatial context

It is frequently difficult to isolate the social function of community from its spatial context, because the two are often synonymous. That is when a group of people are linked together by a common condition of life, be it socio-economic status or a leisure activity such as golf, they often choose to live close together. Such proximity aids the development and continuity of the common condition and in the process gives a physical and symbolic context to the sentiment. This is the philosophy behind the evolution of neighbourhoods and the social planners' attempts to either retain natural neighbourhood clusters because of their self-support and self-reliance features, or to create neighbourhoods in the hope of facilitating such features. Schwilgin (1973: 63) has described such areas as being where:

> the residents commonly recognise some association with each other based on similarities of socio-economic status, or their desires in general for the future of the area; and its shape forms an intelligibly identifiable functional unit.

One way to define a community is to assess whether or not it practices communal decision-making (Mann, 2000). The level of communal decision-making is often a reflection of the size and structure of the group. In a business sense, well organised groups whose members have strong ties to each other and who share a history of cooperation and trust often practise communal decision-making (Roddick, 2000). Therefore, smaller groups can be better positioned to practise communal decision-making than larger groups.

Appropriate planning scale

Neighbourhoods occur in numerous forms and sizes. Planners generally attempt to identify neighbourhoods in a manner that retains the social characteristics and dynamics of a community. Essential characteristics to consider, as identified by Schwilgin and others, include neighbourhoods having sufficient size and capability to become a functional planning unit. In this regard (Suttles, 1970) suggests a need to balance the social function and the spatial planning scale. He offers within his continuum a four-tier hierarchy. This hierarchy ranges from a highly compact and socially comprehensive unit the size of a city block to an expanded community feeling that could extend over a whole city or region. Of these four levels, Suttles recommends his 'community of limited liability' as being suited particularly to community planning.

> The term 'limited liability' is given to this neighbourhood level because participation in the community is a voluntary choice. Most people of the area will participate in organisations and political interest groups, but some will not be activated unless their particular face-block or territory is threatened. (Suttles, 1970: 59)

The limited liability neighbourhood is expected to be the spatial unit to which most people will have some form of commitment. This commitment can take many forms and is often not very visible, such as informal coffee meetings or social group gatherings, but it can suddenly become very obvious if there is a perceived threat to the *status quo*. Incidents such as new land use proposals or changing school districts can galvanise quiet areas into demonstrable action. 'NIMBY' (Not in My Back Yard) and 'NOTE' (Not Over There Either) are just two of the terms commonly used to describe community groups that have developed primarily to stop a particular development they find undesirable. Such reactions are not uncommon when major tourism developments and road changes are proposed in tourist destinations.

Community activists

Community activist groups have their roots in the planning advocacy process that grew out of the political activism of the 1960s (Langlois, 1979). The early community advocacy groups helped to bring more democracy to the planning process by providing an avenue for community input. However, present-day anti-growth groups have been criticised for making the planning process less democratic, especially when their successful complaint campaigns merely shift the 'problem' development to neighbourhoods that are not so well organised, or advantaged (Barbalace, 2000). Therefore, the resources that could have been spent finding a widely accepted solution to a community planning dilemma, such as affordable housing or airport expansion, can be sapped away as opposing sides fight it out.

Core and boundary issues

Just as the concept of community has proved complex, so has the task of describing and locating it on a map. If a community or neighbourhood sentiment exists it is generally evident in the urban landscape, providing signs such as focal points for shopping and recreation within a relatively compact and walkable area. These locations often identify themselves with the neighbourhood sentiment, adopting its name in their business signs or park and recreation centre names. The difficulty emerges not so much with identifying a community or neighbourhood core, as with the mapping of its boundaries. Where does one area of community sentiment and responsibilities end and another begin? In reality those living in the border area are either ambivalent about which neighbourhood they belong to, or they use both neighbourhoods.

Likewise, the spatial description of regions is fraught with difficulties. Tosun and Jenkins (1996) have suggested regions need a 'sense of purpose' for tourism planning or any form of development to take place. But unfortunately such functional regions will vary in size according to the purpose. So we have the situation where any community can be placed in series of overlapping and different regions. This is the case of many small rural communities that are located in the larger Australian shires. They can easily be in one school district, an entirely different political district, sharing a marketed tourist region with other communities and all encompassed within a much larger water catchment region.

Lack of clear boundaries and jurisdictional control can lead to the unrestricted exploitation and conflicting uses of tourism resources. One example is the 'tragedy of the commons' (Hardin, 1969) as it applies to coral reefs, which often stretch across existing jurisdictional boundaries, resulting in a lack of cohesive management and a degradation of the resource. By creating new boundaries to encompass a physiological phenomenon jurisdictions are able to introduce protection and conservation measures that assist tourism and other activities such as fishing. This has been achieved with the Bonaire Marine Park in the Dutch Antilles which in 1992 existed in name only. By exercising sovereignty over the whole area as a park the government has been able to control uses within the park and generate substantial revenue for the island (*The Economist*, 2000a: 106).

Political and economic realities are forcing planners and governments to be more precise in drawing lines between communities for administrative purposes, such as policing or garbage collection. In the United States the rise of the 'incorporation movement', whereby larger political units are broken up into smaller and often exclusive incorporated areas, leads to much debate about where the boundaries for these communities should lie (Husock, 1998). In Florida, as in many other states in the US, there has been a surge in incorporations, resulting in vexatious debates over the boundaries for these 'new communities'. Issues of segregation and social equity are tied to the incorporation movement because the new boundaries for these areas carry with them dramatic taxation, servicing and self-determination implications. In some cases the boundary question has led to so much argument that the final decision has been left to the courts, such as in the Village of Islamorada, in the Florida Keys.

The relevance of a community's spatial context in tourism is very important because as a major and sometimes disruptive commercial activity it takes up space that often intrudes upon existing neighbourhoods, especially those close to a city core. One of the principal social impacts topics studied by tourism researchers has been the visitor–resident interface and the setting for such interaction has often been the neighbourhood. Several studies have found that the distance residents live from the focus of tourism activity often has a bearing on their attitude to local tourism. Generally, those living on top of or next to the tourism activity, with its congestion and noise, develop a negative attitude to the business (Murphy & Andressen, 1988; Sheldon & Var, 1984), especially when it overspills into residential areas.

Examples of this neighbourhood effect occur everywhere. In many towns there is tension between those households in residential areas that operate a bed and breakfast business, their neighbours who put up with the comings and goings of visitors, and the municipality which handles a greater load on its residential services. Another neighbourhood effect can be the loss of local convenience food shops, like a butcher or greengrocer, to souvenir shops as a shopping district changes from its traditional residential base to a more tourism and higher revenue market.

External recognition

The third dimension of community, especially from a planning and development perspective, is the existence of external recognition. Although a group can band together and create a strong sense of belonging, even with an internally recognised spatial context, it is of limited utility unless these two dimensions have been recognised and acknowledged by some external agency. Porteous (1973) gave a graphic example of this in his study of a teenage gang and its turf, as viewed through a cognitive mapping of its members' concept of their 'neighbourhood'. The gang knew their 'turf' but only received a modest acknowledgment of its existence from the local authorities, in part because of the transient nature of the group but mainly because of their lack of political relevance. Such a tenuous external recognition was insufficient to legitimise their existence and territorial claims.

If a community wishes to preserve its way of life and the character of its geographical location it needs to have its existence and right to self-determination acknowledged by others. Just as new nation states and national governments seek the recognition and support from the world's community of nations, so too do neighbourhoods, cities and regions seek the acknowledgment and approval of higher levels of government. Only if their existence has been validated can they expect to receive official jurisdictional status and support. Acknowledging these political entities can include recognising their rights and privileges along with their territorial boundaries. Community planning, whether it pertains to a neighbourhood or complete town, needs to be undertaken 'in parallel with (higher order) development objectives' (Tosun & Jenkins, 1996: 520), especially if it involves seeking some form of public funding.

External recognition of the history and rights of certain groups as communities can in turn empower these communities. Many of the world's indigenous groups are now recognised by non-Aboriginals as legitimate ongoing ethnic communities that deserve to be treated as such. The successful bid of the Canadian Cree to stop the construction of a major dam on their traditional hunting and fishing grounds is an example of how external recognition of a community can empower a group to bring about social justice. The Cree were unable to find a groundswell of support to stop the dam in their home province of Quebec. However, by reaching out to other levels of government and connecting with other communities, most notably environmental groups, the Cree gained substantial recognition and support for their cause (Susskind & Field, 1996). In Australia the growing public recognition and support for Aboriginal communities, as expressed in mass demonstrations across the county involving hundreds of thousands of people, is bringing pressure on the federal government to enter into treaty negotiations with Aboriginal Australians (*The Age*, 2000).

Suttles (1970) included an element of external recognition in the description of his 'community of limited liability', a community scale that he views as fulfilling both the social and planning needs of a community. Suttles (1970: 59) says this should be 'a neighbourhood that is not only recognised and defended internally but also receives outside recognition and sanction, leading to an "official" and more permanent identity'. When a community has such external recognition it can expect to be consulted about potential changes and to be able to seek its share of development funding.

Community empowerment

Another form of external recognition, equally relevant to the treatise of this book, is the rising importance of community empowerment on the world stage. One of those who have commented on the movement away from centralisation to decentralisation is the futurist John Naisbitt. He considers 'the real political power – that is the ability to get things done – has shifted away from Congress and the presidency to the states, cities, towns and neighbourhoods' (Naisbitt, 1984: 108). A part of this process is the growing importance of 'personal geography' – where you live – which is working hand-in-hand with the decentralisation process to enable people 'to tackle problems and create change at the local level' (Naisbitt, 1984: 141).

Someone who would agree with Naisbitt is planning critic and theorist Jane Jacobs. In her book, *The Death and Life of Great American Cities*, Jane Jacobs (1962) promoted the worthiness of maintaining and developing active residential neighbourhoods in central cities. Jacobs considered 'a city's very wholeness in bringing together people with communities of interest is one of its greatest assets, possibly the greatest' (1962: 119). But in order to function properly a city needs to operate at several levels and she recommends there be street and district neighbourhoods to act as functional building blocks to overall city life. To Jacobs these would provide the metropolitan areas with local caretakers, people who would look after the general security of property and safety of people because it was their home territory.

In her later work Jacobs (1984) championed the cause of small communities that in the global economy have become dependent on the metropolitan juggernauts of the modern economy. She suggests many communities can foster greater self-reliance and local employment by substituting more locally produced goods and services for their traditional imports from these distant suppliers. She illustrates how economies of scale advantages in the metropolitan production centres have now been eroded by customised demands and rising transport costs in a growing number of cases. Hence, small communities should check their existing trade relations with larger centres and see whether the economics of traditional trade patterns still hold true.

Social capital

Jacobs and others who have investigated community action and its contribution to a variety of activities have introduced the term 'social capital'. The origins of the term have been attributed to L.J. Hanifan who, as a supervisor of rural schools in West Virginia in 1916, advocated community involvement for the development of successful schools by using 'local social capital . . . the goodwill, fellowship, sympathy and social intercourse among the individuals and families who make up a social unit' (as cited in Putman, 2000: 19). Since then the concept of social capital has been extended to other community oriented topics, including its economic and social development contributions, but not without some debate (De Filippis, 2001; Putman, 1993). While it involves local knowledge and commitment that would be helpful to tourism development social capital cannot replace the fundamental advantages of possessing sufficient financial capital and skilled labour. However, its principles of teamwork and networking (Anderson & Jack, 2002) fit in well with the additional business strength that can be gained from agglomeration and clustering processes, as discussed later in this book.

Community Tourism Definitions

In 1980 as the result of a symposium on tourism development in Canada and his experience with tourism expansion around the world, Murphy described tourism as: 'An industry which uses the community as a resource, sells it as a product, and, in the process, affects the lives of everyone.' (1980a: 1)

This statement, which has been quoted extensively since it first appeared, clearly links the two terms discussed above, but in the process the concept of community tourism becomes bigger than the sum of its parts. The community under consideration is no longer just a home with a communal sense of belonging, it has become an actual or potential profit-making commodity in the global tourism market. If the community enters that market it will need to adjust and change in order to compete and to survive. The community will be promoted as a type of destination product that is expected to attract visitors but this may not appeal to all residents. These same residents will be involved in the successful delivery of the promoted product, whether they work for the industry or not, because they are part of the community that is now on show.

The interest in community tourism has been building over the past two decades. Pearce and Moscardo (1999) refer to its growing status in research and planning agendas. They demonstrate this through reference to:

> the World Tourism Leaders' Meeting on the Social Impacts of Tourism suggests that countries should, as a first priority, 'support greater involvement of communities in the planning, implementation, monitoring and evaluation processes of tourism policies, programmes and projects'. Similarly, the Asia Pacific Ministers' Conference on Tourism and the Environment suggested that tourism should foster local community involvement and integrated tourism planning for sustainability. (Pearce & Moscardo, 1999: 31–2)

In their review of past analysis Pearce and Moscardo note that while there has been much and varied research into community tourism there has been a tendency to focus on individual variables rather than many attempts to link the various facets into a theoretical framework.

More recently community tourism has been defined by the US based Ecotourism Society as: 'tourism that involves and benefits local communities' (Mann, 2000: 26). This definition places the involvement of local people and how they are affected by tourism at the centre of discussion, rather than including them as a mere addition to the economic components of the industry, or worse yet – as an afterthought. Such definitions bring together the previously mentioned autonomous terms 'community' and 'tourism' into a strong and intertwined partnership.

Responsibilities

There has been a general increase in the attention paid to community tourism, both from an academic and pragmatic point of view. In the academic arena much of the concern has been over the impacts of tourism on the local residents and environment. The true impacts of tourism on host communities are often a matter of perspective that can be biased by personal impacts and reveal themselves in unexpected ways (Mathieson & Wall, 1982). Power structures of traditional societies can be threatened when those who benefit directly from tourism employment, such as young guides who earn more money than their elders, can threaten the authority and prestige of traditional leaders (Mann, 2000).

Tourism researchers with a social science background or emphasis have analysed resident–tourists interactions around the world. Apart from a relatively few tense situations, where there is open conflict between tourism developments and community aspirations, these studies generally reveal more support than opposition to the development of local tourism – an aspect to be discussed further in the 'residents' chapter. However, even where there is support for tourism it is generally not boundless, in the sense that residents don't exhibit excessive or irrational enthusiasm for the industry. Rather, residential support for tourism tends to be tempered and balanced as it draws on their first hand tourism experiences and learning about other destinations.

Increasingly a pragmatic approach to community tourism is being developed and adopted. One of the early leaders in this was the extension service of the University of Missouri-Columbia, who's College of Public and Community Services produced a guidebook for community tourism development (Weaver, 1986). The purpose of the book is 'to assist local communities in assessing and developing their tourism potential as a component of their economic development plan' (Weaver, 1986: iii). As part of the general guidelines the contributors identify three essential components of the industry which are listed below.

(1) *The community*
    This supplies the local public services and infrastructure, plus the personnel and volunteer labour for the local destination organisation, and the leadership needed to direct the local industry's product and marketing development.

(2) *Attractions and special events*
    This sector interacts with both the community and the tourist market. It plans and manages the tourist attractions and promotes them and the community to the outside tourism market.

(3) *The tourist market*
    This is the segment(s) willing to buy what the community is selling. To serve this market properly and create satisfied customers the commu-

nity must have the appropriate facilities and service standards for the targeted segments.

If we use Weaver's approach as a guide we can see evidence that all three elements – the host community, the tourists and the industry are beginning to play a combined role in striving for a form of community tourism that is attainable and acceptable to all.

Communal interests

While in the words of Tonge and Myott (1993: 7) 'confusion still reigns supreme' in how to best handle local tourism development, there are signs of progress in this area. Increasingly awareness of the need for tourism management is leading many communities to empower themselves in developing successful tourism products that reflect and promote their goals and values. This empowerment is fuelled by local commitment to tourism management, that involves planning for tourism development and drawing upon available resources to implement the plan. These resources include the following: knowledge, expertise and funding of tourism from the host community; data collection and analysis from local institutions of tertiary education; plan creation and implementation assistance from experienced government officials and consultants; and partnership opportunities with governments and businesses.

Examples of host communities taking a more proactive role include the African communities that are being given more control over the wildlife safaris and parks operating in their homeland. Baker (1997: 275) observes 'the concept of community-based conservation evolved in the 1980s to bolster support for both consumptive and non-consumptive uses of wildlife resources. The concept recognises that wildlife conservation is not just about animals but also people'. She notes that while a communal approach could lead to a 'tragedy of the commons' there is now sufficient knowledge and incentive to avoid this historic trap. After reviewing several national programmes in Africa she identifies five 'optimum conditions' for community-based natural resource management in that part of the world, which are listed below.

(1) Resources need a *focused value* to determine whether the benefit of managing a resource exceeds its cost.
(2) Those *bearing* the *higher cost* of living with the resource must benefit more than those who do not bear this cost.
(3) There must be a *positive correlation* between the quality of management and magnitude of derived benefits.
(4) Proprietorship (*ownership*) should match the unit of production, management and benefit.
(5) Proprietorship (*ownership*) should be as *small* as practicable, within ecological and socio-political constraints. (Baker, 1997: 282–3)

The application of such principles would be a better representation of eco-logical process, and a reduction of the leakage to middlemen and central governments.

More 'self-help' tourism development guidebooks for small communi-ties are being produced to assist these communities in establishing viable tourism ventures and obtaining maximum long-term benefit from the industry. Two recent Australian examples are *Developing Ecotourism: A Community Based Approach,* by Wearing and McLean (1998), and *Protecting Local Heritage Places: A Guide for Communities* (Australian Heritage Com-mission, 1999). The latter states 'this guide contains information to help individuals and groups working locally to identify, conserve and protect heritage places' (Australian Heritage Commission, 1999: 2).

Critical appraisal

Despite this growing development of community tourism interest and action there has been criticism of this approach to research and planning. Taylor (1995: 489) queries whether 'in the end, (community tourism) is different from any other kind of tourism development'. In coming to this conclusion he basically criticises the dual role seen for residents, in that they are expected to be outsiders and at the same time part of the local tourism product. He doubts whether they share the benefits along with the substantiated costs. Furthermore he also doubts whether a community approach to tourism can turn back the clock and allow communities to reverse the destination lifecycle, although we know of no one who has made such a claim.

Such views seem to miss essential points of the community approach to tourism. Community tourism is an attempt to integrate the interests of all community stakeholders, including the residents as an important group, in its analysis and development proposals. A dual or multi-functional role for individuals is not uncommon in modern society and if the tourism–host expectations are appropriate and properly communicated they should not form an impossible burden. The issue of balancing benefits and costs for the community at large and its residents lies at the heart of Murphy's (1983) ecological model that highlights the need for balance. It is true that the benefits, like the costs, will not always be tangible on an individual basis, but they do occur and need to be assessed by all involved. It is even possible with this approach to slow down or stop development, so while it may not be able to reverse a destination's lifecycle, it could help to mitigate its evolu-tionary progress. Thus a community tourism approach could place the host community at a stage it feels is more compatible with its aspirations.

In a response to Taylor's article Baum (1996) reports how community tourism has become a major research and planning focus in Canada and how an important ingredient is an education process for local residents. Such educational components within a community tourism perspective have been 'initiated at government level, in destinations such as Hawaii and Hong Kong (which) illustrate how this process can operate' (Baum, 1996: 149). However, Baum demonstrates such educational programmes need to be undertaken with care. Others, like Madrigal (1995) and Murphy (1991) now emphasise the need for more internal marketing by the industry, so that it demonstrates convincingly what net gains the industry can bring to the community.

Burr (1991) cited in Pearce *et al.* (1996: 27–8) gives some indication of the struggle ahead by observing 'the concept of what constitutes a community (in community tourism) has not been considered carefully by researchers'. In a review of 25 empirical studies on tourism impacts and communities Burr found a disappointing lack of clarity concerning definition and approach. In fact he argued that there are four possible theoretical approaches to the study of community in tourism impacts analysis. These are listed below.

- The *human ecology* approach emphasises the community living to-gether and adapting to the setting.
- The *social systems* approach stresses the roles and institutions that govern society.
- The *interactional* approach that sees community as the sum of individual social interactions.
- The *critical* approach emphasises the power of key groups in the deci-sion-making process.

Burr is quoted as favouring a combination of the interactional and critical approaches, as this 'focuses attention on the dynamic processes that create and alter community structure' (Pearce *et al.* 1996: 28). Such is the focus of this book, as it extends beyond the human ecology approach of *Tourism: A Community Approach*, to examine the interaction of business principles and stakeholder aspirations that leads to conflict resolution and collaborative decision-making processes.

Regardless of the definitions used and theoretical approach taken, few deny the need to concentrate more on the development of theory in the area of community tourism. If the growing academic and practical interest in community tourism is to take on a more solid form it needs the structure of a theoretical framework. If it is to take its place in the lexicon of tourism research it also needs to be positioned within the developing general theory of tourism.

Tourism Theoretical Developments

Like all relatively young academic fields of enquiry, tourism research has been building slowly toward a level of understanding that can lead to the prediction of behaviour and outcomes. In this process the inductive approach has been dominant. So far most research has concentrated on descriptive empirical analysis of particular case studies that lead, either directly or indirectly, to the proposal of a theory. Many of the tourism theories to date have focused on the challenges that can arise from a lack of management or mismanagement of tourism resources. Since tourism is such a broad and multi-dimensional subject many of these theories have their roots in other disciplines.

As inductive research activity has developed and matured there is now more evidence of a deductive approach, where the research and analysis is guided by a priori hypotheses based on earlier literature in both tourism and related fields.

Two outstanding examples of how the inductive approach can lead to theory and prediction are Doxey's (1975) 'irridex' model and Butler's (1980) destination area cycle of evolution. Doxey noted from his experience as a consultant in several Caribbean and Canadian communities that local residents' tolerance of tourism changes with its growing size and dominance. Consequently in his 'irridex' model of resident reaction to tourism he charts a continuum ranging from euphoric acceptance of the industry to open antagonism. Butler describes the development characteristics of a selection of well-known tourist destinations. He then demonstrates how they follow a lifecycle that moves from an exploration stage to a stagnation stage resulting in either rejuvenation or decline. Marketing research has proposed a similar product lifecycle model where the stages pass from introduction to decline (Figure 1.2). Both of these theoretical concepts are based on critical observation of actual experiences and have suggested a pattern of behaviour that can apparently explain many of the differences. It is interesting that such strong parallels exist in two separate academic fields, yet not so surprising since both are linked by a business emphasis. It should be apparent also that Butler and Doxey are describing the same phenomenon but from different perspectives. Butler is focusing on the industry and its development, while Doxey is recording the changing reactions of the host populations to this development (Figure 1.2).

Examples of the deductive approach are appearing more regularly now in tourism research, where the authors develop a theory of behaviour or outcomes based on either past research findings or their own intuition. They develop a series of hypotheses based on these theories and test them with respect to a particular case study. A good example of this can be seen in Palmer's (1998) evaluation of marketing groups' governance style. After reviewing the literature on collaborative tourism destination marketing he puts forward the following hypotheses.

H1: Local tourism marketing associations are more effective where they are associated with a 'tight' governance style.

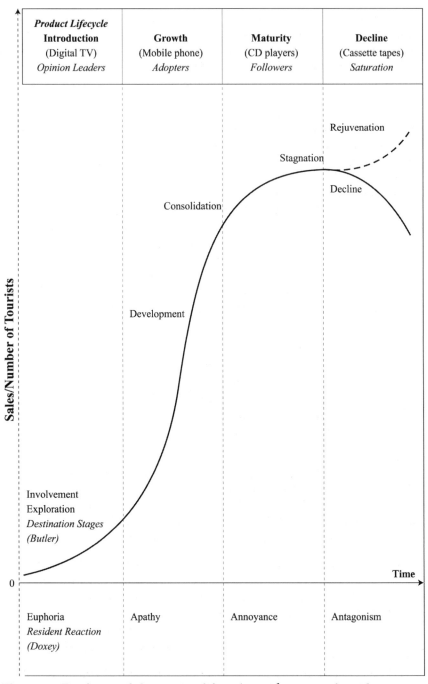

Figure 1.2 Product and destination lifecycles with potential resident reactions

H2: The effectiveness of local tourism marketing associations is greatest where there is a high level of compatibility among members.

These deductive statements were put to the test by developing an appropriate measurement scale and applying a statistical analysis. 'The results of the quantitative analysis strongly supported the hypothesis (H1) of a link between tight governance style and perceived effectiveness' (Palmer, 1998: 196). However, 'the hypothesis (H2) of a relationship between high levels of compatibility and effectiveness is not accepted' (Palmer, 1998: 197). This is because the statistical analysis indicated the actual relationship went in the opposite direction to that predicted in H2. Hence such studies take tourism research a small step forward by ratifying some concepts and raising doubts about others.

In addition to developing various approaches to the development of theory, tourism research demonstrates a growing sense of direction and responsibility. Jafari (1990) identifies four different themes in tourism research over time, that he calls tourism's platforms in the sense that they represent stepping stones. These platforms are described below.

(1) *Advocacy*
    The advocacy platform appeared during the economic reconstruction following World War II. This type of research emphasises the benefits associated with tourism, with a strong focus on economic benefits and is dominated by government reports.
(2) *Cautionary*
    The cautionary platform developed in the 1970s along with growing academic interest in the field of tourism research. This platform challenges the overly enthusiastic stance of the advocacy platform by highlighting the evidence of growing negative impacts.
(3) *Adaptancy*
    The adaptancy platform emerged during the late 1980s and focuses on alternative forms of tourism, that can avoid the principal problems of mass tourism by emphasising a more harmonious scale and functionality.
(4) *Knowledge-based*
    The knowledge-based platform is the fourth and present platform. It attempts to build on the previous work, using a multi-disciplinary approach to guide the development of tourism on a more harmonious scale. This 'new platform aims at positioning itself on scientific foundations' (Jafari, 1990: 35). It will hopefully combine the best of the previous platforms, which still exist in various forms, with modern multi-disciplinary scientific research.

It is this multi-disciplinary and scientific approach to theory building that Tribe (1997) embraces and embellishes in his critical analysis of tourism as an academic discipline and his proffered model regarding the creation of tourism knowledge. He presents tourism knowledge as a band of concentric rings. Proceeding from the outer rim to the core are a series of circles that represent the principal components of tourism knowledge, detailed as below.

- The *outer circle* represents the multitude of disciplines that have some bearing on and interest in the development of tourism knowledge and theory.
- The thin *inner circle*, called 'band k' is where these disciplines interact with each other and contribute to the field of tourism knowledge. This middle circle represents the field of tourism study, which Tribe has broken into two parts – TF1 (business related topics) and TF2 (non-business related topics such as social impacts). TF1 is 'the business world of tourism, pushing out at the expense of other parts of the diagram' (Tribe, 1997: 654), because it has a unifying theme that makes it dominant both in an academic and pragmatic sense. Tribe has trouble labelling TF2, beyond describing it as 'non-business' related. This is due in part to an apparent lack of a unifying thematic approach between the social and other sciences to tourism.
- The *core* of his model is referred to as 'mode 2', and represents the ultimate goal of tourism knowledge production – its own distinctive contribution to knowledge. Tribe describes this core as 'extra-disciplinarity' and quotes Gibbons *et al.* (1994: 168) in support of this view:

> Knowledge which emerges from a particular context of application with its own distinct theoretical structures, research methods, and modes of practice but which may not be locatable on the prevailing disciplinary map.

Important points to note according to Tribe are that mode 2 knowledge production occurs outside of higher education and that it is developing its own epistemology. Its success is judged 'by its ability to solve a particular problem, its cost effectiveness, and its ability to establish competitive advantage. Its results are highly contextualized for a specific project' (Tribe, 1997: 652).

We concur that tourism knowledge and theory should be viewed in such a multi-disciplinary or trans-disciplinary fashion because of its extensive variety of forms and impacts. Therefore, we offer strategic community tourism management as a way of filling some of the gaps in Tribe's model. For instance we suggest the 'community setting' for *TF2*. Host community resources attract the business of tourism in the first place while the community must live with the consequences of such engagements. The physical, social and cultural settings of a location are given form and substance to its host community and create the foundation for tourism development. Such a proposition fits with Tribe's core – mode 2, as his tourism knowledge production point is highly contextualised according to his own words. This recognises the folly in separating any tourism activity and analysis from its setting. Since destinations are the principal setting for tourism activity a host community approach to tourism theory building seems most appropriate.

The development of theory for strategic community management tourism will involve joint consideration of the tourism activity and its setting. Thus it will build on the TF1 and TF2 distinctions outlined by Tribe and in the process combine the tourism business interests with those of the physical and social sciences. In this way such research and development will combine the perspectives of several interest groups and help to create the 'extradisiplinary' approach Tribe thinks tourism study should be generating.

Community-business combination

As early as 1979 Rosenow and Pulsipher (1979: 43) produced a book with the wonderful and apt title – *Tourism: The Good, The Bad, and The Ugly*. In this book they recommended a *personality planning process* that attempts to identify those elements which make a community unique and brings this tourism appeal into a meaningful package for both residents and the tourism industry. A key aspect of this type of tourism is to emphasise a destination's sense of place.

In the view of Rosenow and Pulsipher (1979: 43) 'almost every area in the United States has certain elements of its setting and heritage that are unique'. It is this uniqueness that contributes to tourist interest, especially as tourism becomes more associated with the need to escape the routine experiences of daily life and the tourist market has shattered into many special interest segments. Consequently, more tourists are seeking something different or something that is a new example of their special interest. So this unique setting and heritage of individual places, that geographers call its 'sense of place' (Johnston et al. 1988: 425), becomes an important tourism resource.

While local residents may or may not perceive the significance of their unique qualities to tourism they are both important and fragile community elements that need to be protected in the face of progress and growth. Rosenow and Pulsipher (1979: 63) claim this can be a clear starting point for community action, by quoting from William K. Reilly's book – *In the Wake of the Tourist*:

> The principal advantage of having, or believing that you have, a place that is special is that planning can begin from an agreed-upon point of reference. Consensus, always elusive in land-use planning, is more attainable when special qualities have been commonly recognized.

So they proposed a 'personality planning process' that builds on any area's sense of place. They suggest a simple 'community planning process' that identifies those elements that constitute the local sense of place and assist in formulating policies to enhance its uniqueness. It basically consists of the following four steps.

(1) Delineate distinctive *features*.
(2) Plot critical *zones*.
(3) Establish use *objectives*.
(4) Formulate specific *action* programmes.

This recognition of the importance of a community's sense of place and the need to include and safeguard these features in the general business planning process is a major step toward the development of a strategic community tourism management approach.

Researchers have developed a range of strategic tourism planning models as a way of explaining the developmental potential of tourism destinations in various situations. These models have been tested around the world as a means of better understanding the impacts of tourism on communities and to develop appropriate strategies for managing tourism developments. The tourism models reviewed in this section include the following:

- Ecological tourism planning model,
- Harmonised travel model; and
- Planning modes.

Ecological tourism planning model

Murphy (1983) attempted to present community tourism in a theoretical context by developing an ecological model of community tourism planning that had five essential components (Figure 1.3).

Ecological process The first was to equate tourism planning and development with an ecological process, where a tourism destination could be treated as a living ecosystem. An ecosystem is seen as 'any area of nature that includes living organisms and non-living substances interacting to produce an exchange of materials between the living and non-living parts' (Odum, 1970: 262). Thus, tourism can be viewed as an exchange of materials between the living (human) and non-living (cultural and physical environment) substances of a community.

Community focus Within this ecological setting the model attempts to highlight some fundamental processes. The second component was the recognition that the model would need to involve the consideration of several dimensions of community life if it was to be as comprehensive as the

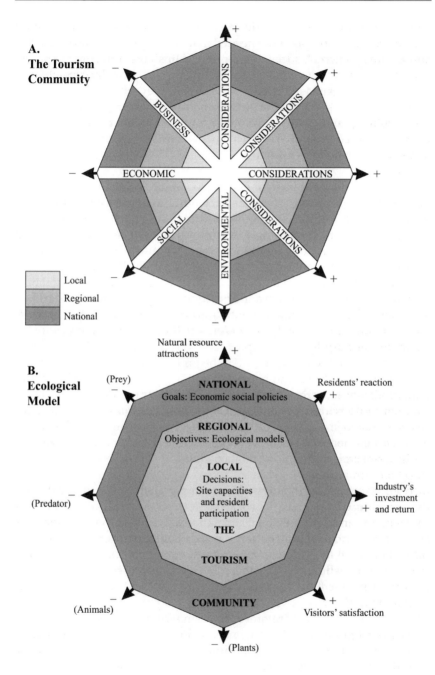

Figure 1.3 Ecological model of tourism planning
Source: Murphy (1985: 168)

term 'community' merited. In this respect Murphy suggested community tourism research and planning needed to focus on the following considerations: environmental, social, economic and business. While resident and visitor surveys are two widely used techniques for providing insight into local considerations associated with tourism, they often only provide a small 'quantitative' part of the picture and can leave out personal and private insights (Hughes, 1995). To obtain a full assessment of what tourism can mean to a community requires more extensive surveys and the inclusion of other stakeholder groups.

Stakeholders The third component was to identify principal actors associated with these four considerations in community tourism and in keeping with an ecological emphasis points out similarities with the features of natural environments. Accordingly, Murphy proposed that environmental and social considerations should focus on the natural attractions and the social/residential response of a tourism destination. These were equated with the native plants and animals of natural environments, that combine to create its overall ecosystem and attraction to potential visitors. The business consideration was equated with tourists, who come to experience the attractions and interact with the residents. In the natural setting the tourists are viewed as the prey, which come to feed on the natural environment and intermingle with the residents but in the process expose themselves to the tourism industry. The economic considerations were represented by the industry, which serves the tourist and provides the travel experience, which in the natural environment is viewed as the predator that feeds off the tourist as its prey. In this case, of course, the goal is not to consume the visitors, but to satisfy them and send them home as repeat visitors or goodwill ambassadors for the destination and its people.

Connectivity The fourth acknowledged component is that this ecological community can exist at a variety of levels. Murphy identifies three such levels of community: local, regional and national. Each level has its own goals and priorities which should be harmonised for maximum effectiveness. Local and regional levels in a community planning context hold particular relevance for destinations. It is these levels that represent the 'coalface' of the industry, where the tourists and the environment and its inhabitants will intermingle.

Interestingly, several prominent tourism writers have advocated more research and planning at the regional and local levels. Krippendorf (1982) has recommended that the most appropriate scale for the development and marketing of tourism would be a combination of local and regional levels. Getz (1983) has recommended more attention be given to planning and initiatives from the bottom up, meaning from and by the people directly affected rather than from higher levels of government, such as state or national legislators. Gunn (1997) has long been championing a corridor and node approach that brings together individual attractions of small communities into regional packages for modern mobile tourists with specific special interests.

Balance The fifth and most important component of the suggested model was that all these considerations, actors and scales had to be brought into balance if the ecosystem is to continue and prosper. This was illustrated by showing all the considerations had both positive and negative poles, and that a central point of balance starting at the local levels was the most desirable outcome. In this sense the model was championing the concept of sustainable development that came to the fore with the Brundtland report in 1987. Goodall and Stabler (2000) make a case for combining the top-down and bottom-up planning approaches to achieve a more balanced and appropriate environmental management on both local and global scales.

Application Murphy recognised that the above model was both a simplification of a complex entity and untested. Therefore, he put his ecological tourism community concept to the test in several empirical case studies and practical situations around the province of British Columbia, Canada over several years. The findings from these experiences were presented in a paper entitled 'Community driven tourism planning' (Murphy, 1988). The evidence from the four cases, involving communities ranging from small rural communities to the provincial capital, revealed some consistent patterns of behaviour. First, it showed the public were well aware of tourism and its potential impacts, so residents could hold their own in debate and discussions. Second, within the case study communities it was often small groups of people who became involved with tourism planning and 'in some cases it may be one determined person' (Murphy, 1988: 98). Third, there was evidence of goodwill in that the industry, local government officials and active residents often had more interests in common than many had suspected, and that given an early chance to express these interests led to a more community oriented perspective in the planning suggestions.

Independent calls for more community participation in the tourism planning process have come from a number of researchers including Krippendorf (1987) and Haywood (1988).

Harmonised travel model

Krippendorf (1987) utilising his extensive European, and particularly Swiss, experiences has suggested that if tourism is to survive and prosper it needs to humanise travel and bring about *greater harmony between hosts and visitors*. He advocates a 'soft and humane tourism' so those who are tourists and those who depend upon them can develop common goals. These goals are to bring 'the greatest possible benefit to all the participants – travellers, the host population and the tourist business, without causing intolerable ecological and social damage' (Krippendorf, 1987: 106).

Tourism Truisms As part of the process to achieve this goal he reminds us to remember some truisms about tourism. First, for many people tourism is the last bastion of freedom, so regulations should not be overly burdensome. There can be a great feeling of release when you are able to act without those who know you being aware of your actions. However, taken to the extreme a tourist's release of inhibitions can lead to behaviour that is degrading to tourists and their hosts. Therefore, limits need to be set and conditions formulated so that tourism leads to more and not less consideration of others. Second, most people wish to relax on their holiday, so we must acknowledge this as a driving and unifying force for most tourists. Third, tourism is highly seasonal so institutional efforts by governments and education authorities must be made to break down the old Victorian and industrial based calendars. Fourth, we must ensure that there are fair economic transactions, with the advantages and disadvantages being equally distributed between hosts and guests.

Balanced tourist development To bring about the humanisation of travel and greater harmony between the hosts and guests Krippendorf proposed a concept of balanced tourism development. This was to be achieved by focusing on the needs and interests of the tourists and locals, and by coordinating them. The first step was to ascertain the interests and priorities of each group; if there was a reasonable match then planning and development could proceed, with the following provisos: 'One of the most important factors in a balanced development is the principle of local sovereignty in matters concerning the use of land' (Krippendorf, 1987: 119). Planned investment is best when both the industry and local interests are involved; in other words they have some form of community partnership. The local workforce should be used wherever possible to maximise individual benefits and to give locals an incentive to improve service. Last, but certainly not least, is the recommendation to 'emphasize and cultivate what is typically local' (Krippendorf, 1987: 123).

Planning modes

Haywood (1988) notes the growing interest in encouraging greater public participation in the general planning process, and he feels the community destination would make an ideal scale and forum for such a process in tourism planning. He considers:

> Tourism and tourists are consumers and users of community resources (which) implies that the community is a commodity ... Whenever communities become venues of and for consumption, 'social sensitivity'

comes to the fore and a call goes out – often unheeded – to incorporate democracy into the planning process . . . Well developed and stronger tourism planning at the community level is vital if any region or country wishes to deliver exciting and novel tourist experiences in which there is an emphasis on quality and high value-added components at the destination points. (Haywood, 1988: 106).

However, Haywood considers that given the diversity of planning situations around the world it would be better to seek *varied planning modes* rather than a particular type of planning model.

Planning perspectives Accordingly, Haywood (1988: 110) calls for a more applied situational approach, based on local planning realities and situational difficulties, in encouraging real community participation. Within this process he hopes to see five basic perspectives of the planning process enhanced, with the particular mix being guided by local conditions. He sees planning as a process for the following:

- designing the future;
- innovation;
- learning;
- influencing; and
- managing

Since management is the focus of this book it is germane to look in some detail at Haywood's suggestions in this area.

Haywood notes that at the community level tourism is more than a purely economic phenomenon. Therefore, tourism planners should reformulate a more sensitive and viable role for this activity within destination communities. He offers a schema to illustrate how the various interest groups within such communities could share their hopes for the future, their learning, their innovative ideas and attempts to influence others in a general process of management. One outcome of such a planning process would be 'a legitimacy strategy'; defined as:

A clear delineation of the role of tourism within a community. This will permit the establishment of guidelines outlining what needs to be done to make tourism more socially, ecologically and economically responsive and responsible. (Haywood, 1988: 115)

Such external recognition of the community and its planning process is one of the key elements of community planning referred to earlier. Haywood cites an example of such a planning process happening in Canada's Northwest Territories (NWT). There the territory government has attempted to legitimise community based tourism by promoting tourism as 'an industry which reflects the interests and aspirations of the communities in which it is located' (Ahmed, 1986, cited in Haywood, 1988: 115). This is achieved by encouraging the type of tourism activity that stimulates NWT purchases and profits for NWT residents, employs NWT residents in jobs compatible with traditional lifestyles, is environmentally sensitive, and offers tourists a variety of quality offerings at a fair price.

Like many discussants of tourism management Haywood declines to define this term, but he does indicate the actual planning process is only one step. '(T)he focus in community tourism is not merely on the formulation of strategy as a problem solving process, but on the problem of implementation and control' (Haywood, 1988: 115). In his concluding paragraph he recognises that for community tourism to be effective it must enhance the operating effectiveness of all parties. To ensure mutual effectiveness requires a more comprehensive management that incorporates elements of monitoring, such as visitor surveys and environmental audits, and controls, such as land use zoning. We will be returning to these management approaches in Part II of this book.

Agent of change

Despite the growing interest in community tourism most researchers and writers have tended to focus their discussions on particular aspects of the topic. For example, many have focused on the impacts of tourism on host populations in destination communities. Within those impact studies the major topic is either socioeconomic or sociocultural in its emphasis. Such a breakdown is natural given the need to concentrate on a specific question or issue in much modern research and that the research is seldom value free, meaning that social scientists will gravitate to social issues and physical scientists to environmental concerns. But the net effect has been to divide into segments that which needs to be managed as a whole.

To illustrate this point, one needs only to examine the multitude of social impact studies that have attempted to analyse the perceptions and attitudes of residents in a variety of tourism destination communities. In an article on host perceptions of sociocultural impacts Brunt and Courtney (1999) have constructed summary impact tables from the tourism literature. While not everyone would use the same classification structure, a condensation of their findings indicates that the social impact will be felt in several ways, differing with respect to diverse aspects of the tourism industry and the quality of the interactions. From their listing one theme emerges strongly, and that is tourism will be an agent of social change in destination communities. However, whether tourism initiates or is simply a facet of ongoing change is a subject of debate. As Brunt and Courtney (1999: 497) observe:

Because the (tourism) industry is highly visual it has often become the scapegoat for sociocultural change. The dynamic character of all societies and cultures should thus not be overlooked and the potential (global) influences must be considered against this background.

In their personal study, Brunt and Courtney found local residents referred frequently to many of the key impacts that their literature review had identified. This caused them to conclude 'while there are some specific differences, the general analyses of the sociocultural impacts of tourism can be applied to the perceptions of residents of a small British coastal tourist (resort)' (Brunt and Courtney, 1999: 511).

While individual research studies of this kind are useful in building up a general knowledge base of what is happening when residents and tourists meet in a tourist destination community, we need to pull such empirical strands together and develop theories that help to explain and predict these interactions. This was the thinking of John Ap, when he introduced social exchange theory as a possible theoretical base for understanding residents' perceptions of local tourism. Ap (1992: 667) states 'the advantages of using social exchange theory are that it can accommodate explanation of both positive and negative perceptions, and can examine relationships at the individual or collective level'.

Social exchange theory

An exchange process is a unique temporal relationship, where each transaction is linked to a history and future for the involved actors, emphasising a more or less durable social relationship between the two actors that is modifiable over time (Ap, 1992: 677–8). The basic components of any exchange process are seen as 'need satisfaction', in that exchanges are engaged in if they satisfy the needs of the involved parties. Linking these components is a set of processes that are presented as flows. These are (1) initiation of the exchange; (2) a positive exchange formation or; (2a) no exchange takes place; (3) an exchange transaction evaluation; (4) a positive evaluation of the exchange consequences or; (4a) a negative evaluation of the exchange consequences and a withdrawal from the process.

Need satisfaction In terms of community tourism Ap suggests several motives within the area of need satisfaction. These motives could include key community actors who may like to encourage tourism depending on local circumstances, such as civic officials, local business people, or residents wishing to improve economic conditions; on the other hand there may be similar groupings opposed to further tourism growth, because of perceived problems with congestion. This identified need satisfaction initiates the actual exchange process, which consists of antecedents and an actual form.

Antecendents The antecedents are those opportunities perceived by one of the actors in the exchange process, whereby they determine 'what's in it for me'. Such returns can cover a wide range of motives. They could be the rational choices of economics, such as increasing income. They could represent satisfying behaviour, where a merely satisfying outcome like a successful festival is regarded as a sufficient return. They could be a perceived win-win situation for both or more parties, such as when the tourism industry provides tangible benefits to residents as well as tourists. The returns could also be viewed as a form of justice, such as the recognition of native land title.

Actual form The actual exchange has two potential forms, in that it can be balanced or unbalanced regarding the sharing of benefits and costs. The actual outcome at this point is highly dependent on the respective powers of each actor. As the description of social exchange indicated, such powers can change over time. For instance, Ap and others consider that when a community embraces tourism it is placing itself at an exchange disadvantage with respect to the industry, because it is clearly signalling its desire to see growth. However, once the industry is established with a considerable equity investment in place the industry becomes more dependent on the cooperation of the host community, and the power relationships of the exchange process become more balanced.

Consequences When the exchange has been completed its consequences are evaluated. This can occur at several levels. The outputs refer to the physical, social or symbolic creations, such as increased income or amenities. Action refers to the behaviour of the two actors involved. Ap (1999: 685) states that:

> The extension of hospitality, courtesy, and friendliness toward tourists, or opposition to newly proposed tourism development are actions that residents may exhibit as a result of favourable and unfavourable encounters with tourists and the industry.

Outcomes refer to how the actors feel about the exchange. If the actors' needs have been satisfied the exchange reinforces the behaviour and encourages continued engagement.

Such a theoretical perspective would appear to hold considerable promise, in treating community tourism as a system of individual exchanges that combine to form a collective assessment which can change over time as circumstances change. It is one which is anchored in sociological theory (Emerson, 1972; Levi-Strauss, 1969), that is 'concerned with understanding the exchange of resources between individuals and groups in an interaction situation' (Ap, 1999: 668). That is certainly the situation in tourism, where the travel business has been described as a series of 'moments of truth' between the traveller and an industry representative (Carlzon, 1987). Furthermore, the community has been described as a commodity in a sales exchange (Haywood, 1988). So it seems perfectly reasonable to place the whole process into a social exchange paradigm. However, there have been few empirical studies that have tried to implement all or part of the social exchange theory and there is some criticism of its true utility.

Application One study that has put social exchange theory to the test is a survey of residents living in five counties surrounding the Mt Rogers National Recreation Area of southwest Virginia (Jurowski *et al.*, 1997). Their social impact survey attempts to refine and clarify previous direct social impact assessment studies by incorporating elements of the social exchange theory. They develop a path analysis to explain the screening process that residents use to weigh and balance factors that could influence their support for nature based tourism in the area. The analysis reveals that the three traditional tourism impact assessments of economic, social and environmental impacts could be influenced by exogenous (screening) variables.

Residents who see a potential for economic gain develop a stronger level of support than those who have an 'ecocentric' attitude (environmentalists) regarding their impact assessments. Those who use the same local resources as the tourist are relatively neutral in their support. Those who have a strong attachment to the region, as measured by their 'attitudinal feelings for the area', are relatively positive about the economic and social returns from local nature based tourism but are negative about its environmental impacts. Consequently, Jurowski *et al.* (1997: 9) consider 'the findings confirmed the interactive nature of the(ir) four exchange elements (economic gain, resource use, community attachment, and ecocentric attitude) and three types of perceptions (economic-, social -, and environmental impacts)'

Pearce *et al.* (1996: 20–7) have three major problems with Ap's support of social exchange theory. First, they feel that the social exchange theory is too simplistic. The proposal that individuals balance the costs and benefits of tourism to guide their support for the industry fails to give adequate acknowledgment to the complex nature of tourism and its relationship with the host community. Second, they doubt that the equity condition and social justice principle occur very frequently. Third, they find Ap offers no techniques with which to ascertain how an individual balances personal conditions with community costs and benefits.

The question of how individuals calculate personal and community costs and benefits of tourism is still largely unanswered. This is a major conundrum with respect to resident reactions to local tourism impacts, where many empirical studies have shown the majority of their samples are positive about tourism even though they receive no apparent personal benefits. Rather than simply offer a criticism of a refreshing attempt to introduce a theoretical framework by which to examine resident reactions to tourism, Pearce *et al.* proffer a social science theory of their own.

Social representations theory

They recommend that researchers and practitioners consider social representations theory (Moscovici, 1984) with respect to tourism – community relationships. This theory 'focuses on both the content of social knowledge and the way that this knowledge is created and shared by people in various groups, societies or communities' (Pearce *et al.* 1996: 31). Social knowledge is a combination of individual and societal values, ideas and practices that individuals use to describe and react to a stimulus. This knowledge becomes their social representations or public evaluation of that stimulus. Pearce *et al.* (1996: 38–40) claim Moscovici sees two key functions operating within these social representations. First, they establish an order by which individuals orientate themselves to the world – their 'orb'. Second, these representations enable an individual to communicate with other members of a community, by providing them with a code for identifying and classifying 'unambiguously' the various aspects of their world. Further, they claim social representations are 'particularly valuable' for explaining social conflict and individual reactions to issues, because it is conflict that brings social representations out into the open and in the process social representations help to turn the unfamiliar into the more familiar.

Social representations theory is seen as being more than personal attitude creation. It emphasises more of the social influences and interactions of community and society than simply relying on personal interpretations of events. The theory contains two major components that could be particularly useful to community tourism research and development – its objectification and anchoring processes.

Objectification process First, there is an 'objectification process' where abstract concepts or ideas are turned into more ordinary reference points to create a personal and understandable image of the concept. Thus, when a tourism development proposal includes references to economic multipliers and impacts, local residents will consider these terms as individuals and groups and give them a more personal and local meaning.

Anchoring process The objectification process leads to an 'anchoring process', which enables individuals to identify and classify an event or proposal by comparing it with what is known already. As such it involves comparisons with previously identified categories and draws upon existing social and cultural knowledge held by the individual and the group. This enables people to gauge the significance of concepts and proposals.

These two components could be equated to the cognitive and evaluative functions of attitude formation (Fishbein & Raven, 1967), but in a more socially determined context, and have been incorporated into the individual's orb. Objectification can be seen as the initial stage of individual reaction, as the person attempts to place the new concept within their own and group experiences. Having interpreted the concept in more personal and meaningful terms the individual categorised it as beneficial or not, based on their own interpretation and that of the social group to which they belong.

Application In their summary of the social representations theory Pearce *et al.* (1996: 56) emphasise the theory is opposed to either a completely individual or social deterministic approach to understanding social knowledge, but prefer to stress its 'emic' approach. This is where study 'draws upon the actor's interpretations and local inside knowledge of the meaning of the behaviour under study' (Pearce *et al.*, 1996: 4). This mutual individual and group assessment and response to situations is well illustrated in their summary of the theory's key features, and is illustrated in their selection of community tourism examples. Some of these features include the use of images, supplemented by the use of metaphors and analogies.

They offer two sets of examples. International cases, based essentially on secondary data, whereby they translate and reinterpret the cases in light of social representation theory; and Australian cases where the authors have been more directly involved with the research and have applied aspects of the theory. Examples of the Australian social representations research include the empirical studies of resident views in two different types of Queensland destination.

Australian social representations cases Port Douglas, a fast-growing resort, serving the growing market for visits to the Great Barrier Reef as well as providing its own tropical experiences, demonstrates a threefold grouping of resident sentiments. Based on responses to questions regarding general tourism impacts along with personal and community service impacts the analysis reveals three social representation groupings could be identified as positive, low negative and high negative groups. The low negative group consists of those who have broad concerns about the environment and economy, yet within this group many are moderately positive about items such as job opportunities and the scenic beauty associated with the tourism industry. When these three groups are compared with various development options significant differences are noted.

Townsville, a coastal destination that has experienced slow and steady growth, presents a different picture. There, questions relating to the type of visitor and industry desired by the local community along with the usual tourism impact and development questions failed to uncover any distinctive groupings. Rather the homogeneity of responses indicated its 'social representation could be characterised as "tourism for the community" since a dominant emphasis on the developments and facilities which were seen as desirable for tourism also served local citizen needs' (Pearce *et al.* 1996: 177–8).

The utility of the social representation theory is that its combination of individual and community assessments provides clearer directions for planning and development. The results from the Australian studies and the other empirical studies according to Pearce *et al.*:

> Direct attention away from the dominant concern with the impacts of tourism and how these are seen by the community to how hosts understand, define and evaluate the future of tourism. This concern with providing planning-relevant information, rather than assuming that a study of impacts per se provides planning-relevant material, is an important evolutionary step which the study of community attitudes needs to take. (1996: 178)

This is certainly the approach and purpose that has been taken by Beeton (2000) in her study of community response to film-induced tourism at Barwon Heads in southern Australia.

Beeton (2000) has examined the residents' reactions to the filming of a successful television series, *Sea Change*, on a small village of 800 households using the social representation theory framework. She utilises the three-staged approach advocated by Pearce *et al.* (1996) by first looking for a consensus among the residents concerning their views on the local tourism situation. This was followed by an examination of the links between the stated tourism impacts and residents' related ideas; the final stage being to cluster the core of images which portrayed residents' social representation of this feature in their lives. This methodology produces seven social representation clusters that were linked to three major factors – average length of residency, ex-city dweller, and the consideration of tourism as a preferred industry. These results indicate to Beeton (2000: 135) that differing attitudes towards economic development, costs of living and crowding have 'the potential to divide and destroy a community as it is today'. Social representations could become a useful planning tool for future community planning in that the theory helps to identify disenfranchised clusters and points to potential uniting strategies.

Summary

The above review indicates that tourism data definition and research are evolving and that certain academic fields are being tapped for inspiration and guidance. The data issues are being addressed by a combination of government and academic interests. These interests are primarily economic and taxation based but in the process we are developing a clearer picture of tourism's size and complexity.

Most of the analysed models and theories draw their inspiration from a single or small range of social science disciplines, primarily sociology and economics, and in some cases the broader fields of geography and ecology. However, to date there has been little evident use of the growing field of business management. This is surprising, given that tourism is a business and if any community is to succeed in this industry and to be sustainable in an economic sense it needs to incorporate business principles into its portfolio of management techniques.

Chapter 2

Key Business Management Functions

While we find many tourism studies referring to and extolling the virtues of management, we seldom find explicit definitions of this term or descriptions of the principles and functions they involve. Even though tourism is recognised as a business very few authors of tourism papers and texts have attempted to incorporate business principles into their research. On the other hand, many authors refer in one way or another to the concept of management that sometimes includes a passing reference to tourism's business perspective. It is the purpose of this chapter to indicate there are indeed some highly relevant business management principles that can have a major bearing on how community tourism operates and to show how similar they are to many of the concepts espoused by non-business authors, such as social scientists.

If tourism is to develop and fulfil its potential it will require careful and detailed management, as many authors have indicated. The need for such management is particularly relevant to community tourism, which will need to involve a wide variety of interests and opinions. However, because most authors have failed to define what they mean by the term 'management', including those who place it in their titles, we are forced to interpret their evidence and advice in terms of traditional dictionary definitions. Most dictionaries define management as the process of managing, where the verb 'to manage' is defined as to guide the running of an activity like a business or household. While such a definition may cover the general purpose and intent of most past uses by academics and government officials, it is no longer satisfactory as a guide to the complex business and environmental management needed for many aspects of tourism development.

Strategic community tourism management will involve a host community deciding which elements of its local 'sense of place' resources to sell as a community product to tourists and the tourism industry. Such a process needs to include a variety of stakeholders with a common understanding of what is meant by management if they are to operate in successful collaboration. Given that tourism is a business, and the principal motivation for community tourism is to determine how to enter this business so as to achieve the best return for the community at large, one of the logical places to start this process is with the concept of business management.

Business Management

The field of business management is relatively young by academic standards and has come to the fore in the post-war reconstruction era, when businesses like tourism have become more complex and global, and the business environment more competitive than ever. Like all new academic fields of inquiry it has struggled to identify and distinguish itself from other academic disciplines and fields, and like most other academic areas it is now composed of a variety of sub-fields. One of business management's key differentiators has been to develop a scientific business management approach that leads to general principles of behaviour and outcomes. Within this approach the sub-field of organisation theory has focused on the total organisation of a business rather than individual worker–manager relations, leading to the current differentiation between organisational behaviour and human resource management studies. This interest in the total organisation has identified four principal functions of management that can be applied to an extensive range of situations, including areas like community tourism, that wish to combine business returns with other objectives.

One of the clearest descriptions of classical business management is offered by Daft *et al.* (1992: 5), who consider:

> Management is the attainment of organizational goals in an effective and efficient manner through planning, organizing, leading and controlling organizational resources.

This definition stresses the need to start with organisational goals, which will be both the signposts to later decision-making and the yardsticks by which to measure the success of subsequent actions. It identifies four basic functional steps in the process: planning, organising, leadership and controlling. These management principles are often used as the structure for many business texts and courses because of their general validity. All of which is encompassed in the pragmatic perspective of being effective and efficient, rather than presenting unattainable utopian systems.

A visual representation of the definition is presented in Figure 2.1. It shows how any organisation, be it a destination or single business, needs a vision of the future and its place within it. This vision needs to be converted into general goals and specific objectives through a *planning* process. To attain these objectives requires *organising* one's resources and assigning responsibility for different tasks and functions. An important task in any management process is *leading* staff through motivation and mentorship. Finally, there is a continuous need for *controlling* the efforts and outputs of

Figure 2.1 The process of management

the organisation, to ensure they are on track with respect to the original objectives and changing conditions.

This description is a compartmentalisation of continuous process, as indicated by the circular flow of the diagram, and as such is an artificial aid to highlight the individual importance of all four functions. One could argue about the placing and number of functions, and we have highlighted the need for *leadership* in all areas by placing it at the centre. This has been done because in the modern business world the only constant is change. It will require leadership to envision the new obstacles and opportunities, to assign tasks in a flexible and effective manner, and to select the appropriate forms of monitoring, as well as continue to motivate and retain key staff in a turbulent and competitive environment.

Four business management functions

Planning

The first management function of planning is needed to select which of the considered goals are more realistic and the possible ways to attain them. Such a process of selection should be guided at this stage and throughout by the need to be effective and efficient; effectiveness being viewed as the degree to which the organisation can achieve its stated objectives, and efficiency as indicated by the minimal use of resources to produced the desired outcomes (Daft, *et al.* 1992: 10–11). So the selection of which goals to pursue involves being realistic about potential returns rather than being overly optimistic about what one has to offer. Consequently, for community tourism this stage requires analysis that is both demand and supply driven. This stage also necessitates an objective assessment of their competitive position and not simply a reiteration of community pride. It is essential at this juncture to review and incorporate input from a range of stakeholders, especially those familiar with budgeting, marketing and community resources.

Organising

The second management function is organising. It is needed to assign specific task responsibilities to different departments, groups or individuals and to allocate sufficient resources to enable them to accomplish the selected planning goals. This should involve the matching of interests and capabilities with the assigned tasks. Increasingly in business, as well as tourism, the final delivery of the product or service requires a multitude of groups or individuals to combine their talents and skills. Similarly, in these competitive times everyone is being asked to 'do more with less', so the issue of resource allocation is a major one in all types of business.

Leadership

The third management function is leadership, which involves the motivation of people to achieve an organisation's objectives. Although Daft *et al.* have isolated leadership and identified it as the third function, this aspect of management is one which should and does pervade every function. It involves innovation and risk-taking and the ability to communicate ideas and enthusiasm.

For some this has become the most important element of modern management. *Time Magazine* reports:

> Once, the CEO had to run the business and watch the bottom line.Now he or she has to be a strategic visionary, an operations hawk and the chief salesman meanwhile keeping Wall Street investors happy. (Kelly, 2000: 58)

Such high expectations are now mirrored in the large salaries and benefit packages being paid to Chief Executive Officers (CEOs) of major companies and institutions, but they 'are also paying with their job for any big strategic failure' (Kelly, 2000: 58). Leadership is finally beginning to be recognised as an important element in tourism, and an example of this is presented in the case study at the end of this part of the book.

Controlling

The fourth function is controlling, which involves the monitoring of an organisation's activities to ensure they are on track with respect to the stated goals. Where deviations are detected, due to internal conditions or external factors, corrections are made as needed. Internal conditions needing correction in tourism could involve problems of communication and coordination between the different sectors, or unforeseen environmental and social impacts. External factors, like economic business cycles, currency fluctuations, and terrorism that cannot be predicted but can have significant ramifications on tourist destinations, require quick corrective responses on behalf of those destinations.

The tourism oriented terrorist attack in Bali required quick corrective responses from several parties and directions. The Australian government felt impelled to issue travel alert warnings to its citizens, advising them to avoid Bali and Indonesia in case of further incidents. Faced with a dramatic decline in business, the Balinese tourism industry developed a promotion campaign and adjusted prices to counter declining business. The airlines connecting Australia and Bali quickly reduced the number of flights until the shock and fear waned and travel numbers began to recover.

Tourism application

An example of these four functions at work in a community tourism situation can be seen in the Laws and Le Pelley (2000) article on managing tourism in the walled city of Canterbury, England (Figure 2.2). Although the authors do not specifically mention or advocate a complete business management approach involving the four functions, their review of the situation and current planning processes indicates these functions are present and being implemented to varying extents. Laws and Le Pelley (2000: 232) observe that the management challenges of a historic walled city are extreme, given that the different patterns of space usage by residents and visitors in such a confined area result in regular congestion and conflict. Consequently, the city of Canterbury has embarked on a series of initiatives that incorporate the four functions of business management.

They report that Canterbury's heritage tourism product was 'beginning to show signs of stagnation and decline' and that 'Canterbury can be considered to be approaching the zenith of its tourism life cycle, as the pressures of visitors is beginning to drive local people away'. Consequently, the city's *planning goal* is to reverse its decline as a tourist destination and sub-regional shopping centre by revising its visitor management strategies (Laws and Le Pelley, 2000: 234). To achieve this goal the city has *organised* a special legal entity, called the Canterbury City Centre Initiative (CCCI). This organisation is designed to 'develop a sustainable management strategy for tourists and shoppers that complement the

Figure 2.2 Canterbury's walled city catering to residents and visitors

qualities of life of Canterbury's residents by involving the tourist trade and residents in its evolution' (Laws and Le Pelley, 2000: 236).

Within the management structure of the CCCI Laws and Le Pelley identified a *leadership role*, and one which changes over time. They claim:

> the city visitor manager is the key individual who draws the partners together and administers the partnership and projects. In Phase 1, the manager was a quiet consolidator who built trust between the partners. In Phase 2, the new manager is a more outgoing personality who will 'sell' Canterbury's management initiatives and the benefits of the partnership. (Laws & Le Pelley, 2000: 236)

Such leadership changes are not uncommon in business or community ventures. The development of Victoria, Canada's successful 1994 Commonwealth Games, went through three different leadership needs and leaders. The first initiated the idea of hosting the Games and put together a team that eventually won the bid over Cardiff and New Delhi. Once the right to hold the Games had been won a different sort of leader was required, one who could coordinate the various municipalities and agencies to build the range of facilities that were needed to host this major event. The third and last leader was one who marketed the event to both domestic and international markets; especially to the challenging adjacent and lucrative United States market which has a limited understanding or appreciation of this major sporting event.

Control over the CCCI initiatives involves a comprehensive monitoring of its progress by an independent researcher based in a local college. This has resulted already in a revision to the original plans with 'the evolution of coach park management arrangements in conjunction with the users of the coach park' (Laws & Le Pelley, 2000: 241). In terms of results Laws and Le Pelley report most stakeholder groups are pleased with the current outcome of this management initiative, as shown in Table 2.1. Such evidence they feel 'demonstrates the value of partnership working, supported by a full-time manager and a sense of common purpose, in empowering a destination to manage its tourism industry in an environmentally and culturally sustainable manner' (Laws & Le Pelley, 2000: 243).

Environmental Scanning

As the above example indicates, any community tourism management will need to integrate tourism business needs with the host community's environmental setting and its tourism character. But that is true of any business, for all businesses are part of an open system. Business management regularly takes place within an open environmental situation that requires constant scanning if the business is to maximise its opportunities to succeed. Consequently the four functions of management cannot be

Table 2.1 Impacts of Canterbury's stakeholders

Stakeholders	Indicative tourism problems	Responses	Observed impacts
Residents	Congestion	Attract tourists into less visited areas	Group visit pressure dispersed on to four alternative pedestrian routes. Decrease in complaints from residents living on original route. Initial complaints from residents living on new routes have now decreased.
Tourists	Congestion Limited range of attractions	New walks Signing Maps Pedestrianisation New attractions	Increased tourist pressure in High Street as Cathedral management measures imposed. Tourists attract pedlars and buskers – complaints from shop keepers. Maps and signing effective in dispersing tourists.
Coach operators	Restricted and undeveloped parking	New coach park Visitor Shepherds	Complaints about length of walk to town centre and price of parking from some operators. Behaviour of tourists and congestion in town is modified by Visitor Shepherds welcoming tourists.
Cathedral	Crowds detract from experiences of visitors and worshippers	Shepherding scheme Entrance charges Burning incense	Ambience of Cathedral much improved. Visitor pressure is deflected into the town centre.
Environment	Air pollution Litter Inappropriate changes to historic buildings Wear and tear	Air quality monitoring at selected sites Park and ride to reduce cars in city New location for coach park Special planning controls	Air quality in town centre improves with increased pedestrianisation. Increased air pollution at new coach park. Drivers asked not to run engines whilst passengers away from coach. Special planning controls effective in maintaining historic ambience. Sheer volume of tourists overspills and widens paths provided.

Source: Laws and Le Pelley (2000: 242)

developed in isolation from the immediate setting of the host community or the wider context of our global economy, and must be viewed from the perspective of a business' overall organisational environment.

An organisational environment includes all the environmental elements that have the potential to affect an organisation. It is commonly drawn up into three major spheres of environmental influence, that also have particular relevance to tourism.

Internal environment

The internal environment is the area within the organisation's boundaries where it conducts its business. It is the corporate entity that manages its own affairs. It represents the opportunity to operate the four functions of management directly, but since no organisation operates in isolation, which is certainly true of tourism, it is influenced in its management options by the surrounding task and general environments.

Task environment

The task environment is the setting surrounding the actual organisation and consists of the sectors that 'conduct day-to-day transactions with the organisation and directly influence its basic operations and performance' (Daft *et al*. 1992: 68). In terms of community tourism this would be the host community setting, with its local labour pool, its supportive businesses, and visitors. In a community setting there are likely to be competitive businesses such as other attractions and hotels, but interestingly these competitors are sometimes collaborators.

Collaboration occurs in the development of partnership marketing, where individual and sometimes competitive businesses combine some of their marketing resources to attract visitors to their community destination. In the northwest corner of the United States the city of Seattle has periodically attempted to boost its attractiveness to distant urban markets in the rest of the country by linking with Victoria and Vancouver, British Columbia, to form a 'Discovery Triangle'. The strategy is that three different yet close destinations could present a combined product that would tempt Americans to travel the thousands of miles needed to reach Seattle and the Pacific Northwest.

General environment

The general environment is the outer layer representing the indirect affects of national policies and major global market and societal trends. In tourism such 'external' factors have long been recognised as major determinants of industry success, as demonstrated by Wahab's (1975: 94) assessment that 'tourism demand is highly sensitive to socio-political conditions and to changes in travel fashion'. For example, national policies regarding tourism marketing, currency exchange levels, and infrastructure such as international airports can have a major bearing on visitor volumes.

In the global and political arenas tourism has been shown to be susceptible to the insecurity generated by political instability and terrorism. Tourism in Fiji has suffered considerably from its series of political coups, and in Egypt terrorists have purposely targeted tourists in order to pressure their government into change. The 11 September terrorism in New York was aimed at corporate America, but it used a major tourism business – air travel, to destroy its targets.

Approach comparisons

As in all classifications of human behaviour the above definition of management with its four functional categories and the related environmental scanning factors should be viewed as simplified photographic snapshots of an ongoing and fluid process. Once planning goals have been selected and the management process put into operation it will take time to monitor the results and decide if corrective measures are needed. 'In this complex and dynamic environment, managers must continually adjust to changing conditions' (Stoner *et al.*, 1995: 18). In the past such a process traditionally was given a five-year period in which to unfold. But with the acceleration of the global business tempo and almost instantaneous communication of the modern media and Internet it is often no longer possible to stick to set time periods of any size. Tourism Victoria in Australia recently completed a standard five-year strategic plan for the state's tourism industry, that is discussed in more detail as a case study. Included in the five-year plan is a call for an annual review process:

> to evaluate the performance of strategies so that appropriate action can be taken if required. It may be necessary to change strategic directions within the plan in reaction to unforeseen events, or shifts in the global environment. (Tourism Victoria, 2002: 8)

This need to be flexible and to consider a series of decisions has led to strategic applications of the management processes discussed above. Henry Mintzberg (1979: 60–1), a major theorist in organisational structure, describes strategy as involving a stream of decisions that incorporates 'a complex multistage process' involving several elements, including 'a change in the environment'. So it is not surprising to see a strong link between our chosen definition of management and its associated need for environmental scanning with strategic management.

Strategic Management

The four business functions have much in common with the concept of strategic management, which is a business management process that has significant utility to the communal decision-making of community tourism. Mintzberg's view of strategy as 'a pattern in a stream of decisions' has two implications that have particular application to tourism, with its many sectors and exposure to significant external factors. First, this vision of strategic management consists of a series of decisions with some consistency between them based on pursuing the organisation's goals. Second, it means the organisation must consider decision alternatives, for 'strategy may be viewed as the rationale that governs the organisation's choices among its alternatives' (Stahl & Grigsby, 1992: 5).

Deliberate and emergent strategies

Mintzberg differentiates between deliberate strategy and emergent strategy, because changing business conditions are especially relevant given the fluid nature of our global economy. When strategies are the result of the management planning function they are a *deliberate strategy*, designed to achieve the organisation's goals. However, there are occasions when businesses do not intentionally set a specific strategy, but may simply fall into one as a reaction to outside forces or as the result of internal control procedures, which is the *emergent* approach.

If Athiyaman's (1995) assessment of tourism's use of strategic management is still valid then it would appear that many tourism businesses and destinations are in the emergent category. His study of tourism and hospitality research publications reveals few are concerned with strategy implications and he considers that this is due either to a reluctance to publish sensitive business information or a lack of activity in this area of management. He notes, however, that previous research did indicate 'tourism businesses lag behind manufacturing firms in strategic planning and the research necessary to support strategic planning' (Athiyaman, 1995: 452). This would indicate it is an area of weakness in many tourism businesses – including destinations.

Decision steps

A strategic management process according to Stahl and Grigsby (1992: 5–6) involves the entire range of decisions that an organisation makes to fulfil its purposes. It consists of the following three *procedural steps*:

- *Strategy formulation*, where a set of decisions determines the organisation's mission and establishes its specific objectives, strategies and policies.
- *Strategy implementation* that refers to decisions creating either a new strategy or reinforcing an existing one.
- *Evaluation and control*. These are the activities that keep the strategy on track and provide an information feedback loop to the first step.

Tourism Strategic Management

The tourism industry focuses on meeting the needs and expectations of visitors. To do this it needs to follow the four functions of management internally, and to undertake such procedures strategically in light of its task and general environments as well as its internal circumstances. In setting its goals the industry needs to work with the host community because it is selling the community as a commodity. In organising to welcome and accommodate the visitor the industry needs to include resident and community priorities and to look for leadership within the community as well as the industry. Finally, it needs to monitor the situation via visitor and resident surveys, environmental and financial audits, to ensure the stated industry and community goals are being achieved. While these essentially internal and task environment features are being considered and acted upon, both the industry and community need to be aware of the more general and external forces that can influence their management strategies. Features such as economic cycles or government policies need to be anticipated, and surprises, such as the Asian financial crisis of 1997 or the more recent terrorist attacks in New York and Bali, require contingency plans.

To operate tourism management strategies along business lines at the community level requires a strategic approach operating within an open system that can incorporate as many considerations as possible with input from different stakeholder groups. Such management cannot be highly detailed and specific, for it needs to be flexible enough to consider the evolving wishes of the community and tourism market, plus leaving itself enough room to meet changing outside forces. However, at all times it should be able to present clear community tourism objectives, outline a series of strategic steps to achieve those objectives, and be measurable so as to be accountable.

An example of this is seen in a South Australian award-winning strategic tourism plan (Tonge & Myott, 1993: 45–6). The Eyre Peninsula Tourism Association developed a simple *seven point plan* as outlined below:

(1) Establish a *structure* with multiple stakeholder representation.
(2) Establish an effective *communication* network.
(3) Create high *visibility*.
(4) Focus on *product development*.
(5) Establish/maintain necessary *funding* base.
(6) Ensure that there are *courses* to train industry participants.
(7) *Advertise* and promote.

The key to their success is that they have built the foundation for the presentation and operation of their tourism resources in a logical and practical manner.

Social responsibility

Clearly this form of community tourism management will be a major challenge, but it is not one that is unique nor is it that unusual in today's global economy. Many businesses have adopted the functional strategic management perspective outlined above and in the process have developed techniques and perspectives that can be of assistance to the goal of strategic community tourism management. Gordon *et al.* (1990: 90) refer to a trend toward 'social responsibility' where business executives 'see themselves as legitimate servants of a variety of constituencies'. This involves being more responsible to society at large and developing stronger and clearer ethical standards. Their motivations are not entirely altruistic as Klein (2000) points out in her book *No Logo*, for companies are under increasing pressure to act responsibly as their failures and shortcomings are noted and acted upon by knowledgeable consumers.

In the process of serving more constituents and acting ethically three particular business ideas have considerable applicability to the goal of strategic community tourism management. One is the concept of stakeholder analysis, whereby the interests and views of those affected by an organisation's activities are analysed and taken into account. This includes those outside of the organisation's internal environment, and is particularly germane to those living and working in the task environment which can be considered the equivalent of the host community. Another is the technique of portfolio analysis and strategy that brings together a variety of individual and business considerations to guide strategic planning. The other is the concept of corporate culture that reflects the shared values, beliefs and habits of an organisation that interact to produce behavioural norms and expectations.

Stakeholder analysis

As business has become more complex and now serves a multitude of interests, it is no longer sufficient to consider only those within an organisation. Now managers must not only consider profit margins and shareholder returns, but working with local communities and contributing in some way to the betterment of society. This need to think 'outside the box' stems from both pressures to include outside groups in decision-making and opportunities that arise when a broader perspective is taken. Community activism is assisted by the easier spread of information through modern technologies and legal precedents supporting community participation in local initiatives (American Planning Association, 1999).

Companies that observe and adapt to emerging global trends can position themselves appropriately and reap the benefits, as AT&T did when it transformed itself into a global communications company (Callenbach *et al.* 1993).

Gordon *et al.* (1990: 87–8) reflect this thinking in their *'primary roles of business'*, which they identify as consisting of three levels.

- *Level 1* 'represents the traditional economic functions of business'. It is where the business produces needed goods and services that in the process provides employment, contributes to economic growth and earns a profit for shareholders.
- *Level 2* represents the social responsibilities of business, to its workers in the sense of a safe working environment and to the surrounding community in terms of minimising the negative impacts of its operation, such as using resources carefully and reducing pollution.
- *Level 3* is concerned with business' 'responsibility for assisting society in achieving such broad goals as the elimination of poverty and urban decay through a partnership of business, government agencies, and other private institutions' (Gordon *et al.*, 1990: 88).

The parallels between the primary roles as identified above and environmental scanning's three zones are clear, and very relevant to the tourism business. The primary objective in each situation is to establish a healthy business that produces employment and profit within the organisation. But this is no longer the only role for business. It must now operate in a socially acceptable way and contribute to the general welfare of the task and general environments of society.

Proactive business practices

In many respects these broader social and environmental responsibilities have been placed on business by legislation, but some business scholars are demonstrating how a more proactive stance by business with regard to the Level 2 and Level 3 roles can lead to more harmonious relations between stakeholders. Howatson (1990) cites a study by the consulting firm of Arthur D. Little Inc. that in a survey of environmental management practices among United States' corporations found three *stages of development*.

- *Stage 1* represents those businesses that respond to problems only as they arise; in other words possess a 'reactive management' philosophy.
- *Stage 2* occurs when businesses establish systems and programmes to comply with legislation and regulations, which is compliance management.
- *Stage 3* occurs when businesses attempt 'to foresee hazards and regulations and, therefore, work systematically to minimise the effects of their operations on the environment, the health and safety of their workers, and the local community' (Howatson, 1990: vii).

The number of businesses at Stage 1 were thankfully small. Most businesses in the survey were classified as being at Stage 2, but a growing number of 'progressive firms' were moving into Stage 3 – 'beyond compliance'. Howatson considers this last stage is preferable from a business point of view, because they can be proactive, that is 'actively managing, rather than letting events force them to respond' (Howatson, 1990: viii).

From an environmental perspective there is a call to move beyond compliance, because this can be seen as 'shallow environmentalism' that focuses merely on meeting current environmental regulations and standards. 'Deep ecology', which strives to adopt a more progressive and holistic approach to management, is held up as the new ideal. These principles of deep ecology have found expression in the business community with firms such as The Body Shop and the Pantagonia Clothing Company (Callenbach *et al.*, 1993).

With these broader roles and responsibilities business has to consult and work with a larger group of stakeholders. Such stakeholders will vary from situation to situation, but in general terms researchers and practitioners have identified a manageable number of key groups. In Howatson's (1990: 11) review of Canadian businesses he identified four *stakeholder groups*. These included the following:

- *regulators* and *policy makers* in governments at all levels;
- *employees, investors* and *local communities* whose economic fortunes are tied to the corporation's well-being;
- *firms' customers* and *suppliers*; and
- *general public*, who watch 'The Journal' (the Canadian equivalent to 'Sixty Minutes' or 'Panorama'), support environmental groups and vote.

In one of the few tourism papers on the subject, Robson and Robson (1996) provided two examples in the tourism industry. In their schematic for a tour operator they identified 12 possible stakeholder groups, but it is possible to locate all of them within Howatson's broader framework. For example, we would place stakeholders in the following categories:

- central government bodies, national tourist organisations, regional tourist board;
- employees, local government tourism marketer;
- end users, transport providers, hoteliers, local and national attractions, travel agents; and
- Pressure groups and media.

Obviously in the modern world where individuals have multiple functions and responsibilities there can be some overlap between such groups. To a large extent this depends on which hat some stakeholders put on for the issue under examination. For example, in Robson and Robson's tour operator example the media could be functioning as an advertising forum or as the 'fourth estate', protecting the public's interest with its news stories.

Conflict issues

Regardless of the exact number of stakeholder groups identified in any particular analysis there is also the question of how they are to participate in any corporate decision-making. This has become a major issue in business management and general planning, for 'whenever people work together in groups, some conflict is inevitable' (Daft, *et al*. 1992: 529). Consequently, we are starting to see more research and experimentation with conflict resolution and facilitation processes.

Conflict types

In business increased attention is now paid to conflict causes, negotiation, and resolution. Conflict has been defined as 'antagonism or opposition between or among persons' (Gordon *et al.*, 1990: 532). It can take two forms. 'Substantive conflict' occurs in fundamental disagreements over goals and the means to accomplish them. 'Emotional conflict' involves interpersonal difficulties involving feelings of anger, dislike or resentment, and is commonly referred to as a 'clash of personalities' (Schermerhorn *et al.*, 1995: 203).

A key feature of modern business management is to manage both forms of conflict, so that the best possible outcome is achieved. Five potential conflict management approaches have been identified by Schermerhorn *et al.* (1995: 207) in Figure 2.3. The ideal outcome is the central box, when all parties view the decision as a 'win-win' situation. However, this may not always be obtainable, especially under the increasing circumstances of zero-sum situations, where the demands for more resources by one group can only be met by reducing another group's resources by a similar amount.

Negotiation

In the process of resolving such conflicts it is common to invoke a negotiation process. Negotiation 'is the process of making joint decisions when the parties involved have different preferences' (Schermerhorn *et al.*, 1995: 208), and two key goals are at stake in any negotiation. Most often attention is given to the *substance goals* that are concerned with the outcome relative to the content issues at hand, such as wage agreements or land use decisions. However, equally important are the *relationship goals* that indicate how well the parties will work together in the future, to make the negotiated settlement work. If the process of negotiation has been acrimonious it is unlikely that the final decision will be truly supported by all

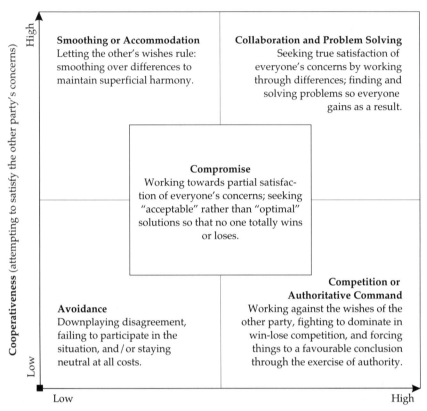

Figure 2.3 The conflict management grid with five conflict management styles

Source: Schermerhorn *et al*. (1995: 206)

parties, and in community tourism such an outcome will be reflected in sub-par products and service.

Participatory power

In planning, attention has been placed on securing real participation from various groups. Sherry Arnstein's (1969) now famous ladder of participation reveals how easy it is to dupe oneself and others into thinking there has been participation and not tokenism involved in a decision-making process. So planning agencies are now attempting to develop more open and effective processes by which to encourage participation and negotiation. One process that has been used effectively in land use planning situations and is being advocated for tourism is the nominal group technique (Ritchie, 1994). This technique facilitates the expression of individual views in a non-hostile situation, leading to the development of group priorities via a process of consensus building. More discussion of this technique and others will occur later in the book.

Portfolio analysis and strategy

A technique that has been developed in business management to provide information on a variety of dimensions that can guide strategic decision-making for a number of business units is portfolio analysis and strategy. Luehrman (1998) demonstrates how portfolio analysis is a common feature of general life as well as business life. Like anyone planning for the future when 'executives create strategy, they project themselves and their organisations into the future, creating a path from where they are today to where they want to be some years down the road' (Luehrman, 1998: 89). Such strategies become a series of options, and one of the most common facing everyone involves whether to take action or not. Action may be needed immediately, or deferred so as to benefit from circumstances as they evolve, or redundant because the opportunity has truly passed. These represent 'portfolios of real options' and can apply in everyday situations, as well as in business.

In business, the technique focuses on key dimensions such as market criteria or relative competitiveness, and applies those dimensions as criteria by which to judge the performance of various business units within a corporation. With that information strategic decisions regarding the best mix of business units can be made with respect to the corporation's goals and competitive advantage. In terms of community tourism the community can be considered the corporate entity and the business units its respective tourism businesses.

Boston Consulting Group matrix

One of the best known examples of this form of analysis and strategy is the Boston Consulting Group (BCG) matrix (Haspeslagh, 1982). It organises business units along the dimensions of market share and industry growth rate, and offers four distinct cells. Those business units that have a high market share in an industry with a high growth rate are called 'stars'. They will be attractive investments because they are already significant, maybe dominant, in the market and that market is growing. In the 1990s this description would have fit the cruise ship and gaming companies of the tourism industry. At the other extreme are the businesses in the low growth industries and which have a low market share of this stagnant or declining industry. These are the 'dogs' that have no bright future and if not currently profitable should be discarded, because their prospects are dim. Despite tourism being a significant growth industry over the past 50 years, there are some areas that could fall into this category. These would include some old-fashioned seaside resorts, with their piers and pinball arcades that have been forsaken for the sunnier climates and brighter lights of new destinations around the Mediterranean and Caribbean seas (Butler, 1980; *The Economist*, 2000b). However, it should not be forgotten that certain 'dogs' in tourism have rebounded by marketing their kitsch appeal as in the case of New Jersey's 'Jersey shore' or reinventing themselves such as Times Square in New York.

General Electric screen

A more sophisticated portfolio matrix has been developed by General Electric; this is their nine-cell GE screen (Daft *et al.*, 1992). This screen is based also on two composite dimensions – industry attractiveness and business strength – and offers the three options of low, medium and high scores. Industry attractiveness is a composite variable made up of factors such as market size and growth rate, plus industry profit margins, seasonality, and economies of scale. The business strength variable is composed from relative market share, profit margins and technological capacity. Such a screen in a tourism context could provide a more detailed assessment of individual business and destination prospects by equating a destination's position with industry attractiveness and a business' position with business strength.

Organisational strategy typology

Miles and Snow's (1978) organisational strategy typology indicates how business managers can formulate general strategies that are congruent with their organisational structure and external environment. It is significant in that it suggests strategies that combine the internal characteristics of a business with the external environment, and thus tries to pull together the three elements identified earlier in the environmental scanning process of this chapter. Their typology, as presented by Daft *et al.* (1992: 190), proposes four strategic positions and how they best relate to organisational characteristics and the task and general environments. These include a *prospector* strategy of innovation to create new markets; a *defender* strategy to protect existing markets; an *analyser* strategy to maintain current markets while encouraging moderate innovation; and a *reactor* strategy that simply reacts to changing conditions. Such strategies are particularly relevant to destinations entering the stagnation and beyond stages of Butler's tourist area evolution cycle, because they indicate possible options for businesses and the host community at that critical juncture.

Competitive strategy

Another portfolio typology that has received extensive interest, including from tourism writers, is Porter's (1980) competitive strategy.

Porter contends there are three ways to make a business competitive in this intensely competitive global environment. These are to emphasise its differentiation, overall cost leadership, and focus. The resulting competitive strategy has several components:

Differentiation

Differentiation is necessary to distinguish a business' products and service from those of its competitors. In tourism there is very little that a business or destination can offer that is truly unique, and hence one of a kind. Consequently many businesses and destinations have attempted to differentiate themselves from the competition by emphasising specific images and qualities. However, there is a growing appreciation that each destination does have something unique to offer – its sense of place. This is the essence of Rosenow and Pulsipher's (1979) place personality planning process.

A sense of place is the character and lifestyle that has evolved in each community and is the sum of local people interacting with the local environment and their history of this association. This has led to local building styles, traditional costumes, and local customs. If these traditional links with the past can be maintained in the face of increased global homogenisation then a destination has something 'unique' to offer the tourism market.

Cost leadership

Cost leadership is important in a free market situation, where the market determines prices and businesses can only influence their profit margins through the cost control of their operations. Cost control should be considered in real terms, which is the level of productivity associated with the costs involved, so it does not necessarily equate with minimising wages.

In a labour intensive industry such as tourism this is an important consideration. But rather than thinking simply of monetary costs tourism should consider real labour costs. These are the costs to be compared with the level of sales and service achieved, that in turn can be linked to the professional skills of the workforce. If cost considerations incorporate the skill levels of employees the chances of meeting or exceeding tourist expectations are increased, and tourists will return home satisfied and happy customers. Such happy customers become the goodwill ambassadors for a business and a destination, and spread the good news by word of mouth to their friends and relatives.

Investing in training and rewarding employees with higher wages or bonus systems have been shown to increase the levels of productivity and service quality in tourism. Some studies comparing German and British tourism workers have found the Germans, who received more training and higher salaries, are more productive and provide better service than their British counterparts (Scottish Tourism Research Unit, 1998 cited in

Nickson, 2000). The Butchart Gardens is one of Victoria, Canada's most successful tourist attractions and has a worldwide reputation for quality. One of the reasons for its success is the training it provides its young front-line staff. This not only produces knowledgeable and enthusiastic employees but also contributes to a low staff turnover rate from season to season, thereby reducing future staffing costs.

Focus

Although the first two dimensions of Porter's portfolio strategy are key to competitiveness they cannot be expected to work to the same degree on every market. A destination's 'sense of place' product, for example, will appeal to only a certain segment of the tourism market. The type of tourism developed in a destination will influence the expectations and hence the cost factors of the operations. So the expectations and costs involved in operating a heritage attraction like Colonial Williamsburg in the United States will differ significantly from operating a seaside resort, where the principal attraction is the public beach and not restored buildings and antiquities with first person interpretation.

Hence Porter's third dimension is to focus on a specific regional market, product line or buyer group. This involves matching the product with a market segment that will bring sufficient business to make the exercise worthwhile. An up-market product and price would appeal to certain special interest segments; whereas a more generic and low priced product would appeal to a mass market. This process equates to the common seg-mentation strategy of modern marketing, in that 'a market segment consists of consumers who respond in a similar way to a given set of marketing stimuli' (Kotler & Armstrong, 1989: 42).

To focus on a segment or several segments it needs to be possible for des-tinations to identify the following four segmentation characteristics.

(1) They should be *measurable*, in the sense one can determine their size and purchasing power.
(2) They should be *accessible*, in terms of being reached by any promotion and able to visit the destination.
(3) They should be *sustainable*, in that they are a long-term proposition and not a short-term fad or 'one-day wonder'.
(4) Finally, they should be *actionable*, in the sense that effective marketing programmes can be designed to attract and serve the targeted seg-ments.

While all of the above business techniques and management strategies have been discussed in isolation, it should be appreciated that they often operate in conjunction. In addition, these decisions not only influence the form and direction of a business; in turn they are influenced by the values and beliefs of the business operators themselves. Hence, any strategic management must consider the corporate culture of the organisation involved if it is to be implemented rather than left on a shelf.

Corporate and Community Culture

A corporate culture is 'the set of key values, beliefs, understandings, and norms that members of an organisation share' (Daft *et al.*, 1992: 540), and is frequently cited as a major factor in the success or otherwise of many businesses. The reason is that most businesses and certainly all communities are made up of a variety of people performing different tasks, and how they view events and proposals is strongly determined by the history and norms of their organisation.

Certain corporations, such as The Body Shop, are gaining profits and respect through the development of caring cultures to guide their businesses. Anita Roddick (2000: 58), founder of The Body Shop sees:

> The old views of business as a jungle where only the vicious survive will, I hope, soon be giving way to a new view of business as a community where only the responsible will lead. If your values are heralded and if your heart is in the right place, if your feelings are recognized and your spirit at play I believe there will be footprints out there for all of us.

Thus, once again we have a close parallel between business management and community tourism aspirations, in that both need to consider the background and feelings of their constituents.

Schein (1992) has suggested that there are three levels of culture in most organisations. The invisible yet basic building blocks of a corporate culture are its *fundamental underlying assumptions*. These are the unconscious and often taken-for-granted beliefs, perceptions, thoughts and feelings of those working in the organisation. They become the corporate body's source of values and interpretations and they influence how people will react to events or proposals. As such it leads to the sort of social representation that Pearce *et al.* (1996) identified as being important to community reaction to tourism.

The underlying assumptions of the organisation's personnel lead to their *espoused values*, or the reasons given for doing things the way they are done. Stoner *et al.* (1995: 185) relate how DuPont stresses the value of safety, based on its original business of making gunpowder; and in the cited words of a past chairman 'Either you make gunpowder safely, or you don't make it for very long'. Peters and Waterman (1984) in their book and video on company excellence reveal that the driving force for the Disney organisation is to make people happy, and this is the principal stated value for their theme parks.

Both of the preceding levels create the *artefacts* of a corporate culture, which are the visible forms of products, services, and the behaviour patterns of organisation members. These represent the external image of the organisation and its products and services. As such they indicate to consumers what the organisation publicly values and is willing to bring to the marketplace. It may be as mundane as a dress code or a company uniform, but it is part of the corporate culture that delivers the final product. For example, McDonald's is in the fast food business, but many weekend sports coaches know it also welcomes children and has clean toilets. In terms of community tourism a host destinations' artefacts, such as well-maintained facilities, good service and a friendly atmosphere, will signify visitors are welcome. Perhaps the prime example of this is Hawaii's famous 'Aloha' spirit.

Corporate game culture

Corporate culture has been described by some business analysts as a game (Gerber, 1995) and their description of the process makes it particularly relevant to the mood of tourism businesses. Businesses are considered to function well when their organisation produces the product and service as a game, and the corporate culture becomes one of creating fun and enjoyment. This enthusiasm and loyalty to the corporate culture has been nurtured and developed in some prominent tourism companies, such as Disney, Club Med, and McDonald's. From such evidence Gerber (1995: 204–6) identifies eight rules to create a *successful corporate game culture*. These are:

(1) Start with a *game strategy* (be prepared).
(2) *Know* and *play* the *game* yourself (be a team player).
(3) *Create ways* for *winning* without ending the game (create a reward system).
(4) Periodically *change the tactics* of the game, but not the strategy (be flexible but always stick to your ethics and beliefs).
(5) Keep the *game going* (remind staff of goals, roles and rewards).
(6) The game has to *make sense* (keep it interesting, effective, and simple).
(7) Keep it *fun* (fun as defined by the team).
(8) If you *can't think* of a *good game, steal one* (copy the corporate culture of a benchmark company in your industry).

With the many challenges tourism presents, like demanding work schedules and numerous community impacts, it is important that those involved create a corporate culture that strengthens their business and community. Achieving the 'right' corporate culture takes hard work to establish and requires a sensitivity and responsiveness to customer-, staff- and environment needs. Since an important component of tourism is fun, it makes sense for individual tourism businesses to incorporate an element of fun into their corporate culture.

Multicultural dimensions

Another feature of corporate culture that is emerging, as the workforce changes due to demographic trends and legislation, is *multiculturalism*. This recognises there are now 'many different cultural backgrounds and factors that are important in organisations, and that people from different backgrounds can coexist and flourish within an organisation' (Stoner *et al.* 1995: 191). The multicultural factors that have come to the fore include consideration of ethnicity, race, age, gender, physical ability and sexual orientation. While much of the public and press attention in this area has focused on organisations like the armed forces, the police and firefighters, it is particularly germane to tourism.

Tourism is a global industry that has a world market, which means customers come to a destination from a variety of ethnic and racial backgrounds, and they don't all speak or read English. If a community is to engage in tourism it must not only be prepared to serve such a varied market; it should be excited by the prospect. One of the best ways to meet the expectations of international visitors is to have staff from similar backgrounds or trained to speak and understand the different languages and cultures they will meet. Another rising market is the seniors' market, where personal needs can change dramatically over a 20- to 30-year period of retirement. But it is not only the global market that is changing and growing; in many parts of the world the sources of labour are changing. Many of the front-line positions in tourism are filled traditionally by young people, but as populations in the Western economies age the pool of such suitable labour has shrunk. This has encouraged some companies (the fast food sector in particular) to turn to other groups; and has seen the rise of part-time work for seniors. The tourism industry is only just beginning to adjust to such changing conditions and to recent legislation encouraging the hiring of minority groups, but if it wishes to survive and serve it needs to take on a more multicultural perspective.

Implementation

The four-function definition of business management along with the application of a strategic management approach holds great promise for the combination of community aspirations with the business interests of tourism. This book is not alone with such an assessment, for Swarbrooke (1999) in his recent book, *Sustainable Tourism Management*, has come to a similar conclusion. He notes that use of the term management has been rather casual and incomplete in the past and he too advocates a more complete model of strategic management that incorporates monitoring, evaluation and control mechanisms.

To date there has, perhaps, been too much emphasis placed on strategy generation rather than strategy implementation. Yet unless it can be implemented there is no point in having a strategy . . . Most existing strategies tend to be public-sector led destination strategies or rather academic, generic strategies for the tourism industry as a whole. (Swarbrooke, 1999: 355)

For any strategy to be implemented on a community basis it needs to address many of the business management principles and techniques outlined above. One of the best ways to illustrate the points of this argument is to conclude with an actual case study.

The selected case is of a small business in Victoria, British Columbia, Canada. The business – Victoria Harbour Ferry – has faced many of the issues discussed above and illustrates the close connection that can develop between a tourism business and its host community. It exemplifies the majority of tourism businesses in that it is an owner operated small business, it is dependent on the appeal of its host community, and it is seasonal in nature.

Case Study: Victoria Harbour Ferry

(Paul Miller, Victoria Harbour Ferry)

The Victoria Harbour Ferry Company operates a small water-bus system with a tourism rather than transport emphasis in and around the harbours of Victoria, which is the provincial capital of British Columbia on Vancouver Island and receives over four million visitors a year (Figure 2.4). It was started by Paul Miller in 1990 and by 2002 consisted of 10 small boats, a staff of 32, which handled around 150,000 passengers a year. In the years of its existence Paul has won several plaudits, including the GEM (Going that Extra Mile) Award from the Victoria Hospitality Society and becoming the President of Tourism Victoria (the destination tourism association) in 1999. The internal environment of the company exemplifies the *four functions of business management*, as outlined above. This case study is gleaned from several class presentations by Paul Miller and subsequent conversations. The interpretation of the facts is the sole responsibility of the authors.

Planning

In the *planning* stage Paul's initial goal was to provide a water-bus transport system around the three interlinked harbour areas of Victoria. Like most small business operators he was not in a position to undertake a detailed market analysis, but he did use his eyes and his head.

My market really consisted of a study of the way the system in Vancouver worked and in the isolation of differences and similarities with my proposed market (in Victoria). I thought at the time that what was required was a large mass of people in one place and an attraction or

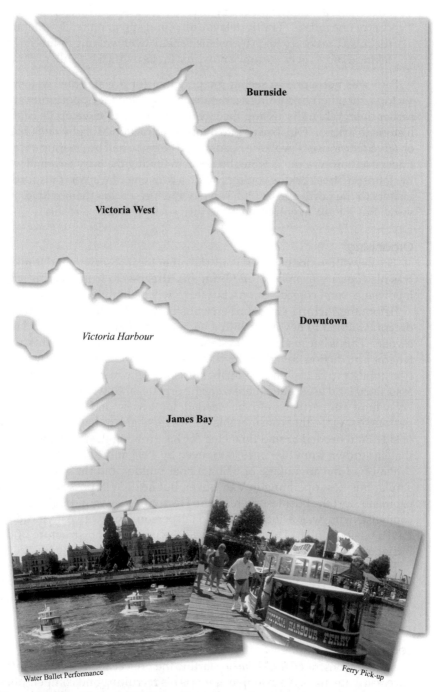

Figure 2.4 The Victoria Harbour Ferry operations

attractions in another place or places, across a body of water not in excess of one mile . . . Traffic delays didn't and still don't really enter into the mix. The choice to go by boat is usually over walking or bussing or taking a cab . . . or as we now know, just for its own sake. (Miller, 1998)

Paul was not alone in seeing the potential for a water-bus system in Victoria, for others, including academics, had spotted the opportunity at an earlier date. When discussing the city's aspirations to develop its central historic district of 'Old Town' into a tourist attraction Murphy (1980b: 71) observed the tourists' walking needs could be cut in half by creating a water transportation system. 'A water bus system linking the ferry terminal with the Johnson Street Bridge could provide a convenient way of transporting visitors to the north end of Old Town, while presenting them with a new vista'. But it took an entrepreneur to turn such ideas into a reality.

Organising

The key difference between Paul and other local observers and thinkers was his capacity *to organise* and bring his 'dreams' to fruition. This stage involved several considerations, but three will be highlighted here.

Before the Victoria Harbour Ferry business could become more than a dream Paul had to negotiate with a wide range of jurisdictions and landowners. This is because a ferry system links land and water elements, with federal jurisdiction covering the rules and regulations of sea transportation, while provincial and municipal jurisdiction cover the shoreline and associated land uses. Then there were the private landowners and developers whose property would be needed for access and as a source of passengers. Once this considerable and diverse group had been brought onside Paul needed to find financing for his growing fleet of boats: a fleet that has grown from two in 1990 to seven by 1994 and 10 in 2002.

Paul had the advantage of being a boat builder and the example of a similar business operating in Vancouver, but he did not possess sufficient capital to start the business on his own. His solution was finding a venture capitalist, who was a local professional person, and was convinced by Paul's business plan. This plan outlined the purpose and structure of the business, along with realistic financial projections.

Finally, Paul insists a key to this stage of business formation was the support he received from his wife who is an accountant. In all his presentations to students Paul emphasises what a blessing it has been to have such support and such important skills at home.

Leadership

Paul demonstrated *leadership* in starting the project and building it into a successful business. An example of this is his recruiting and compensation procedures. Like all tourism businesses he relies heavily on the quality and enthusiasm of his staff, for it is the single employee in charge of each boat – the 'skipper', who presents the company's face to the public. Skippers needed to be skilled people who possessed, or were willing to achieve, the appropriate master's certification needed to pilot his boats. They needed to be customer- and service-oriented, who knew and loved their local community. They needed to be available for seasonal employment, generally extending from April to October. What he found were retired airline pilots, retired navy officers and business people who were happy to work on the water during Victoria's warmer months and to take up to five months' vacation over the winter months. In recognition of his staff's contribution to the success of the business Paul instituted a profit-sharing system in addition to a regular salary. This system encourages each skipper to treat his boat as his personal contribution to the business and has helped the business develop a staff retention rate of 80%, which by industry standards is excellent.

Control

Paul's *control* over the business is demonstrated by his participation as one of the skippers in the early years, as a continuous observer of the operation, and as an auditor of its progress. As a skipper he was able to see how the business operates on the frontline, and as an external observer from points around the harbour he can see how well the transport system and schedule is working. It was based on these experiences that Paul changed the entire marketing direction of the business after its first few years of operation, as will be discussed in the next section. By auditing the business' progress Paul could determine when he needed to change from a partnership arrangement with the venture capitalist into a sole proprietorship. Which is also discussed in the next section under strategic management.

Strategic management

Strategic management, as exemplified by strategy formation, implementation, evaluation and control, can be seen in the evolution of Victoria Harbour Ferry. At its formation the initial goal of the business was to be a transport company, with an expected 50:50 split between locals and visitors using the service. However, by the end of the third season, an evaluation of the company's experience and observations from Paul and other skippers suggested transportation was not the company's main business. It became apparent that the major customers were tourists and these people had a thousand questions about what they were seeing.

As a result of this evaluation it was decided to change the focus of the business from transport to tourism. Paul and his skippers developed talks that provided a tour guide to the harbour waters and surrounding points of interest. Unlike the Disney example cited in Peters and Waterman (1984), where a set drama and script is composed for the boat guides in the 'Jungle River Cruise', 'each skipper lends his own style, personality and experience to his unique tour' (Miller, 1998). It is this paradigm shift in presentation, from a transport focus to a tour business, that Paul credits with much of his subsequent success.

Success also caused Paul to make a strategic change to the business' ownership. A key issue in working with silent partners, like the venture capitalist, is to know when to cut the umbilical cord and buy them out. Paul maintains that if he had not bought out his partner's share of the business when he did, after four years of operation, he would never have been able to afford to own his company outright. The reason was that as the business grew older and more successful it became more valuable, and to buy back the percentage owned by the venture capitalist would eventually have become too onerous. So a key element in the strategic relationships with external stakeholders is timing – knowing when to enter and exit such partnerships.

Stakeholder analysis

Besides concerning himself with internal stakeholders such as his staff and partner, Paul had to be aware of the interests of *external stakeholders* such as his customers and community partners. As a result of changing the business focus to tourism and listening to his customers Paul has extended the initial route structure to incorporate some additional tourism attractions. One of the longest runs now takes his small boats to the inner reaches of the harbour, where a renovated pioneer home – Point Elice House, which now nestles among the industrial uses of a 'working harbour', has become a local tourist attraction.

In tourism individual businesses do not operate in a vacuum. They are part of a destination (task environment), where the approach should be 'sell the destination first and your business second' if a business wishes to attract sufficient customers. To do this Paul networked extensively with existing tourism businesses and the destination association of 'Tourism Victoria'. In fact, one of the authors first met Paul on a Tourism Victoria committee that was attempting to boost interest in local events and festivals. However, such networking is not all business related. This community orientation revealed itself in several ways; including the rescuing of some competitor vessels and shuttling convention delegates from their hotel to a conference function at the provincial museum when an interconnecting road bridge was put out of commission. It was for acts like these that Paul won the GEM award.

Portfolio analysis

As part of his strategic planning Paul is a great advocate for one particular form of portfolio analysis, that being Covey's (1989) time management matrix. In this case the two dimensions under consideration are whether an activity should be classified as important or urgent. The resulting four-cell matrix indicates different time management priorities. Those in Quadrant 1 are both important and urgent so have been termed crises and require immediate attention. Those in Quadrant 2 are important but not urgent. As such they allow deliberation and the search for best solutions. Quadrant 3 activities are not important but urgent. We could add the insistent presence of e-mail to this category, in the sense that most e-mail messages are not vital but they carry the expectation of a quick response. In Quadrant 4 the activities can be classified as neither important nor urgent, thus allowing them to be postponed and attended to at convenient times. 'Effective people stay out of Quadrants 3 and 4 because, urgent or not, they aren't important. They also shrink Quadrant 1 down to size by spending more time in Quadrant 2' (Covey, 1989: 153).

For business and Paul it is in the 'important and not urgent' Quadrant 2, where a manager places emphasis on the long-term issues and require-ments that are essential to the health and prosperity of the company. Although tourism businesses are open to the influence of external factors over which they have little control, Paul believes that preparation can help to mitigate their negative effects and to enhance their positive ones. Hence he supports Covey's management emphasis on focusing on matters that are 'important and not urgent'. In this regard he uses the business' down-time to service and refurbish his boats to minimise any mechanical problems during the season. Paul always has a spare boat or two to cover for any internal or external emergency that should arise. Since the tourist season is determined to a large extent by the weather Paul has developed a flexible scheduling system that enables him to have a soft start or ending to the season.

Corporate to community culture

To guide his company's strategic management and make it stand out in a crowded marketplace Paul decided to create a strong and definite mission statement. When he started the ferry business in 1990 his original mission statement was 'To become the best loved business in town'. Which meant it had to be noticed and appreciated, not just by its customers but also the host community.

Given the above evidence it is apparent that the Victoria Harbour Ferry has taken a very proactive role in its community relations, but none that compare to the returns received from one generous gesture. At one of the Tourism Victoria meetings discussing events and festivals Paul volun-teered to have his 'fleet of five boats' open the spring boating festival with a water ballet. This meant he had to choreograph the performance and provide loudspeaker music to the inner harbour where the ballet was to be performed in the prime tourist district 15 minutes before the start of his regular schedule.

This offer was accepted with alacrity and seeing these small boats bob and weave to the strains of the 'Blue Danube Waltz' proved to be the hit of the festival. It was such a hit that it has been retained and is repeated each Sunday morning from mid-June to mid-September, before the start of that day's schedule. For this goodwill gesture Paul considers he has been repaid tenfold. As an example he cites a travelogue put together by a Seattle television station to demonstrate Victoria's potential as a weekend 'get-away' holiday destination. In their short two-minute presentation they refer to and show Paul's funky ferry boat water ballet six times. No small business could afford to purchase such advertising, but in this case it came for free.

Summary

This chapter notes that use of the term management by tourism researchers and writers has been rather casual in the past, and despite tourism being the largest industry in the world there has been a disappointing level of discussion of business management principles in the literature for this industry. Hence, this chapter attempts to demonstrate the relevance of many business functions and concepts to tourism in general and to strategic community tourism management in particular. Starting with the four basic functions of business and proceeding to strategic management with its portfolio analysis and other techniques, it is possible to show the direct applicability of many business concepts and techniques to tourism. This has been illustrated further by concluding with a detailed case study of one small tourism business that has been community oriented and successful.

Part 2

Key Business Management Functions in Tourism

Management Functions

A key feature of modern tourism and this book is to view tourism as a business providing value for its host community as well as its owner. To understand how we can arrive at such a symbiotic state between a business and its context requires a preliminary overview of management theory and tourism's place within this evolving discipline.

Management theory is an academic discipline of the twentieth century and it has evolved into several established specialisation sub-fields over time. According to (Stoner *et al.*, 1995) its early stirrings were associated with the need to increase productivity and efficiency which led to the development of the Scientific Management School. This in turn evolved into the Classical Organisational Theory School as the emphasis focused on large corporations. From these beginnings sprang the Behavioural School and Management Science sub-fields, as large corporations became global organisations requiring their own forms of technical and human management. As business functions became more complex and interrelated the Systems Approach was advocated as a way to direct the various component parts, and the Contingency or Situational Approach became necessary with the cross-cultural influence of international business. Finally, Stoner *et al.* identify the current era of management theory as one of Dynamic Engagement, where circumstances 'are forcing management to rethink traditional approaches in the face of constant, rapid change' (Stoner *et al.*, 1995: 49).

One who would agree with that last assessment is Normann (1991), who has championed the new era of service management. He maintains that management of services is different from the predominantly manufacturing management concepts because there are some basic differences between the two types of business. The ways service differs from manufacturing include:

- the service is tangible;
- the service product/experience cannot be resold;
- the service product/experience cannot be pre-demonstrated because it does not exist until the actual purchase;
- the service product cannot be stored;

- production and consumption generally coincide, and always coincide with a tourism experience;
- production, consumption and often even selling are spatially united;
- the service product cannot be transported;
- the buyer/client takes part directly in the production/experience;
- in most cases direct contact is necessary;
- the service cannot normally be exported, but the service delivery system can.

(Normann, 1991: 15)

To incorporate these distinctive service components into management theory Normann advocates a service management system that incorporates a new service culture combining a market segment with an image and delivery system that emphasises service. As such this is a perfect description of the modern tourism business.

Tourism is a service industry that sells travel experiences. It is made up of numerous components to provide the complete experience, and an important part of the travel experience is often the economists' 'free/public goods' – the landscape, amenities like beaches, parks and toilets, and access via roads or hiking trails. The economists are referring to goods that do not need to be purchased by an individual because they are provided as a public service by the host community, but these goods and services are not free. They cost host communities and local residents many dollars through their taxes. This makes tourism a distinctive service industry, for to function it not only requires a partnership between host and guest, it often depends on a symbiotic arrangement between the public and private sectors.

Another distinctive feature of tourism, and one that distinguishes it from much of the past management theories and literature, is that it is the realm of small business and not large corporations. Although it is the multi-national companies that first come to mind it is really the small to medium-size enterprises (SMEs) that form the bulk of this industry; and they are maintaining their dominance as the market fragments into a myriad of special interest segments. Hence, one of the new 'dynamic engagement' areas of management has particular relevance to tourism, and that is the growing sub-field of entrepreneurship.

Tourism needs to be viewed as a multi-disciplinary subject that incorporates management principles with environmental, social and political considerations and this is the approach taken and explored in this part of the book. Its development should involve management – 'the process of getting things done through the efforts of other people' (Gordon *et al.*, 1990: 4) in a business and community sense. The management principles that are considered to be particularly relevant in this case are those general requirements that need to be considered by business and organisations of all sizes, namely the four generic functions of planning, organising, leading and controlling.

Part Outline

The four functions of business are an artificial division of what should be a continuous management process, but have been isolated and discussed in the following order to demonstrate their individual importance. The order generally represents a chronological sequence of management events, but the placement of leadership is somewhat arbitrary. One could argue that leadership is needed at all stages and at the planning stage in particular. Therefore, some authors feel all ambitious management processes should begin with leadership.

This part gets underway with a discussion of the planning function in Chapter 3. It examines how planning is used in a business context before moving on to how it has been applied in a community tourist context. Chapter 4 demonstrates the importance of organisation to put plans into operation and the increased difficulty of this step in community situations where there are so many different interests and opinions. What helps in situations where there is a wide variety of opinions is leadership, and this is discussed in Chapter 5. Although leadership is a fundamental function of management it has proved to be difficult to categorise and explain. However, there can be little doubt about its significance to tourism as the examples in this and other chapters so clearly illustrate. Chapter 6 discusses the importance of control, both in a business and tourism sense. The chapter demonstrates how controlling has moved from an emphasis on the operational and environmental features in tourism to a more comprehensive concern over matching consumer and community interests.

To demonstrate the effectiveness and interaction of the four business functions to strategic tourism management the part ends with a case study. The case is drawn from a recent strategic tourism plan in Australia. It highlights not only the business functions but the growing use of IT and the government's role as an important facilitator for the strategic management of this industry.

Chapter 3

Planning

The first step in any management process is planning. Although the first step is always crucial, in management the planning stage is only the beginning of a decision-making sequence. While this chapter will examine planning as a separate entity it should be appreciated that it is linked with the other three functions of management in a continuous exchange of information and ideas. This is particularly true when a business organisation's or community's participation in a global industry needs to be planned and integrated with various levels of government planning initiatives.

In a business sense, the increasingly global and competitive tourism market means the planning options and techniques outlined below should be viewed as general guidelines that can be customised to suit local environmental and market conditions. Given this competitive market and tourism's susceptibility to external forces, the ideal planning structure needs to be flexible and dynamic rather than rigid and sacrosanct. An important part of this flexibility and openness to change will be determined by planning's links to the information flowing back from the other three functions of organisation, leadership and control. In this way individual businesses and destinations can hope to adjust to changing market and social conditions in both a responsive and responsible manner.

As we are examining strategic planning options for a community tourism industry they will need to incorporate more than business concerns. Since the tourism industry will be selling a community the planning phase should be more oriented to the external task environment and more consensual in nature than normal business planning. This responsiveness involves consideration of land use and social planning principles in conjunction with the standard business objectives. Hence, as in the subsequent chapters of this part, this review will focus on concepts and techniques that have broad applicability and will attempt to blend business and societal planning principles that will provide for a solid strategic community tourism management approach.

Business Planning Process

The standard business approach to the planning process is to complete five steps that set the direction for the subsequent functions, realising that those functions in turn can and will impact on the planning phase. Although planning is an internal business function it needs to respond to and anticipate those forces in the task and general environments that can influence the organisation. Thus it is a dynamic process that should be continuously evaluated and adapted to conform to the unfolding situation faced by an organisation.

The first step is to determine the organisation's *vision* of the future and its place within it. A company's vision involves looking to the future, attempting to assess what is needed and the best ways to supply those needs. Visions are often the result of a documented consultation process, primarily consisting of market research and competitive analysis that are used to pull together the views of various people in an organisation regarding future prospects and alternative actions.

The second step is to establish a *mission* for the organisation. This represents its continuing purpose or reason for being. At its core a mission statement describes in a general sense a type of organisation and why it is needed. Published mission statements generally relate to the service of customers and a desire to be a benchmark company, that is one that sets the standards for its particular industry. The unpublished and assumed mission is to make a profit for shareholders and in order to survive. But according to some, corporate missions need to encompass a number of constituent groups besides the shareholders. These include:

> Employees should be assured of continuing, profitable employment under conditions conducive to good health and personal growth. And the right of society to have good corporate citizens – who obey the laws, produce economic output efficiently, and sustain the environment must not be neglected. (Gordon *et al.*, 1990: 109)

In business the mission need not be published or promoted outside of an organisation but it needs internal promotion to be clearly understood by managers and staff at all levels. Small businesses and those run entirely by their founders are less likely to have a formal mission statement, or even a loosely defined long-term plan, but the more focused they are on a specific approach or plan the easier it will be to make all subsequent decisions.

The third step is to create *goals*. Goals are the very purpose(s) that an organisation strives to achieve, and they are either identified directly within a mission statement or are implied. While the mission statement represents the overarching ambitions of the company, goals provide a sense of direction. They are put in place to guide plans and decisions and help in focusing efforts and evaluating progress.

The fourth step in the business planning process is to establish objectives. These are the desired results. There are three types of objectives that are relevant to both individual businesses and to a community development situation. These are:

(1) *Economic objectives*, concerned with survival, profit and growth. These represent the engine of any business organisation that has to compete in an open market.
(2) *Service objectives* relate to the creation of benefits for society. These reflect the external relationships of the organisation and particularly its contribution to the wellbeing of the task environment of its host community.
(3) *Personal objectives* that are the objectives of individuals and groups within the organisation. These acknowledge the importance of teamwork and the importance of recognising individual contributions to the organisation's success.

Hence, this typology of objectives reveals the profit motivation is not the only consideration in business planning, many managers also recognise their obligation to society and the need to consider the personal aspirations of individual units and people within their organisation.

Good objectives possess the following *four basic characteristics* (Gordon *et al.*, 1990):

(1) They should be expressed *in writing*, so there can be no doubt as to what is proposed.
(2) They should be *measurable*, so it is possible to determine whether they have been achieved.
(3) They should be *time specific*, so it is known by when the objective should be accomplished.
(4) They should be *challenging but attainable*, so that some effort is needed to achieve the stated objective.

Such objectives should be set by top management and should be consistent with the overall mission of the organisation.

The fifth and final step in the business planning process is the actual act of *planning*, or stating how the objectives are to be accomplished. Three levels of planning are commonly recognised in business management. These are strategic planning, tactical planning and contingency planning.

Strategic planning

Strategic planning from a business perspective is concerned with developing practices that can attain the stated objectives over a period of time. 'One characteristic that strategic planning shares with budgeting/control and long-range planning management systems is that it is largely based on a periodic planning system, usually an annual (or even longer) system' (Aaker, 1992: 11). While annual planning periods suit most tourism businesses due to the regular seasonal nature of the business, there are times when more extensive planning or faster responses are needed.

Certain business practitioners and researchers would like to replace the term planning with all its time period and cycles ramifications with the broader term of management. Aaker (1992: 11) maintains that:

> Strategic management is motivated by the assumption that the planning cycle is inadequate to deal with the rapid rate of change that can occur in the environment facing the firm. To cope with strategic surprises and fast-developing threats and opportunities, strategic decisions need to be precipitated and made outside the (regular) planning cycle.

Consequently, Aaker suggests a continuous real-time process of decision-making to complement the structured periodic analysis of strategic planning. Thereby companies can still be counted on for their mandatory reviews, while having the flexibility to conduct further reviews and modifications as unforeseen circumstances arise. This is the process advocated in this book for all tourism businesses and destinations.

Strategic planning or management is often recommended, but given the complexity of modern business and the daily demands on managers' time it often receives only lip-service. However, in a study by Yip (1985), cited in Aaker (1992), of the strategic development of 13 companies, he found that strategic planning approaches had particular relevance for those businesses that are dependent or involved in the following:

- *multi-functional strategies*;
- *synergy* among multiple markets;
- *coordination* of strategies for *multiple brands*; and
- complex markets with multiple distribution channels, regional variation and multiple elements in the marketing mix.

What better description could one have of a tourist destination? Such places need to satisfy the strategic objectives of many sectors, plus the aspirations of the host community. A tourist destination needs to accommodate the various tourism and resident markets. It needs to coordinate the activities of its constituent parts into a corporate destination image and product with which they can all collaborate. Finally, a tourist destination needs to present this corporate destination image and product to a global and highly competitive marketplace.

Tactical plans

Part of this call for more flexible planning and management in business makes use of the other two planning approaches – tactical planning and contingency planning. Tactical plans are the more detailed plans designed to implement the strategic plans of top management. They often relate to specific functional areas, such as sales or personnel, and encompass a shorter time span than strategic plans. In tourism tactical plans often occur with the seasonal hiring, where in preparation for the upcoming 'high season', businesses hire and train the additional casual labour needed to handle the anticipated increase in business.

Contingency plans

Contingency plans need to be in place to be ready for a surprise break in the pattern of events. Certain changes, such as the slow season and a need to adjust staffing and service provisions, accordingly can be more easily anticipated and planned for than others. For example, Paul Miller's Victoria Harbour Ferry operation has nominal opening and closing dates for its season, but in reality these dates are determined by the weather and its customers' associated interest in taking a water trip. In tourism with its exposure to external forces over which it has no control some form of contingency planning is essential. With the Asian currency crisis of 1997, Australia's tourism industry faced a dramatic decline in some of its principal overseas markets. Fortunately, many companies and government agencies were able to implement contingency plans that shifted marketing and packaging toward the still buoyant North American market, and thus ameliorated the downturn of their Asian markets.

Policy

Those plans that are intended to have some permanency often develop policy statements on how objectives are to be accomplished. Policies are used to provide direction to the decision-making process, and can be referred to for guidance when dealing with new situations. 'As such, policies should be based on a thorough analysis of corporate objectives. Separate policies cover the important areas of a firm such as personnel, marketing, research and development, production and finance' (Gordon *et al.*, 1990: 117).

Several general principles associated with appropriate policy design are recommended:

(1) They should be based on *factual information*.
(2) They should *support* the organisation's *objectives*.
(3) Where different divisions or departments are involved they should be *coordinated*.
(4) They should be *definite*, understandable and preferably in writing.
(5) Given the dynamic nature of modern business they should be *flexible and stable*. This is not an oxymoron according to Gordon *et al.* (1990: 117) because 'stable policies change only in response to fundamental and basic changes in conditions'.
(6) Policies should be as *comprehensive* as possible in their scope, so as to maximise their utility to the decision-making process.

Challenges

While planning is widely recognised as a crucial component of management, understanding and committing to this process can be problematic. As we have seen, even this initial step in the management process involves several interrelated components that require clear delineation and development if the final planning phase is to be effective. Differences in interpretation and difficulties in arriving at consensus can challenge the process. Such difficulties need to be appreciated and avoided, where possible, if the planning process is to present the guidance value that is intended.

Three problems can be encountered in setting objectives within an organisation (Gordon *et al.*, 1990: 114–15), and these can be magnified within a community setting given the wider range of stakeholders and responsibilities. First, the real objectives may differ from the stated objectives, as a result of internal tension or as a response to external forces. To determine the real objectives one needs to look beyond the words of a document to the actual resource distribution and specific actions taken. Second, it is common for organisations to have multiple objectives, and given the limited resources available some priority needs to be established, which again will indicate the true objectives. Third, those objectives that are easier to quantify will receive the greater attention and pressure for completion. So when the forest industry and the tourism industry argue over the value of a tree, the forestry industry's 'hard data' regarding its market value in board feet always carries more weight with the politicians than the tourism industry's 'estimated' scenic value.

Aaker (1992) has identified several problems associated with business planning that have extensive relevance to the planning phase of tourism management. These include a financial or spreadsheet dominance that has a tendency to turn strategic plans into annual financial forecasts. These forecasts, in turn, become dependent on the projections of past performance rather than on visions for the future. The dominance of short-term financial returns to satisfy stockholders and banks can lead to a milking of the business and under-investing in its future. Plans can become too rigid and take on a life of their own, and in the process stifle innovation. Plans that are too vague or have little practical relevance to an organisation will not be utilised, but end up on the shelf.

Rather than fighting against the natural inclination of businesses to focus on monetary flows and short-term performances, a planning process can be responsive to these priorities. By incorporating planning processes into budgeting, a business is both recognising the importance of planning and responding to the consequences of its actions. Two budgeting styles that have particular relevance to business planning are performance budgeting and zero based budgeting. Both can raise the profile and effectiveness of planning. *Performance budgeting*, also referred to as management budgeting, sets performance goals and objectives and then uses performance measures to asses the extent to which these goals and objectives are achieved (Bertsch, 1999). The focus of this approach is on evaluating and ranking the options by ranking measurements that are based on economic and non-economic factors including technical feasibility, legal requirements, intangible benefits and opportunity costs. *Zero base budgeting* draws on goals and objectives to build a results-orientated, priority-setting budget within existing resources. Zero base budgeting involves the identification, ranking and commitment to alternative packages of actions as they reflect the priorities of the organisation. Each decision package is reviewed in terms of the intent of the package: what will be done, how much it will cost, how it meets the goals and objectives of the organisation and the cost of not adopting the package. The final rankings and approvals of decision packages, which are tied to long-range plan objectives, are contingent upon available funds.

Performance budgeting and zero based budgeting offer planning advantages to a business. While these budgeting techniques have a strong monetary focus, their ultimate success lies in their acting as a measure of how well the company is meeting its overall goals and objectives. Both of these planning techniques are usually conducted on an annual basis; however, this yearly review can act as a longitudinal monitor of organisation progress towards achieving its long-term goals and objectives. These two budgeting techniques are responsive to changes in the external and internal business climate of an organisation, and as such can be a practical and effective way to combine planning with monetary policy.

Community Tourism Planning Process

While the planning processes for community tourism follow similar steps to the business planning processes, differences can be found in terms of priorities and processes. The main priorities for a business are often straightforward and easily quantifiable, involve a limited number of stakeholders and are flexible in application and implementation. In contrast the priorities for a community can be complex, difficult to quantify, involve multiple stakeholders and can be onerous to prepare and implement. The desire to generate profits over the long term is one shared by business and community tourism planning organisations, as is the need to consider multiple stakeholders and external factors. Community tourism planning, as with business planning, looks at missions, goals and objectives. The primary difference between the two is one of scope. Community tourism planning is accountable to a wider range of stakeholders and as such additional factors need to be reviewed and included in their planning processes.

The motivating factors behind creating a community tourism plan can vary widely, from responding to a sudden influx or decrease in tourists to taking advantage of available funds and expertise for such planning exercises. Generally, one can identify two types of planning effort that relate to when the planning process starts:

- Retroactive
- Proactive

Retroactive

Certain tourist areas allow their tourism potential to evolve in an organic and unstructured way until a particular turning point is reached. This turning point could involve substantial damage to tourism resources or a substantial drop in tourism revenues. Typically an area that develops a tourism plan in a retroactive fashion is responding to tourism development that started on a small scale and evolved into a major industry. Once locals recognise the scope of the industry they begin to seek ways of controlling and guiding it, such as partnering with tour providers and retroactively integrating tourism planning into their community plans. Mann (2000: 24) refers to this type of tourism planning as 'demand led', since local tourism is driven by consumer demand. It is the type of tourism planning commonly associated with Butler's (1980) destination evolution model.

Proactive

Certain areas are identified as strong potential sites for tourism growth by outside interest groups. Such groups can primarily have a business perspective and profit generating motivation, such as hotel and resort chains, or they can primarily have a developmental, environmental or social perspective, or even an altruistic motivation, such as national developmental agencies and non-government organisations. Proactive community plans lay down the groundwork for tourism development, such as providing the necessary infrastructure and designating areas for concentrated tourism growth, before the development takes place. Proactive tourism planning can be referred to as 'supply led', since the 'supply' of tourism services and products are in place before the 'demand' comes from tourists (Mann, 2000: 24).

Determining the vision, goals, objectives and strategies for a community tourism planning process involves a great deal of organisation, commitment and resources. Public meetings and discussion groups need to be arranged and widely attended. Extensive amounts of background material that provide context to the impending planning decisions need to be gathered and shared with community members. Stakeholders need to be identified and able to contribute in a meaningful manner. Finally an organisational structure needs to draft, adopt, implement, monitor and adjust the resulting plan. A general framework for this process is presented in Figure 3.1. It shows the planning phase's individual components, operating

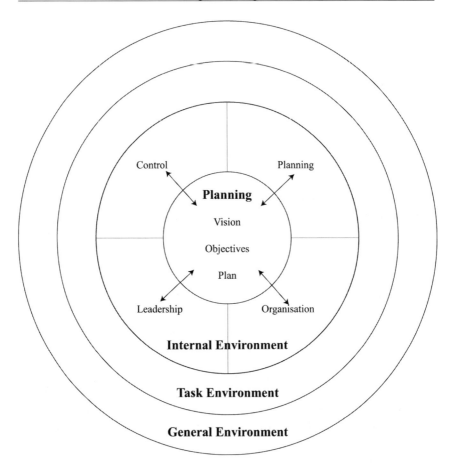

Figure 3.1 Planning tasks and environment for community tourism

within the four management functions and within the internal environment of local government. This internal environment has to be responsible to the task environment of its community and responsive to outside pressures from the general environment of its state government and world events.

To illustrate the steps of the planning process we offer examples of possible visions, mission, objectives goals and strategies for the fictitious community of Appleton and actual tourism examples in the following paragraphs.

Visioning

Visioning is a projection of what is desired that is unhindered by the constraints of reality (Becker, 1999). While businesses are often able to proceed with a largely personal and guarded vision of their future, community visions by their very nature are based on communal interests and aspirations for the future. As such, community visioning processes often involve community workshops and facilitated meetings at which the public can share their hopes and concerns for the future, and from this great diversity an inclusive and responsive future vision for the community is formed.

The visioning process is widely used in community planning. According to Bosselman *et al.* (1999: 26):

> When a community is considering ways to manage its tourism development and the use of its shared resources, it needs to create a process for meaningful participation by disparate parties with different objectives. In modern planning parlance, this is often referred to as a 'shared vision' theory of planning or even, to the disgust of language purists, as 'visioning'.

While the term visioning may strike some as being too whimsical, the practice of visioning can be a powerful tool for bringing diverse sections of a community together. Visioning can be especially useful in laying the foundations for an inclusive and supportive planning environment, as all participants are invited to share their views in a relaxed and non-binding manner. Visioning does not require an extensive gathering or review of data detailing current conditions; however, a certain awareness of such conditions is necessary to ensure that the visions for the future are not so far-fetched that they could never be realised (Becker, 1999). (See Box 3.1). A recent paper by Smith (2003a) examines how a visioning process has been used to refocus Canada's tourism industry and help it to become more competitive in a global market.

The increased use of the term 'vision' is associated with a growing concern over the future and in particular our environmental impacts on this globe. In suggesting their Tourism Opportunity Spectrum as a more long-term management tool for tourism and environmental planning Butler and

---

Box 3.1   Vision Statements:
- Appleton will be the premier tourist destination for the entire region.
- Residents of Appleton will enjoy a wide range of rewarding and sustainable economic opportunities.
- The Appleton Tourism Association will be an umbrella organisation that works with government, businesses and community groups to promote, protect and enhance the area's tourism resources for the enjoyment of visitors and residents.

Waldbrook (1991) recommend moving away from the traditional and rather static master planning approach to one that seeks to implement a process of continual reassessment within community-defined social and environmental carrying capacities. Others have gone further and called for an 'integrative vision' of long-term care for the natural environment that must flow through all environmental management and tourism-related activities (Coccossis, 1996; Hansen & Walker, 1997). Examples of tourism planning developing such visioning exercises and documents are presented below.

The Ministry of Tourism in the province of British Columbia developed a vision statement in 1992 because it considered it had reached a crossroads. After consulting with numerous bodies and businesses the Ministry felt it needed to ensure future economic success so it had to 'identify our options and clearly define our priorities and strategies' (Ministry of Tourism, 1992: 11). To do this it proposed general goals that encourage sustainability, improve the product, increase competitiveness, increase revenue genera-tion and the sharing of benefits, encourage greater cooperation and communication. This vision is to guide subsequent business plans and forms the basis of the province's tourism growth management strategy (Tourism British Columbia, 1995).

Telfer (2000) reports on the visioning activities of a regional tourism activity in another part of Canada. Telfer talks about the successful alliance that has been created between the agricultural sector of the Niagara peninsula and the food processors, distributors, hotels, restaurants, wineries and chefs of the area, under the heading 'Tastes of Niagara: A Quality Food Alliance'. This programme 'started in 1993 and evolved out of the Agri-Hospitality Committee of Vision Niagara Planning and Develop-ment Inc., a non-profit, volunteer organisation' (Telfer, 2000: 76), a vision of various groups to enhance the image and productivity of this rural region close to major metropolitan markets like Toronto, Ontario and Buffalo, New York, that could tap into those market's desires for rural experiences and products.

Jamal and Getz (1997) have reviewed the vision-based experiences of four different community types: Jackson Hole (Wyoming) and Aspen (Colorado) as resort destinations, Calgary (Alberta) as an urban tourist des-tination, and Revelstoke (British Columbia) as an emerging tourist destination. They reviewed the visioning exercises of these four communi-ties from both a process and content perspective. In terms of the visioning process, they found it was customised to suit local needs and resources, and not surprisingly the community concerns mentioned in the resulting vision statements varied in specificity with respect to the community's character-istics, values and aspirations. Of the resulting vision statements Aspen, as the most developed resort community, produced the most detailed and comprehensive vision statements. For Calgary the emphasis was economic and tourism viewed as an important supplement to a varied urban economy and lifestyle. While neither Revelstoke nor Jackson Hole 'made direct reference to the role of tourism in their community's future' Revelstoke was interested in opening up more opportunities for visitors (Jamal & Getz, 1997: 211).

Based on their review of these experiences Jamal and Getz (1997: 215–16) present three propositions:

(1) A well-articulated, community-based vision statement offers effective direction to the public and private sector for managing a community's tourism-related resources over the long term.
(2) The success of a community-based vision statement in achieving community consensus on destination planning and development is directly related to the level of community involvement in the vision formulation process.
(3) The effectiveness of a community visioning exercise to aid public and private planners will be enhanced by the existence of an ongoing representative body or bodies, to ensure implementation, monitoring and revision of the vision and/or of the strategic outcomes of the visioning exercise.

If such propositions can be achieved they feel a community visioning process would be invaluable in bringing together the various destination stakeholder groups and 'crafting' a joint direction for their community's future.

The third proposition that the visioning process will be aided by the presence of a representative body – has been confirmed by King *et al.* (2000), who have also demonstrated that such a process can operate in less developed countries. Their study of a new approach to tourism planning and development in Niue, an island in the South Pacific, revealed that consultants must now work closely with local residents and industry stakeholders. They must do this to ensure 'the tourism "product" reflects domestic social and cultural concerns and not simply the needs and aspirations of international tourists' (King *et al.*, 2000: 409–10). An important and constant element in this planning process is the Program Steering Committee made up of public servants, industry and community representatives. 'All proposals need endorsement by the steering committee prior to ratification by the Cabinet' (King *et al.*, 2000: 413), which means this body is central to the planning and implementation of future community tourism developments on the island.

Probably the most complete visioning exercise in the field of tourism is the one recently completed by the late Professor Bill Faulkner in the Gold Coast on behalf of the Australian Cooperative Research Centre for Sustainable Tourism. Key findings of this research process are that most residents have a positive perception of tourism; while the majority of tourists are domestic it is the international markets that will provide the highest growth rates; and there are several hinterlands to the main beach focus of the region. Given this information, the resort destination developed a vision for the next 20 years that incorporates:

- strengthen the Gold Coast as Australia's most preferred holiday destination;
- increase its knowledge, stewardship and development of its unique tourism advantages;
- develop Australia's most successful, concentrated tourism industry cluster;
- increase yield;
- provide ethical and sustainable tourism practices;
- develop greater dialogue, cooperation and partnerships between the public and private sectors.

Evidence of this last vision is exemplified in the vision and drive of Bill Faulkner and was acknowledged by the Chair of the Gold Coast Tourism Visioning project. In that visioning exercise Bill Faulkner states 'We cannot create a future unless we first imagine it' and the project was designed to enable a wide range of stakeholders to share their image and vision of the destination's future.

Mission

Missions, goals and visions are relatively new concepts in tourism planning. Much of tourism planning is based on the senior administration's and experts' interpretation of community mission and goals, and these interpretations have moulded subsequent objectives. Therefore, with tourism planning, as with other forms of community planning, one can see an evolution from plan formation being the domain of 'experts' and elected officials to that of the general public (Susskind & Field, 1996).

The mission step is vital to tourism management for it sets the scene and indicates what sort of destination a community wants to be. It requires an assessment of the community's tourism resources and potential, plus an analysis of stakeholder opinions. It is this type of auditing that will indicate whether a community is potentially competitive and whether the necessary industry and public support is present. If there is insufficient competitive advantage or public support for the changes a tourism development policy would bring, then it would be better to invest a community' time and resources elsewhere.

If you equate visioning with dreaming of the type of place you would like to be, then a mission statement is the actual destination that you plan on reaching. A mission statement which is a statement of purpose, can be seen as a declaration of self-determination. Without a mission statement businesses and communities can have difficulties prioritising their actions and can find themselves constantly reacting to events, rather than progressing towards their desired end state.

In terms of community tourism development use of the term mission is not very common, as yet, but we can find reference to its component parts. An illustration of this appears in Goeldner *et al.* (2000: 455), where they state:

> Although a 'tourism philosophy' sets out the overall nature of tourism in a destination, it is the *destination vision* (their emphasis) that provides the more functional and more 'inspirational portrait of the ideal future' that the destination hopes to bring about in some defined future (usually 5, 10, 20 or 50 years) . . . Visions can take many different forms. Some are very concise (the equivalent of a corporate 'mission statement'); others are much more extensive and idealistic.

They do not go into any detail regarding how such visioning is to be accomplished beyond the fact that 'the "crafting" of a destination vision is a stimulating, intellectual process that often attracts and involves the relevant stakeholders of a destination' (Goeldner *et al.*, 2000: 457). Nor do they indicate how visions become a mission statement.

The literature review of the business experience with mission statements indicates community tourism planning should reflect the priorities, resources and capabilities of the host community along with the expectations of the types of tourist that they hope to attract. Mission statements for community tourism planning can build upon existing community visions, or new visioning processes can be undertaken with the intent of creating a foundation for a community tourism plan. A mission statement should be succinct, realistic and ambitious. The mission statement for a community tourism plan should act as a mantra and a reference point to ensure that planning efforts stay on track (see Box 3.2.)

Box 3.2 Mission Statement:
The Appleton Tourism Association is the destination's umbrella tourism marketing organisation that will work with government, businesses and community groups to promote, enhance and protect the area's tourism resources for the enjoyment of visitors and residents.

Goals

A community tourism mission statement needs to be supported by goals, objectives and strategies in order for a community to realise its ambitions for the future. Goals are the broad statements of intent that underlie a mission statement. Goals, which are more specific than the mission statement, stake out the territory that will be covered by the organi-sation. Setting community goals can be difficult given that goals reflect values, aspirations and concerns and such feelings often differ widely among various people and groups. As such, developing attainable and acceptable goals for a community tourism plan that reflect the sentiments and resources of that community and its tourists can be especially challenging.

While developing community visioning and a mission statement is often conducted via a series of large public meetings, developing specific goals, objectives and strategies is often best accomplished using a smaller group that is representative of the wider circle of interests and expertise (Susskind, 2001). The stakeholders involved in developing community tourism goals need to be informed of the current context in order to develop realistic goals. Existing sources of information, such as tourism patterns and revenue, census data and existing plans for the area, should be utilised where available and appropriate. (See Box 3.3.)

Box 3.3   Goals:

(1) Increase Appleton's community awareness and support for tour-ism.
(2) Increase visitation yield.
(3) Effectively manage tourism impacts.

Although the business term 'mission' is not commonly used in tourism planning its associated components of goals and visions are becoming more accepted and commonplace. Bosselman *et al.* (1999: 10–11) talk of goals, claiming:

> the goal of any sensible community should be to maximise the benefits and minimise the risks of tourism . . . the goals of each destination is the same: to secure those benefits that the community most desires; to avoid those impacts that the community deems harmful; to share the benefits and burdens in an equitable way; and to be resilient enough to adapt the chosen strategy to future changes.

The thrust of this goal has remarkable similarity to the broader constit-uent description of business goals provided earlier by Gordon *et al.* (1990). Both see a goal as a trade-off, maximising the positives such as employ-ment and personal growth, while minimising the dangers of poor health and safety. Each emphasises the long-term goal of sustainable development.

The link between community goals and business goals can be seen very clearly in many tourism development plans. This is illustrated in Goeldner *et al.*'s (2000: 20) review of tourism development goals, where their five destination goals can be linked to regular business goals. (1) Providing a framework to facilitate the economic benefits of tourism is the same as a business organising itself to offer a product and service. (2) Developing an infrastructure is identical to a business creating its facility to appeal to tourists and residents alike. (3) Ensuring the appropriate type of development is the matching of customer expectations with what the destination and its individual businesses are prepared to offer. (4) Establishing a development programme that is consistent with the culture and history of the host area suits the sense of place emphasis of tourism business. (5) Optimising visitor satisfaction is in the interests of individual businesses and the host area at large, for it ensures repeat business and strong recommendations.

Objectives

Objectives are derived from and support the goals of a community tourism plan and should be clear and specific desires. Objectives represent real commitments and as such they usually have a quantitative component, relating to what exactly needs to be accomplished and when (Tonge & Myott, 1993). Developing community tourism goals and strategies can be stressful, since they involve the allocation of communal resources across a wide range of values and aspirations, plus the fact that opportunities and constraints created for other activities need to be considered.

Using a facilitator can be especially helpful in drawing out ideas, setting priorities and reaching consensus for establishing objectives. Such roles are becoming more in demand and generally are being filled by lawyers or professional facilitators. However, in the authors' experience, these early visioning exercises leading to specific objectives provide local universities with an excellent opportunity to link 'town and gown'. Murphy *et al.* (1985) have outlined one example of this approach when he and several graduate students took a large number of tourism and community interest groups through a workshop to identify local tourism priorities.

In community tourism management the objectives of a wide cross-section need to be considered and matched wherever possible. The various sectors and individual businesses within a destination must feel they are receiving equal attention and have an equitable opportunity to make a profit. Various areas of a community or region must feel they have the opportunity to participate in the tourism market, to the extent and style that they desire. It is not uncommon, therefore, to find tourism destination associations attempting to spread local tourism activity to a variety of businesses and areas. (See Box 3.4.)

Box 3.4 Objectives:

1.1 Create community oriented workshops and committees.

1.2 Survey and publish industry results.

2.1 Increase annual occupancy rates in local accommodation to an average of 75% over the next five years.

2.2 Increase revenue yield per visitor by 20% over the next five years.

3.1 Reduce taxi waiting times at Appleton International Airport by 50% over the next two years.

3.2 Reduce noise and light pollution around Appleton's waterfront centre.

3.3 Enter 'Tidy-Town' competition.

In terms of traditional land use planning the use of objectives, rather than goals, has been a common starting point. Inskeep (1991: 51) observes:

> As typically used by planners, goals refer to the more general aims of development and objectives to the more specific ones. Because the distinction between goals and objectives can be confusing to many users of planning studies, the approach used in this book (and in many actual planning studies) is to refer only to development objectives and not use the term goals.

In one respect there is no difference between the business and technical planning approach to the planning process in that both require clear and concise objectives to guide their subsequent actions. To achieve this state objectives should be SMART according to McDonnell *et al.* (1999: 61) in their book on festival and event management. *SMART* is the acronym for the following features of good objectives:

- *Specific,* carefully focused on the mission.
- *Measurable,* expressed in a concise and quantifiable form so they can be assessed after the event/plan is concluded.
- *Achievable,* the objectives can be realised given the resources available.
- *Relevant,* applicable to the current environment in which the tourism planning takes place.
- *Time specific,* to be achieved by a designated time.

Without such principles objectives run the danger of becoming 'immeasurable vague hopes and desires, without benchmarks for success' (McDonnell *et al.,* 1999: 62). An example of developing tourism objectives can be seen in the Canadian government's initiatives for the 1990s. After conducting a nation-wide discussion of the challenges facing Canada's tourism industry at the end of the 1980s, the government, in conjunction with industry and public sector representatives, drew up a strategy to help it grow and prosper through the next decade. This consultation exercise confirmed for the government that Canada's tourism stood at a crossroads, facing a number of significant challenges that included increasing international competition, shifting markets, new technologies, an ageing infrastructure and fragile environments in some key tourist destinations. To meet these challenges the Canadian government (Canada, 1990) identified eight tourism areas that needed attention if the country was to remain competitive. Among the objectives were the creation of the 'right products', 'sustainable development' and the 'development of new markets': concepts that have universal relevance to tourism planning at any level.

In tourism, as in any business, one needs products that the customer wants – the right products, and as we have seen, tastes change and products have an associated lifecycle. Hence a major objective of the Canadian tourism study was to develop products that would be in demand during the 1990s and beyond. To do this the government proposed priorities that included building on existing facilities and attractions, and assisting visitors by creating packages. It then listed specific activities to be undertaken, such as increased collaboration within the industry to build competitive packages, increased collaboration between government departments and agencies to assist the development of tourism, and closer working relationships with the provinces in order to spread the economic benefits of tourism.

Sustainable development is regarded in some circles as an oxymoron and in others as a dream, but with the above mentioned example we see an attempt to integrate this concept into specific planning objectives. The priorities to achieve this objective are striking the appropriate balance between business opportunity and community responsibilities. The industry is given the opportunity to self-regulate, but if that is not forthcoming or is inadequate there is the promise and threat of government regulations. Activities to support a community tourism planning objective and its priorities include the following:

- disseminating the action plan and recommendations at major conferences and other venues with a wide audience;
- support of jointly developed 'environmental' and 'conduct' codes; and
- dissemination of information from best cases and benchmark communities.

Planning

Strategic planning is the foundation of later management functions, without which the objectives, goals, missions and visions of a community tourism plan would not come to fruition. Strategies are the actions necessary to implement objectives, and as such are used to identify and resolve more immediate issues than long-term goals. 'Strategic planning (in tourism) is more oriented to rapidly changing future situations and how to cope with changes organizationally' according to Inskeep (1994: 9), who differentiates between this form of planning and long-range comprehensive planning that projects future development patterns 10 to 20 years ahead. (See Box 3.5.)

Box 3.5 Strategic Planning:

(1.1.1)   Provide Appleton residents with discounts at government owned and operated tourist attractions, since they support these facilities already through their taxes.

(1.1.2)   Create a 'be a tourist in your own town' promotional day, whereby residents can visit local tourist attractions for a minimal cost on a set day during the slow season. The purpose being to increase their awareness of what the community has to offer, and hoping they will recommend attractions to visitors or bring along their visiting friends and relatives.

(2.1.1)   Partner with regional tour operators to encourage a steady flow of tourists throughout the year.

(2.1.2)   Schedule conferences and other special events for off-peak tourist times.

(3.1.1)   Issue more taxi licences and restructure taxi parking and flow at Appleton International Airport.

(3.1.2)   Prohibit tour buses from certain congested parts of the downtown core and residential areas.

(3.1.3)   Create attractive walkways and pedestrian only streets linking accommodation to attractions and shopping districts.

(3.1.4)   Establish a 'Tidy-Town' committee and place more rubbish bins in popular areas, with a daily collection policy

---

Most of the published planning reports in tourism have been of a strategic planning nature, because these represent the culmination of a lengthy decision-making process that often requires public reporting. It is less common to see tactical and contingency plans in a published form because these are often internal documents that are to be used either by sub-units in the operational process or in response to crises. However, they are meant to be supporting the policies outlined in the strategic document.

Tourism planning has become more prevalent as the industry has grown and its impact problems have become more apparent. Although champions of more comprehensive tourism planning like Gunn (1994) and Inskeep (1991) have demonstrated the benefits that systematic planning can bring to destination areas it is still in its infancy as a specialisation. There are few planning departments with a tourism specialist but more community administrations are hiring tourism development officers to act as a liaison with the industry and to advise planning departments and councils. As a consequence, more communities are starting to include tourism considerations as part of their comprehensive economic and land use planning.

Despite its relatively short history, strategic tourism planning has been identified as passing through several phases. Getz (1987), as cited in Hall (1998) identified four approaches to tourism that could be placed in a rough chronological order. The earliest approach was 'boosterism', with its blind faith in any activity that brings visitors and their money to a community. This was followed by an economic/industry-oriented approach, which emphasises land use zoning and site considerations: a physical-spatial approach, which attempts to either concentrate tourism activity to minimise its disruption of local lifestyles or to spread its activity to peripheral areas with tourism potential of their own, or a combination of these two strategies. A community-oriented approach, which places more emphasis on the role the host community does and could play in the successful delivery of a tourism experience. Although Getz (1987: 5) points out these four approaches 'are not mutually exclusive, nor are they necessarily sequential' it has not stopped others, such as Hall and Kotler, engaging in similar classification exercises.

Hall (1998) has adopted Getz's typology of tourism planning approaches and added a fifth phase – that of sustainable tourism planning. Given the increasing concern over what is happening to our environment and tourism's dependency on a healthy and attractive environment Hall indicates that the issue of sustainability is now receiving more attention. Sustainable tourism planning is seen as 'an integrative form which seeks to provide lasting and secure livelihoods with minimal resource depletion, environmental degradation, cultural disruption and social instability' (Hall, 1998: 12).

Examples of this fifth and integrative strategic planning approach can be seen in the growth of various environment-oriented management strategies.

The Tourism Opportunity Spectrum (TOS) developed by Butler and Walbrook (1991) provides a framework within which information and data can be examined with respect to the tourism activities that should be allowed or prohibited, and the kind of facilities which should be developed. This has been augmented by the Ecotourism Opportunity Spectrum (ECOS) with respect to the growing ecotourism market and its ramifications for host communities, particularly the smaller and more isolated communities (Boyd & Butler, 1996).

Boyd and Butler's concept of the ECOS can be applied to the resource opportunities of a potential destination. Their template views eight factors as being worthy of consideration by communities. These are:

(1) Accessibility to major markets.
(2) Relationship between ecotourism and other resource users, such as forestry.
(3) Attractions in a region, their type and number.
(4) Presence of existing tourism infrastructure, such as roads and accommodation.
(5) Level of user skill and knowledge required, indicating whether it is a difficult or easy ecotourism product to undertake.
(6) Level of social interaction expected between visitors and the host community (ies).
(7) Degree of acceptance by local community of the impacts and controls associated with ecotourism products.
(8) Type of management needed to ensure the viability of areas on a long-term basis.

Such factors can and should be applied to a variety of tourism development opportunities.

To overcome the technical issues of calculating carrying capacity Stankey *et al.* (1985) have developed the Limits of Acceptable Change (LAC) approach, which allows community decisions to be made on a more general and perceptual basis. In the national parks of North America, which face the challenging dual mandate dilemma of conservation and recreation, two separate yet similar strategic approaches have been taken. The Visitor Activity Management Process (VAMP) of Canada (Graham *et al.*, 1988) and Visitor Impact Management Process (VIMP) of the United States (Loomis & Graefe, 1992) have been developed to establish a balance between these two contradictory, at times, objectives.

Kotler *et al.* (1993) have identified similar phases within strategic marketing, which is the broader type of management approach recommended earlier by Aaker. In terms of the strategic marketing of places they see three phases. The first is 'smokestack chasing', which is similar to the 'boosterism' and economic-industry phases in that the emphasis is on luring facilities to the area. The focus is on creating a friendly environment for business that could include government subsidies. One of this book's authors well remembers a welcoming sign on one of the freeway entrances to Ohio in the 1960s that read: 'Profit is not a dirty word in Ohio'. The second phase is 'target marketing', where planning and management moved to a multiplicity of goals – retention, start-ups, tourism, export promotion and foreign investment – during the 1970s and 1980s. The third, and current emphasis, views places as moving to product development and competitive niche marketing. Locations are seeking to define themselves as special places, with specific competitive advantages for their target industries.

The result of this evolution is that tourism is now one of those target industries for many communities and they are planning how to integrate this function into their overall comprehensive plans. The traditional process is to incorporate tourism issues into the objectives, survey, analysis and synthesis, policy and plan formulation, recommendations, implementation and monitoring, as outlined in Inskeep's comprehensive tourism development planning process (1988: 364). But this book is closer to the views of Kotler *et al.* (1993: 79), who claim 'places must begin to do what business organizations have been doing for years, namely strategic market planning'. Such a strategic market planning process puts tourism planning squarely in a business context, but from both an industry and host community perspective. According to Kotler *et al.* (1993: 81) it should consist of five stages to answer the following questions:

(1) *Place audit* – What is the community like today? What are its major strengths/weaknesses, opportunities/threats? What are its competitive advantages?
(2) *Vision and goals* – What do residents want the community to be or become?
(3) *Strategy formulation* – What broad strategies will help the community reach its goals?
(4) *Action plan* – What specific actions must the community undertake to carry out its strategic objectives?
(5) *Implementation and control* – What must the community do to ensure successful implementation?

We would suggest one modification to the Kotler process and that is to include policy statements as part of the strategy formulation, thereby providing clear guidelines as to what constitutes each community's tourism approach.

Policy

Policy creation is the most detailed and exacting component of the overall planning process. Whereas, the general plan and strategies lay out what needs to be done, the policies are the final step in the overall process. While the content for community tourism policies will be dependent largely on the circumstances particular to the community in which they will be adopted, there are some useful guidelines for policy formation.

Netter (1981) offers some guidelines for policy language and formation, that are provided below:

- comprehensive;
- precise;
- clearly stated;
- responsive to community needs as outlined in the vision, missions, goals and objectives of the plan;
- based on sound research and technical studies; and
- consistently applied.

Policy involves the establishment of local regulations, guidelines, development and promotion incentives that provide a framework to guide individual and collective decisions in the fulfilment of the overall strategy. 'In effect, tourism policy seeks to provide high-quality visitor experiences that are profitable to destination stakeholders while ensuring that the destination is not compromised in terms of its environmental, social, and cultural integrity' (Goeldner *et al.*, 2000: 445). With a ubiquitous industry like tourism, policy needs to be interrelated with other industry development plans and with community infrastructure priorities.

Challenges

The biggest issue with developing visions, missions and goals within community tourism will be creating an appropriate and real consultation process within the host community. As has been indicated, this will be a more challenging step for communities than for business, but given the growing trend to more inclusive planning and development it should not be insurmountable. Woodley (1992) in her study of tourism development in the isolated community of Baker Lake in the Canadian Northwest Territories noted that the concept of community planning existed in the region but had not spread to the visioning stage for tourism planning. She cited several barriers to a local visioning and goal setting process for this Inuit community, some of which will have broader relevance.

First, 'residents must have a basic level of awareness of the potential benefits and costs of tourism and of what is required to develop a successful tourism industry. . . . In Baker Lake, the concept of tourism is not well understood'. Second, a 'lack of trained tourism planners within peripheral communities has resulted in planners of a different cultural background being brought in to lead the process'. Third, language differences as well as cultural differences also mean 'that standard participation techniques are not effective'. Fourth, 'in most peripheral communities financing for tourism development is not available and must come from outside interests' (Woodley, 1992: 143–45). This not only reduces local ownership and control but leads back to the first point of lack of knowledge.

In community tourism there will be many stakeholder groups with different objectives and there will inevitably be power struggles leading to hidden agendas and a possible difference between stated and real objectives. One can expect some resistance to change from the established power groups, as Jackson (2002) has illustrated with respect to the difficulties in developing golf tourism within the Scottish countryside.

Although various government papers and acts have promoted the concept of rural recreation that has a benign impact on the countryside, golf has had a struggle to participate in such visions. Part of the cited problem is that 'the planning system remains better equipped for yesterday's problems of rural depopulation and urban sprawl than for the complex problems of what has been called the "contested countryside" in the 1990s' (Cabinet Office, 1999, paragraph 4.24 cited in Jackson, 2002: 190). Hence, visions to build on the status of St Andrews, as the home of golf and to spread golfing opportunities throughout its surrounding countryside, have created tensions. The countryside has become contested between those who wish to preserve their current built and natural environments and those who wish to develop a new economic and employment base in the countryside.

Planning in tourism is criticised sometimes for promising more than it delivers. While there will always be an element of scepticism concerning strategic planning effectiveness, 'during three decades of empirical research, strategic planning has been proven to be an essential prerequisite in successful organizations' (Phillips & Moutinho, 2000: 370). Such research, however, indicates the effectiveness of strategic planning should not be taken for granted.

In their study of hotel organisations using strategic planning Phillips and Moutinho (2000) found there were six key attributes that made this form of planning effective. First and foremost, a plan has to be implemented rather than left on the shelf, and to implement it a team should be drawn from all levels and departments. Strategic planning also needs to be focused on performance, necessitating extensive use of financial and other data. The exchange of information between parties is essential to effective planning, so the greater the functional integration of information and needs the better. The setting of specific and measurable goals via benchmarking or investment appraisal techniques helps to indicate levels of success and whether the plan is on track. To succeed, planning needs adequate resources and support from senior management, so that middle and line managers can devote the necessary time to this function.

While this study relates to the hotel industry there are many features that can relate to strategic planning for communities, especially when one considers that running a large hotel is very much like managing a small community. Based on their research Phillips & Moutinho (2000: 376) recommend the following steps to enhance strategic planning effectiveness:

- setting explicit goals;
- assigning clear responsibilities for implementation;

- obtaining a high level of commitment to the strategic plan;
- involving all levels of management;
- obtaining adequate functional coverage;
- using modern analytical techniques;
- obtaining a suitable level of staff planning assistance.

All of these are pertinent to the planning for community tourism, and should be kept in mind in order to make such strategic planning efforts more effective.

The community tourism planning process outlined above is a structured and detailed planning template for tourism management. However, in real world applications it is not always necessary or advantageous to follow all of the steps outlined above. The list of steps for strategic community tourism planning and management outlined in this section should be viewed more as a 'best practice' model from which elements can be chosen to suit the needs of the community, business or organisation that will be using them. The main reason for this is that many of the steps can be condensed, or folded into each other, such as combining the creation of community visions, missions and goals into one step. The desire to condense the steps makes practical sense given that many of the terms are used interchangeably, and it can be argued that some of the differences between these steps are based more on semantics than process.

It should not be assumed that the creation of community tourism plans and their subsequent application will be a straightforward or easy task. As detailed throughout this book community tourism planning involves the establishment of consensus among a wide range of stakeholders, and change will always be perceived as a threat to some.

Combining Approaches

The planning process in tourism has evolved with the industry's changing business needs and with changing emphases within the planning fields. Initially the focus was on growth and how to develop the industry and the destination areas. This was the era of centralised planning and master plans, and was dominant in both national and international spheres (Tisdell & Roy, 1998). With the growing scale and competitiveness of the industry, business interests changed to competitive strategies and destinations started to focus on minimising tourism's negative impacts (Gunn, 1997; Inskeep, 1991). Now the emphasis is on sustainable development and the integration of tourism planning into the overall planning objectives of host communities (Wahab & Pigram, 1997).

Throughout this evolution the business approach and host community approach to planning have generally run parallel courses, but given the growing convergence of a more societal orientation by business and a more fiscally creative approach from government administration the opportunities for a working partnership between the two have increased immensely. Consequently we are seeing an increasing use of business planning terms and approaches in the overall planning of this industry, from the higher order central planning agencies to the local planning processes of host communities.

Business planning has long been criticised for being too profit focused (MacArthur, 1999). However, community tourism planning initiatives also need to be concerned about profit generation for they need financial resources to meet the needs and expectations of residents and visitors. Lack of a business focus can be seen as one of the major pitfalls of community planning. Much can be gained, though, from combining the strengths of a business approach – economic viability and flexibility – with the strengths of a community planning approach – heightened concerns for social and environmental impacts and inclusive decision making processes. By adopting economic self-sufficiency, fiscal planning and market responsiveness from business, community tourism planning is in a stronger position for fostering a more equitable distribution of tourism's benefits and costs to a community.

Summary

This chapter examines the planning process as it is used in business management and applies it to the present research and practitioner perspectives of community tourism planning. It reveals that the initial steps of visioning and the creation of mission statements have been practised less frequently in tourism, in a formal sense. However, with the growing realisation that tourism has significant community impacts and in response to the growing demand for broader community input, the concept of community visioning is starting to become more evident. As such, the community tourism planning phase is beginning to replicate the management planning function even more closely than in the past.

There will always be one major difference between the business and community planning functions and that is the number of stakeholders and the need to seek broader consensus in the community setting than in the boardroom. However, these questions of scale and complexity do not negate the procedural steps outlined in the business management approach to planning, because the need for a logical and clear process becomes even more paramount in a community setting. Hence the need for visioning exercises that bring the community together, from which will emerge consensual goals, that in turn can be formulated into clear and measurable objectives, are all essential building blocks to a solid strategic plan.

Although the final step of the planning function is to create a plan, it is noticeable that more writers, in both business and tourism, prefer to use the

term management because it symbolises increased flexibility and responsiveness. Given the increased pace of change, especially in a business
context, managers are seeking plans and guidelines that permit contingency planning and rapid response. This is still a proactive procedure in
that it attempts to anticipate change through the establishment of objectives
and courses of action by which to best manage the organisation and its
mission. The move from a planning mindset to a management one is
germane also to the complexities of ecosystem management, where the
interrelated nature of the system requires constant vigilance and adjustment. Such an approach is required not just of ecotourism but for all
tourism that sells a community as a commodity.

It should be appreciated that in terms of management the strategic plan
is only the first step, so even when considering the planning function the
next step and other management functions must be borne in mind. The
stakeholders who develop the strategies for their community plans must
ensure that the appropriate organisational structures are available and are
able to implement the plans, otherwise all will be wasted.

Chapter 4

Organising

To implement a strategic plan requires the allocation of resources and effort, which will involve many people. These people and their individual tasks need to be coordinated – and that involves organisation. 'A key aspect of implementing strategy is the need to institutionalize that strategy so that it permeates daily decisions and actions in a manner consistent with long-term strategic success' (Chon & Olsen, 1990: 213).

This chapter will start by examining some of the principal concepts in business organisation and then proceed to analyse their applicability and use within the strategic community tourism management context. It will focus on organisational structures that have developed to assist in the implementation of organisational goals and plans, and how they are changing in face of the growing complexity and dynamism of the business environment. It will review how the activities, responsibilities and interrelationships must be organised in a manner consistent with the chosen strategy, and how that in turn helps to mould the organisational culture. Finally, it will discuss the importance and role of leadership in this process.

Business Organisation Processes

In business the principal task is to fulfil the mission of developing a product and service that meets the needs of customers and provides a profit for the organisation and its shareholders in the process. Hence the first organisational task is to structure the business' people and resources in the best way possible to support that principal objective and any other ancillary planning objectives developed through its mission statement. Consequently an organisational chart outlining the different responsibilities and contributions of various individuals and departments to the overall planned outcome is an essential step.

Organisational structure

The traditional view of organisational management is that authority and responsibility flow from top management downward in a clear and unbroken line, following what is known as the *scalar principle* of management organisation. Within this system the ideas and responsibilities flow from the top, and it is senior management who not only contribute to the strategic plan but take principal responsibility in securing its implementation. This forms the basis of traditional organisational management and responsibility within both business and government. It explains why in the past a chairman or government minister felt obliged to tender his or her resignation if something went awry in their company or department – even if they were not personally aware or involved. However, like many traditions this philosophy of overall responsibility is no longer so sacrosanct.

Although the responsibility and accountability components of the scalar principle may be weakening, its effect on organisational structure is still very evident. It has produced the *line organisations*, those with 'direct and vertical relationships between different levels within the firm (that) include only line departments' (Gordon *et al.*, 1990: 251). This produces the standard pyramid organisational chart with the president or Chief Executive Officer (CEO) on top, supported by a few senior department managers, who in turn are supported by a larger number of department heads.

In recent times this standard structure has been criticised as being more appropriate to internal order and efficiency than in meeting the chief objective of many organisations – serving the needs of its customers. Consequently, instead of placing the president at the top some businesses, especially those in the service sector, are now inverting the pyramid and placing the customer on top, supported by the departments that bring the product or service directly to them, and placing the president or CEO at the bottom. Figure 4.1 offers a general inverted pyramid of a line organisation for a resort. The chain of command and directional control of senior management is not diminished by this inversion, for they still have the responsibility to implement the plan and meet customers' wishes.

As some businesses have become more complex and have started to serve a wider range of customers they have developed a *matrix organisational structure*. This uses teams of specialists from different functional areas within an organisation to work with specific product or project managers. Such structures imply the product or project managers have roughly the same power and authority as line managers of such key departments as finance and human resources. It can lead to special arrangements like the creation of 'skunk works', where certain individuals are given free reign over a certain period to develop a new idea or product, without the usual reporting responsibilities. Such arrangements can create 'the possibility of conflict and frustration, but the opportunity for prompt, efficient accomplishment is great' (Gordon *et al.*, 1990: 258).

An even more flexible form of organisational structure is the *open-systems* approach which facilitates interorganisational links to achieve planning objectives (Benson, 1975; Hall *et al.*, 1977). This concept is based on two major approaches to creating a more efficient organisational structure for these changing times. These involve taking advantage of exchange

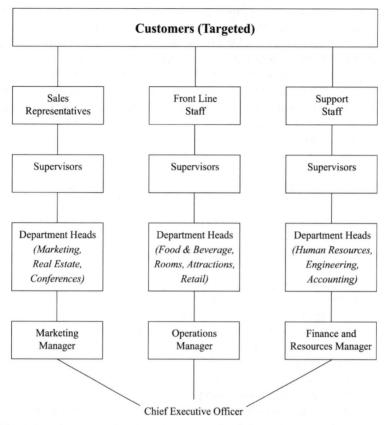

Figure 4.1 Inverted line organisation for a resort

theory or stressing power-dependency relations. Organisational exchange is 'any voluntary activity between two organisations which has consequences, actual or anticipated, for the realization of their respective goals or objectives' (Levine & White, 1961: 588), and forms the basis of many business partnerships. Power and dependency involve the issues of money and authority, and are closely linked to an organisation's concerns over domain and market share (Benson, 1975). Open-systems, therefore, encourage organisations to look beyond their own resource base to fulfil their objectives, and to look for partners to help meet the needs of their stakeholders and customers.

Organisational culture

While a structure and organisational chart outline the approach to be taken in implementing the strategic plan, it says little about the actual process and commitment. How individuals and departments react to their assigned *responsibilities* in the organisational chart structure will dictate the likelihood of success in implementing the plan. Certain people will have the authority to make decisions and to direct others to achieve the planning objectives. At times they can assign responsibilities to others through delegating work internally or out-sourcing certain responsibilities to outside specialists, such as accountants or advertising agencies. Their beliefs, values and expectations regarding the plan will influence their effort and will be reflected in the organisation's culture and commitment.

Along with responsibility goes *accountability*, which is where the individual or department becomes responsible for the way in which they operate and the success of their particular contribution to the organisation's objectives and mission. A commitment to the tasks at hand will be reflected in more enthusiastic and responsive effort in meeting the needs of the plan. With everything else being equal such an approach should lead to the successful implementation of the plan and positive business results.

Organisational leadership

Leadership has little to do with charisma or other so-called 'leadership qualities', according to Drucker, who is one of the most respected writers on business management. Rather, according to him, it 'is mundane, unromantic and boring. Its essence is performance' (Drucker, 1993: 119). Performance definitely is needed to turn the 'dreams' of a strategic plan into a reality, and Drucker outlines some key characteristics that need to be present to achieve such leadership performance.

The first and foremost requirement is a work ethic. 'The leader sets the goals, sets the priorities, and sets and maintains the standards' (Drucker, 1993: 121). An example of this was provided to the authors by a family member who attended a school with a renowned principal. When asked what made this principal so special, she responded 'he is everywhere', and one could certainly see the results in the quality and enthusiasm of the staff, the clean facilities and tidy grounds, and the strong after-school activities.

The second requirement according to Drucker (1993: 121) is 'that the leader sees leadership as responsibility rather than rank and privilege'. One CEO of a major tourist attraction once related how when he was first hired his jobs were to clean the toilets and pick up the cigarette butts. He still picks up the cigarette butts if he spots any on his regular tours of the facility. It means that leaders should be willing to 'pitch in', to make the tough decisions and to take the blame if things go wrong. Knowing that a team effort helps the organisation to be successful and helps the leaders to cope as an individual, effective leaders need strong associates who can share the burdens of management and carry on with the tasks in their absence

The third and final requirement identified by Drucker is to earn trust. 'Otherwise there won't be any followers – and the only definition of a leader is someone who has followers' (Drucker, 1993: 122). People within an organisation need to have confidence in their leaders as well as the plan, and a key element in this confidence building is consistency between words and actions. Leaders do not have to be liked, or even agreed with, but their word has to be trusted.

Drucker (1993: 123) concludes with the observation that many see these qualities of leadership as being synonymous with the requirements for an effective manager. To which he replies – 'Precisely'.

In order to create a structure and system to implement a strategic plan requires *champions* for the cause. That is people who believe in the plan and will use their energy and influence to ensure it is accomplished. Such people become the 'battlefield' leaders in the sense that they steer the necessary changes through the various committees and decision-making steps, plus take on the responsibility for ensuring that the required resources and staff are in place.

Leadership is expected to come from the top, but it need not be confined to senior management. If there is opportunity for junior members of an organisation to present ideas on implementation based on their more immediate knowledge of the market or suppliers then this should be incorporated within the overall implementation scheme. In the service industries in particular, with their thousands of daily 'moments of truth' between the customer and the company, the emphasis is on finding ways to *empower* line staff to take the initiative where necessary to ensure customers' needs are met.

Challenges

The choice of organisational structure should be determined by the objectives and tasks at hand, but in real life the choice is also strongly influenced by the resources available and any structure that is already in place. Responding to new planning directions and objectives often requires additional resources and sometimes requires new skills. To finance such adjustments means securing additional funding or transferring funds from existing programmes. In today's business and administrative world it is generally the latter, and this naturally causes resistance or opposition regardless of the merits of the proposed strategic plans. It is a rare situation where an organisation has a clean slate with respect to fulfilling its strategic plans, so in most situations the organisational structure to implement new planning objectives must be grafted onto existing systems and integrated with ongoing obligations. Consequently any organisational restructuring must take into account the power of inertia and existing commitments.

While a series of organisational structures has been discussed above they should not be viewed as being mutually exclusive. Given the increasing number and variety of objectives that large organisations, in particular, face there is often a combination of structures in place. While the move to matrix and open-system structures is a direct response to the growing market complexities, the traditional philosophy of management responsibility ensures that line-management systems still apply.

The presence of a suitable organisational structure to implement strategic plans represents only the skeleton of the organisation and its chances of overall success. The heart of the organisation and what will bring the structure to life is the organisation's corporate culture. This culture will determine the level of effort and degree of flexibility staff and management will apply to the new objectives, which reaffirms their involvement in the initial planning stages. However, such consultation needs to continue within the organisation phase, because department managers and line staff can contribute insights based on their closer experiences of serving the customer.

Throughout the whole process of implementing new strategic plans there has to be leadership. Leadership is crucial at all levels if strategic planning objectives are to be met, and this is strongly influenced by the corporate culture that exists within the organisation. Stimulating and facilitating leadership is one of the major challenges for business today and is becoming a more significant topic of research and teaching within business studies. As such we will explore this topic in more detail in the next chapter.

Community Tourism Organisation Processes

When it comes to implementing a strategic tourism plan within a community all of the above business concerns and methods will be at work, but on a more complex and comprehensive scale. To implement the plan will require the support and involvement of three major interest groups – the government, the tourism industry and the broader community. Within these three groups there will be specific interests and priorities that will need to be considered and integrated into the actual organisational delivery.

While the dominant government sector for community tourism will be the local level of government, because it has the responsibility for land use zoning and facility licensing, the direct and indirect interests of state and national governments cannot be ignored. These higher forms of government are directly involved when they offer various development inducements or assistance with grants and expertise, and through the promotional efforts of the National Tourist Offices and their state equivalents. Their indirect involvement with any implementation largely comes about through their influence over infrastructure developments, such as the location and state of the local road system and airport or ferry connections.

The tourism industry should be represented by a local destination association, where the various sectors of the industry have come together to form a united front of interest groups. The prime motivation for such associations is acceptance of the principle that any tourism business, regardless of its size and sector, must sell the destination first and its own business second. This means the individual competitors must collaborate in order to entice visitors to their destination, so the principal function of these associations becomes partnership marketing. However, as they take on the responsibility of marketing a community as a destination their tasks and responsibilities broaden accordingly. Unfortunately, due to the competitive and fragmented nature of the tourism business and relative newness of the industry in some locations not all communities have a destination association to represent the industry.

No tourism plan can be implemented successfully within a community without the support of the other business interests in the community and its citizens. Consequently an important step of the visioning and goal creation of the planning stage is to develop objectives that coincide with and, wherever possible, support other existing or latent economic activities within the community. The implementation of the tourism plans will be that much easier if it can be demonstrated that the proposed objectives have only a benign impact on existing businesses in other areas, such as on fisheries, agriculture, forestry or manufacturing. Or better still that it will have a supportive role for these industries, such as producing an increased demand for their products. It is this overall assessment of the benefits and costs that the residents will consider in terms of their endorsement, as suggested by Ap's social exchange theory.

To integrate these different yet related interests into a coordinated community tourism strategy will require the development of an organisational structure. Such a structure should build on what has worked in other areas of tourism and business, but should be modified to reflect the broader stakeholder framework of community tourism.

Organisational structure

Despite the significance of organisation as a major business management function little has been written on this subject in the tourism literature, and where it has occurred it is often related to the senior levels of tourism organisation – the National Tourist Offices (NTOs). In terms of textbooks Pearce's (1992) coverage is the most comprehensive, with an emphasis on national and regional destination organisations (defined as being between the national and local bodies) in the USA, Western Europe, and New Zealand. This work has been supported by chapters on tourism organisations in other texts, such as Middleton (1988) and Mill and Morrison (1992), and more recently by Morrison et al.'s (1995) study of overseas NTOs operating in North America.

The major conclusion from these studies is that a range of functions has emerged in these NTOs, such as marketing, development, planning, and research; but the dominant function by far is to promote the national product to overseas markets. The standard NTO brief is to promote national destinations *per se*, that is as places in their own right (Pearce, 1992: 7), without obvious favour to any particular region or product since it is taxpayer funds which essentially support this expensive process. The end result is broadly appealing images that are designed to attract international visitors to the country, supported by branch offices in the country's prime tourist generating markets. Good current examples of this are the New Zealand promotions, built around the success of the 'Lord of the Rings' films and the natural beauty of the country.

Middleton (1988) has identified two steps within this international destination marketing. These are *destination promotion*, whereby a primary level of awareness is created by the NTO promotions. This can be leveraged through *market facilitation* that enables regions and private companies to promote their own product, via processes like joint marketing or packaging. Once the international visitors arrive they become the responsibility of regional and local destination organisations, which must tempt them to their specific areas and products.

In addition to these prime marketing responsibilities NTOs have developed other functions. In the developing world they are often used to encourage and facilitate product development, acting as a conduit for government grants and subsidies designed to increase the nation's offerings and competitiveness. In some countries the NTO's close link to government, its knowledge of international markets, and all embracing coverage of the national product has encouraged some involvement in the actual planning of tourism development. 'Here again, united action is required to draw together the different operators and agents of development within a given destination, a role appropriate for a destination organization' (Pearce, 1992: 12). Another function that has developed in some NTOs is research. Most frequently this research arm is associated with market research, but in some cases it includes impact studies.

An often unstated yet very real function, for NTOs and all tourism organisations, is political lobbying. Tourism organisations need the acquiescence and support of government for their existence, and this does not come about without constant reminders of how much tourism is contributing to the local economy and quality of life. Too often legislators are blinded by the very ubiquity of tourism and the difficulty of measuring its direct impacts, so a regular function of tourism organisations is to maintain the awareness of the industry in the minds of politicians and administrators.

Some of the functions and characteristics associated with NTOs do spill over to organisations operating at the community level of individual destinations, as can be seen in the more recent research into the principal destination associations operating at this level. Morrison *et al.* (1998) have examined the structural profiles of Convention and Visitor Bureaus (CVBs) in the USA and have found several parallels with the NTOs. 'Strong local destination marketing organizations, typically known as convention and visitor bureaus in the USA, have emerged with the mandate of promoting their communities by bringing in more meeting and pleasure travellers' (Morrison *et al.*, 1998: 15). While their primary function is to promote the local destination, 'more of their attention is now being given to acting as a catalyst for development, facilitator, and supporter' (Morrison *et al.* 1998: 15).

In Europe destination associations have been called City Tourist Offices (CTOs) and surveyed by Wober (1997). In his analysis of 61 such associations he detects the same marketing and promotional emphasis as elsewhere. In addition to direct advertising most CTOs invite travel editors, writer and agents on 'familiarisation tours', because 'these groups are multipliers and it is of prime importance to stimulate their interest in selling the city' (Wober, 1997: 7). But marketing is no longer the only function of these CTOs. Many (76%), have become involved in product development, and a good number (41%) have become involved in the actual planning of tourist attractions. Several CTOs operate various tourism enterprises, such as guided walking tours (69%), bus tours (57%), and sell concert and theatre tickets (55%), but 'only 18 per cent maintain or manage tourist attractions' (Wober, 1997: 8).

Most of the organisational structures discussed in the tourism literature have been the traditional line organisations, responsible for the promotion of a single destination through a single umbrella organisation. There is usually a president or CEO, supported by line (department) managers responsible for finance, marketing, product development, and sometimes research. The organisation answers to an elected board that represents the cross-sectoral interests of the industry and usually has a few local politicians to liaise with city hall.

As the business of tourism management has become more complex and intertwined with community life some tourism associations have taken on a more matrix form of organisational structure. This occurs when the destination association attempts to be more than an umbrella organisation for the local industry by taking responsibility to contribute to the well-being of the whole community. An example of this is can be seen in Canada's Tourism Victoria (1995: 4) business plan priorities (goals), one of which reads:

To enhance member and community services for Greater Victoria.

This will be achieved by providing quality membership services to businesses and professionals in the tourism industry ... Enhancing services for Greater Victoria communities will be achieved by increasing community awareness and support of tourism through improved communications and active grassroots involvement in the community by all facets of the local tourism industry.

What this organisation has done has been to create 'additional to the norm' working committees that are as concerned with the general community environment as with local tourism issues. Hence, thanks to the initiative and pressure of its 'Environment Committee', Tourism Victoria became the only business group in the city to support and commit to the expense of upgrading the local sewage treatment system. It also led to some of its prominent board members joining protests against the continual use of clear-cut logging elsewhere on Vancouver Island. In addition, the organisation has committed to an annual spring clean-up of the city centre and has hired a professional organiser to assist local community groups in operating their events and festivals.

None of this is completely altruistic. The tourism industry will gain from a more wholesome environment and from more professionally operated local events. But the drive for such initiatives has often come from the non-tourism members of this broad based community organisation and then been endorsed by the local industry.

Examples of open systems are beginning to emerge as various destinations see the advantages of collaboration that alliances and partnerships have brought to different industry sectors and firms within those sectors. A strategic alliance allows parties to invest their resources into mutually beneficial pursuits (Johanson *et al.* (1991). Consequently more organisations, including destination associations, are taking up the challenges of developing the synergistic opportunities that exist in mutually serving the tourist and enhancing their travel experiences and company revenues in the process (Crotts *et al.*, 2000).

However, research shows that interorganisational partnerships are not always easy to achieve. Selin and Beason (1991b: 641) point out two alternative theories have been used to explain interorganisational relations. One views organisations as voluntarily interacting to achieve mutual synergistic goals, and is commonly called an exchange theory. The other sees a dominant organisation inducing the interaction of various organisations, which is called the resource dependency theory. In their study of a potential exchange theory partnership, between the United States Forest Service and local tourism associations in an area of Arkansas, they found this type of relationship was impeded by several barriers. These included differing ideologies between the resource managers and the tourism associations, and a lack of awareness of each other's issues, but they felt that these difficulties could be overcome.

Palmer and Bejou (1995) have compared the effectiveness of marketing alliances between the private and public sectors in the UK and USA. They examined the coverage of such alliances, in terms of their functional competencies and geographic coverage; the *form* of the alliance, whether it was a joint promotion or a joint venture; the *mode* of the alliance, whether it was the responsibility of senior or junior staff; the *motives* for the alliance, whether it included the possibility of an exchange or dependency relationship. Their results from a survey of 67 visitor and convention bureaus in the USA and 24 tourism development companies in the UK reveal that the U.K. alliances have 'a greater domain coverage which included more strategic marketing activity, compared to the operational and promotion-focused domain of US collaboratives' (Palmer & Bejou, 1995: 627). They noted also that the alliances reflected the stakeholders' work environment, with the small business operators in the USA exhibiting a stronger 'self-centred entrepreneurship' compared with their UK counterparts who had more trust in their government agencies. Consequently they feel 'the most important generalizable conclusion from this research is that no one unique approach for creating marketing collaboratives is applicable in all business environments' (Palmer & Bejou, 1995: 628).

Selin and Myers (1998) explore one tourism marketing alliance in depth. Their case study of the Coalition for United Recreation in the Eastern Sierra (CURES) of California examines those factors that contribute to an effective interorganisational alliance or constrain such an alliances. Contributing factors include improved communication, strong leadership, trust, and personal investment. Constraining factors include turf protection, restrictive personnel and accounting procedures, the lack of a formal agreement, and a loss of momentum. An analysis of 45 coalition members' sense of effectiveness and satisfaction reveal some significant correlations. The highly correlated variables with members' 'effectiveness rating' are the level of administrative support, sense of belonging, personal benefit and level of trust. When it came to the members' level of 'satisfaction' all of those variables remain highly correlated to satisfaction, but are joined by such variables as leadership, give and take, inclusion and issue importance.

Several members provided some significant observations in this study, based on their interorganisational experience with CURES. One reported 'In this day and age, the only way to get anything funded or done is to have partners'. While another observed that barriers are always going to be there, but 'the real challenge is keeping the initial enthusiasm alive and producing beneficial results so people stay involved' (Selin & Myers, 1998: 93).

Organisational culture

As indicated in the business literature and confirmed in the above tourism studies the success of organisational structures depends to a large extent on the culture that is developed within and between organisations. Where there is encouragement and openness the various contributors feel more comfortable with the implementation process. Selin and Myers' (1998) study of tourism marketing alliances shows that the significance of administrative organisational support, give and take, a sense of belonging, feeling of interdependence, and level of trust are important variables.

These are all elements of a corporate culture and confirm the importance of common bonds.

Effective organisations are those that encourage innovative and responsive behaviour on the part of their staff, leading to levels of performance beyond the standard requirements needed to accomplish organisational functions. These include cooperative and collaborative acts, expressing ideas for improvement and promoting a positive organisational climate. Organ (1988: 4) has called such cooperative acts 'organizational citizenship behaviours' (OCBs) and defined them as 'individual behaviour(s) that (are) discretionary, not directly or explicitly recognized by the formal reward system, and that in aggregate promote the effective functioning of the organization'. Organ theorised there are five forms of organisational citizenship behaviour, these being altruism, conscientiousness, courtesy, sportsmanship, and civic virtue.

Walz and Niehoff (2000) have recently examined the relevance of Organ's five forms of OCB to corporate culture and organisational effectiveness in terms of the restaurant industry. Their findings 'clearly support the idea that aggregated OCBs are related to organizational effectiveness indicators. Specifically, as employees exhibited helping behaviours, food cost percentages were lower, and revenue to full-time equivalent employees, operating efficiency, customer satisfaction, and perceived company quality were higher' (Walz and Niehoff, 2000: 314). Furthermore, sportsmanship and civic virtue were associated with fewer customer complaints.

Based on this admittedly small and sector specific study Walz and Niehoff (2000) feel encouraged to recommend that managers consider what they can do to foster the OCBs and the associated positive corporate culture. They recommend that managers:

- clarify personal and organisational expectations during interviews and orientation, and periodically throughout the period of employment;
- remember and keep promises that are made to employees – document if necessary;
- provide needed resources so that employees can carry out their job responsibilities;
- make sure procedures used to allocate important organisational rewards are perceived as fair and equitable;
- be supportive of employees' well-being and considerate of their needs;
- provide an appropriate model for employees to follow;
- empower employees;
- foster the acceptance of group goals.

Such guidelines have wide applicability and can certainly assist in the effective implementation of strategic plans by the varied staff of any authorised organisation or inter-organisational association.

Organisational leadership

As we have seen above, many studies of organisational effectiveness in delivering strategic planning objectives come down to the type and quality of leadership. Selin and Myers (1998: 89) in their study of the CURES organisational experience claim 'several CURES members noted the importance of "strong leaders" and "the contributions of outstanding folks" in explaining the success of CURES efforts'. These are becoming common sentiments in tourism and will be explored briefly here and in more detail in the next chapter.

One example of leadership in developing an interorganisational structure in tourism has occurred with the development of the French ecomuseum concept. This approach to community tourism involves presenting the best of the past with the best of the present, so that the host community's future is assisted by the consideration of its heritage. An example of this approach occurred in the Cowichan and Chemainus Valleys Ecomuseum, located on Vancouver Island, Canada, with an area of 1000 square kilometres and a population of 57,000 in 1991.

Under the leadership of Wilma Wood the existing 12 museums, other heritage sites, the tourism industry, government, local industry and businesses, unions, cultural groups and organisations were brought together to form an 'ecomuseum' (Wood, 1993): a museum without walls that would develop a new heritage/cultural tourism industry for the region. The theme uniting all these groups was the 'forest legacy' of the two valleys. The past was remembered with individual museums and heritage sites, such as the Duncan Forestry Museum and the Native Heritage Centre. The present was portrayed by the forest management display projects throughout the region, outlining the sequence of clear-cut followed by replanting, thinning and re-harvesting. The future was represented by the forest research station which is developing faster growing and disease resistant trees, along with the championing of a community forest, where small local logging enterprises could maintain specialised forestry production. To bring all these elements together became the responsibility of the ecomuseum director – Wilma Wood. She liked to refer to the whole project as a living museum, 'to initiate an improvement in the quality of life at the request of and with the participation of its community members' (Wood, 1991: 449).

Challenges

Organisational structures do not always work smoothly because combining the work of many individuals and in some cases different and independent organisations can be a real challenge. There have been a few tourism studies that have reported on such difficulties and disappointments. Holder (1993: 219) reports on the frustratingly slow progress of the Caribbean Tourism Organisation in meeting the goals given to its predecessor the Caribbean Tourism Association some 40 years earlier 'to market the Caribbean as a region, as opposed to individual countries'. She lays the blame for this on the dominance of island over regional cultures, even though most outsiders view the Caribbean area as a whole. This in turn led to a lack of sufficient human and financial resources needed for the task.

Sometimes the problem is the reverse, with the higher order organisation assuming that what is beneficial for it would also benefit lower order organisations and meet their needs. Mutch (1996) reports on the demise of the English Tourist Network Automation (ETNA) project. Only 17% of the 500 English Tourist Information Centres went on-line within the start-up phase, so the original concept was 'shelved (and) replaced by the use of two private sector software houses' (Mutch, 1996: 604). Among the reasons given for this failure was that the regional tourist boards served several stakeholders and that the thrust of ETNA only satisfied some of these. At the local level tourist information centres are designed to serve local residents with information on local council services as well as the tourists. Plus, there is a powerful disincentive to invest heavily in a computer reservation system that handles not only local tourists but at times sells them products in other regions.

These difficulties in implementing strategic plans indicate that the second function of management – organisation – requires careful consideration and operation if it is to fulfil its function. Pearce (1992) has indicated all tourist organisations will face a number of constraints to their effective implementation of tourism plans. The biggest of these is that 'tourist organisations generally exercise only limited control over the product' (Pearce, 1992: 12). He feels that most organisations lack an adequate legislative base and apart from their leadership role in promotion and marketing they are relatively powerless to influence the direction and form of this fragmented and competitive industry. Indeed, Pearce feels (1992: 12) 'in general it is easier to plan to prevent something from happening than to ensure that something does take place'.

Not everyone would agree with Pearce's rather dismal assessment of the potential effectiveness of tourism organisations. As indicated in his use of the words 'control' and 'power' much will depend on local circumstances and the legitimacy of the organisation. As we have seen in the Palmer and Bejou study, tourist organisations will reflect their home environment and local needs, so in some areas all that is expected of these organisations is to coordinate destination promotion. Even if the situation envisaged by Pearce is correct, it signifies that at a minimum tourist organisations can be expected to coordinate the promotion and to police the image and product that has been selected for the destination – very important functions for community tourism.

However, in order for tourism organisations to become effective, even at the minimal and basic capacity outlined by Pearce, they need to possess the legitimacy to act. Legitimacy has been defined by Suchman (1994: 574) as 'a generalised perception or assumption that the actions of an entity are desirable, proper or appropriate within some socially constructed system of norms, values, beliefs, and definitions'. According to Lawrence *et al.* (1997) firms and organisations within tourism need to be perceived as legitimate by key stakeholders in order to access critical resources and the authority to fulfil their mandate.

> From a managerial perspective, the process of legitimacy management is the process of managing stakeholder perceptions of corporate and industry activity, managing the evaluative frameworks – the expectations – that stakeholders bring to bear on the firm or organization, and managing issues as they arise to ensure that they do not damage the carefully tended image of the firm or of the industry. (Lawrence *et al.*, 1997: 311)

Thus, if a tourist destination association is to implement a strategic plan its legitimacy to do so must be recognised as the first step, to be followed by the appropriate resources and authority needed to carry out the tasks. In some locations this legitimacy may be limited to promotional activities, while in others it may be more comprehensive, including the leadership and control functions discussed in later chapters.

Continuing in this vein is the work of Palmer (1998) on the governance of destination organisations. He has studied the effectiveness of destination marketing in terms of the various levels of control that the organisation has been able to use in pursuing its promotional objectives. He suggests the literature indicates that governance systems can be placed along a continuum which runs from loose and informal authority and control through to tight and formal. 'The results of the quantitative analysis (of his study) strongly supported the hypothesis of a link between tight governance style and perceived effectiveness' (Palmer, 1998: 196). Consequently Palmer recommends the development of a tight governance style that is more likely to emerge with the legitimacy needed to implement the marketing and other requirements of a strategic plan.

Throughout the discussion of organisations in general and in tourism in particular is the significance of recognising and responding to a growing number of stakeholder groups. Among the list of stakeholders that need to be considered in any organisational structure involving community tourism are the volunteer and non-profit groups, who in pursuing their individual or group interests contribute to the individual character of a destination's product offerings.

According to Drucker (1993: 213–21) volunteers have some specific demands they will make of non-profit or other organisations in which they devote their time and energy. 'Their first and most important demand is that the non-profit have a clear mission, one that drives everything the organization does', so they know their concerns are compatible with the organisation's objectives. The 'second thing this new breed requires, indeed demands, is training, training, and more training', so they can really contribute to the cause. 'Supporting all this activity is accountability', both on the part of the organisation and their own contribution.

The growing involvement of volunteers in tourism organisations is due to the attraction of unpaid staff and the rising numbers of retiring professionals who are seeking some interesting and useful part-time activity. However, as Deery and Jago (2001: 58) report 'the issue of service quality and reliability of volunteer attendance has become a concern'. They note the use of volunteers in visitor information centres requires special consideration, given that volunteers are not present at all times and may not be included in regular communication processes; that their roles need to be differentiated from, yet integrated into, those of the regular staff; and that their contribution needs to be appreciated and noted. Based on their research they propose several ways to improve the organisational management of volunteers. These include:

- developing clear job descriptions for both paid staff and volunteers;
- maintaining regular induction programmes:
- providing clear communication channels between management and staff/volunteers and between the staff and volunteers;
- managing the balance of power between paid staff and volunteers;
- training the workforce in understanding the needs of both paid staff and volunteers;
- training the volunteers in areas such as computing skills and cultural differences. (Deery & Jago, 2001: 66)

All of this leads to a type of organisation and board that is broader and more varied than found within a regular corporation, as illustrated by the structure of many tourist destination associations. But it requires a special structure and culture to tap the energy deriving from such volunteer activity. Drucker (1993: 209) acknowledges this in the following observation:

Precisely because the non-profit (as are most destination associations) is so committed and active, its relationship with the CEO tends to be highly contentious and full of potential for friction. Non-profit CEOs complain their board 'meddles'. The directors, in turn, complain that management 'usurps' the board's function.

All of these feelings have been experienced or witnessed by the authors and have been referred to at times in the tourism literature. But insufficient attention has been paid to its ramifications on developing a more effective implementation of community tourism objectives.

Summary

Organisation can be seen as the structure required to put the original vision, objectives and plans into operation. As such it needs to bring together various elements and stakeholders in a united effort to deliver the plan's promise. This can become a complicated process in large organisations and in terms of communities, where large numbers of stakeholders can have conflicting interests.

Although a tourism organisation will vary in size and scope according to its location and situation the evidence suggests there are several key components to consider. The structure of most organisations is one of line departments, undertaking the various primary functions of the organisation's purpose and plan. These in turn report to department managers who are coordinated by a CEO, who reports to a board of directors. In the service industries more organisations are inverting their structure to place the customer on top.

Another feature of tourism organisations is the growing awareness of the need to collaborate, both internally and externally. To compete on the global stage a destination association needs to coordinate the various elements of its tourism industry, to produce a united image and product. In order to be competitive smaller destinations need to seek external alliances to build up their critical mass of attractions and activities, to make their regions more appealing.

Such adjustments to the traditional and insular organisational structures are responses to changing market conditions, but it requires leadership to recognise this and to implement the changes. Leadership will be examined in more detail in the next chapter.

Chapter 5

Leadership

In business and in tourism it takes many people, and sometimes many separate units or sectors, to provide the customer product or experience. This necessitates a team environment and those teams look for leadership to help them fulfil their individual contributions to the overall plan and success of the organisation. Leadership is required at all levels and is now recognised as being a significant feature in helping organisations to develop their full potential and to become successful in competitive markets. For example, professional sports teams pay huge sums to their managers for their overall leadership of the team's structure, preparation and game tactics; but leadership is needed also on the field of play as the game unfolds and this becomes the formal responsibility of the team captain(s). Within the team and game situation there are generally some players who stand out by contributing above the average, and these 'stars' are the individual leaders who regularly stand out in their area of the game, whether it be on attack or defence.

So it is in a service industry like tourism where the CEOs of individual firms may develop the strategic plans for their businesses, but if they wish to see them implemented effectively, they need to involve their managers and key line staff during strategy formulation. In this way leadership will involve communication and motivation along with the hard work recognised by Drucker, to bring about a greater commitment to the new strategy. In the process it may well change the corporate values and culture of the organisation.

One particular type of leadership that is very important to the tourism industry is entrepreneurship, because so many of its individual components are small businesses owned and/or operated by an individual. The definition of business size differs from country to country, but generally micro businesses employ under ten people, small businesses employ fewer than 50 people (Page *et al.* 1999) and medium sized businesses employ less than 200 full-time employees (National Office for the Information Economy, 2000). In this regard it comes as no surprise that 80% or more of tourism business around the world can be classified as small to medium enterprises (SMEs). Indeed, in the United States Edgell (1993: 13) has claimed '98 percent of (travel related business) can be classified as small business'.

To make these small businesses successful the skills and leadership qualities of the owner/operator become vital, for they often have no one else to turn to for assistance within their own organisations. To lead these small businesses the qualities of entrepreneurship would be extremely helpful in today's competitive markets, 'but to be entrepreneurial, an enterprise has to have special characteristics over and above being new and small' (Drucker, 1985: 22). According to Drucker these characteristics involve creating something new, something different that changes the organisation's values. Drucker (1985: 26) goes on to declare 'entrepreneurship is behaviour rather than personality trait. And its foundation lies in concept and theory rather than in intuition'.

While leadership has become important in a business sense it becomes far more complex and vital in a community sense, because in that setting it involves many organisations and different groups with different priorities. Very often those communities seeking tourism as a means to replace dying industries or to broaden their economic base require leadership to set them on the path. Examples of this can be seen in Chemainus, British Columbia; where one man – Karl Shutz – helped to raise a community out of the economic and psychological depression associated with the closure of its one remaining wood processing plant. He achieved this by encouraging the town to recall its past forestry heritage and industrial glory by depicting them through murals that could, and did, attract thousands of tourists (Beyer & Bunbury, 1993: 10) Figure 5.1.

Likewise, the growth of New Zealand's tourism industry has been linked to a few pioneers, whose leadership helped to transform this agricultural and isolated nation into a broader-based economy, where tourism plays a growing role. Watkins (1987) has identified the efforts and achievements of several New Zealand in-bound tour operators and travel agencies, including Ron Guthrey of Guthrey's NZ Tours which developed into one of the country's leading in-bound tour operators. Guthrey started his business after World War II with his war gratuity of £500 and built it into a multi-million dollar business that has offices around the Pacific Rim selling coach tours, self-drive holidays, adventure tourism, farm stays, and educational and special interest tours around New Zealand.

Business Leadership

Leadership definitions

Leadership has proved to be both an important and elusive concept in business management. Organisational theory and behaviour studies and human resource practices and research have explored the subject and come

Figure 5.1 Murals of Chemainus

up with a variety of definitions. Among those that are germane to the purpose of this book are:

Leadership is the behaviour of an individual when he (or she) is directing the activities of a group toward a shared goal. (Hemphill & Coons, 1957: 7)

Leadership is the interpersonal influence, exercised in a situation, and directed, through the communication process, toward the attainment of a specified goal or goals. (Tannenbaum *et al.*, 1961: 24)

Leadership is an interaction between persons in which one presents information of a sort and in such a manner that the other(s) becomes convinced that his (or her) outcomes (benefits and costs) will be improved if he (or she) behaves in the manner suggested or desired. (Jacobs, 1970: 232)

Leadership is influencing others to do what the leader wants them to do. (Gordon *et al.* 1990: 553)

Leadership is the process in which an individual influences other group members toward the attainment of group or organisational goals. (Shackelton, 1995: 2)

Leadership is about harnessing people's energy towards achieving organisational goals. (Van der Wagen & Davies, 1998: 37)

From such definitions it is evident that much of the variation in leadership concepts and models can be accounted for 'by differences in who exerts influence, the nature of that influence, the purpose for the exercise of influence and its outcomes' (Leithwood *et al.*, 1999: 6).

Research and instruction in business management has generally focused on four aspects of leadership, moving from the most basic description of observable features to more complex interactional theories. Throughout these studies it has become apparent that there are strong similarities between management and leadership, since both involve getting tasks done through the efforts of others. The main distinction between the two is that leadership concentrates on human interactions, while management is more concerned with procedures and results. Kotter (1990) goes so far as to maintain leadership and management are two distinctive and complementary systems, which are both necessary for success. However, the general consensus is that 'no one leadership style is the most effective' (Gordon *et al.*, 1990: 577).

Leadership traits

One of the earliest approaches to studying leadership was to search for those physical and psychological characteristics or traits that identified leadership potential. A common, yet often unstated, assumption of much trait research has been that leaders are born, not made. Consequently, research has attempted to demonstrate correlations between leaders and their physical or psychological traits, producing appearance models and personality tests to indicate leadership potential based on these correlations. However, more recent research has demonstrated such simple correlations are not necessarily foolproof in that different leaders have different traits, both in their appearance and psychological make-up (Clancy & Webber, 1995). For example, while the image-makers would have us believe that leaders need to be tall and good-looking males, real life has provided a more varied profile via the likes of Napoleon, Ghandi and Margaret Thatcher to balance the likes of Ronald Reagan and John F. Kennedy.

Despite the difficulty in creating definite links between certain characteristics and leadership 'the trait approach to the study of leadership is not dead' according to Gordon *et al.* (1990: 556–7), who offer the evidence of Ghiselli's (1971) research. They identify six of Ghiselli's most significant traits related to effective leadership, which can be applied to most management situations, including tourism development. These are:

(1) *Supervisory ability.* The ability to perform the basic functions of management, which includes planning, organising, influencing and controlling the work of others. In other words the four management functions being discussed in this book.
(2) *Need for occupational achievement.* The desire for success and willingness to work toward such a goal and to seek the responsibility associated with it.
(3) *Intelligence.* Creative and verbal ability that includes a capacity for judgement, reasoning and thinking.
(4) *Decisiveness.* The ability to make decisions and solve problems capably and competently.
(5) *Self-assurance.* The extent to which individuals view their capability to cope with problems and their degree of comfort with such responsibilities.
(6) *Initiative.* The ability to act independently and develop courses of action not readily apparent to other people.

Evidence that trait research is still being pursued and championed can be seen in the publication of Goleman's work in the *Harvard Business Review*. Goleman (1998: 94) maintains 'effective leaders are alike in one crucial way: they all have a high degree of emotional intelligence'. The five components of his 'emotional intelligence' are self-awareness, self-regulation, motivation, empathy and social skill. These have considerable overlap with the six traits identified by Ghiselli.

Leadership styles and behaviours

Another of the descriptive models of leadership is based on leadership styles and behaviours, where four fundamental styles have been identified and recognised. One is *autocratic leadership*, where senior management instructs subordinate staff what to do and expects to be obeyed without question, as in the military. Another is *participative leadership*, where the leader involves subordinates in decision-making, but retains the final authority and responsibility for any decisions, as in government cabinets. One is *democratic leadership*, where the leader does what the majority of sub-ordinate's desire, as in the case of committee chairs. Lastly, *laissez-faire leadership* occurs when someone not involved in the regular operations is brought in to offer expert advice, as in the case of outside consultants. However, such advice does not have to be acted upon.

Leadership involves communication and motivation, so a key concern has been to study leaders' behaviour in directing the effort of others toward organisational goals. One focus has been on two separate and distinctive dimensions of leadership behaviour, namely the: *initiating structure (task oriented)* – the extent to which leaders establish clear goals and structure their roles and those of their subordinates to achieve those goals; and *consideration (employee oriented)*– the leaders' relationships with subordinates as characterised by their consideration of employees' ideas and feelings and the development of mutual trust and respect.

Using these two dimensions it is possible to develop a leadership grid that indicates four potentially effective leadership styles (Stoner *et al.* 1995: 476–7). For example, those leaders who rank high on initiating but low on consideration could be identified as 'authoritarian' types, while those low on initiating and high on consideration could be labelled 'democratic' style leaders.

This model does not purport to provide the most effective leadership style for all situations, because the significance and magnitude of influence along its two dimensions will change with varying situations. For example, if an organisation expects and wants authoritarian leadership behaviour, it is more likely to be satisfied with that type of leadership, as exemplified by the 'high structure and low consideration' box. If an organisation is highly dependent on volunteers then it will need to emphasise the consideration dimension and, depending on the stage of development and experience within the organisation, will be in either the high or low structure box; the high structure and high consideration approach to leadership being more appropriate to those community festival groups that have considerable experience with past festivals and events. This is one reason why the management of international hallmark events is based on a professional and experienced core, who move from one event to another to help the host community put on a successful Olympic or Commonwealth Games.

A frequently cited behavioural leadership style theory along the same lines is Blake and Mouton's (1985) 'Managerial Grid'. This grid involves two basic dimensions of leadership in management, namely a concern for production and a concern for people. These dimensions are assessed along nine point scales from low to high concern, producing a 9 × 9 grid. Within the grid five cluster types of leadership style have been identified. These are:

(1.1)   *Impoverished Management* – where the manager has little concern for either people or production matters.

(9.1)   *Authority-Obedience* – where the manager stresses operating efficiency and controls above all else. Where the people element has little consideration and even less input.

(1.9)   *Country Club Management* – where the manager is people oriented and has little concern for output.

(9.9)   *Team Management* – where the manager seeks high output through working closely with and listening to his/her subordinates, developing mutual trust and respect in the process.

(5.5)   *Organization Man Management* – where the manager attempts to balance and trade-off concern for output in exchange for a satisfactory level of staff morale.

According to Blake and Mouton the most effective leadership style is '9.9 Team Management', in that it will result in improved performance, lower employee turnover and absenteeism, and greater employee satisfaction. This is certainly a laudable objective and many organisations strive to achieve it, but its attainment can be difficult, especially when the two considerations are in opposition. For example, a common problem in tourism is that staff need to be at work and on peak form during public holidays like Christmas and New Year, when their hearts and minds may be elsewhere with family and friends.

Situational theories

Situational theories of leadership emphasise that different styles of leadership will be needed for different situations and with different people, so they attempt to move beyond the normative nature of the trait models. An example of these is Hersey and Blanchard's (1974) situational leadership theory, which has been outlined by Gordon *et al.* (1990: 571–4). This builds on the Ohio State work and the Managerial Grid by arguing 'an effective leader is one who can diagnose the demands of the situation and the level of readiness of the followers and use a leadership style that is appropriate' (Gordon, *et al.*, 1990: 571). This theory recognises that *work tasks* and priorities will change over time, much as we have described with the product and destination lifecycles. That in organisations with a high reliance on skilled and motivated staff the *task-relevance readiness of followers* will change with the stage of development, the targeted market segments and the seasons.

That a leader has to be cognisant of these variations and adjust his/her *task behaviour* style accordingly.

A simplified version of the Hersey and Blanchard situational model in Figure 5.2 shows how this flexible form of leadership style can be equated to the regular product lifecycle pattern of a tourism product or destination.

Stage 1

In the *early stage of development (S1)* when everything is new there will be a high task load, with many tasks needing to be done with much uncertainty regarding the best approach. At this stage the relevant task preparedness of staff will be low with respect to the organisation's specific needs. Under these conditions the leader will need to *tell staff* what to do and how to do it, in order to reach the organisation's goals and objectives.

Stage 2

At the *second stage (S2)* the leadership style must still deal with a high task load as the business and destination enter the rapid growth phase and new products or facilities are created. Now some staff have more experience and training so they have higher task relevance preparedness and can be used to supervise new or casual employees. At this stage the leader should be *selling* and embellishing the business goals to all staff by encouraging them to utilise their training and to increase their personal potential returns from the evolving business opportunities through career development.

Stage 3

In the *third stage (S3)* the staff continue to build on their training and high task preparedness, becoming more experienced and skilled in the process. Hence the level of task relevance remains high and becomes more diverse. The number of new tasks diminishes as the business and destination reaches maturity allowing leaders to focus more on selective quality product delivery and selecting staff for supervisory roles. Thus a more *participatory leadership* role should emerge at this stage.

Stage 4

In the fourth and *final stage (S4)* there are very few new tasks and little need for new staff, as the business or destination enters the stagnation and possibly declining stage of its product lifecycle evolution. The skill level of most staff should be at its highest level, therefore there is little need for new training and skill development. Hence there is a low relevant task readiness once again, but in this case it is because the staff are generally well prepared and not because of inexperience as in the S1 situation. Due to this high level of experience and skill the most appropriate leadership style at this stage would be to *delegate* more responsibilities to staff, to build on their

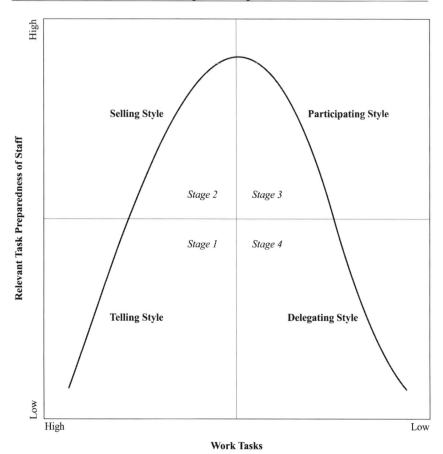

Figure 5.2 Changing leadership behaviour style
Source: After Hersey and Blanchard (1974)

individual expertise and provide them with the satisfaction of career development to middle or senior management.

As with the original product lifecycle theory this situational leadership theory appears logical and simple, but it is difficult to operationalise. For example, it is not always possible to identify when the stages of development and their associated leadership changes take place. Nor is it necessarily true that all businesses and employees proceed through the evolutionary cycle in a regular and unbroken sequence. This is especially true in tourism where the strong seasonal patterns often disrupt the steady progress of skill development for many staff. Tourism also struggles with staff turnover, which makes it difficult to build up the task and supervisory skill levels anticipated in this model. Furthermore, the logical and objective assessment process associated with the situation model has been challenged by some who feel it does not provide enough credence to the personal nature of leadership. One of these alternative theories is the attributional theory.

The *attributional theory* of leadership suggests that leadership exists only in a person's individual perception and assessment of a situation, rather than as an objective and measurable fact (Bartunek, 1981). This approach is linked with the phenomenological approach to research in the sense that what is true is only that which is perceived and accepted by the individual. Hence in this theory a leader's judgement about tasks needing to be done and who to assign to such tasks is influenced by their personal assessment of follower's attributes and behaviour. While championing individual perceptions and assessment of leadership, it is only natural to find followers attributing certain causality to the leader's behaviour. 'Subordinates tend to view leaders as the cause of group behaviour and, depending on members' attitudes to group behaviour, they develop either positive or negative attitudes about and reactions to the leader' (Gordon *et al.* 1990: 575).

New leadership theories

The term 'New Leadership' has been used to categorise a number of leadership styles that emerged in the 1980s and 1990s when business was experiencing major changes in structure and emphasis, especially in the US. According to Clegg *et al.* (1997) writers used a variety of terms to describe these new types of leadership, including 'transformational leadership', 'charismatic leadership', and 'visionary leadership'. The overall perception of these leaders or industry was

> as someone who defines organisational reality through the articulation of a vision which is a reflection of how he or she defines an organisation's mission and the value which will support it. Thus, the New Leadership approach is underpinned by a depiction of leaders as managers of meaning rather than in terms of an influence process. (Clegg *et al.*, 1997: 280)

The impact of these new leadership approaches was a dramatic rise to 'stardom' as stock markets rose and stock options increased, but come the bubble burst there has been a major reassessment of its desirability. Some have become concerned over the focus on heroic leaders, the preoccupation with leadership at the highest levels, and the focus on individuals rather than teams (Clegg *et al.*, 1997). Now there is a return to leaders being coaches, by building commitment and confidence, removing obstacles and creating opportunities for the whole team.

With this range of theories associated with leadership, business texts regularly conclude that there is no single leadership style that is the best or most effective. Four basic leadership styles have been identified in the literature, and all work effectively at certain times and for certain individuals. The trait approach has evolved from an emphasis on physical and psychological characteristics to a search for how leaders should behave, as exemplified by the Ohio State leadership studies and the Managerial Grid. Situational theories assert no single leadership style is sufficient, for leadership needs will change with the evolution of the business. Attributional theory runs counter to the normative nature of the other theories in promoting the significance of the individual to concepts about leadership, and shows how both leader and follower perceptions and assessments of situations can influence attitudes to leadership. This individualisation of leadership styles has led in the recent past to a business and media fixation on 'successful' leaders who participated in the recent stock market boom. However, many of them failed to see the big picture and others seemed to have exaggerated their business acumen through questionable accounting procedures.

Consequently, we find business texts recommend managers choose a technique and style that best suits the needs of the organisation and their own personality. One particular type of leadership that is beginning to emerge as a significant factor in both business and tourism is that of entrepreneurship.

Entrepreneurial Leadership

In both developed and under-developed countries the powerhouse of national economies has been the small to medium enterprises (SMEs). These have grown substantially over the past few decades. In part this trend is due to push factors such as a response to the downsizing of some of the major international corporations or to local high unemployment. In part it is due to the pull factors of seeking individual opportunity or new lifestyles, to introduce innovative ideas that permit enterprises to be more flexible in their responsiveness to changing global markets and business situations. In either case, to achieve the levels of success recorded around the world has required leadership and very often that leadership has come from the individuals who have started these SMEs.

Entrepreneurship definitions

In this chapter we will examine entrepreneurship as an aspect of leadership, a behavioural concept that is capable of being analysed and integrated into the business management process. 'The concept of entrepreneurship can best be understood by deconstructing it into three main overlapping components' (Shaw & Williams, 1998: 236). These are innovation, risk taking, and managerial capabilities. *Innovation* can be seen as a way to 'change the yield of resources' which is the basis of entrepreneurship, according to J.B. Say who originated the term (Drucker, 1985: 33). *Risk* is involved in any business venture, but especially in those that are new and innovative. Accordingly, Vesper (1996: 234) advises 'a business plan should be designed with maximum realism, and in real life risk is a part of the picture'. *Managerial capabilities* are needed to capitalise on the preceding components, and the classical process is operationalisation of the four business functions that form the structure of this book.

Entrepreneurship is synonymous with leadership, especially within the setting of small business enterprises (SBEs) where many are owner operated with a small staff. Early recognition of this came from the renowned Joseph Shumpeter, who described entrepreneurship as:

> Consist(ing) of doing things that are not generally done in the ordinary course of business routine; it is essentially a phenomenon that comes under the wider aspect of leadership. (Schumpeter, 1951: 255)

Similar expressions of the linkage between entrepreneurship and leadership can be seen in the following definitions:

> In . . . entrepreneurship there is agreement that we are talking about a kind of behaviour that includes: (1) initiative taking, (2) the organizing or reorganizing of social economic mechanisms to turn resources and situations to practical account, and (3) the acceptance of risk of failure. (Shapero, 1975: 187)

> Entrepreneurship is the ability to create and build a vision from practically nothing: fundamentally it is a human, creative act. It is the application of energy to initiating and building an enterprise or organization, rather than just watching or analyzing. This vision requires a willingness to take calculated risks – both personal and financial – and then to do everything possible to reduce the chances of failure. Entrepreneurship also includes the ability to build an entrepreneurial or venture team to complement your own skills and talents. (Timmons, 1994: 5–6)

> The entrepreneur is the aggressive catalyst for change in the world of business. He or she is an independent thinker who dares to be different in a background of common events. (Kuratko & Hodgetts, 1995: 4)

Such definitions include many of the leadership trait characteristics identified by Ghiselli and others, plus they reinforce the strong links to the other three functions of business management – namely planning, organising and controlling.

Entrepreneurial traits

Timmons (1994) has included leadership among the desirable attributes for entrepreneurs who reveal its importance to this form of business activity and its strong links with the other attributes. He has clustered various indicators of entrepreneurial activity into six dominant themes, which he calls 'desirable and acquirable' attributes. The second of these is leadership qualities, but if one considers the previous business definitions and studies of leadership one can see considerable overlap with his other themes, such as commitment, creativity and risk. Such a listing of attributes should be viewed as a critical mass of characteristics that can combine into different forms of entrepreneur and leadership, for 'effective entrepreneurs come in very different combinations of qualities which work for them in a particular context' (Morrison *et al.*, 1999: 42).

Morrison *et al.* (1999) also make the point that entrepreneurial leadership can be very different from the leadership characteristics and qualities outlined for corporate situations. While differences in organisational size and complexity can explain some of these leadership differences, they feel that the common autocratic and commanding style of entrepreneurial leadership is more closely linked with the psychological nature of the entrepreneurs themselves. 'One major reason for this is rooted back in the entrepreneurial personality and traits such as need for achievement, strong internal locus of control, and a driving ambition. They expect others to work at the same level and pace as themselves' (Morrison *et al.*, 1999: 137). Indeed, this may be one of the factors that make it so difficult for many small entrepreneurial businesses to grow into successful multi-unit and corporate structures. To make such an adjustment requires a change of leadership styles along with the evolution of the company, as indicated in the Hersey and Blanchard (1974) situational model of leadership. For a large number of small business entrepreneurs this proves to be a major challenge.

Role in small businesses

It should be appreciated, however, that entrepreneurial activity is only one of three key factors in managing small businesses, according to Longenecker *et al.*'s (1994) book on *Small Business Management*. Citing previous studies in the field, they consider the three important dimensions to small business management are:

(1) *Entrepreneurial values* – including intuition, risk-taking, creativity and flexibility.
(2) *Managerial skills* – including the selection of a niche strategy, effective cash flow and budget management, organisational structure and education.
(3) *Interpersonal skills* – including good relationship with one's banker, good customer and employee relations. (Longenecker *et al.*, 1994: 18).

Others agree that entrepreneurship plays an important role in small business development, and some feel it is the crucial element to success. One of these is Gerber (1995). He feels that people going into business should possess three characteristics: the best features of being an entrepreneur, a manager and a technician. According to Gerber (1995: 24) the entrepreneur within us is 'the innovator, the grand strategist, the creator of new methods for penetrating or creating new markets' and represents our 'creative personality'. But to be successful the creativity and leadership of the entrepreneurial spirit needs to be coupled with 'pragmatic' management and the technical ability to deliver the ideas. Gerber contends that many small businesses fail because the owner is more a technician than an entrepreneur, and too busy working at the job s(he) has created for themselves, rather than working to create a business.

The *Harvard Business Review on Entrepreneurship* supports the need for entrepreneurship that encompasses multiple skills. In the introductory paper Bhide (1999: 24) states that entrepreneurs must balance their bias for action with concern over the management issues of goals and strategies, and their resource capabilities to deliver the product. This is supported later in the same volume by Rock, who examines entrepreneurship from the viewpoint of a venture capitalist. He feels that 'good ideas and products are a dime a dozen. Good execution and good management – in a word, good *people* – are rare' (author's emphasis – Rock, 1999: 137). So he focuses on the quality of the business plan and the management skill ability of the entrepreneur to carry out their ideas. In some cases this may include the out-sourcing of particular functions, due to the lack of particular technical skills on the part of the entrepreneur or due to a realistic time management assessment on their behalf.

Regardless of the style and character of leadership in business and entrepreneurial settings, its significance and impact remain unchallenged in this era of intense global competition. Its role within the four-function model of business management extends beyond its individual functional box to influence the other three functions in terms of priorities and style. Nowhere is this more evident than in some of the management trends that have been noted by business analysts. Peters and Austin (1985) in their book *A Passion for Excellence* consider the concept of leadership is so crucial they recommended discarding words like 'managing' and 'management', with their associated images of controlling and arranging in favour of 'leadership' because it connotes unleashing energy, flexibility, building and growing. In a review of innovative business practices in Australia it was determined that 'sustained success with innovation is the product of consistent, concentrated efforts by people in enterprises around five key factors: customers, supply, leadership, resources and systems for innovation' (Carnegie & Butlin, 1993: xxxvii). All of these factors will be examined in terms of tourism and community tourism.

Tourism Leadership

Leadership within entrepreneurship and SMEs is a relatively new area of research interest within business management studies so there are few tourism specific studies as of this date. However, certain entrepreneurial and SME management studies would appear to have particular relevance to the tourism situation and we are beginning to see the extension of such research into the field of tourism. So we will examine those which appear to have particular relevance to the development of community tourism.

After a slow start the significance of leadership is beginning to be appreciated and starting to appear in the tourism literature, especially with respect to one area of tourism – entrepreneurship. This has occurred with the growing interest in business management studies links to tourism research and theory, as described by Tribe (1997) earlier in this book, and to a rise in interest in these topics within the field of business management. Their importance has also been demonstrated by various biographies of successful entrepreneurs in tourism related businesses and case studies into tourism development. These have acknowledged the important role played by individuals and the influence of entrepreneurs in developing the opportunities presented by the appearance of new consumer interests and destinations.

Examples of the impact of pioneers in tourism can be seen in the studies or biographies of some famous entrepreneurs who changed the face of the industry in various ways. Walt Disney (Capodagli & Jackson, 1999) created the modern theme park concept out of the traditional fairground milieu. Ray Kroc developed the modern fast-food industry with his McDonald's franchises (Love, 1995). Sir Richard Branson (Branson, 1998) created a new type of airline based on increased customer service.

There are equally important pioneers also at the other end of the tourism business spectrum, where individuals give birth to successful SMEs. A good example of this is Walsh-Martin's (1998) book on how 25 rural women have turned ideas into small owner-operated businesses. Included in that book are accounts of how these women developed a variety of SMEs, some of them tourism related, for a variety of reasons. For example, Lynne Bullen planted a maze on her country property, and 'provided an environment where everyone can indulge in the simple pleasures of life – eating, music, nature, literature, art, horticulture and socialising – in a friendly, comfortable, and exciting atmosphere' (Walsh-Martin, 1998: 41). In another example, Jeanette Basset-Pearse and her husband developed host farming in order to 'diversify just to bring in the extra income so we could remain on the farm' (Walsh-Martin, 1998: 171).

The linking of leadership with entrepreneurship and SMEs has occurred because so many of the leadership characteristics outlined above have been observed in tourism entrepreneurial behaviour, and as many of the SMEs in tourism are owner-operated they reflect the characteristics and priorities of their leaders. The dominance of the owner-operator is revealed in the work of Goffee and Scase 1983, cited by Shaw and Williams (1994: 134), who identified four types of SME firm characteristics of which three are owner-operated. Their organisational categories are 'self-employed', 'small employer', 'owner-controllers', and 'owner-directors' where there is a separation of ownership and management.

In their book on *Entrepreneurship in the Hospitality, Tourism and Leisure Industries*, Morrison *et al.* (1999: 44) state that leadership in these industries ranges from authoritarian to participative in style, but that all leaders require the same skills. 'These include the ability to select appropriate team members, communication, mediation, negotiation and persuasion skills.' These skills are generally developed over time and with experience rather than through formal education channels, either because such information sources are lacking or because individuals have entered into tourism entrepreneurship primarily for non-economic reasons.

Echtner (1995) maintains that tourism development has been held back in developing countries, and one could add in the peripheral regions of developed economies, by a lack of appropriate tourism education and training. Part of her proposed three-pronged model for such education and training is 'the development of entrepreneurship or the initiative to *work for oneself*' (author's emphasis – Echtner, 1995: 121). In addition, she maintains education should focus on professional management education and vocational skills. Such a model for education and training can prepare more people for the realities of entrepreneurship, and would be beneficial even if it convinced students such risk taking and hard work was not for them. For it will not be an easy process in developing countries or regions, that face 'issues such as inadequate financial assistance for new ventures, complex bureaucracies, and traditional barriers (that) may inhibit small scale entrepreneurship' (Echtner, 1995: 128).

Prime non-economic motives for becoming an entrepreneur in tourism are lifestyle and location. In the developed economies, where redundancy packages and retirement planning are providing more people with a lump sum to invest, more people are considering a small business in their retirement or semi-retirement, and want to live in an attractive part of the world. Such motivation often explains the choice of small bed and breakfast operations. They are often uneconomic business propositions in themselves, but provide the owners with some activity and interpersonal relationships during their retirement and may help to justify the expense of a larger home in an attractive destination than they could otherwise afford. Shaw and Williams (1998: 248) confirm both of these trends in their summary of studies on small-scale tourism entrepreneurs. Based on their own work and the work of others in various seaside resorts throughout England, Shaw and Williams (1998) show there is often little formal training undertaken to prepare for this type of activity and that a strong incentive is to live in such surroundings.

Leadership and entrepreneurship occur in various forms and settings within an industry as diverse as tourism. In a review of innovations and

entrepreneurial activity within sustainable tourism, which was represented by nature tourism, Hjalager (1997) identified entrepreneurial
enterprises in terms of nature tourism products, equipment sectors, professional tours and supplementary products. In fact she notes that many
'innovations in tourism and leisure are predominantly linked to innovations in the other sectors supplying it with products and services' (Hjalager,
1997: 40), revealing the strong links between tourism's entrepreneurial
leadership and that of other business sectors. Such links can be seen also in
cultural and urban tourism like festival and event management, where a
plea can be made for more consideration of leadership in the management
of festivals and events that depend so heavily on volunteer assistance.
These 'volunteers are not just unpaid labour but people with needs, who
probably present a greater leadership challenge than paid employees, since
the rewards they seek are intangible and intrinsic to the job itself; they do
not seek the extrinsic reward of salary' (McDonnell *et al.*, 1999: 83). The
effectiveness of appropriate leadership and concern can be seen in the
success of the Sydney Olympics, which depended on thousands of volunteers drawn from all over Australia.

Most of the leadership and entrepreneurship studies in business and
tourism have been retrospective accounts of setting up a small business and
developing it into a success. Such analytical approaches have revealed
some broad generalisations regarding the characteristics of business
founders (leaders), but as Davidsson (2000) has pointed out such post-
event analysis could be tainted by selective memory. Consequently he has
recently completed a study of nascent entrepreneurs in Sweden to test
among other things if the generalisations hold true. Since nascent entrepreneurs will be at the creativity and innovative stage of leadership his
findings are of particular interest to this book.

The general characteristics that have been associated with entrepreneurs, according to Davidsson (2000: 3–5), include:

(1) Parental occupations – a large proportion of self-employed people
    have parents who were themselves self-employed.
(2) Gender – self-employment is a male-dominated career choice.
(3) Ethnicity / race – some ethnic groups have demonstrated a higher pro-
    pensity to self-employment, such as the Indian, Pakistani and
    Bangladeshi communities in the UK and the Jewish and Asian commu-
    nities in the USA. The main explanation being that groups like these
    have access to critical resources such as financial and human capital
    (education and networks) before they enter a new country or new sec-
    tor.
(4) Education and work experience – the level of education has a positive
    impact on self-employment, especially with regard to knowledge-
    intensive businesses, and previously self-employed individuals or un-

employed individuals are two occupational groups over-represented among business founders. The first category could be considered as pull motivation and the second as a push motivation to self-employment.

(5) Psychological profile – the individual's value system and cognitive mechanisms conditioned by their social context helps to explain the career choice of self-employment.

A sample comparison between nascent entrepreneurs, determined by whether they had undertaken one business gestation activity such as doing market research or saving money to start a business, and a control group produced the following results.

The importance of a parental role model is confirmed by the significant positive impact of 'having self-employed parents and a positive impression through observation of self-employed family members and friends'. The effects of education and experience are confirmed as well, with '41.2% having a university degree or at least some university education, compared to 26.4% for the control group'.

Males are over-represented among the nascent entrepreneur group, as are those already self-employed. There are some surprises, however. 'Interestingly, the unemployed did not show a higher probability of being nascent entrepreneurs.' In contrast to previous generalisations this study did 'not find a very strong over-representation of immigrants among the nascent entrepreneurs' (Davidsson, 2000: 12–14). Based on this evidence Davidsson (2000: 14) concluded 'the results imply that previous, retrospective studies have not been grossly misinterpreted, which increases their value'. Consequently, we can feel more secure that the characteristic indicators identified above are likely to be relevant generally, including to tourism and its SME leadership.

Community tourism applications

The rise of local leaders and their link with entrepreneurial activity in tourism has been seen as a positive factor in terms of community tourism. Koh (2000: 164) observes that 'touristic enterprises do not just sprout up from the earth but are creations of people . . . We call these touristic enterprise creators tourism entrepreneurs, and in their collectivity, they shape a community's touristscape, scale and impacts (economic, sociocultural, and physical)'. By responding to market opportunities or creating innovative concepts and products these entrepreneurs become as much tourism's agents of change as the tourists themselves, and thereby significant influencers of a community's future.

Two authors who feel that entrepreneurial leadership and community have a special relationship are Russell and Faulkner (1999). They make the point that those entrepreneurs who can be described as 'movers and shakers', or as leaders in our terms, can have a phenomenal impact on the local community. They note that the 'butterfly effect' of chaos theory, so dramatically demonstrated in Stephen Spielberg's movie 'Jurassic Park', can apply equally well to the activities and impacts of mover and shaker entrepreneurs. This happens 'in terms of (the) leverage entrepreneurs achieve from small advantages through their ability to identify opportunities and create the organisations and alliances required to maximise the benefits derived from these opportunities' (Russell & Faulkner, 1999: 417).

To illustrate their point Russell and Faulkner examine changes in Queensland's Gold Coast, which is Australia's largest resort destination by size and visitor number. They feel 'the sequence of changes that the Gold Coast has experienced can be interpreted in terms of the tension between the entrepreneurs (the chaos makers) and the planners and regulators (the dampeners), whose actions are generally focused on moderating and controlling change' (Russell & Faulkner, 1999: 411). They indicate that the innovative and risk-taking entrepreneur will constantly be battling the bureaucracy because an administration's mandate and style is different from that of the SME leader. However, when conditions are conducive, as they were in Queensland during the 1980s, when the state government 'was particularly accommodating to free enterprise and favourably disposed towards the Coast's development' (Russell & Faulkner, 1999: 420) substantial changes and development could and did occur. They offer the life experiences of two major 'movers and shakers' from the Gold Coast's developmental period – Bernard Elsey and Keith Williams, to illustrate how these men, as chaos makers, challenged the system. In the process they brought about a sequence of changes that transformed this area and created an international destination with its own worldwide image.

A key issue at the community level is the origin of local tourism entrepreneurs and their impact on the community's economy and lifestyles. 'The balance between external and local entrepreneurs is at the heart of the debate over ownership and control of the tourism economy and, in turn, which benefits from such economic growth' (Shaw & Williams, 1998: 238). On the whole it is considered that if entrepreneurs are local people then their impacts are likely to be more beneficial than harmful, due to the small scale of the enterprises, their dependence on local resources and labour, and their sociocultural links to the community. Dahles (2000: 156) reports:

> Liberal market theorists believe that prosperity is the outcome of successful individual entrepreneurship. Local ownership implies that economic success for the entrepreneur results in benefits to the local economy. Tourist developments based on local entrepreneurship are much more likely to rely on local sources of supplies and labour and are much less likely to produce negative socio-cultural effects associated with foreign ownership.

In contrast, a reliance on outside entrepreneurs, especially big business from distant metropolitan centres or foreign countries, often is seen as an initial economic booster that has little beneficial long-term effects on the local economy because of the leakage and dependency created in such relationships. Relying on external capital and entrepreneurship naturally weakens the local returns and control, as dividends flow back to the capital's source and expatriate management follows the transnational organisation's practices and corporate culture (Britton, 1982; de Kadt, 1979; Pearce, 1989).

A key issue in this debate is balance, and along with that the question of timing. Based on fieldwork and observations in the Caribbean, Lundgren (1973) has demonstrated that the arrival of a transnational business in a community does not necessarily have to mean a total leakage and loss of control. Using a transnational resort hotel as an example, Lundgren has developed a model that shows different community relationships can develop over time (Figure 5.3). In the initial stage of development the hotel will be dependent on overseas suppliers for most fittings, food and beverage supplies, and management. By the intermediate stage local wholesalers will have started to replace overseas sources with produce and supplies from local producers who can match the quality and quantity needs of the hotel. Certainly the hotel would welcome this, because it would save on the transport costs for such items and provide them with the greater flexibility and reliability associated with JIT supplies delivery. At the advanced stage the hotel will have a regular source of local suppliers, some operating directly with the hotel, and its dependence on overseas supplies will be limited to those which still retain a cost advantage or are linked to the parent company image. By this stage there should also be associated local businesses that complement the hotel's offerings, like local tours, and more local staff should be at the management level. Thus over time an outside entrepreneurial activity can act as a stimulus to local entrepreneurship, demonstrating the potential of an area and encouraging local participation.

In a similar vein the early dominance of local entrepreneurs does not guarantee long-term community success and harmony. Rothman's (1998) historical account of the growth of ski resorts in the American West indicates several examples where local business people first saw the skiing opportunity and developed small-scale resorts, only to be bought out by major corporations which could turn regional resorts into national or even international destinations.

The increased importance of skiing changed the structure in which both local elites and communities functioned. Bill Janss (local developer of Snowmass in Sun Valley, Colorado) served as a precursor. His developments, the improved transportation to resorts, the growing

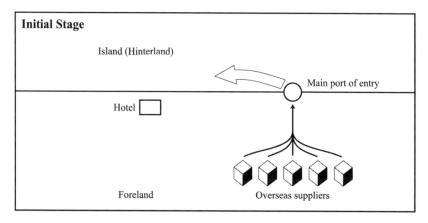

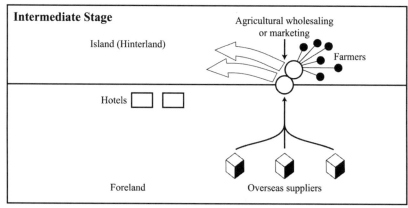

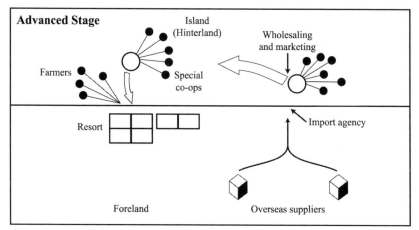

Figure 5.3 Lundgren's model of entrepreneurial development and hotel linkages

Source: After Lundgren (1974)

profits that could be realized, and other cultural factors attracted the interest of emerging multinational corporations. When CEOs noted that between the 1967–1968 and the 1970–1971 ski seasons, average pre-tax profits at ski resorts grew from 1.2 percent to 10.5 percent, they sought to join the expansion. As in other forms of tourism, the rise of skiing made the sport too lucrative to be left to locals or idiosyncratic private entrepreneurs. Ski resorts could become part of a corporation's image, a way to meld assets with a high-status capstone that served as a magnet for consumers. (Rothman, 1998: 254)

Thus we can see a reverse flow to the picture outlined by Lundgren, which only goes to emphasise the importance of timing and balance if a community wishes to exert some control over its tourism development. However, the degree of local control under these circumstances will be dictated by how open the host community is to the influences of the free market and local laws concerning property rights. Some communities have attempted to prevent the intrusion of major transnational corporations, at either end of the time spectrum, and have had mixed success.

Another factor to consider when discussing entrepreneurship at the community level is the presence of more than one economic system, especially in developing countries. In her investigation of small tourism enterprises and community development in Indonesia, Dahles identified a dual economy at work. Some entrepreneurs, like owners of guesthouses, restaurants and transport businesses, operate in the formal economy and rely on private property resources and work closely with government planning. Others, like street vendors or brokers of services to tourists, operate mainly in the informal sector and depend on personal networks and tolerant local officials to provide their services. Both types of entrepreneur are 'extremely flexible in using changing consumer preferences and government regulations to their advantage', but both need to 'be supported and to a certain extent controlled by the state' according to Dahles (2000: 166).

The issue of state control raises the possible contribution of government to the entrepreneurial process. A number of governments around the world have espoused the idea of encouraging free enterprise to stimulate their economies, but how to do this without the heavy hand of government legislation distorting or destroying the freedom and flexibility of entrepreneurship and SME development has proven difficult. It is notable that a leader in this approach, the Thatcher government of Britain, faced a philosophical dilemma when it attempted to stimulate free enterprise activity while committing to less government interference in the economy. It is apparent also that 'the costs of intervention have to be carefully assessed and the benefits estimated. To date there has been no such cost-benefit analysis in the UK' (Morrison *et al.*, 1999: 77). So it is doubtful how effective such government intervention can be.

Many writers now think governments should focus on encouraging entrepreneurial leadership and activity indirectly, by creating a supportive environment for its development. For example, Michael Porter (1980, 1998) who is the champion of developing a competitive advantage is now advocating a supportive, yet non-direct, government presence in his cluster theory. The type of policies considered helpful in this direction includes:

- Macro policies that dictate general conditions, like lower interest rates and taxation or education policies that facilitate entrepreneurship.
- Legislative deregulation and simplification that cuts the bureaucratic red tape or exempts small business from certain legislative requirements.
- Sector-specific legislation that tackles the problems associated with a particular industry, such as licensing and smoking laws for bars and restaurants.
- Financial assistance, such as start-up funds or loan guarantees.
- General assistance, such as information and incubator facilities.

In addition to these political measures a supportive environment needs to include sociocultural conditions that encourage individual enterprise and a free market approach to producing goods and services. Furthermore, these contributory factors need to be effective at all stages of the entrepreneurial process: at the formative stage when entrepreneurs are considering their ideas and the potential for success; at the mobilisation stage when they first attempt to seek financial help and premises or equipment; at the operational stage when they seek to establish themselves in the market place and attempt to operate in the business world of rules and regulations, including the burden of becoming a government tax agent with the spreading adoption of the VAT/GST tax systems.

One model to guide government and individual decision-makers in developing community tourism entrepreneurship has attempted to map the entrepreneurial process and identify the types of community assistance that would be helpful at each stage. Koh (2000: 207) feels entrepreneurism at a community level is dependent on two interactive factors – 'the differences in supply of tourism entrepreneurs and the perceived attractiveness of the investment climate for launching tourism enterprises'.

These factors thereby combine the individual nature of entrepreneurship and the environmental setting in which it must take place. According to Koh's conceptualisation the interaction of two factors, a P-factor that represents a community's propensity to enterprise, and a Q-factor that indicates the community's investment climate as perceived by nascent tourism entrepreneurs, can produce four basic types of community-entrepreneurial activity.

The four cell matrix indicates where community tourism entrepreneurship is likely to be successful or unsuccessful. In Quadrant 1 both resident and external entrepreneurs will be attracted by the record and culture of entrepreneurial activity along with the supportive investment environment created by the community. In Quadrant 3 the low record of individual enterprise and lack of community encouragement will deter much entreprenuerial activity.

To put this model to the test Koh examined the record of two comparable rural Texas communities (Athens and Mount Pleasant) along his two dimensions or factors and traced their enterprise record over a five-year period which was then compared to the state average. His measure of the P-factor was residents' attitudes to entrepreneurship and his Q-factor was measured by assessing the views of local tourism entrepreneurs. The analysis of this information placed the two communities in Quadrant 2 – high on the propensity to enterprise but low on creating a supportive environment. This should have placed these communities around the mid-point of the state's annual tourism enterprise birth rates for the five-year period, which 'ranged from 1.48 percent to 2.47 percent with a mean birth rate of 1.93 percent' (Koh, 2000: 212). Which is what happened, with Athens recording a mean enterprise birth rate of 1.87% and Mount Pleasant a mean of 1.6%. Consequently, Koh (2000: 214) felt 'the results of this study seemed to offer some empirical support for the model' and seem to support the notion that leadership in entrepreneurship at the community level is going to depend on a combination of individual initiative and community encouragement.

One example of leadership, entrepreneurship and government support at work, in a different country and at a different scale, is the experience of the London borough of Southwark. The local government of this dockland area had been struggling with declining business and employment for many years, but generally ignored tourism as a potential saviour because of its past commitment to an industrial way of life. It was not until the arrival of Jeremy Fraser as the Chairman of Southwark's Development Committee that 'tourism found a champion within the Council, not for tourism's own sake but as a means to economic regeneration' (Tyler, 1998: 57). In the 1990s Southwark began to emphasise its tourism potential, hired a tourism officer and joined other boroughs and agencies to promote the south-east area of London. The council developed a five-point strategy to guide its tourism development, of which a key area was education and training because of the change from industrial to service employment. 'Training has been given a top priority, as creating jobs that are not taken up by local people is of little benefit to a borough that at the last census point in 1991 had a male unemployment rate of 21.3% compared with 13.5% for the whole of London and 11.2% nationally' (Tyler, 1998: 60). The actions of Fraser and the teams he put together helped to transform Southwark from an inward-looking area concerned with hanging onto an industrial way of life into a more diverse and vibrant community where tourism became one of the platforms for its resurrection. According to Tyler (1998: 62), 'in 1991 a newly emerging leadership with a willingness to widen the vision and appreciation of the nature of economic decline and regeneration led to tourism being accepted as part of the post-Fordist service economy of London, which Southwark could not ignore'.

Summary

Tourism is an extremely competitive business and to attract tourists to a community needs not just people to plan and serve but people who will be innovative and develop new or better attractions. Such people will be leaders.

This chapter reveals that leadership types and styles will be diverse and variable. Research has moved from simple descriptive models of individuals to contextual situations where the stage of development and market forces will also be strong determinants of ideal leadership for a particular place or time. Leadership has been studied in the form of entrepreneurship because in tourism 80–90% of businesses are SMEs where owner operators make the key decisions that affect not only their own businesses but can impact the future of the host community.

Entrepreneurial leadership is an important agent of change for a community. The elements of innovation and risk taking embedded within entrepreneurs will have dramatic impacts on the host community. With the prospect of major change it becomes important to monitor events and impacts in order to control and direct change as much as possible. This issue of control becomes the focus of the next chapter.

Chapter 6

Controlling

In many tourism settings the establishment of a strategy and its associated operational conditions has been enough to exhaust the initiative and energy of those involved. Even if all the elements for a successful endeavour are in place, without the vigilance of regular monitoring and the willingness to adjust to changes and emerging weaknesses, such an endeavour can fall apart. In planning texts and diagrams there is often reference to monitoring a plan's progress and the provision of a feedback loop in the systems diagram. But how often is there detailed coverage of this planning stage so that the reader can appreciate its importance to the overall success of the endeavour? This chapter attempts to redress this imbalance, by emphasising that the fourth function of 'control' is necessary to ensure the planning, organisation and leadership that have gone before are all on track and providing the type of outcome initially envisioned in a community's tourism goals.

'Controlling' is a business term relating to how an organisation goes about establishing its standards or expectations, how it evaluates its actual performance, and how it takes corrective action where needed. It is a necessary step in any business to ensure its objectives are clear enough to be appreciated by the customer and its product or service able to meet their expectations. It should regularly monitor its performance not just in terms of the balance sheet but with respect to customer satisfaction. If its performance is proving disappointing in some respects and if the market expectations are beginning to change then it needs to consider ways to respond to these issues.

While tourism involves many sectors and different players this same controlling function is required, especially within destinations that are attempting to present a united image and product. Within a voluntary alliance the need for a controlling function will remain the same, but its actual form and delivery will have to take into account the commercial and political realities of the destination's situation. In community tourism it will need to consider a range of stakeholders and how their combined standards and performance are to be evaluated. If deficiencies are noted and it becomes necessary to take corrective action it should not always be left to government and legislative bodies to initiate corrective action because they are often too tardy and blunt an instrument of change.

Controlling in Business

In business management the control function is applied at all three phases of the manufacturing or service process – the input, processing, and output stages. At the input stage the main control concerns are the quality of materials and staff. In the processing phase attention turns to the most efficient and effective way to deliver the promised good or service. At the output stage an organisation needs to ensure the customer is satisfied with the quality of the product or service, and will either become a repeat customer or an invaluable advocate of the business. In the tourism industry a good example of this process would be the international airlines.

In terms of inputs international airlines put heavy emphasis on their materials and personnel. The chief material is the modern passenger plane that costs millions of dollars to buy or lease and must be kept flying as much as possible if it is to provide a good return on the investment. One airline – Singapore Airlines – has made a branding statement in this regard by claiming to have the youngest and most modern fleet of aircraft in the world. Another important element in their inputs is the quality of staff. International airlines have some of the highest selection standards in the world for their personnel and they spend millions of dollars on training and re-training them.

In tourism the actual travel component is an important part of the total experience and this part is the core business of international airlines, but as with many tourism businesses they can only deliver their service in conjunction with partners. The operation of a modern airline business is a complex process that required early and extensive use of IT to link the myriad of systems needed to deliver passengers to their destinations. These systems include the computer reservation systems, the scheduling of aircraft maintenance and delivery, the varying dietary needs of passengers, luggage handling, and frequent flier accounts. Besides ensuring that internal processes are in place to deliver passengers safely and comfortably to their destination, airlines need to work with others to make the whole operation possible. Governments are responsible for the quality of infrastructure that links each airport to the world, they control the permitted hours of operation and are responsible for traffic control. Airport authorities are responsible for the design and operation of the airport, including the provision of parking and location of facilities. Other important components of a trip that seem to be very difficult to control are the truly exogenous variables, such as the weather, to which some would add taxi drivers and customs-immigration officials.

Control of the outputs for international airlines extends beyond providing a satisfactory flight experience for individual passengers, to include maximum financial return and loyalty. The airlines have pioneered two important management techniques in these areas that have been adopted extensively by other sectors of the industry. To maximise their financial returns in a very time sensitive business, they introduced 'yield management'. This is a technique for maximising the sales revenue from time-perishable assets like a seat on a particular flight. To encourage loyalty in a very competitive business they introduced a rewards system of frequent flier points. This system builds on satisfactory performance by making an airline the first choice in future travel plans, and has now been extended to alliance partners and associated businesses in accommodation, transport and resorts.

An important element in business controlling is where to introduce such measures so they are effective but non-intrusive in the manufacturing or service process. According to Gordon *et al.* (1990: 314) critical control points must possess a number of characteristics:

- relate to key operations or events in the process that will have a bearing on other parts of the process;
- permit early identification of problems before serious damage or difficulties occur;
- indicate clearly the level of performance over a broad spectrum of key events;
- emphasise efficiency and utility in the amount of information collected;
- permit a balanced assessment of all three phases.

In the tourism industry this approach to control has become a regular feature of hospitality management, particularly with respect to food preparation and delivery. In this sector a Hazard Analysis Critical Control Point (HACCP) system has been developed to monitor and control contamination risks within facilities (Spears, 1995). Within this process a HACCP/ Servsafe method is used to identify points at which contamination or the growth of micro-organisms can occur and indicates the control procedure required to eliminate such a hazard. For example, critical control points have been established where temperatures are taken during the cooking and storage phases to ensure food is cooked safely and handled appropriately.

Within the financial and operational literature of business studies are several control techniques that have relevance to tourism. Some basic budgetary and financial control techniques that need to be considered by businesses include the following. A cash flow analysis, to ensure the business is receiving enough revenue to pay its own bills. This can be a problem when major accounts take a month or more to process and pay an invoice, and to overcome this difficulty more small businesses are turning to factoring, which is explained in more detail in Chapter 8. Activity ratios, such as 'profitability ratios', that measure the operating efficiency and overall financial return of an organisation can be useful indicators for developing greater control over daily operations. Key ones in this regard include 'return on total assets' and 'earnings per share'. In terms of operational efficiency concepts like inventory control, using techniques like 'just in time' (JIT) delivery have been introduced to reduce asset costs and warehouse space. Likewise, 'critical path analysis' which displays the network of interactions needed to produce a product or service can be used to highlight crucial steps in the process or even to simplify it.

An important aspect of controls in today's competitive business world has been the rise of quality controls, which are designed to ensure a promised standard of excellence is delivered by an organisation. An example of this type of control is Total Quality Management (TQM), which is a proactive management approach designed to bring about continuous quality improvement. It has 10 main principles (Flood, 1993: 48), and these are as follows:

(1) There must be agreed requirements, for both internal and external customers.
(2) Customers' requirements must be met first time, every time.
(3) Quality improvement will reduce waste and total costs.
(4) There must be a focus on the prevention of problems, rather than an acceptance to cope in a fire-fighting manner.
(5) Quality improvement can only result from planned management action.
(6) Every job must add value.
(7) Everybody must be involved, from all levels and across all functions.
(8) There must be an emphasis on measurement to help to assess and to meet requirements and objectives.
(9) A culture of continuous improvement must be established.
(10) An emphasis should be placed on promoting creativity.

The central element of this concept is the achievement of 'quality' goods and service, with 'total' referring to a necessary wholeness for the process to be effective, and 'management' indicating the need to have everyone responsible for managing their own contribution to the overall quality goal.

The success of this approach has encouraged the development of several accreditation systems. One of the most recognised is the International Organisation for Standards, with its check marks/ticks logo. The ISO 9000 series of certification for various industries provide a series of standards for various aspects of an organisation's operation. Under the 'management responsibility' are four main areas of concern (Flood, 1993: 58), which all indicate the relevance of a controlling function. These are:

(1) Control and maintenance of the quality system
(2) Control functions to eradicate quality deficiencies.
(3) Feedback to ensure effective operation of both controls is being achieved.
(4) Review of the declared quality system to ensure that it reflects policy.

Such certification systems have their origin in manufacturing but have been extended to the service sector with varying degrees of success. This is due to the complexity of providing experiences to accompany products and the variability of priorities and expectations that a customer brings to any interactive service process, like a tourism experience.

However, there has been one outstanding tourism success with respect to a standards system that has generated a lot of interest and some action. In 1992 the Ritz Carlton Hotel Company won the prestigious Malcolm Baldridge National Quality Award that is offered annually to a recognised leader in quality achievement in US business. The Baldridge award tests companies on seven categories (Hart & Bogan, 1992). These include:

- leadership;
- information and analysis;
- strategic quality planning;
- human resources utilisation;
- management of process quality;
- quality and operational results;
- customer satisfaction.

The Ritz Carlton approach to these seven categories or standards demonstrates that a tourism-oriented company can indeed benefit from a quality management approach.

Controlling in Tourism

In her inaugural lecture as Professor of Tourism at Erasmus University in Rotterdam Myriam Jansen-Verbeke (1994) provided a reflective address on the development of tourism. She considered that tourism had reached a critical stage where it had to move from 'business as usual' into a form of 'crisis management'. The cause for the crisis is found in tourism's phenomenal success and growth, that now places many areas of natural beauty and some societies under stress. Noting that tourism has become a two-edged sword Jansen-Verbeke advocates tourism businesses must start to change from pure developers to become controllers, if tourism is to sustain itself and contribute to global sustainable development.

Jansen-Verbeke (1994: 15) maintains there are two global trends that tourism now needs to consider if it is to manage the current crisis of overdevelopment or inappropriate development. These are the growing

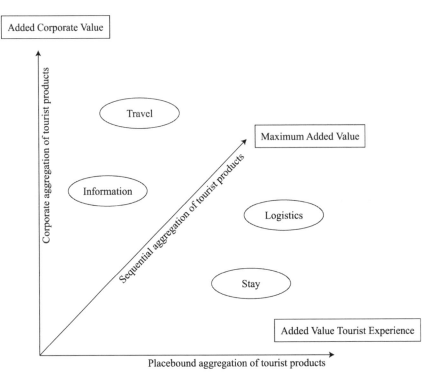

Figure 6.1 Strategic alliances and quality circles in the tourism sector
Source: Adapted from Jansen-Verbeke (1994)

concern for environmental quality and the growing demand for quality products. In both cases it requires a move from the old business management styles of independent growth strategies to one which involves more collaboration and a greater emphasis on controls to provide the quality experiences modern tourists are seeking in an environmentally benign way.

To move in this direction of sustainable quality experiences, Jansen-Verbeke (1994: 15–16) recommends a focus on eco-management, which aims at 'reducing the negative and damaging environmental impact of the various tourist activities . . . and requires more specific guidelines (controls) than the ideological concepts now to hand'. To provide the quality experience she recommends collaboration through 'strategies for assuring that all tourist products are geared to one another and hence improving the quality of the (total) tourist experience' (Jansen-Verbeke, 1994: 18). To do this she suggests greater use of strategic alliances and the use of 'quality circles' from the TQM techniques (Figure 6.1). The figure shows how corporate and community concerns, as the axis, need to be incorporated in the development of value. To bring these two groups together the quality circle concept from TQM could be used with respect to specific issues, such as 'stay' that would include consideration of local attractions, accommodation and culture, or 'travel' that would involve consideration of road and air links, connectivity to local airport and attractions, and the service quality of local transport and taxi operations. This allows 'research into the quality of tourist products by all actors involved in the entire chain of 'conceptualisation-production and commercialisation', which implies an understanding and responsibility concerning the entire process as targeted and managed' according to Michaud *et al.* (1991) as quoted by Jansen-Verbeke (1994: 25). As such it is a cry for greater control to serve the needs not only of the tourist but also of the host community and global environment.

Environmental controls

A large part of meeting customer expectations and providing satisfaction is related to the quality of the destination environment. Consequently the tourism industry is becoming more concerned with monitoring the state of the natural and cultural environments that attract the visitor, and should be attempting to integrate a control process into the overall goal of sustainable development. In the recent past environmental impact assessments have been required for proposed and new tourism developments, but little has been said or done about the more numerous existing facilities and the need for 'continued monitoring and revision of possible (environmental) objectives and operational procedures' according to Ding and Pigram (1995: 4).

Environmental impact assessments (EIAs) are carried out to ascertain the likely environmental effects of a new project proposal. EIAs are a legislated requirement of the preliminary planning process for major developments in many countries. However, the techniques involved are still in their infancy and clouded by the human element. Humans become involved as a direct feature of the impact process when they are tourists, with their own perceptions of when environmental stress is occurring that may not always match the scientific views. They are also the assessors of the presented environmental data, which means objectivity is sometimes difficult to guarantee. Inskeep's (1991) review of several large-scale EIAs provides an illustration of the mixture of scientific and human assessments involved. His example of an EIA matrix indicates clearly the scientific measures along the rows, as revealed in measures of air quality and road traffic; but the assessment of these measures is purely human and therefore more vague, as indicated by the 'minor', 'moderate' or 'serious' impact columns.

Environmental scientists have been attempting to devise a range of scientific measurements that can be used to assess environmental impact, so that the matrix approach is now only one of several available techniques. Williams (1994: 427–31) has demonstrated that EIA functions can be divided into three groups based on their primary (human) purpose. A key control purpose is to *identify and describe* what is happening in the environment, by monitoring changes in its condition. There are three major techniques in this category:

- Checklists that describe the presence and size of a particular feature via physical measurement where possible.
- Matrices that are two-dimensional checklists, with an evaluation of the potential impacts added to the physical measurement.
- Networks examine the secondary and tertiary effects associated with a project, such as following a sequence of outcomes up the food chain.

The second category involves *predictive* methodologies that are designed to forecast the probable outcomes of an activity or project. They often involve laboratory simulations like wave machines on different forms of coastline or river bank. The third category is *evaluative* methodologies that attempt to demonstrate the net result of a project development. This can be an assessment of trade-offs between various forms of development or group interests, or through a benefit–cost analysis. Despite this range of options however, most of the control work to date has been limited to the identification and monitoring category.

Due to the past emphasis on EIAs for major planned projects Ding and Pigram (1995) have recommended that greater attention should be paid to existing facilities that may be either at risk themselves or contributing to general destination wide environmental stress. They advocate a continuous application of environmental auditing that should involve:

- an ongoing process of self-monitoring;
- the collection and documentation of data that are relevant evidence of the environmental condition;
- a focus on environmental performance and direction;
- a comparison with predicted environmental performance and impacts.

This is starting to happen in a number of settings as businesses recognise the self-serving need for some form of environmental control and as destination authorities appreciate the need to consider environmental carrying capacities and their place on the product lifecycle. The WTO Environment Committee has assisted in this direction with the development of local and destination environmental indicators that include a consideration of the time factor (WTO, 1993). They have developed a matrix that considers different types of environmental indicator and assesses them in terms of a short-term list of existing data, leading to a medium-term set of indicators and finally to a long-term and ideal set of indicators.

Quality Controls

Such a call for more emphasis on quality controls has been gathering momentum as the tourism market became more complex and competitive. In service areas like tourism there is growing awareness that as customers become more experienced they become more value conscious and demanding. The senior author of this book, by age, still remembers his first family vacation just after World War II involved a quick trip to the English seaside, travelling in the back of a van with our own bedding and food supplies because rationing was still in force. Our rented seaside cottage overlooked a beach, but we had to be careful where we went because only part of the beach had been cleared of landmines. In the evening the entertainment consisted of board games and listening to the radio. The holiday was a great success because of the pentup demand and novelty of getting away for a few days. Today the family would not be so impressed, because since then we have experienced such a range of beautiful places and wonderful experiences that we have established far higher expectations.

What today's customer looks for is value, which is a combination of quality and price, and is central to the service profit chain concept developed by Heskett *et al.* (1997). Their concept maintains there is a strong relationship between the quality of goods and services presented and the customer's satisfaction and loyalty, with the two linked by the customer's sense of value received. In tourism, customer value assessment would therefore revolve around a combination of quality and price considerations. For example, budget travellers are only able or prepared to pay a certain amount for their trip experience, but still expect to receive a standard of facilities and service appropriate to basic travel – in that they are clean, safe and friendly as well as inexpensive. Luxury travellers are willing and able to pay far more for their travel experience, but they expect to receive premium products and service in return. The quality process is therefore directly related to value, and controls need to be in place to guarantee that the appropriate levels of value regarding the product and its relevant target market segment are in place.

The concept of value in a tourist experience can be either explicit or implicit, and is often a combination of both. Explicit value is visible and easily defined so it can be measured and controlled readily, such as with the assessment of a hotel room's qualities and associated cost or in the case of coach trip between two points in terms of its comfort, time and cost. Implicit value is related to the customer's perceived image of a product or service and its performance. An example of this would be how different tourists react to the explanations of a tour guide; is the guide 'knowledgeable' and is s(he) presenting the material at an appropriate level? It is a matter of individual taste and preference. Even in the two easily measured and controlled explicit examples provided above there is an implicit element of customer perception. The in-house experts and relevant external accreditation agencies may have agreed on the appropriate price and quality combinations, but if the tourist had a personal preference for a certain standard of lighting or access to a toilet that did not coincide with the norm then they would not be satisfied. Comfort is a nebulous concept, especially when it involves sharing with others, as on a coach trip.

At the customer service coalface, there has been growing dissatisfaction with the treatment of customers and clients in banking, transportation, and health-care services according to Ho (1995). We do not want to see tourism added to this growing list of customer disaffection, because unlike those listed services it is a discretionary activity and not an unavoidable activity. Hence, it needs to fulfil customer expectations and dreams if it wants to have tourists return or to act as goodwill ambassadors. 'There is an old saying in service industries that if customers like the service they will tell 3 people. If they don't like the service they will tell 11 people' (Augustyn and Ho, 1998: 73). So it is imperative to create satisfied customers.

It requires controls to ensure that tourism businesses are offering the quality and value that is expected. Gap analysis is one method for measuring service value whereby gaps between the expectations of customers and service providers are examined and identified. Gaps between the expectations of what groups want and their perceptions of the actual service received have been used to assess tourists' and community members' satisfaction with tourism. The concepts and premises of gap analysis and the applicability of this service quality measuring method to tourism are reviewed in detail in Chapter 12 of this book.

Dual controls

In tourism both the quality of the environment and the tourist experience need to be considered, hence the industry needs to monitor and control both at once. This is a major challenge as there are many variables, both endogenous (internal) and exogenous (external), that need to be considered. But efforts have been undertaken in select environments to try to develop techniques that will manage the visitor experience in such a way as to satisfy their particular needs and to conserve the environmental setting of the experience. Foremost among these are the Visitor Impact Management (VIM) schemes developed by a variety of researchers and well summarised in Glasson *et al.* (1995).

Most of the VIMs have originated from the concept of carrying capacity and the assumption that any tourism development will inevitably lead to some degree of change on the host environment. The traditional concept of carrying capacity is that each ecosystem has a threshold capacity for development and use, and that if a critical threshold level of development or use is breached there would be progressive deterioration in the environment, leading eventually to its destruction. In this respect it is very similar to the economic concept of an equilibrium point of production, beyond which the marginal costs of each additional unit of production (additional visitor) begin to exceed the marginal revenue to the company or destination.

There are several problems associated with the carrying capacity approach to tourism. These include:

(1) The search for a numeric threshold value is akin to searching for the 'holy grail', because to calculate the biophysical carrying capacity of an area or site requires meticulous scientific measurement and knowledge.

(2) Furthermore, the conditions in any area or site are always changing with the seasons and the different demands placed upon it. Hence there can be no inherent use level or maximum absolute capacity.

(3) A measurement without purpose offers no direction to management. This is because a carrying capacity measurement without the prior determinations of goals and objectives leaves it difficult to assess and incorporate into management strategies.

(4) There is no firm evidence in the tourism literature that lowering or raising business volumes around a calculated carrying capacity actually affects a destination's ability to absorb tourism's impacts.

(5) In tourism the critical variable in calculating carrying capacity often has been visitor numbers, but visitors are not constants. They do not behave the same way or have the same impacts on the environment, and therefore form an unreliable indicator of changing use.

(6) In tourism it is the visitor experience that is critical, but too often in carrying capacity calculations the views of the visitor have been ignored. For example, the visitor expectations and priorities of an allocentric type of tourist will be vastly different from those of a psychocentric tourist (Plog, 1973, 1978). Consequently, their personal views of crowds, environmental conditions and stress will vary considerably as will their impacts on the environment.

(7) Finally, the goal of tourism is to provide a satisfactory experience, yet traditional carrying capacity measurement makes no attempt to assess a customer's satisfaction. This is particularly germane in tourism when a customer may be restricted in what s(he) can do due to conservation goals, and need an appropriate communication to explain the situation.

As a result of such difficulties with the traditional concept of carrying capacity Glasson *et al.* (1995: 52) have suggested a modification of the concept and its measurement. Building on the prior work of Williams and

Dimensions   **Perspectives**

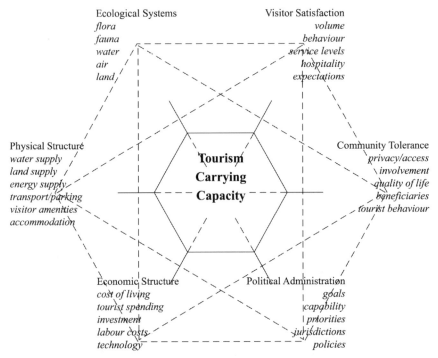

Figure 6.2 Tourism capacity networks

Source: Glasson *et al.* (1995: 52)

Gill (1991) they suggest tourism carrying capacity should be viewed more as a network of factors rather than as a simple direct relationship between usage levels and negative impact. The network involves linking the physical characteristics of the site with visitor satisfaction, community interests and political goals (Figure 6.2). It is this view that sets the scene for the more recent VIM measures.

VIM measures accept the assumption that tourism is likely to create change, but its direction and magnitude are determined by two separate elements: the physical and the human. The physical represents a descriptive component of what is happening to the environment and the human an evaluative component of how visitors and residents are assessing that change. An early exponent of this view is the Limits of Acceptable Change (LAC) methodology introduced by Stankey *et al.* (1985). The LAC technique examines the physical and social conditions in an area and seeks

Figure 6.3 The Limits of Acceptable Change (LAC) planning system
Source: Stankey *et al.* (1985: 3)

to determine the degree of change local people, as stewards of the environ-ment, are willing to accept in their community. It consists of nine steps that combine the previously missing managerial context with physical mea-surement and assessments of visitor and resident views (Figure 6.3).

An extension of the LAC approach is the more recent VIM methodolo-gies, which focus more on human impacts and interactions in the change process. 'It is argued that, first, we need to better understand the nature of impacts and the factors related to their occurrence, and only then can we apply this to management strategies in an attempt to reduce (negative) tourism impacts' (Glasson *et al.* 1995: 57). VIM is also a sequential process that aims to reduce or control the negative impacts of visitor interactions with the environment that may threaten the quality of the destination and tourist experience. Its similarities to LAC may be seen in Figure 6.3, along with the greater emphasis on the tourists' role and responsibilities in Step 6. Graefe *et al.* (1990) have suggested that visitor management (Step 7) may be either direct, in that it regulates visitor activity and behaviour, or indirect when it attempts to influence visitor behaviour through various communications. In many cases it is a combination of both approaches.

Examples of the VIM approach are most common in park environments, where the threat to sensitive wildlife and fragile plant-life from over-visitation is real and evident; but the concept and technique has been extended to urban areas, particularly where heritage attractions have come under stress. National park systems around the world have introduced their own versions of VIM and use the type of impact indicators identified by the WTO. Parks Canada has introduced a Visitor Activity Management Process (VAMP) which, in conjunction with the usual park zoning, attempts to direct and manage visitor experiences and encourage their understanding of the parks' twin mandate (Graham *et al.* 1988). The United States National Park Service has introduced Visitor Experience and Resource Protection (VERP) to create desired ecological and social conditions rather than worry about specific numbers of visitors and measures of maximum sustainable use (Hof *et al.*, 1994). In Australia the various park systems are working on a best practice benchmarking system that incorporates better use of visitor related data in management decisions. 'The purpose of establishing best practice criteria was to assist in the design of a comprehensive Visitor Data Management System' (Archer *et al.*, 2001: 6), one that can link park data with state and national tourism data as well as with park environmental needs.

In the urban arena we are starting to see the introduction of VIM techniques and approach in Venice, Italy. Canestrelli and Costa (1991) have introduced a fuzzy linear programming model that calculates the socio-economic carrying capacity of the centre of Venice, based on the desire of residents and visitors to use the same facilities. According to their impact model Venice could bear about 25,000 visitors a day, which was exceeded on 156 days in 1987 and predicted to be exceeded on 216 days by the new millennium (Glasson *et al.*, 1995: 115). However, a separate resident survey conducted by Glasson and his students in 1993 showed local residents were less concerned about numbers than the experts. For many residents 'the decreasing quality of life in the city is perceived to be more a function of the poor management of the Municipality, than of the excess tourism demand' (Glasson *et al.*, 1995: 114). Hence, it is no surprise that Venice is still struggling with a specific VIM programme to balance its tourist interests with local needs and concerns for the physical condition of this world famous heritage attraction.

Despite the more balanced management controls of the VIM techniques that blend scientific measurement, behavioural modification and business goals to support a management strategy, the world's major attractions still face significant challenges, especially from exogenous factors that are beyond immediate control. A good example of this is the dilemmas facing Yellowstone National Park in the USA. In 1986 Alston Chase wrote a book called *Playing God in Yellowstone*, that as the title suggests and *Newsweek* interpreted 'portrays the Park Service as tourist-minded and scientifically inept' (*Newsweek*, 1986: 52). The basis of this judgement was that this national park, like all others, had placed artificial constraints and bound-aries over a natural and much larger ecosystem. This produced a system that favoured the sensitivities of tourists over the natural order of the wil-derness. One of Chase's major concerns was the elimination of wolves and cougars to protect animals like the elk, because this had led to severe over-grazing when the predators were removed. However, conscious that the park should represent a natural landscape for visitors, the park authorities did apply some hands-off and natural management approaches. But even that type of strategy can have its problems.

One such problem was the fires of 1988, which affected about 900,000 acres or 40% of the park's total land area in a patchwork of blazes that left some forest areas decimated and others untouched (*The Economist*, 1988: 34). These fires were started by lightning strikes and as such could be viewed both as exogenous variables and part of the regular process that forms the park's natural landscape. Consequently the Park Service initially left the fires alone to burn out naturally. Unfortunately several factors worked against this strategy, namely a long drought and the build up of forest debris and waste over the years meant the fires spread much more than usual. In the end 10,000 fire-fighters were called in to save the park and its icons, like the Yellowstone Lodge close to the 'Old Faithful' geyser. It being somewhat ironic that the historic lodge was saved thanks to prior tourist minded planning – 'protected not so much by the (fire-fighters') water as by the quarter-mile-wide paved parking lot that surrounds it' (*Newsweek*, 1988: 18).

However, one should not get carried away by the emotion of the events and should always treat immediate figures and estimates with some caution. Despite the 'inflammatory' titles of the news-stories at the time of the Yellowstone fires later and more objective assessments showed the situation was not as bad as first thought. 'A January 1990 analysis and mapping of burned areas in Yellowstone shows that the total acreage affected by the fire was 793,880. Of that 323,290 acres were 'canopy burn', which means that the trees lost all needles and were blackened. Of the remainder, 281,098 was 'surface burn' – only the forest understorey (the lower layer of the forest) was affected, sparing most of the trees. The rest was sage and grassland burn' (Randhawa, 1990: 7). Not surprisingly Yel-lowstone recovered much of its former glory with the arrival of the winter and spring rains, due to the fact that mineral nutrients in the ash acted as a fertiliser to promote new growth, and the return of the animals to feed on the new lushness. 'All tourist facilities were fully operational as of spring 1989 and, if anything, tourists were intrigued by the dramatic look of Yel-lowstone after the fires. A record number of 2.06 million visited the park during 1989' (Randhawa, 1990: 7). This demonstrates once again that there is life after most natural disasters, as Murphy and Bayley (1989) relate in their assessment of disaster recovery at the site of the St Helens volcanic eruption.

What these Yellowstone experiences demonstrate is the difficulty of implementing controls in open tourism environments. In addition to the normal business difficulties of obtaining timely information on relevant issues in the production and marketing areas, tourism organisations will need to be aware of changing public sentiments and expert opinions as they develop and refine their management priorities and control systems. One way more organisations are trying to set the stage for more acceptable priorities and controls is through the development of codes of conduct.

Codes of conduct

Like many industries facing internal competition and external legislative interest, the tourism industry has been developing a series of codes of conduct to guide its operational practices and hopefully forestall the arrival of outside pressures on how and where it conducts its business. Often the early codes were established by various organisations to encourage a more professional and long-term approach to the industry. They offer guidance to members with respect to 'best practice' and societal responsibilities. They often incorporate some ethical statements and are at times subdivided into codes for operators and customers.

Codes of conduct also have become more commonplace in certain areas of the industry that are deemed to be operating in highly sensitive locations. This is particularly germane to the ecotourism sector, with its intense interactive experiential product. It is often taking visitors into sensitive ecological areas and attempting to offer a high quality educative tourism experience, but the visitors must play their part and be as sensitive and unobtrusive as possible with their surroundings. Hence the ecotourism sector sees the need to ensure all operators act appropriately with respect to the environment and the experiences offered to their customers, with the customers primed as to what to expect and how to behave. To achieve such objectives the Canadian Environmental Advisory Council proposed a detailed code of ethics (Scace *et al.*, 1992). It attempts to set general ethical goals, then indicates the relative contribution that is expected from both the industry and the customers. The Tourism Industry Association of Canada has responded to such a call to action with their own code of conduct for tourists and the industry. Among the objectives for tourists are:

> Experience the friendliness of our people and the welcoming spirit of our communities. Help us to preserve these attributes by respecting our traditions, customs, and local regulations

and for the industry:

> Strive to achieve tourism development in a manner which harmonizes economic objectives with the protection and enhancement of our natural, cultural and aesthetic heritage. (Hawkes & Williams, 1993: 87, 88)

When the quality of tourism development is enhanced by local cultural and political factors it is good practice to set certain ground-rules before the tourism business develops too far to ensure all party interests are respected, including those of the residents. This is what has happened in the Haida Gwai (Queen Charlotte) Islands off the coast of British Columbia, where wilderness and wildlife have been attracting increasing numbers of tourists to this world heritage site and home of the Haida people. The commercial tour operators have developed a code of conduct for their operations in this area, that includes statements regarding etiquette, wildlife observation, treatment of archaeological and cultural sites, and how to handle garbage (Falconer, 1991: 21–6).

All of the above codes of conduct are voluntary and depend on self-policing by members of the umbrella organisation or association that has initiated them. While such monitoring is generally effective because of the political and financial influence of the body concerned they do lack legal authority and what is worse they do not guarantee a standard of performance for the customer. Consequently we are starting to see the development of more formal codes of conduct that incorporate set standards of practice for the environment and the customer in the form of a commercially developed and promoted certification.

These certification processes set out the rules and expectations for operating a business that ensure a customer will receive the promised product quality and associated level of experience. To guarantee this there is regular inspection of the business and assessment of its practices. If the business can maintain the expected standards it is allowed to promote itself as having achieved a certain quality of business, with the expectation that over time the customer will come to associate that particular business with a certain standard of operational quality. This is the basis of most hotel and restaurant classifications but it is starting to expand into more general tourism fields with the introduction of Green Globe Awards by the WTTC. The Green Globe approach offers three levels of accreditation in its benchmarking process, designed to enhance a business' environmental sustainability and its customer appeal. The highest of these is certified status, that involves a developed environmental management system that has been audited and approved by an independent assessor.

However, even these attempts to bring more effective environmental certification into the industry have their problems. Font (2002: 203) considers:

there are too many ecolabels (and codes) with different meanings, criteria, geographical scope, confusing messages, limited expertise and expensive systems, only partly meeting the requirements of the process of compliance assessment.

He feels the future lies in further international accreditation and certification that will provide the tourist with recognised brands and levels of expectation. But even here such systems 'will have to negotiate the difficulties of site-specific and sub-sector requirements, different legislations and levels of support . . . that are likely to (lead) to very generic and vague standards and criteria' (Font, 2002: 204).

A case in point

Robbie Burns' warning that the best laid plans of mice and men can go astray reflects the importance of controlling and illustrates the problems that an American mouse had in France (Burns, 1996). In the mid-eighties, flush with popular support and financial success, the Walt Disney Corporation was very interested in opening a large-scale theme park somewhere in Europe. After narrowing the search to France and Spain, and then seeking the best deal, Disney committed to building 'Euro Disney' in Marne-la-Valee, a rural community in north-west France, about an hour outside of Paris.

Disney had a recognised product and name brand that was already enticing considerable numbers of Europeans into transatlantic flights to Disney World. The Disney theme parks were already widely popular in California, Florida and Japan and the public's love of everything Disney was showing no signs of slowing down. The Disney research and strategic planning followed past successful procedures which placed the new theme park 25 kilometres from central Paris, within a major hub for millions of travellers each year and within three and a half hours drive of 70 million people (Eisner with Schwartz, 1998: 265). Disney had the financing. The Walt Disney Corporation, French banks and multitudes of stock market players invested great sums in the proposed development. Disney had the infrastructure. The French government agreed to major infrastructure improvements including extending express train and subway (metro) service to the front gates of Euro Disney and to improve the freeway that ran near the site. Disney had a good measure of public support. There were only minor and isolated instances of public concern over the new theme park – mainly from the tenant farmers of the area who suddenly found that their 'life-long' government leases had been sold to this international company.

Everything that the Disney Corporation had done to prepare for this major initiative seemed to be appropriate and successful. Euro Disney opened on schedule in the spring of 1992, offering visitors the Magic

Kingdom theme park, a separate restaurant, nightclub and entertainment complex, six massive hotels, a full service campsite and an 18-hole golf course (Eisner with Schwartz, 1998: 282). Its stock opened at US $13 a share, closed at US $16 a share later that day and at its height reached US $30 a share (Eisner with Schwartz, 1998: 269). This Disney venture had so many advantages and was following an established and successful planning strategy that the company and its backers were confident it would be a great success. However, in its first year Euro Disney lost $900 million and there was soon widespread concern over the very survival of the park (*Newsweek*, 1994: 43).

The troubles of Euro Disney can be linked to several issues, but a key one was the lack of controls. This has been admitted by Michael Eisner, the CEO at the time, who states in his autobiography that, 'our primary goal was to control our financial exposure . . . and ensure a substantial share of the profits and management control' (Eisner with Schwartz, 1998: 266). But one can see that a lack of control over these and other factors precipitated the theme-park's woes. There were major cost overruns at Euro Disney, amounting to over $300 million before the opening day (Eisner with Schwartz, 1998: 267). There was insufficient control of known external cultural factors such as those relating to European preferences, like drinking alcohol with meals. There was an under appreciation of Europe's lower discretionary income which led to more economical approaches to travel such as choosing day trips or staying at lower cost accommodation. Furthermore, controlling for unpredictable aspects of the external environment, such as the poor winter weather and contingency plans for a downturn in the economy, were shown to be inadequate. While reports on the quality of the experience were high, Disney could have demonstrated more self-control in its media relations. Confidence slipped into arrogance as Disney officials were quoted as saying 'we are the best' and 'we're building something immortal, like the pharaohs built the pyramids' (Eisner with Schwartz, 1998: 281). Once Disney started having problems the press gleefully reminded the public of these gems.

Disney was able to turn around the situation at its French theme park after making careful adjustments to its control procedures. Disney started to control its costs by restructuring its debt load, adjusting its hotel room supply, laying-off some staff, and putting further development plans on hold. Disney became more responsive to its market by allowing alcohol to be served in the park and making minor changes to the services offered in the park, such as expanding facilities for sit-down meals (Eisner with Schwartz, 1998: 283). Disney responded to the downturn in the economy by lowering prices, cutting back its overhead, and refocusing its marketing. The cultural clash between the Europeans and Americans is demonstrated yet again in renaming the park 'Paris Disney'. American Disney officials felt the term 'Euro' was glamorous and exciting. However, market research showed the Europeans associated the term 'euro' with the slow moving new European currency and bureaucratic red-tape. Paris Disney is now more successful and the plans for expansion more realistic.

Controlling in Community Tourism

At the community level the monitoring and control of tourism becomes everyone's business but seldom anyone's responsibility. It becomes every-one's business because within a destination every individual and area is affected by tourism, not just the businesses engaged in the activity. Local residents not engaged in the industry must put up with the increased congestion and changed lifestyle that comes with thousands of visitors. Areas adjacent to tourist facilities will feel the pressure of business marked by traffic and noise, and if the destination is successful there will be a general increase in land and housing prices as the industry grows and visitors become second home owners or retirees to the destination. But who is to monitor these trends and who has the responsibility to control or legislate this industry?

The simple answer is government, but in free market economies government is generally not keen to become enmeshed in the detailed management control of industries because of the cost and poor track record of central planning. In terms of tourism with its diverse products and settings this would be even more challenging. However, there is always one exception that proves the rule and that has occurred in the Falkland Islands, where political considerations have led to close government control 'to maintain balance between the interests of growth and the environment' (Riley, 1995: 471). The official Falkland Islands Development Corporation has the 'status as the sole agent for change' on the islands and in terms of tourism has applied an absolute ceiling of 500 land-based tourists a year. Thanks to the islands' isolation and the political situation such a restraint had not been put to the test by the mid-nineties according to Riley.

The evidence suggests that control at the community level comes when both the industry and local population see it as a net benefit to all concerned. It is also evident that in this area of tourism management most progress has been made by small communities, often in a mountain resort or coastal setting.

Bosselman *et al.* (1999) refer to the monitoring efforts of several small communities around the world with respect to enforcing various performance and environmental standards in addition to the normal building codes and zoning regulations. Among these was the town of Chepstowe that monitored its tourism performance over a five- year period in order to increase the economic benefits it brought to the community. But the community to catch the imagination of the authors was the success story of

Whistler, British Columbia. To them 'The municipality (of Whistler) has for over twenty years had an active and evolving public community participation process that has resulted in a carefully crafted, and continually monitored, growth management strategy that responds to community needs and goals' (Bosselman *et al.*, 1999: 12).

One of those who observed the evolution of Whistler into an international ski resort with a four-season market appeal and contributed to its monitoring process and community participation has been Alison Gill. Gill (1997: 55) maintains 'few tourism communities have resolved the problems of how to successfully control and manage the balance between tourists and residents in a resort setting', but she feels the chances of success are dramatically increased through a community oriented approach to management and monitoring. She notes that in 1988 Whistler introduced a growth management approach to its tourism development through a comprehensive development plan that shifted the growth emphasis to a more balanced appraisal of resident and tourist needs. 'Community involvement lies at the heart of the growth management approach that underlies the development policy in Whistler' (Gill, 1997: 62), including such features as resident surveys and small group 'living room meetings' between various subgroups of the community and the tourism industry. 'Notably a commitment was made to a comprehensive community and resort monitoring system' (Gill, 1997: 63), that covered aspects of land use and development, and market demand as outlined in Table 6.1.

The type of monitoring system developed at Whistler is designed to provide information to guide both the industry and the community in their development decisions. It is facilitated through the input of primary and secondary data, assembled and assessed by arms-length and objective individuals. In the case of Whistler a nearby university (Simon Fraser University) has assisted the process, and there have been examples of similar successful approaches elsewhere, such as in the Austrian Alps.

In the 1970s the pressure of development on small ski villages in the Austrian Alps was reaching the critical point of threatening 'the ecological integrity and long-run socio-economic stability of the area' (Moser & Peterson, 1981: 68). A test-case of one village – Obergurgl in the Tyrolean Alps, was undertaken by the Alpine Research Institute of the University of Innsbruck as part of UNESCO's Man and the Biosphere (MAB) Project 6 to study the impact of human activity on the mountain environment. 'The MAB–6 Obergurgl Project lasted for about 12 years and has left a definitive mark on the village and on many of the scientists who participated.' Furthermore, 'Obergurgl's experience has been studied by many other communities, and the wider region around the village has been declared by the provincial government a zone of limited development – a move that was strongly supported by Obergurglers' according to Moser and Moser (1986: 102–3).

Table 6.1 Elements of monitoring systems, Resort Municipality of Whistler, 1994

Category	*Indicator*
Land Use/ Development	inventory of residential/commerical development
	construction activity
	hotel accommodation
	resort-related development and other land use changes in Highway 99 corridor
Environment	water system quality
	wastewater effluent quality
	air quality
	vegetation cover
	lakes and river quality
Commercial/ Social	population
	school enrolment
	health unit statistics
	unemployment
	crime, traffic violations
	community satisfaction survey
	selected community/recreational facility usage
Infrastructure/ Transportation	water system – remaining capacity
	sewer system – remaining capacity
	Highway 99 volumes
	transit system ridership
	BC Rail passenger volumes
Market	hotel occupancy, hotel rates
	skier volumes
	conference delegate volumes
	golf-green fees
	visitor satisfaction surveys
	residential sales prices

Source: RMOW, Planning Department

Working in conjunction with local residents, some of whom operated local ski facilities and hotels, the scientists developed a four-dimensional monitor model. The four dimensions considered were:

(1) *Recreational demand* – which examined the actual and potential tourist demands for the area.

(2) *Population and economic development* – which examined tourism's relative economic contribution to the local economy.
(3) *Farming and ecological change* – which measures the impact on the principal resource and activity in the area, its farmland and farming productivity.
(4) *Land use and development control* – which assessed the needs of all groups and industries in terms of their resource base and utility demands.

This process led to the identification of eight major problem areas for Obergurgl according to Moser and Moser (1986: 104). These were:

- Different villager attitudes to land ownership, emigration and economic development.
- Different perceptions of environmental quality between the villagers and tourists.
- Determining the effect of ski development on soil erosion.
- Determining the productivity of alpine pastures with respect to domestic and wild animals.
- Projecting future recreational demands with respect to changing public attitudes and transport options.
- Continual analysis of alternative development schemes.
- Experimental ecological studies involving the manipulation of grazing patterns and trekking routes.
- Economic impact assessment in terms of employment structure and savings patterns.

After examining these issues the scientists and villagers suggested various strategies to improve or alleviate the problems. For example, in the area of recreational demand some hotels reduced the number of guest beds as a quality improvement measure and natural history tours were introduced, guided by specially trained local residents. In terms of population and economic development there was an expansion of the youth education programme, a substantial revegetation of the ski runs, and better management of the summer visitor impacts. In the area of farming and ecological change there was the establishment of quiet zones and nature protection areas. Included among these was a calculation of vegetation resistance to the 'stamping damage' of hikers. In terms of land use and development control the village added a new biological sewage treatment plant to reduce local water pollution and applied restrictions on traffic in the village.

The success of such collaborative efforts has been duplicated elsewhere in Austria. Kariel (1989: 64) reports on the general 'acculturation to tourism and the desire to control growth' that spread through the alpine regions of Austria and he follows the experience of four other mountain communities.

He notes that most villages did not want 'to be totally given over to tourism to become another St. Moritz or Zermatt' (Kariel, 1989: 65), but that in order to control their own destiny they needed to take the responsibility for their development options away from the central government. For the changes they wanted to see 'are more likely to occur when there is local development and control, with suitable guidance from experts' (Kariel, 1989: 68).

Summary

This chapter emphasises the importance of including control measures in the development of tourism, because as an industry with some undeniable negative impacts it is imperative to minimise these effects if the industry is to succeed. It is noted that control measures have become a regular element of business management, and with the shift to a service economy and growing consumer sophistication there has been a change of emphasis from simple physical controls to one emphasising customer satisfaction.

In tourism past discussion of controls and monitoring has either been of a general nature or with a heavy emphasis on environmental issues. However, with the growing awareness of different consumer perceptions and priorities, and examples of successful quality control in the accommodation and transport sectors there is now emerging a broader interpretation of management control. Major companies have embraced the principles of total quality management and yield management, which involve consideration of different stakeholders and overall productivity. This has spread to certain destinations, where there are attempts to involve more stakeholders in the creation of a quality experience and efforts to vary the product and price through the seasons.

To illustrate the relevance of the four functions of business to modern tourism management the recent planning efforts of a state government will be examined. The strategic tourism management plan for the State of Victoria, Australia, is presented in the following case study. This major undertaking has been analysed in terms of the four business functions and with respect to its overall direction.

Case Study: State of Victoria's Strategic Tourism Plan

Tourism has become an important industry to the Australian state of Victoria over the years and it is becoming more important. It is important to the capital city of Melbourne's ambitions to become a world class city and to country Victoria's desire to diversify, as its traditional industries can no longer support previous population bases and amenity levels. Tourism in the state is comparable to the agricultural and communications industries, contributing A\$8.5 billion to the Victoria economy and accounting for 150,000 jobs according to the Minister for Tourism (Tourism Victoria, 2002:

1). To build on this strong base the theme of the plan is to 'Advantage Victoria' by building on its economic, social and environmental advantages (Tourism Victoria, 2002: 4). This case reviews the plan according to the role of the four business functions outlined in this part. The data and quotes are taken from Victoria's Tourism Industry Strategic Plan, 2002–2006 (Tourism Victoria, 2002), but the interpretation is the responsibility of the authors.

Planning

Planning philosophy and statements naturally dominate such a document but certain trends and emphases are apparent. The first is that a state plan has to be as comprehensive and inclusive as possible. To achieve this the plan adopts the triple bottom line approach of considering environmental and social implications in addition to the more obvious economic drivers. It addresses the issue of exclusivity by promoting Melbourne as a gateway to the country and state, and enhancing its position as a world sport event and convention centre. It shifts its promotion of Victoria's rural regions from a general product emphasis to a more specific marketing of primary motivations for travel. Its new emphasis will be on certain 'destinations and attractions, desired experiences, special interest themes, products and touring routes' (Tourism Victoria, 2002: 66).

While marketing remains the dominant interest of the state its management has matured and so marketing is not the only planning interest. In its discussion of strategic marketing the plan considers trends in international and domestic tourism (Figure 6.4), along with branding and psychographic segmentation opportunities. It links these consumer interests to particular products in its section on product development, where it is particularly optimistic about Victoria's food and wine possibilities as well as the more common alpine, nature based and heritage themes of the past.

Organising

For the plan to work Victoria needs to ensure there is sufficient communication and organisational structure in place, for as the Minister for Tourism observes the plan needs to be 'underpinned' by stakeholder and government support (Tourism Victoria, 2002: 1). The plan notes 'there are about 24 tourism industry sector organisations in Victoria . . . There are also about 100 local and regional tourism associations . . . and numerous municipal tourism boards' (Tourism Victoria, 2002: 16), so one of its priorities is to encourage the development of one umbrella organisation to represent the industry. An appropriate body – the Victorian Tourism Industry Council – was created in 2001 and the state government hopes it can interact with this council to promote the plan's objectives.

One important consideration in the organising of Victoria's tourism is to ensure that the relevant information reaches potential customers. To achieve this the state plans to create an information distribution chain to

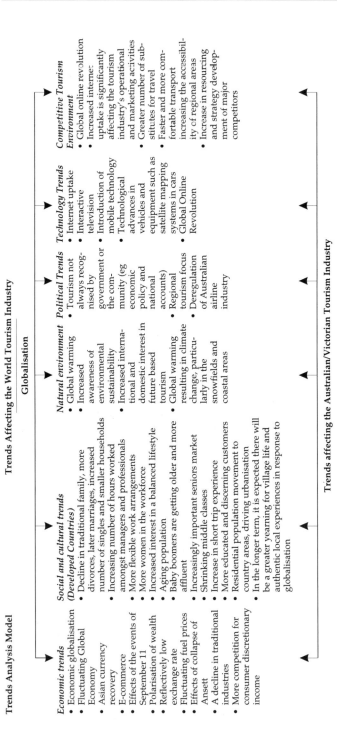

Trends Analysis Model

Trends Affecting the World Tourism Industry

Globalisation

Economic trends
- Economic globalisation
- Fluctuating Global Economy
- Asian currency recovery
- E-commerce
- Effects of the events of September 11
- Polarisation of wealth
- Reflectively low exchange rate
- Fluctuating fuel prices
- Effects of collapse of Ansett
- A decline in traditional industries
- More competition for consumer discretionary income

Social and cultural trends (Developed Countries)
- Decline in traditional family, more divorces, later marriages, increased number of singles and smaller households
- Increasing number of hours worked amongst managers and professionals
- More flexible work arrangements
- More women in the workforce
- Increased interest in a balanced lifestyle
- Aging population
- Baby boomers are getting older and more affluent
- Increasingly important seniors market
- Shrinking middle classes
- Increase in short trip experience
- More educated and discerning customers
- Residential population movement to country areas, driving urbanisation
- In the longer term, it is expected there will be a greater yearning for village life and authentic local experiences in response to globalisation

Natural environment
- Global warming
- Increased awareness of environmental sustainability
- Increased international and domestic interest in future based tourism
- Global warming resulting in climate change, particularly in the snowfields and coastal areas

Political Trends
- Tourism not always recognised by government or the community (eg economic policy and national accounts)
- Regional tourism focus
- Deregulation of Australian airline industry

Technology Trends
- Internet uptake
- Interactive television
- Introduction of mobile technology
- Technological advances in vehicles and equipment such as satellite mapping systems in cars
- Global Online Revolution

Competitive Tourism Environment
- Global online revolution
- Increased internet uptake is significantly affecting the tourism industry's operational and marketing activities
- Greater number of substitutes for travel
- Faster and more comfortable transport increasing the accessibility of regional areas
- Increase in resourcing and strategy development of major competitors

Trends affecting the Australian/Victorian Tourism Industry

Travel Styles
- Growth in combined trips – business/VFR – business/pleasure • More sophisticated high yield markets
- High yield markets travelling more for business • High yield markets more discerning
- Short break trend continuing for managers/executives due to less leisure travel time
- More emphasis upon niche/specialised/tailored tourism product across all markets

Travel Substitutes
- Dining out, events, shopping, staying 'in', renovations…
- Increase in home based electronic leisure activities
- Ever increasing 'Entertain Me' mind set and expectation to be entertained in all areas of our lives

Figure 6.4 Trends analysis of international and domestic tourism *Source:* Victoria (2000: 2)

link all products and regions with potential customers (Figure 6.5). The rising importance of 'electronic/online distribution channels' is evident, as more travel consumers are prepared to move from simply obtaining information via the web to making actual bookings.

The web and IT have become major sources of information in the development and distribution of this strategic plan. IT was a vital component in the extensive consultation and build-up of the plan, as the state sought input from a wide variety of industry and industry-related interest groups, including a small group of academics. The final version of the plan is available on Tourism Victoria's corporate website (www.tourismvictoria. com.au/strategicplan) for the first time, which ensures the widest possible dissemination to the industry and students of tourism.

Leadership

The very presence of a strategic plan epitomises leadership, for it indicates a willingness by the state government to coordinate and guide future tourism development for the benefit of as many as possible. But within this commitment to lead there are some significant innovations proposed for the state's tourism. One is the commitment to Agenda 21 and making tourism a positive contribution to a healthier planet by emphasising sustainable development. Another is the recognition that Tourism Victoria should 'take a leadership role in the tourism industry and encourage professional standards and the development of cooperative arrangements, which maximise industry effectiveness (according to the triple bottom line audit)' (Tourism Victoria, 2002: 15).

The determination that this industry needs to 'raise its game' in the area of professionalism and standards is one that bears repeating and emphasising on a continual basis. The plan recognises the difficulty in recruiting and retaining quality staff and presents several strategies to overcome these difficulties. Among them are the promotion of tourism's attractiveness and dynamics as a career, initiating a tripartite forum of industry, government and education to develop relevant training and education, and supporting the case for professional development courses in this industry. In terms of standards the plan seeks to use accreditation to ensure 'the delivery of an experience in a sustained and reliable manner consistent with promoted expectations' (Tourism Victoria, 2002: 109).

Controlling

The plan recognises the relevance of controlling and monitoring through a discussion of performance indicators and targets, but in addition to this auditing role it also provides insight into other ways the government can and will control the direction of Victoria's tourism. For example, since 'thirty percent of land within the state is Crown Land' the government will explore ways to facilitate the appropriate development of tourism on or

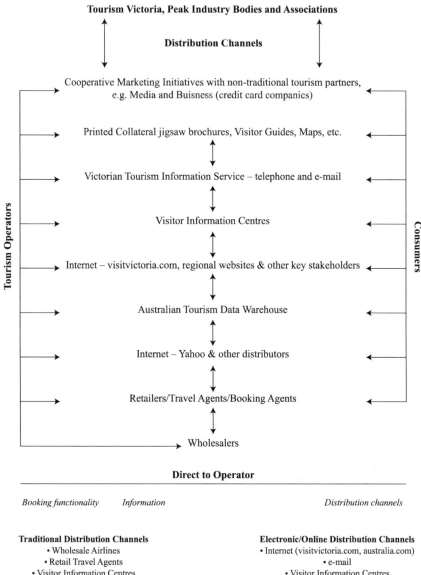

Figure 6.5 Tourism distribution chain

Source: Tourism Victoria (2000: 84)

adjacent to such high value national assets (Tourism Victoria, 2002: 116). The plan also recognises its controlling influence in relation to air transport links and development. Consequently the government commits to 'play a leadership role in Commonwealth (federal) regulatory matters affecting aviation, including input to bilateral negotiations . . . expanded or new air services . . . increasing the competitiveness of the Melbourne sector (airport) to foreign and Australian carriers' (Tourism Victoria, 2002: 129). It is only through such controlled transport development that the state can hope to raise the industry's yield factor and to control the spatial distribution of its important international and interstate tourists.

Summary

Only part of a very extensive strategic plan has been covered in this short review, but within these few pages it is evident that the state government of Victoria has considered and used all of the four business functions within its plan. In many cases these functional elements have been declared structural elements of the plan, in some areas they have been interwoven into other objectives as in the case of the leadership and controlling attributes. But throughout the plan there is a business emphasis which recognises the future of Victoria's tourism must be based on sound business principles, with a focus on serving and satisfying the customers' expectations.

Part 3

Tourism Community Stakeholders

Stakeholders

Widespread support for tourism initiatives will be necessary to success-fully integrate the four business management functions outlined in Part 2 into strategic community tourism management. Communities are made up of many individuals, each with their own interests and priorities. Since this book will be examining individuals' interests and priorities in their community's tourism development, we will use the term 'stakeholders' to describe the grouping of these individuals. The term 'stakeholder' in the business management literature has been defined as: 'Those groups or individuals who are directly or indirectly affected by an organization's pursuit of its goals' (Stoner *et al.*, 1995: 63). Such a definition reflects the concept of managing through organisation and recognising impacts will be more than simply economic when assessing tourism's impacts on a host community.

Stakeholders can have different types of relationship with a business in that they may be *internal stakeholders*, such as owners and employees, or *external stakeholders* such as customers, suppliers or special interest groups. Both of these have been described as 'direct action' stakeholders (Stoner *et al.*, 1995). But in the open system of a global economy with tourism busi-nesses' external environmental impacts affecting communities down-stream or overseas, the existence of an 'indirect-action environment' beyond the immediate community should be acknowledged also. This is where people and places well removed from an actual business site can be affected by that business organisation's actions and thus become indirect stakeholders.

Many stakeholder groups find they have to fight to be included in deci-sion-making processes. However, just because a group is included in a discussion does not automatically mean they will have a chance to partici-pate in an effective and efficient manner in management decisions. The strategy, whether intentional or incidental, of wearing down dissenters with tedious meeting agendas and schedules that fail to produce results can alienate stakeholders from group decision-making processes. Such proce-dural attrition might seem acceptable in the short term as they can clear the way for those remaining to make decisions. However, if important community decisions are made in such a manner they are likely to alienate public opinion and damage goodwill towards the participation process.

Decisions made with only limited community participation and support tend to survive only in the short term, as many underlying issues and opportunities will have been neglected due to the lack of full and vigorous participation by all stakeholder groups. Given the importance of stakeholder involvement in any successful community visioning exercise and the development of a truly communal tourism strategy it is remarkable that so little research attention has been placed on this aspect of tourism activity to date.

Those living in a community with a significant tourism activity will often find they have multiple roles and views regarding the industry. No categorisation of community stakeholders can be mutually exclusive due to the interlinked nature of community living and this industry. There are those who are employed directly in tourism or have a family member who is involved in a core or peripheral component of this extensive industry, as described in Chapter 9. Such people are likely to have a different perspective from those who are simply residents of the same community. This has certainly proven to be the case with many studies of resident attitudes and opinions demonstrating such differences of opinion (Lankford, 1994; Milman & Pizam, 1988; Murphy, 1983; Williams & Lawson, 2001).

In many communities residents with no apparent link to the industry could in effect be indirect shareholders, since so many of their local governments invest in tourism-related facilities such as piers, parks and parades. One example of this indirect shareholder relationship is the growing practice of offering residents a price discount when they enter local museums or a reserved camp ground space because they have contributed to these facilities already through their rates or property taxes.

The occurrence of multiple roles and perspectives is common in stakeholder analysis. Stoner *et al.* (1995: 74) describe the situation as 'multiple stakeholder relationships', where:

> Individuals may need to balance conflicting roles and values when they work for an organization, use its products, perhaps own stock in the company, and live and raise their families nearby. Such multiple stakeholder relationships are not uncommon.

To ensure the survival of a tourist organisation or business, along with the continued prosperity and appeal of the host community requires maintaining a balance among multiple key stakeholder groups and relationships.

To illustrate this point Stoner *et al.* (1995) refer to the McDonald's restaurants attempt to satisfy several stakeholder groups when it introduced its more environmentally friendly packaging. It had to satisfy its customers and provide the sort of convenient packaging to which they had become accustomed. It needed to increase the recycled component of its packaging to show greater environmental responsibility. It had to undertake such change with fiscal responsibility to maintain its market share and shareholder loyalty. Since then McDonald's has entered another key phase in its development by expanding into accommodation, and is experimenting with McDonald's hotels in certain European locations. Once again this will call for the balancing of various stakeholder group interests, including customers, local residents, employees and shareholders.

Like the key decision moments for McDonald's, pivotal questions for many tourism destinations with regards to stakeholders will include the following:

- Who are this community's various stakeholder groups in regards to a proposal?
- What sort of process should be established to incorporate the input of stakeholders into the proposal?
- How will stakeholders participate – will they provide only their separate opinions, or will they be encouraged to develop mutually acceptable options?
- Who will represent these stakeholders?
- What is the optimum number of stakeholder representatives to include in the process to ensure that they are manageable in number with respect to analysis and strategy formation?
- What level of ownership will the stakeholders have in the formation, adoption, monitoring and adjustments of implementation strategies relating to the proposal?

While tourism research has yet to address many of these questions some attempt has been made to identify the groups referred to in the first question. However, even this simple first step has proven challenging and illustrates the difficulty in ensuring all stakeholders receive adequate attention.

Researchers have identified a consistent handful of stakeholder group candidates, but not always the same groups. Wheeler (1994: 648) split tourism interests into three sectors: the commercial providers, the tourists and the host population, not including the providers. Wearing and Neil (1999: 74) divide community ecotourism stakeholders into four groups: the tourism industry, the government, the community, and non-government organisations. Cock and Pfueller (2000) have divided their ecotourism community stakeholders into the four groups of environmentalist, the tourism industry, the host communities and the visitors. Ritchie (2001: 64) has divided her tourism community into four stakeholder groups: the residents, the industry, the visitor, and local government.

Some authors have suggested a more detailed representation is needed than is found among the broad categories of stakeholders outlined above. Jamal and Getz (1995: 187) in their thoughtful paper on 'Collaboration theory and community tourism planning', argue that 'a domain-level (local) focus in community tourism planning is critical due to the interdependencies among multiple stakeholders in a community tourism destination'. They raise the issue of legitimacy and cite Gray (1985) in claiming a legitimate stakeholder is one who has the right and capacity to participate in any decision-making process. Blank (1989) notes that any community should be reasonably reassured that the stakeholders assembled are capable of representing their interests. In light of these and other considerations Jamal and Getz (1995: 198) propose:

> Collaboration for tourism destination planning will depend on encompassing the following stakeholder groups: local government plus other public organizations having a direct bearing on resource allocation; tourism industry associations and sectors such as Chamber of Commerce, Convention and Visitor Bureau, and regional Tourist authority; resident organizations (community groups); social agencies (e.g., school boards, hospitals); and special interest groups.

When the Canadians tried to develop a strategic vision along these lines for their 'global tourism icon of Banff National Park' they attempted to involve all legitimate 'interest sectors' in the process (Ritchie, 1999). The result was a round table composed of 14 interest sectors, each of which were to 'represent the interests of its constituents within the process designed to plan the future of the Banff-Bow Valley region' (Ritchie, 1999: 276).

The discussion paper for a new Australian 10-year strategic plan invites all stakeholders to respond to the challenge and attempts to stimulate a response by asking over 200 questions (Australia, 2002). Stakeholders in this context are identified as 'participants in the tourism, transport, construction, finance and other tourism-related industries, the education and research sector, government agencies and members of the general community' (Australia, 2002: 2). In other words – anyone, so as to be all inclusive at the first stage of this planning process.

When the division into stakeholder groups is undertaken there is no guarantee that the views of each group will have internal consistency. Within each group there will be some variation of feeling toward tourism based on personal values, experiences and opinions. Choy's (1995) study of employment within Hawaii's mature and varied tourism industry indicated some differences between its airline, hotel and restaurant/bar sectors that resulted in different perceptions of job satisfaction and presumably attitude toward the industry. But it should be noted that in this destination, where tourism is the major single industry, 'the quality of tourism employment is much better than that usually perceived by those outside the industry' (Choy, 1995: 137). Similar differences of opinion have emerged in studies of residents living in tourist destinations.

Several segmentation studies of resident attitudes and opinions toward the local tourism industry have revealed a series of internal variations within this single yet general stakeholder group. Davis *et al.* (1988) using cluster analysis segmentation of a sample of Florida residents discovered five segments within this category. These are:

- *Lovers* (20% of the sample) who have no negative opinions of tourism.
- *Haters* (16%) who have extremely negative opinions regarding tourism and tourists.
- *Cautious romantics* (21%) who although being positive toward tourism also agree with some negative features.
- *In-betweens* (18%) who hold moderate opinions, agreeing with statements to a lesser degree than lovers or haters.
- *Love 'em for a reason* (26%) that are pro-tourism but less strongly than lovers.

Ryan and Montgomery (1994) used a similar process in Bakewell, England. They identify three clusters:

- *Enthusiasts* (22%) who support tourism, 'but not excessively so'.
- *Somewhat irritated* (23.5%) who have negative opinions about tourism's impacts and are sceptical about its benefits.
- *Middle-of-the-roaders* (54.3%) who generally score between the other two clusters.

Williams and Lawson (2001) have produced a more recent and thorough analysis of resident clusters, using a sample of 1062 residents from 10 New Zealand towns. Within that large data set they identify four clusters:

- *Lovers* (44%) who approve of tourism the most and believe the benefits are distributed fairly throughout the community.
- *Cynics* (10%) who approve the least, and think tourism has changed their town for the worst.
- *Taxpayers* (25%) who do not feel very strongly about anything to do with tourism except how it has a bearing on their taxes, both good and bad.
- *Innocents* (20%) who seem to be missing both the benefits and problems of tourism because of their lack of direct contact with the industry.

Thus, we can see in this quick global coverage that resident stakeholders can be expected to have a variety of views regarding tourism development in their community and that once again it will require explanation and balance to develop a consensus from this or any group.

Part Outline

Different stakeholder groups all influence each other whether they like it or not. Understanding the positions, motivations, needs and resources of these groups is, therefore, invaluable in developing tourism plans and strategies. This part will try to set the scene for future tourism research and management by applying some basic elements of stakeholder analysis from the business management literature to several key groups in the community decision-making process. It has been subdivided into four chapters representing four different stakeholder groups, but as this introduction has demonstrated there is nothing sacrosanct about this division. It merely represents an attempt to be both comprehensive and compact.

In this part each stakeholder group's general objectives are described in an attempt to isolate their key interests and concerns. This is followed by an examination of the group's needs using the four key business management functions to emphasise the pertinence and potential effectiveness of this management link to tourism businesses' strategic planning at the community level. The involvement of all stakeholder groups might seem like an invitation to agony by some who would rather bypass or minimise the involvement of groups, who they feel have either little to contribute or are outright troublemakers. However, since broad-based community support is necessary for long-term and successful tourism developments it is prudent to invite all affected stakeholders to participate in the process in order to understand their views. Involving stakeholders in a meaningful way allows them to develop a greater understanding of their own group with its internal differences, and the views of other stakeholders. Once such an understanding is reached these groups can discuss the issues and develop strategies that offer a greater opportunity to the whole community.

The customer is examined first because tourism is intended to be a service industry, one which is established to serve the needs and expectations of customers from all walks of life and origins. This is followed by an examination of the industry, which due to its diversity also needs to be examined in terms of various sub-groups. Then comes an examination of the residents who are not directly related to the industry, but who need to be 'on-side' if the efforts of the industry are to be rewarded with a receptive environment. Finally, we will examine the multiple roles and expectations of government and its agencies, which can instigate or facilitate the process of tourism development at the community level.

Chapter 7

Customers

Customers are often referred to as the foundation of business success. While many companies are quick to say they 'put the customer first', what are they really doing to understand and respond to their customers? It has been suggested that despite the big push to develop more customer focused business practices, 'only a relatively small percentage, perhaps 30%, practice what they preach' (Christopher *et al.*, 1991: i). Most businesses are still selling what they produce rather than what the customer wants, so are supply driven rather than market driven.

Since tourism is about selling travel experiences it involves the combined efforts of several organisations and businesses to satisfy the expectations of its customers. This makes the tourism experience exchange more complex than a simple product exchange and causes it to involve more than price considerations. As Kotler (2001: 140) notes 'if customers only bought products and didn't care about services and surrounding benefits, and all products in the category were the same, all markets would be price markets'. This is certainly not the case in tourism where customers value not only the product, but the service with which it is presented, the setting in which the exchange takes place and the knowledge base of the host regarding the destination as well as the product. These become a significant aspect of the total experience and the customers' interaction with these components is an important part of the experience success.

Under the circumstances of a service experience involving customer-tourism industry interactions, the traditional 4P marketing mix has become insufficient in the management and marketing of tourism experiences. As Berry and Parasuraman (1991: 4–5) state the four Ps of marketing are missing an important ingredient for service industries, namely the quality of the exchange. They claim 'service quality is the foundation for services marketing because the core product being marketed is a performance', and in tourism that experiential performance involves the interaction between customer and supplier. Jan Carlzon (1987) astutely calls it tourism's 'moments of truth' and tourism marketing texts have found it necessary to expand the marketing mix to include factors such as packaging, people and partnerships to indicate this more interactive nature of the tourism product (Morrison, 1989: 210–13).

With tourism often operating in public places its sales and operations also need to consider non-profit situations and the impacts on the destination. Non-profit organisations such as governments, non-government organisations like arts and culture organisations, and even universities have become more involved with marketing as the need for customers and a clear message has become more acute. The major contribution of marketing to the customers of non-profit organisations has been to help position them in an ever-growing and competitive market. 'Marketing competition (among such non-profit organisations), at its best, creates a pattern of varied institutions, each clear as to its mission, market coverage, need specialisation, and service portfolio' (Kotler *et al.*, 1987: 13).

This has certainly been the case for cities, which now actively market themselves as ideal and distinctive homes for various businesses, including tourism. Place marketing has been identified and described by Kotler *et al.* (1993: 18), as embracing four activities:

- Designing the right mix of community features and services
- Setting attractive incentives for the current and potential buyers and users of its goods and services.
- Delivering a place's products and services in an efficient, accessible way.
- Promoting the place's values and image so that potential users are fully aware of the place's distinctive advantages

Such activities describe how a destination should structure its tourism marketing, producing a clear and differentiated image of its products and service strengths. Overlooking the marketing and operation of this industry should be the destination, with its formal and informal obligation to ensure customers' expectations are met within the capabilities and aspirations of the destination.

Objectives

The prime concern of the customer is a *satisfactory experience*, one where expectations have been met and possibly exceeded. For this to happen customers will need to receive sufficient value from the experience to make up for the time, money, and energy committed to the exercise. Under such circumstances the customer can be expected to become loyal, not only in terms of repeat patronage but as an ambassador/lobbyist for the business(es) and destination(s) visited.

To achieve this desirable state customers will benefit from:
- research that has identified their interests and needs;
- clear destination images that indicate the prime tourism product(s) and life style of the host community;

- relevant information to targeted consumers whose interests would match the destination image and offerings;
- sufficient facilities and service to match their expectations and to provide a satisfactory experience.

The issues that will arise in meeting customer objectives can be met through the application of the four business functions. First and foremost the customer wants to be understood and appreciated. This requires market research and planning within the planning phase. Business and destination organisation will be responsible primarily for determining what corporate and community image to develop, and how to position their business and this image to relevant target markets. This will require collaboration between many groups and is one of the biggest challenges facing destination marketing associations. The effort to create the right match between expectations and offered facilities and service will be determined largely through individual business and community leadership. Reaching the appropriate customers with the appropriate messages will require a large degree of control over selecting the most effective distribution channels, monitoring the response to current offerings and identifying possible alternate options. For both individual businesses and destination communities this necessitates an ongoing examination of their offerings, and should be linked with consumer research into new markets and opportunities. As such it completes the circle with the market research of the planning phase.

Planning

Consumer choice process

Customer research should be an integral part of the strategic planning process because knowing the needs and desires of customers enables communities to better judge whether they can meet such expectations and how to go about blending consumer wishes with commercial objectives.

A generalised model of a tourist's consumer decision-making process is presented in Figure 7.1. It is based on previous consumer and marketing research, where particular features have been shown to influence travel decisions. The internal factors are those personal traits and situations that affect an individual's propensity to travel. The external factors are those outside forces that impact on everyone's ability to travel such as global economic and political conditions, plus those that have a specific impact on the individual such as the effectiveness of destination marketing. Both have been shown to influence the cognitive processes (thinking and decision-making) that individuals are likely to consider.

The model starts with the various *stimuli* that can create an interest in travel. In this era of consumerism all of us are bombarded with external factors like *general marketing* information, most of it unsolicited in the form

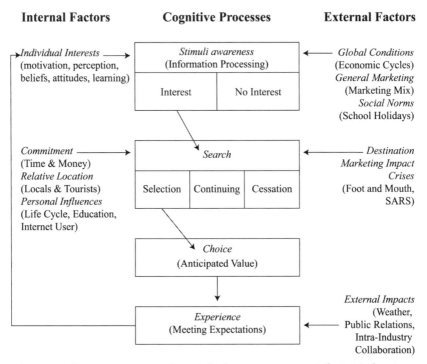

Internal Factors   **Cognitive Processes**   **External Factors**

Figure 7.1 Composite general model of consumer travel choice behaviour

of billboards, media advertisements, junk mail and 'internet spam'. Despite our best efforts some of this bombardment penetrates and starts us thinking about a product or service, how it may fit our needs, and how we can obtain it. The success of such penetration often depends on the 4 Ps of the marketing mix – promotion, product, price and place (Kotler, 1997: 92–4). It also depends on general *global conditions*. For example, the terrorist acts in New York (2001) and Bali (2002), plus the SARS outbreak and Iraq War (2003) all caused temporary declines in the stock market and to the growth of international travel. Cultural factors such as national holidays and customs can have a strong influence on the timing and location of many holiday choices.

Whether and how a consumer responds to such marketing stimuli is conditioned a great deal by internal psychological factors – motivation, perception, learning and beliefs and attitudes that influence *individual interests* (Kotler & Armstrong, 1989: 130–6). Motivation drives a person to satisfy a need and can be initiated by physiological, social or personal forces, as outlined in the Maslow and Freudian theories. In terms of travel, which often involves advanced purchases based on incomplete knowledge, individual perception of potential destinations and their offerings is an important component of the decision-making process. To help broaden their knowledge base most travel consumers attempt to learn more about their intended purchase, especially when it involves a major cash and time commitment. All of these psychological factors are influenced by the beliefs and attitudes acquired by the customer over time. Some of these beliefs and attitudes will be formed through personal experience, but others will be moulded by societal stereotypes.

The importance of individual interests has been recognised in the growing area of psychographic research. Such research attempts to explain why people from the same demographic groups can make very different vacation choices based on their individual interests. One of the early commercial forays into this area of research was the Values and Life Style (VALS) methodology developed by SRI International. Based on US surveys of people's general attitudes and demographic profiles it was considered possible to identify nine lifestyle groups. At the time these were said to include survivors (4%), sustainers (7%), belongers (35%), emulators (9%), achievers (22%), I-am-me's (5%), experiential (7%), societally conscious (9%), and integrated (2%). Another has been the Roy Morgan Value Segments http://www/roymorgan.com.au/papers/1999/1999my1.html) that have been used widely in Australia. Tourism Victoria has identified Roy Morgan's 'Socially Aware', 'Visible Achievement', 'Traditional Family Life' and 'Young Optimism' psychographic groups as core market segments for Victoria's regional market (Tourism Victoria, 2002: 71).

If the above stimuli have created an interest in travel the consumer will enter and *search* a global marketplace, for many countries and their destinations will be vying for the customer's attention and business. Major external factors at this stage include the extensive national and individual destination marketing and promotions activity. Millions of dollars are spent annually on attracting the attention of potential tourists and this has become a principal expenditure item for destinations and individual businesses alike. However, even the best prepared marketing plans and searches can be disrupted by external crises. We have only to look at how the foot and mouth epidemic in Britain changed rural holiday plans, and the Severe Acute Respiratory Syndrome (SARS) deeply affected travel to and within South East Asia. The search process is expected to be a continual process leading to three possible outcomes. One is a selection process that leads to immediate action and a choice. Another is a continuing process that indicates the consumer is still undecided, but is still a prospective tourist. The final outcome is a temporary cessation of search due to an unsuccessful search or a change of circumstances.

The degree of search will depend to a large extent on the consumer's anticipated expenditure of time and money, which is represented in the model as their degree of *commitment*. If the trip under consideration is a 'weekend getaway' it is assumed that this is likely to a regional trip to areas that are well known or referenced through family and friends. It would be a relatively inexpensive option in terms of time and cash, requiring little search and preplanning and could be classified as a minor commitment. On the other hand, if the trip is a 'once in a lifetime' overseas trip it would justify a far greater search for information because such distant places are less known and require much more time to structure into a personal trip. This would be indicative of a major commitment.

While not commonly associated with the tourist decision-making process we have introduced a *relative location* factor into the model at this point. Local residents do not qualify as tourists in terms of distance travelled or overnight stops away from home, but these people are important customers nevertheless, especially in the slower months. Their level of commitment, in terms of the search process, is far less than distant decision-makers, but local people still undergo a selection process and are influenced by the same or similar factors. As such they should not be over-looked and should be included through internal marketing within the destination community. If local people are included in the overall marketing perspective, they not only become more loyal customers, they interact with visitors and can positively influence visitors' overall tourism experiences through their recommendations. Victoria, BC, has recognised this and encourages resident use of tourism businesses and facilities by hosting a 'Be a Tourist in your Own Town' function once a year and offering favourable resident host ticketing deals.

Although the level of commitment dictates the degree of analysis and planning involved in decision-making, the search process will be influenced by both personal and external destination influences. The personal inputs are discussed in some detail here, but the destination inputs are left to the next chapter on the industry, for that is where and how communities can best influence the customer's decision-making process.

Personal influences include the impact of personal circumstances and immediate family and friends on vacation travel decisions. One factor that influences the amount of discretionary time and cash available is the customer's position in the lifecycle. One of life's ironies is that when one is young there is plenty of time to travel but few funds, and when one is older more people find themselves 'cash rich and time poor'. That said, it is no coincidence that two prime long-distance travel segments are the youth and the seniors markets, both with the respective amounts of time and income to pursue their travel interests. When most people make travel decisions these days they are make them in consultation with others. At the household and family stages of the lifecycle it is the partner and children who need to be consulted, because a successful vacation will depend on group consultation and participation.

A growing personal influence in travel decisions is the ability to use the Internet. This relatively new and rapidly expanding form of information technology has revolutionised customer access to the global market of tourism and has been equated with the jet engine as having the most significant impact on modern tourism by Buhalis (2000). By the end of the last millennium large numbers of consumers had access to and were using the Internet. Taylor (1999) cited in Buhalis (2000: 166–7) claimed Norway is the largest Internet user nation (34% of its population) followed by the US (27%), Australia (23%), UK (14%) and Germany (9%). However, these figures represent a snapshot of a rapidly evolving situation, for the number of computers and their Internet sophistication has grown remarkably since then. Furthermore, use of this feature is strongly linked to other personal influences like being well-educated professionals with higher disposable income which are key contributors to travel interest (Smith & Jenner, 1998).

After searching the alternatives and taking into account the solicited and unsolicited advice from family and friends, via personal research and potential destinations' marketing efforts, the travel customer makes their *choice*. It is not clear in tourism or other areas of consumer behaviour whether this choice process is a rational or emotional one. It can be highly rational in the sense that some customers calculate the opportunity costs of one choice over another, and select the best value with an emphasis on its financial aspects. For some it is an emotional response to a personal crisis or success, and the need for a break or to celebrate. However, given the large number of influential variables and the frequent group decision-making involved more attention is being given to the role of satisfying personal and group interests. So rather than striving for the perfect vacation, whatever that may be, the majority of travel customers are looking for a satisfactory return on their time and money investment and something that will satisfy all members of the travel party. They are selecting based on perceived value.

In tourism, unlike most other businesses, there can be a substantial lag-time between making the trip decision, including a commitment of money, and actually experiencing the product. But it is the *experience* which determines the success or otherwise of the whole process and impacts later judgements and decisions. Once again the tourism industry is not in complete control of its own destiny. While its emphasis on quality and service will contribute significantly to a satisfactory experience there is little it can do about the weather. However, it can work to collaborate with associated or peripheral activities, such as the agricultural or forestry industries, and it can place more emphasis on internal marketing to host communities to foster good community relations.

A good experience is one where expectations are met or exceeded, and will create a loyal and possibly a repeat customer in tourism. The repeat customers are of great value to tourism destinations as they spread positive word of mouth advertising and often return to spend more money and stay longer (Alford, 1998; Ross, 1993). Destinations and tourism businesses can expect much higher returns for their advertising dollars when they target repeat as opposed to new customers (Christopher, *et al.*, 1991). However, loyalty does not necessarily transform into repeat visits, for in some situations like that 'once in a lifetime' overseas trip it would be unrealistic to expect much repeat travel. In fact for many the long-haul trips are generally separate excursions to different parts of the globe, to take in as much of this earth's diversity of landscape and customs as possible. But a good experience will always create a loyal ambassador, who will take up their role as a consultant to family and friends with the same vigour as they received when making their decisions.

The above model is presented as a general simplification of a very complex decision-making process. It is necessary for destination communities to consider models like this in order to guide their research into customer needs, and to adopt a customer oriented marketing and development approach to this industry. Having analysed their prospective market a destination needs to organise how it will approach its potential customers. One immediate adjustment that a destination should make is to optimise the model's potential through organising its marketing resources and efforts into a focus on specific target markets.

However, a note of caution is necessary with respect to the model in Figure 7.1 and all other 'grand models' of consumer behaviour, according to Hudson (2000). He notes that they are not predictive, but only general guides. They cannot predict specific customer choice because they are broad generalisations, and they do not include a time-line. Therefore they cannot indicate when and how to intervene in the process so as to actually influence the decision. What they are intended to do is to highlight the relevant areas for market research regarding types of activity and types of destination.

Organising

Segmenting tourist types

No business or destination community can be all things to all people, and it should not try to be. Rather the destination should segment its potential market into more or less homogenous subgroups, or tourist market segments, based on certain common characteristics and/or behavioural patterns, that they can serve and satisfy. The underlying reason for market segmentation is efficiency (Court & Lupton, 1997) and it takes organisation to match the product with the most appropriate market segment.

Tourists tend to be segmented according to their socio-demographic, psychographic or behavioural characteristics or some combination of these categories, as a way of predicting their travel interests and spending patterns. Any target market must be:

(1) *Measurable* – marketing objectives should be set in numerical terms so the results can be measured and the value of the investment assessed.
(2) *Substantial* – the target market should be large enough to warrant the investment.
(3) *Accessible* – it should be possible to identify and to reach the intended target market through specific channels.
(4) *Defensible* – the target market should be sufficiently different in character to justify its individual attention.
(5) *Durable* – it should be a long-term market segment, not necessarily the same people, that is worthy of the attention and investment.
(6) *Competitive* – if the first five criteria can be met, a destination must ascertain whether it can offer something distinct or unique to attract these targeted customers.

Segmentation methods

The most common form of market segmentation is to examine actual and potential visitors' *socio-demographic* characteristics, such as their gender, age, home location, income, education, occupation, marital status and stated travel purpose. This is because it is both an effective differentiator of tourist choices and it is easily accessible. A study of tourists' decision-making processes conducted in Belgium grouped travellers by the following socio-demographic categories: singles, couples, families with children and friend groups (Decrop, 1999). Each market segment was found to have its own set of priorities, personality traits and product experiences. For example, singles wanted to interact with other singles during their vacations and families with children were more concerned with safety than other groups. It has been noted that wealthier and more educated travellers tend to be more mobile (Hanson & Hanson, 1981), while older travellers and travellers with children tend to be the least mobile (Driver & Tocher, 1979).

Much of the socio-demographic information can be obtained from regular government publications such as the census and annual reports, from government-industry national surveys, and from the regularity of past survey results. Such information is easy to understand and lends itself readily to comparisons of groups that are segmented according to clear and quantifiable characteristics. Unfortunately, when a destination comes to use such material it will often find that the information is not broken down to the level of their particular area or township, or is out of date, or does not ask the exact right question for its market situation. Consequently, many destinations will need to conduct their own surveys to supplement this important aspect of market segmentation.

The main drawback with using socio-demographic data to track and predict tourist's actions is that this data only tells us about who the tourists are, not what they want and why they want it and what factors make them buy. Certain market researchers, like Cameron (1992) feel the key to understanding how to attract visitors is by 'examining their values and linking both values and attitudes with actual and intended behaviour' Cameron (1992: 155). This approach supports the examination of *psychographic characteristics*, whereby actual and potential visitors are grouped according to their beliefs, attitudes, and values. A study in the UK conducted by Schul and Crompton (1983) used psychographic information as a way to analyse and segment the search behaviour of vacationers who used the Internet. A factor analysis revealed six composite psychographic dimensions, including 'cultural interest', 'convenience' and 'knowledge seeker' along which these travellers were described and evaluated. Analysis of the results led to the creation of two different psychographic profiles in the tourist consumer choice process: active and passive planners.

Perhaps one of the most commonly cited psychographic techniques is that developed by Plog (1998). Utilising the concept that all societies have a central tendency toward certain beliefs and behaviours Plog examined travellers in terms of how closely they fitted their society's psychological norm for any behaviour. As a result of his studies Plog developed a pattern of psychographic segments that had a normal distribution surrounding the mid-centric norm. Moving away from the central mid-centrics Plog (1998: 254–6) identifies an *allocentric* group who are more venturesome and self-assured individuals who seek out more novel and unique destinations.

At the other extreme are the *psychocentric* group, who are self-inhibited and anxious personality types seeking dependability in all that they do. These individuals are very conservative about travel, either selecting to stay close to home or if they try international travel, preferring to travel in the safe environmental bubble of a tour group that maximises the use of home language and facilities. However, this classification is a snapshot and individual categories can and do change over time. It is noticeable that the early American tourist ventures into Europe after World War II were dominated by tours – leading to the 'If it's Tuesday it must be Belgium' film topic. But with experience and survival many of these earlier psychocentric tourists became free independent travellers (FIT market) and moved to the mid-centric or allocentric areas of Plog's continuum.

The main benefit of using psychographic information for tracking and predicting tourist actions is that such information can be used to create a context for understanding traveller motivations. Understanding the motivations of travel market segments and preparing tourism offerings to satisfy them is the most direct route to pleasing customers and turning them into a loyal client. The main drawback with using psychographic data to track and predict tourist's actions is that while this data helps to better understand what tourists want, it is incomplete. This is because it only addresses the 'individual interests' section of Figure 7.1. There is not always a direct or obvious correlation between personal attitudes and actual behaviour, as various psychology studies have indicated (Mayo & Jarvis, 1981; Ross, 1994).

Another problem some destinations have experienced is translating the factor or cluster analysis groupings into meaningful and reachable subgroups. For example, how helpful are identified groups with catchy titles, if you do not know how stable these groups are or how best to reach them through the media. In addition, the commercial emphasis and proprietorship of some of the key psychographic techniques has prevented independent scholarly assessment of their validity and reliability (Ross, 1994). To overcome such limitations psychographic segmentation is now closely linked to other techniques, such as behavioural segmentation.

Behavioural segmentation focuses on past actions as a way of predicting future actions. 'Behavioural segmentation divides customers by their usage rates, usage status and potential, brand loyalty, use occasions, and benefits sought' (Morrison, 1989: 150). Woodside and Carr (1988) have used past behaviours as a way of segmenting markets according to their established 'decision styles', which they define as the ways in which people make their travel decisions. One problem with behavioural segmentation is that past actions will not always serve as a good predictor of future intentions, especially when personal conditions, needs and associated circumstances change over time. Hence, once again the best form of market segmentation is a combination of techniques.

Market positioning

To achieve a competitive edge in market segmentation will require businesses and destinations to position their product. *Positioning* is the 'development of a service and marketing mix to occupy a specific place in the minds of customers within target markets' (Morrison, 1989: 175). As such it is a prime way to differentiate the local product and to set it firmly in the mindset of the targeted market. Judd (1995) notes how US cities have been forced to promote and position themselves for the tourism market with the reductions in federal urban renewal funding in the early 1980s. This was one way they could raise their profile in the eyes of potential visitors and investors, and revitalise certain districts in their central areas.

According to Morrison (1989: 191) effective positioning requires five 'D' steps. These are:

(1) *Documenting* – identifying the benefits that are most important to your customers.
(2) *Deciding* – selecting the image that you want your customers to have within your chosen target markets.
(3) *Differentiating* – identifying the competitors from which you want to appear different and the things that will make you different.

(4) *Designing* – providing product or service differences and communicating these in positioning statements and via the marketing mix.
(5) *Delivering* – making good on your promises.

Part of preparing for customers is organising tourism offerings, to gain and maintain a distinctive position in the marketplace for a product, service or destination (Lovelock, 1992). If this process is successful and people come to associate a product, service or place with its marketed image, such as equating Florida with sunshine, then the commodity is referred to as 'branded'. That is it has common recognition and acceptance. As such it has a distinct advantage when customers come to consider their options.

Kotler (2001: 55) has linked positioning and branding as a two-phase process in his steps to develop a strong brand. His first phase is to develop a 'value' position by:

- choosing a *broad positioning* for the product;
- choosing a *specific positioning* for the product;
- choosing a *value positioning* for the product;
- developing a *total value proposition* for the product.

This then leads to the brand development by:

- choosing a *brand name*;
- developing *rich associations and promises* for the brand name;
- managing all the customers' *brand contacts* so that they meet or exceed the customers' expectations associated with the brand.

It has been demonstrated that when there is a clear recognition of a brand and its position (offerings) in the market it is possible to develop a loyal market following, as in the case of Wal-Mart. This worldwide chain has grown from a single store in Arkansas to 4600 stores across 10 countries on the basis of low prices and a wide range of products (Saporito, 2003). At the destination level the Mt Buller resort in Australia believes 'companies with a strong brand perform better. Their customers are more loyal and the brand is top of mind for the market when they go to make their purchasing decision' (Hamilton, 2002). Consequently its brand name 'Mt Buller My Mountain' attempts to build on its strong ski club history, its easy access to Melbourne, its leadership in tourism education and the warm hospitality of its village.

Destinations need to position themselves appropriately with their preferred customers to ensure they maximise their return on tourism investments. Procedures for a general positioning strategy include detailed analysis of the following elements:

Market

All businesses need to understand their customers in order to better meet their needs, but with the intangible service experiences of tourism and the collective nature of a destination visit who is going to find out this information and how? In many instances it has become a responsibility of the local destination-marketing organisation, which has various options open to it. To search for the appropriate market segments it can utilise state and national surveys that reveal market trends and interests. To identify potential visitors it can join the regular consumer omnibus surveys that use established panels of consumers or those annoying telephone surveys. A destination can purchase several questions in those consumer surveys relating to their potential appeal as part of general consumer and marketing questions. To determine how well it is serving its current customers a good method is an 'exit survey' of visitors, as they are leaving the area and their memories are sharp.

Determining a destination's market potential should start by examining the current travellers to the area. Visitor surveys, as well as interviews with tourism providers and focus group discussions with tourism stakeholders in the community can provide data to understand what attracts the tourists and how satisfied they are with the current product. Surveys can both confirm conventional local wisdom and reveal some unexpected nuggets of information.

Competition

All businesses and destinations should be aware they are not operating alone in the tourism market and should know who their competition is and what they are offering. Many businesses hire 'secret shoppers' to scout out what rivals are offering and doing to attract their customers. In business being copied is not viewed as the highest form of compliment but as one of the greatest threats to long-term success. To minimise this risk they must focus on an aspect that will differentiate them and would be difficult to emulate.

For most destinations the competition is local, with nearby communities offering similar landscape and heritage products. But it does not have to be that way. Tourism, like certain retail establishments can build upon the drawing power of agglomeration and the provision of a critical mass to entice tourists to visit a destination area (Jones & Simmons, 1987). Just as the retail sector has found it advantageous to place similar outlets together at times to facilitate comparison shopping, as with fashion and car sales, tourist destinations can benefit from aligning themselves with other destinations in a region. This could provide sufficient combined attractiveness to draw visitors and to hold them overnight somewhere in the region, especially for those visitors travelling a long distance.

Internal operations

To operationalise the above market research and develop a competitive image requires the organisation of resources and development of a marketing strategy. Community and industry cohesion over issues of tourism development can be challenging due to the large number of affected stakeholders and the uncertainties that surround tourism growth. The information gained in assessing an area's market potential and principal competitors needs to be organised and assessed within the context of what's best for the industry and the community. Consultative meetings with stakeholders can assist in developing appropriate tourism strategies and plans, which in turn will direct the marketing position of the destination.

The importance of organisational structure and collaboration has become more evident as the tourism industry has become increasingly competitive and the need for collaboration more evident. Pearce (1992) has outlined the growth and complexity of various levels of tourism organisation that have evolved over the past decades. Selin and Beason (1991a: 208) have been pioneers in examining ways to enhance collaboration between tourism organisations and note that 'while the tourism industry has become increasingly competitive, there are strong incentives for tourism organisations to collaborate under certain conditions'. These conditions include the benefits of combining forces to draw visitors to a region.

Top of mind awareness

Even if a destination has what tourists desire, they are unlikely to visit unless the destination is one of their top destination choices. It has been documented that many people considering a vacation will consider approximately four destinations prior to making their holiday plans (Bronner & de Hoog, 1985; Thompson & Cooper, 1979). 'First brand awareness', which is also referred to as 'top of mind awareness (TOMA)' has shown itself to be a strong predictor of consumer purchasing in general (Axelrod, 1968: Woodside & Wilson, 1985).

Woodside and Carr (1988) conducted a study to assess the awareness of foreign travel destinations by US vacation travellers, as a means of determining the relationship between TOMA and travel choices. They asked respondents which countries outside of the US first came to mind when they thought about taking a vacation. The top four countries that came to mind for the survey participants were the UK (27%), France (10%), China (9%) and Australia (8%). Upon comparing this data with actual international travel choices by US tourists, they found a strong correspondence between a high awareness of a destination and high visitation rates for the top two destinations. However, countries that were not even mentioned, including Canada and Mexico, received far greater US tourist numbers than either China or Australia. One needs to realise that while certain places will stand out in people's minds, even in a very positive way, other factors such as time, distance, cost, and a lack of information regarding distant destinations can keep dreams of visiting such places from becoming reality. This is represented as the search cessation in Figure 7.1.

Positioning involves three interrelated customer focused components: image, market segmentation and priority promotional features (Aaker & Shansby, 1982). Given the importance of image, it is not surprising that a considerable amount of attention has been paid to this specific aspect of destination development.

Image

An important aspect of positioning is the image a destination wishes to develop and portray of itself. Deciding on what image to develop and designing the relevant promotional material generally has been left to industry or government experts, with little input from local residents who have to live with the outcome. At times this can lead to some unfortunate and unpopular choices that can create embarrassment all around. As Metelka (1977: 4) observed in an old, but still relevant, paper 'past and present marketing practices reflect the fact that destination area residents are overwhelmingly unaware of how their homeland is described in pro-motional material'. At other times the experts have hit the right button for residents as well as visitors. For example, British Columbia in Canada has long positioned itself as the 'SuperNatural' province; that describes its scenic wonders concisely and fits with its residents' views of their homeland. Likewise, the state of Victoria in Australia has positioned its variety and heritage very well with its 'Jigsaw' campaign, that invites visitors and locals alike to explore every piece of the state.

The more that destinations and individual service providers understand the image their target markets have of them then the better suited they will be to meet visitor needs and fulfil or exceed their expectations. Visitors have been found to prefer destinations that have strong, salient and benign images (Hunt, 1975: Woodside & Lysonski, 1989). Providing a strong, clear image that resonates with selected target markets in a positioning strategy helps potential visitors to establish a 'mental fix' on tourism offerings. The intangibility of the vacation experience makes this type of explicit position-ing strategy necessary, as it provides both a means of differentiating tourism offerings from one another and an incentive to purchase.

Within the general positioning strategies tourist destinations have payed particular attention to the development of an appropriate and com-petitive image to assist the customer's search process. Gunn (1997: 37–8) describes images of tourist destinations as either being *organic*, in that they are formed from one's previous information, such as news coverage and books, or as being *induced*, in that they are formed as a direct result of marketing and promotion. Before setting out on a vacation customers'

image of a potential holiday destination will likely include some precon-
ceived ideas of what they can expect, supplemented by promotional
materials and travel advice from others.

The attention to image is increasingly combining research into customer
expectations, their reactions to the proffered images, and how these images
compare to their real experiences and assessments. Customers tend to look
for clues about a provider's capabilities and qualities prior to making
purchases (Berry & Clark, 1986; Shostack, 1977). This tendency increases
with the cost and uncertainty of the commodity in question. In regard to
tourism, these clues play an important role in forming destination images
(Pearce, 1982). Since taking a holiday can be costly in terms of time, money
and energy people explore their options to help them make the right
holiday choices (Schul & Crompton, 1983).

Once the choice has been made the tourist-customer will experience the
realities of the destination environment and will judge how well they
support the promoted image. Bitner (1992) used the term 'servicescape' to
describe the ability of a working environment to affect customers. She
found that servicescapes can either assist with or detract from the organisational and marketing goals of a service provider, including the promoted
image. Bitner found that the physical design of service industries assisted
with their positioning and segmentation strategies and enhanced certain
marketing objectives, including customer satisfaction and attraction.
Servicescape elements that can influence customer behaviours include the
following:

- *ambient conditions* – such as lighting, noise, and smells;
- *spatial layout and general functionality* – the appearance of the physical
  setting and how well the elements work together; and
- *signs* – these can include written signs as well as more subtle indicators of values and appropriate codes of behaviour.

A good example of this process at work on a micro-scale is McDonald's
interior design work, developed to create an attractive, friendly and clean
environment that is welcoming to their families target market. On a larger
plant scale there is the example of the Disney theme parks. Their attention
to access and parking, convenient transfers to the park gate, theme areas
within the park, and a queue management process that converts an
unpleasant activity into a bearable experience has helped to make these
attractions world leaders in their field. The benchmark examples set by
these successful companies have been noted and copied by a variety of
tourist destinations, and have worked even when the destination did not
possess the full control of a private company. York, England, has turned an
archaeological find into a major tourism attraction using Disney principles
at its Jorvik Centre. Williamsburg, Virginia, has restored and recreated a

pioneer settlement in the midst of a modern city. Kyongju, in South Korea, has surrounded its tomb mounds of Shilla dynasty kings with beautiful gardens and restored artefacts and attractions (Figure 7.2).

As has been noted elsewhere, customers of the tourism industry will include employees and local residents, so the servicescape should also consider their needs. It has been found that the environments of service organisations affect employees as well as the customers they serve. Work environments that meet employees' needs have been found to increase their motivation, satisfaction and productivity (Bitner, 1992; Davis, 1984). Furthermore, it stands to reason that an attractive tourism environment in their community can affect residents' support for local tourism. Resident surveys that will be reported more fully in a later chapter indicate strong support for tourism where it has contributed to the appearance and amenities of the community.

Bramwell and Rawding (1996) have presented a clear delineation of the importance of imagery and how different perspectives influence its assessment. Geographers emphasise the importance of local 'landscape, history and traditions, cultural patterns, community values and power relations, and these come together in a unique way within the locality' (Bramwell & Rawding, 1996: 203), creating its 'sense of place'. Shaw and Williams (1994) recommend that places need to project their distinctive local and 'unique' place images in order to enhance their tourism appeal. This would respond to Urry's (1990) argument that modern tourists are seeking cultural and landscape features that draw them out of their everyday lives through their 'tourist gaze'.

Marketers emphasise the issue of place/destination substitution and advocate images that build on the unique benefits of a destination, be they natural or artificial, to enhance its competitive advantage. By integrating place images into a planned brand identity approach to positioning, it is expected to build visitor and investor confidence in the area by its contribution to a planned cohesive marketing strategy. An example of this approach is provided by Rouse's festival marketplaces and harbour redevelopment projects throughout the US (Kotler *et al.* 1993: 125–6). Gilbert (1990) has recommended that places use images to position themselves as status areas rather than as commodity areas. A status area is one that promotes its special attributes that cannot be found elsewhere and thus appeals to up-market visitors who wish to be associated with such status. It is the difference between a resort that emphasises its villas, exclusive casinos and yacht clubs, and one that promotes its beaches and inexpensive accommodation and entertainment.

Critical sociologists contend that as tourism becomes more global the pressures to differentiate through image increase, and as mass tourism loses its appeal the marketing emphasis is shifting more to individual consumption (Urry, 1990). However, at the same time the challenge is to stand

Figure 7.2 Kyongju, old capital of the Shilla dynasty in South Korea

out in an increasingly homogenised global economy while respecting the needs and desires of local residents (Britton, 1991; Harvey, 1989). As one can see from recent World Trade Organisation meetings around the world on advancing the global economy, some people feel the threat to local economies and ways of life is too high a price to pay for such progress and have demonstrated against such globalisation.

In their analysis of the tourist images created for five old industrial English cities Bramwell and Rawding (1996: 217) conclude 'tourism marketing images have a wider significance than initially may be apparent'. They note there will be both 'winners' and 'losers' in the development of community tourism images. Consequently, they call for a broader multidisciplinary approach that analyses images in relation to their distribution of benefits among residents as well as with respect to regular business accountability.

At the community level one of the biggest challenges is to coordinate the numerous individual business and personal interests into a united message that will promote the community in the tourism marketplace. To achieve this more communities are organising themselves into destination-marketing associations that have the mandate to create a corporate community image and positioning strategy to present to the world. These are just one of the elements in the general organisation of the travel trade, which has the role of connecting tourism products with prospective customers through a variety of distribution channels.

When Gunn (1979: 145) noted that 'one of the weakest links in all tourism is that of imparting information', his words spoke of the need to analyse and improve the performance of the tourism industry with particular regard to consumer awareness and response. To create such improved industry performance in this area will require leadership.

Leadership

New and emerging theories of customer behaviour and marketing are starting to re-shape the ways tourism operators and destinations view their target markets. The growing sophistication and individual demands of increasingly knowledgeable and experienced travellers is forcing the industry to not only segment the market into sub-groups but at times down to specific individuals, or a market of one. The Internet is providing new ways to reach customers and for them to book directly. Finally, destination-marketing organisations are taking on a greater leadership role in that they are becoming the focal point for tourism research, analysis, marketing and planning for the industry in their area. This leadership, taking place across the many spectrums of tourism development, provides a guide to improve the functioning of the tourism industry.

Marketing leadership

The intense level of competition for modern consumers has led to some marketing innovations that destinations need to consider. According to *The Economist* (2001b: 9) 'only happy customers will be loyal ones – and loyalty is something companies desperately need if they are to survive in today's difficult climate'. It goes on to say 'The right approach to retaining customers starts with trying to understand more about them, and then to work out what to do with the knowledge'. This advice and some recent marketing trends have particular relevance to tourism destinations.

Relationship marketing is one relevant strategy because it addresses 'the twin concerns (of) getting and keeping customers' (Christopher *et al.*, 1991: vii). It is a strategy of building long-term satisfying relations with key parties such as customers and business partners (Kotler, 1997) and involves the development of quality products, customer service and marketing into a combined and total approach to customer relations. In tourism it is a process of detecting prospective customers, turning them into first-time visitors, then into repeat visitors who become 'clients' and advocates for the destination – in effect partners in its success. As such relationship marketing is based on the premise that important customers and associates require continuous and focused attention.

Some people consider that if relationship marketing is taken to its full extent it becomes the *marketing of one*, focusing on each customer as an individual with their own needs and expectations to be fulfilled. The power of individual consumers, with their own wishes and schedule, has become an important factor and meeting such needs is one important way to differentiate a destination. However, one should always remember the 80:20 rule adopted from Pareto, that says it is best to concentrate on those customers (the 80%) you can please rather than spend too many resources on customers (the remaining 20%) who will be difficult if not impossible to satisfy.

Catering to one or a few individuals is an expensive personal service and not every community can afford such a strategy. Butler (1990) was one of the first to point this out as a major pitfall to the alternative or green tourism market ideal and the experiences in many parts of the world have borne him out. Consequently, many destinations need to find ways in which to appeal to individual or small group interests, but in such numbers as provide sufficient returns on the investments made by the host community. One possible solution is the concept of *mass customisation* that 'involves the selling of highly individual products but on a mass scale' (*The Economist*, 2001c: 63).

Mass customerisation can be seen as an extension of the 'built-to-order' process in manufacturing. Where companies such as 'Dell Computer and Renault already make extensive use of BTO systems, shortening delivery times and trimming work-in-progress ... that means turning a production-push industry into a demand-pull one' (*The Economist*, 2001c: 63). In tourism this can be and is being, achieved by developing guest profiles to ensure their needs are anticipated and by variable packaging that enables more customised products for the visitor. This move to mass customerisation is a real boon to small businesses with local contacts, for they can adjust schedules and improvise more easily than large corporations that are often locked into long-term contractual arrangements.

Since such long-term and customer oriented marketing strategies would undoubtedly have significant impacts on the type of image and product developed by a destination, they can be seen as worthy of *macro-marketing* analysis. 'Macro-marketing refers to the study of (1) marketing systems, (2) the impact and consequences of marketing systems on society, and (3) the impact and consequences of society on marketing systems' (Meade II and Nason, 1991: 73). In such a context the marketing strategies of a destination would be assessed in terms of a two-way interaction, between the customer and the destination. This would recognise two customers – the visitor and the host, and could help to minimise some of the false expectations that have been created in the past for both parties.

As indicated in the above marketing relationships, to reach and satisfy today's demanding customer will require more effort and partners. Day, who is an advocate of using marketing to create value, has identified three positioning themes to help make customer-oriented marketing more successful. For him a business should strive to be:

- *Better* – through the provision of superior quality and service.
- *Faster* – by being able to sense and meet shifting customer requirements quicker than its competitors.
- *Closer* – with the creation of desirable linkages, relationships, and even partnerships which channel members and customers. (Day, 1990: 173)

Responding to customer wishes is still the main route to success, but in terms of modern marketing it now involves a combination of individual customisation with the higher total returns of less noticeable mass production, all within the setting of destination accountability.

Technology

One of the first to highlight the significance of technological development and leadership to tourism was Poon (1993). She noted 'By far the most important area of impact of technology will be in the areas of marketing, distribution and sales' (Poon, 1993: 176), and went on to demonstrate what significant strides in efficiency and productivity had been achieved with the introduction of computer reservation systems (CRS). However, most of her examples relate to major corporations and destinations, where the high cost of CRS development and IT infrastructure in the 1980s encouraged strategic corporate linkages and a significant delay to the return on investment. What has occurred since Poon's important work is the rise of the Internet and the marketing power this is placing in the hands of the small operator and less well-known destinations to reach their targeted customers.

The Internet's interactive capabilities have assisted in the delivery of quality products and service by creating opportunities to monitor what aspects of a tourism product, service or destination appeal to customers (Tierney, 2000). The raw interest or appeal can be measured through 'hits per site', which is the number of times a site is viewed by customers browsing the Web. Such basic information can be enhanced by including interactive elements in website designs to measure specific customer interests. This can be achieved by providing options for the down-loading of particular features or attractions, as well as offering direct purchase and booking services.

There is an opportunity to combine information and sales with customer surveys over the Web that has the potential to produce more customer intelligence for individual operations and destinations in an efficient and relatively low cost manner. However, some methodological weaknesses have been found with such surveys; such as response and non-response bias, and multiple and unwanted entries (Schonland & Williams, 1996). In his study of the research effectiveness of tourism websites Tierney (2000) suggests that while the Internet can provide more frequent and targeted contact with customers, the greatest challenge with the tourism surveys on the Web is low response rates. He suggests these could be bolstered by providing incentives, such as prize drawings, to attract people to complete the survey. However, care should be taken to ensure the prize is not too grand, which may tempt people more interested in the prize than the topic to enter more than once.

One point that Poon makes is that destinations will be dealing with 'new tourists' and will have to market accordingly. These new tourists are 'consumers who are flexible, independent and experienced travellers, whose values and lifestyles are different from those of the mass tourists' (Poon, 1993: 114). These new tourists have the following key attributes that require different focuses and approaches.

- More experienced – their travel experiences have made them more aware of quality and more demanding, they now seek more variety and wish to fulfil their special interests.
- Changing values – they are more educated and have a greater appreciation of global differences, they search for authentic experiences, are sensitive to the environment, and wish to become involved.
- Changing lifestyles – they are healthier, have more flexible hours, more income, and view travel as a way of life.

- Products of changing demographics – the aging population of Western countries, fewer children, longer retirements with sufficient funds for travel.
- More flexible – they are better informed and freer of constraints so they can be spontaneous, flexible and unpredictable leading to hybrid consumption patterns.
- More independent-minded – they want to be 'in charge', are more willing to take risks, and to break out of the mould. (Poon, 1993: 114–15).

Examples of some of these new tourists and their relevance to destination marketing are presented below.

Adventure tourists

Adventure tourists are those who seek some excitement in their activity, including a sense of danger for some. This segment ranges from 'soft' adventures such as bird or whale watching activities, to 'hard' adventures such as overnight wilderness hikes or sea kayaking, scuba diving and ski sports. Such tourism opportunities can be provided in a variety of destinations and can involve a range of business types and scales. One issue which is impacting this sector, however, is the growing number of insurance claims and court cases that are causing liability insurance rates to skyrocket and generating the need for strong risk management.

Backpackers

Backpackers are young travellers, who prefer budget accommodation, long and informal independent vacation experiences (Ross, 1993). Such travel takes them beyond the major cities and tourist icons to the regional areas of overseas destinations; as they seek to learn more about the country and its people or casual work, often both. This market has become a major international tourism segment for Australia, and is one segment that is holding up well despite the world terrorism of the past two years.

Ecotourists

Ecotourists are tourists who visit natural areas and engage in some form of education-based field excursion (Wight, 1996). This special interest group does open up many new areas to tourism, including the Arctic and Antarctica, and provides business opportunities to small businesses and communities. However, Butler (1990) has cautioned industry enthusiasts about the need to maintain small-scale development for this market segment, and Price (2003) has noted that the education component needs far more development.

Education market

The biggest element of the large 'Meetings, Incentives, Conferences and Events' (MICE) sector are the small corporate or local association meetings. These are designed to bring together members on a regular basis, but outside of their normal work environment, so they can interact and learn without interruption. Accordingly, resort businesses and destinations that are different yet convenient make ideal locations for such business. This provides significant opportunity to resorts and destinations which surround major urban centres to provide business meeting getaways that can supplement their regular tourism business and help even out the seasonality of pleasure travel.

Seniors

Today's seniors are significantly healthier, better educated and financially more secure than in the past, plus many can expect 10 years or more of active retirement. Thus, they are becoming an important tourist segment. Many are travelling as FITs, to visit with global friends and relatives or to catch up with long-awaited vacation dreams. Some are settling down with their favourite sport (such as golf) or moving to their favourite climate and holiday spot (Florida, Queensland, Mediterranean), while others are increasing their knowledge through group tours and university level instruction (Elder Hostel and Odyssey Travel). Therefore, this market is proving to be as diverse in its interests as the fragmenting mass market, making many different destinations and tourism activities attractive to the seniors.

Controlling

To understand how well a business and destination are satisfying their customers requires regular monitoring of customer experiences and the outcomes of current marketing and operational strategies. Both the individual businesses and the destination community need to develop indicators of achievement with which to measure their programmes and products. These should be applied in such a way as to minimise customer inconvenience and conducted on a regular basis to provide a realistic profile of customer experiences and reactions.

A good place to start is with the image and positioning strategy, to see if the customer is aware of the business or destination message in a very crowded marketplace. To determine whether current advertising practices are meeting performance objectives will require a marketing audit. 'A marketing audit is a comprehensive, systematic, independent, and periodic examination of a company's environment, objectives, strategies, and activities to determine problem areas and opportunities and to recommend a plan of action to improve the company's marketing performance' (Kotler & Armstrong, 1989: 540). Among these broad objectives is the 'marketing functions audit' that includes an assessment of advertising and sales, and the effectiveness of the distribution system (Kotler, 2001: 197).

Conversion studies

A logical method to assess the effectiveness of advertising is to determine the level of enquiries, patronage or sales generated by a specific advertising campaign, which is called its conversion rate. Unfortunately, conversion studies have generally been internal operations so there are relatively few in the public domain, and those that have been published reveal it is a challenging task to link customer behaviour with specific marketing campaigns. In fact conversion studies can become misleading to the uninitiated.

Burke and Gitelson (1990) have written a cautionary tale about the pitfalls of conversion studies. They note that in the past some rather questionable claims have been made of 60–80% conversion rates and returns on advertising investment ratios of $23–100:$1. Such results often occur due to a lack of rigorous research standards, so Burke and Gitelson's article points out potential research design pitfalls and ways to bring more rigour and objectivity to these measures. They advocate the following 10 steps for developing better conversion rate studies.

(1) Understand the travel decision process is an information search that is influenced by a host of variables and not just advertising. As shown in Figure 7.1 at the beginning of this chapter.
(2) Recognise the limitations of conversion studies, to minimise their misuse and misinterpretation.
(3) Understand that accomplishing the goal of increased 'return business' will reduce the 'net' conversion rate from advertising.
(4) Select proportionally representative and randomly selected research samples.
(5) Determine an acceptable sampling precision for the study.
(6) Address non-response bias by determining if respondents are representative of all enquirers.
(7) Differentiate between those who were influenced by an advertising campaign to visit ('net' conversion) and those who had already decided to visit.
(8) Define the destination area in detail so that actual visitor numbers and spending are attributed correctly.
(9) Identify the portion of a tourist's spending that produces economic benefits for the destination.
(10) Include all costs (not just advertising, production and placement) in

determining the return on investment of a promotional campaign. (Based on Burke & Gitelson, 1990: 50)

It is challenging to accomplish all the steps, but simply striving for such goals will improve the quality of a conversion study and the accuracy of its findings.

A specific conversion return study of a British Columbia 'Spring Visit campaign' aimed at the California market reveals the utility of this audit approach. The study by Pritchard and Swanson (1993) sampled 1205 Californians who had responded to advertisements placed in their state by using a toll-free telephone number supplied by Tourism BC. Pritchard and Swanson's postal survey of the California residents revealed a 23% conversion of those callers who made specific enquiries. They estimated that each Californian traveller to BC that season spent an average C$1005.32, resulting in a total revenue of C$2,200,977 from the campaign. This compares favourably with a C$303,199 expenditure on various Californian media outlets used in the campaign, representing a sevenfold return without taking into account the cost of assembling and designing the advertising campaign. However, examination of the return from the various distribution channels reveals the return on investment varied significantly across the different media outlets (Table 7.1). Even though the major city newspaper was the most expensive media outlet used, it presented one of the better returns due to its prestige and circulation. But the best return came from the city magazine and the worst from radio advertising.

Satisfaction audits

Once customers are at the place of business or destination it is important to determine how well the travel experience is matching their expectations and how satisfied they are with their experience. To find out how happy

Table 7.1 Return on investment

Media	ROI ($CN)
Big City Newspaper	$11.06
Community Newspapers	$4.37
Big City Magazine	$11.11
Bus Sides/Other	$9.93
Radio	$4.09
Direct Mail	$7.91
Total	$7.26

Source: Pritchard and Swanson (1993), BC Tourism 1993 Advertising Effectiveness Study, Victoria BC, Tourism BC and School of Business, University of Victoria, 10

customers are, operators need only to use their eyes and ears. They should study their customers by 'walking the talk' and working alongside their staff at times. They should place themselves in the position of a customer and see how the approach to their business will be viewed by a stranger and what sort of welcome they receive when they come through the door. A lot of this is 'common sense', but it is remarkable how rare this intuition has become.

A common problem is adequate and appropriate signage, but fieldtrip experiences with tourism students has revealed some amazing experiences. These include:

- wrong instructions on a directional sign;
- a blank wall separating a tourist attraction from the major highway link;
- lack of things to do or buy at transport terminals;
- lack of product knowledge;
- lack of instruction and care with certain adventure tourism activities.

If the business operator wishes to investigate beyond surface levels s(he) will need to interrupt the service experience with some form of survey. This could be a casual enquiry through striking up a conversation with customers that includes some questions regarding their experiences with the business and destination, or through simple survey questionnaires as are found in many restaurants and hotels. Either way this form of information gathering should not become intrusive, to the extent that it interferes with the experience.

The importance of marketing audits to destinations has been emphasised in Mazanec's (1997) book on city tourism. Within this review of organisational needs and processes in Europe, Wober (1997: 26–38) noted the need for local destination marketing associations to gather data on accommodation usage, visitor activities spending patterns and origins, that should be coordinated with published national and state statistics. By combining local primary data with published secondary data a destination can develop a long-term profile of its visitors and industry performance. This type of information can be used to identify shortcomings and to guide future promotion and development. This has certainly been the case within the city of Victoria in British Columbia, Canada.

Victoria's destination marketing association – Tourism Victoria – has been collecting data on its visitors since 1989. It has been aided in this by the support it has received from its constituent members, especially the transport sector that has assisted with its visitor exit surveys and the hotels and motels that have participated in the regular occupancy – charges surveys conducted by a local accountancy company. Victoria is particularly fortunate in having an ideal situation for exit surveys, because it is on an island and most visitors need to wait for a certain period of time for their ferry or airline connection to the mainland. Under these circumstances a short survey of their recent travel experiences is a welcome diversion, so excellent response rates have been the norm.

Data from the visitor exit surveys have revealed both problems and potential opportunities for future development. An early problem was disappointing visitor responses to the question regarding 'value for money'. This is a major issue for an industry that depends on tourists incurring the extra travel costs to reach Vancouver Island while mainland destinations like Vancouver and Seattle were becoming more aggressive and competitive for the tourism business. Tourism Victoria shared this information with its members and encouraged them to focus on changing the situation. It was gratifying to see a steady rise in the evaluation of Victoria's value for money over the years, to the point where the clear majority of tourists now feel they receive good value for money. Potential future developments have arisen from questions regarding 'what is missing' or what type of attractions 'would attract tourist back' to the city. An early identified 'missing' element was the opportunity to view the local whales and seals. This has now been rectified with the development of several whale/ wildlife watching tours. Another was the popularity of the British Columbia Provincial Museum's early 'block-buster' exhibits. These generated such a favourable response that they have become a regular feature, giving locals and visitors a reason to return to this outstanding attraction.

Risk management

An important aspect of delivering the promised and anticipated level of experience is an appropriate 'duty of care'. If businesses or destinations fail to deliver reasonable care and attention in their operations they can expect to be sued for unsatisfactory experiences, injury or death in this litigious age. 'Between 1998 and 2000, the number of public liability claims Australia-wide rose by 60% to 88,000; total payments rose by 52% to A$724 million' (Feizkhah, 2002: 46). The cost of protecting themselves against lawsuits is causing many businesses, community groups and destinations to limit activities like adventure tourism and festivals. It has become so bad that a *Time Magazine* article on the subject cites the following experience. 'Can I sue' asked one wit in a letter to the Sydney *Morning Herald* "if I walk into a warning sign if there is no warning sign warning me of the warning?' (Feizkhah, 2002: 46). Consequently, another relevant audit for today's customer is the risk management audit.

There is an element of risk in almost every undertaking or decision people engage in, but the key in law is that business operators must demonstrate they provided 'reasonable care' for 'foreseeable acts or situations' with respect to their customers. Consequently, tourism businesses and destinations need to show they have established a reasonable duty of care toward the safe enjoyment of their products and experiences, and the best way to achieve that is to manage the risk. This is accomplished by identifying potential risks involved with the tourism business. Measure the frequency and magnitude of loss due to those risks, using established records or own data, to determine their degree of seriousness. Develop systems (physical or human) to either reduce or eliminate the risks. Determine, when there is an incident, whether to absorb the costs through direct compensation or to call upon insurance companies, to whom the risk has been transferred through an insurance policy and premiums.

In his book on risk management in adventure tourism, Cloutier (2000: 104–5) cites some advice from Will Leverette that has wide applicability. Leverette recommends six easy risk management steps for tourism operators:

(1) Develop a means to prove that guests were adequately warned and informed.
(2) Any guarantee of safety made in a business' literature, or marketing materials is an open invitation to be sued.
(3) All field staff must have current training in basic first aid.
(4) The business should develop a written emergency/evacuation plan for all areas and activities to be used.
(5) One good witness statement will shut down a frivolous lawsuit faster, more cheaply and less painfully than will anything else.
(6) The business must use a properly drafted liability release form.

He goes on to make the point that such management should be motivated by the desire to ensure a tourist has the best possible experience. The fact that this same planning will reduce the chance of a frivolous lawsuit is simply a bonus.

Summary

It is essential in this competitive business world that businesses put the customer first.

Their needs and priorities will need to be considered and wherever possible met, if individual tourism businesses and destinations are to draw sufficient numbers and revenue to survive and prosper. An important planning step in reaching that goal is to understand how customers choose their options and how individual businesses and destinations can identify those segments they feel best able to satisfy.

The organising component of this chapter provides an in-depth look at how the marketing positioning of destination influences the likelihood that desired tourists will visit these places. Destination awareness and preferences are strong factors in predicting what types of tourists and how many of these tourists a destination can hope to attract. The value of emerging theories and technologies in marketing and organising, and their relevance to community tourism, are a focus of the leadership component of this chapter. Finally, the control component in this chapter looks at the scope and scale and impact of tourism advertising. Particular attention is paid to the challenges inherent in taking the appropriate care of tourists once they arrive, to ensure their visit is both enjoyable and safe.

Questions that destinations need to ask themselves are which customers are likely to be attracted to us, which of these customers do we want and how can we better attract our desired markets? Once these questions have been answered then the questions to explore include which customers are actually visiting us, how satisfied are they with their experiences and finally what are the appropriate changes to be made to the travel destinations products, services and marketing in order to remain competitive. The following chapter explores the role that industry can play in the development of community oriented tourism destinations.

Chapter 8

Industry

The popularity of the phrase 'tourism industry' in both scholarly and industry publications implies there really is such an industry. However, this is 'not the case' claims Smith (2003b: 1). Because the 'tourism industry' cannot be captured statistically by a system of national accounts and census definitions Smith would rather consider tourism as an 'economic constella- tion – a grouping of numerous industries in the transportation, accommodation, food service, recreation and entertainment, and travel trade sectors that creates a picture of something more than the simple col- lection of the parts' (Smith, 2003b: 1). Consequently Smith would prefer to speak of 'tourism industries'.

While the current facts support Smith's perspective, the shape of modern industry and spirit of innovation would not. Most of the standard industrial classification (SIC) systems developed around the world have their origin in the Victorian era when the emphasis was on primary and secondary manufacturing processes, not on service. Consequently, if we examine one of the SICs used by Smith in his paper to determine the scale and structure of Canada's tourism we find under the classification 'Educa- tion Service Industries' only one entry – Museums and Archives. Although these represent a tangible achievement of the Victorian era and we have all benefited from this legacy, it is no longer an adequate description of this important tourism sector. Where are the Visitor Information Centres, the tertiary education departments that specialise in tourism, or the myriad of consultants? All of these groups earn a living by contributing to the knowledge base of tourists and providers.

This one example of the inadequacy of official statistical classifica- tions for the tourism industry is repeated in every SIC because tourism is a modern service industry that has witnessed innovations in service and products that were unheard of in Victorian times. Developments such as sub-orbital space flights and tram/trolley dining are difficult to place in any of the current transport or dining categories. The growing interest in space tourism, where the tourist expenditures can make the critical dif- ference between launch or no launch, is probably still classified as scientific research rather than transportation, and certainly not as tourism.

The spirit of tourism activity has been innovation but one of the major shortcomings in its operators has been a tardiness to come together and work as one industry with one voice. This has not been helped by government bureaucratic statistics and the suspicions of established industries to the newcomer on the block, nor by the small business orientation of most operators and the ubiquitous nature of tourism activity. But if one is to look at various definitions of industry there is hope and direction as to how this situation may be changed. The *Macquarie Dictionary* (Delbridge and Bernard, 1988: 490) defines industry as 'any large-scale business activity: the tourist industry' as well as the more traditional definition of 'a particular branch of trade or manufacture'. The *Webster New World Dictionary* (1962) also offers the origin of the term industry as 'intelligent work, skill, cleverness and the application' and it is these features that will be crucial to the success of the industry.

This chapter will focus on these foundation attributes of industry and treat tourism as a conglomerate industry that focuses on serving a common customer – the tourist: one that will require lots of personal intelligence, hard work and skill to meet the various demands of the customer while meeting individual business objectives and community priorities; and one that requires intensive collaboration between its component parts in order to supply the expected travel experience.

Australia's new tourism strategic plan intends to consider tourism as an industry, although it recognises its constellation qualities. It has chosen to treat the tourism industry in the sense of managing its supply and demand factors.

> Unlike many industry sectors, tourism is unable to be defined simply as a group of businesses that produce particular, similar products. Rather, the 'tourism industry' embraces a diverse range of providers and users of a variety of goods and services, and overlaps with other sectors of the economy.

> However, the elements of tourism may be described in the conventional terms of 'supply' and 'demand'. 'Supply' involves the companies which deliver tourism products and services, including tour operators and travel agents, and companies for which tourism is not the main focus of business . . .

> Tourism 'demand' is usually measured in terms of the number of tourists, the number of nights they stay in hotels or other types of accommodation and the money they spend. (Australia, 2002: 4)

This generic and official use of the term 'tourism industry' is adopted in this book.

Objectives

To succeed and survive all businesses must develop sufficient business volume and yield to produce a profit. In addition for tourism industries, they will need to demonstrate external benefits, especially the more they are reliant on public resources. This certainly applies to the non-government organisations that have developed to serve and coordinate the industry.

To achieve the above state of success businesses and destinations need to *target* the appropriate market segments, those segments whose needs and interests they can meet. This will take careful research and planning, ensuring the destination community's image and development coincide with customer expectations and desires.

To satisfy those customers who visit and turn them into loyal supporters will require the basic fundamental of business – provide a product and service of *value*. Porter's theories of competitive advantage are based on finding ways to produce value, whether it be by cost leadership, differentiation or niche marketing. Others emphasise quality as a path to value differentiation. To provide any of these features of value for the customer will involve considerable internal organisation and management, and in tourism much of this depends on the entrepreneurial skills of the small business owners.

As noted in the introduction, the tourism industry involves a range of businesses to produce a tourism experience, therefore an essential ingredient to customer satisfaction and value will be the level of *external coordination* that individual businesses and destination can develop. This will involve a broader and more collegial form of organisation of the sort advocated by Porter (1998) in his cluster model of industrial development. It is in this area that tourism leadership particularly comes to the forefront, and it is notable how many successful small business operators are contributing to the general appeal of their destination.

Since tourism can be identified as a community industry that makes extensive use of public resources it should be contributing to the host community's quality of life as well as ensuring it is on track to corporate success and sustainability. To assess how well the industry is meeting its own business goals of satisfying the customer and its *broader obligations to the host community* requires some form of monitoring. Control measures will be needed, therefore, for both internal operations and external impacts.

Planning

The range of attractions for tourists is extensive and incorporates both natural and created artefacts. Major attractions include marvels of the natural world and the intriguing aspects of human culture. Many tourist attractions were not created for tourism purposes; rather they were originally used or built for other purposes and were later adapted for tourism. As fashions and tastes change tourism products and services need to adapt to meet new market conditions. Accordingly we find a variety of industry classifications that represent the variations in the industry by location and over time.

One aspect which helps this industry to stand out is that it is a service industry that depends on developing the appropriate service skills in its labour-intensive delivery. The ultimate product – the service experience, involves an interaction between the tourist customer and a staff provider. The provider needs to be knowledgeable, efficient and friendly, which means people make a big difference to the success of tourism regardless of what form and structure the industry takes.

Industry structure

Tourism products and services can be categorised into sectors within the tourism industry, yet there is no agreement on how this categorisation should be done. The created divisions often reflect local interests within the more regular divisions. We offer two examples of this.

The six interconnecting sectors of the tourism industry, as described by Funnel and Ainsworth (1996: 248) are as follows:

- transport;
- property and business service;
- personal and household goods;
- accommodation;
- food and retail;
- recreation service,

This division of the industry reflects a business and suppliers emphasis and could be associated with big city tourism.

The Pacific Rim Institute of Tourism (PRIT) in Canada, which was a non-government organisation designed to facilitate the linkage between industry and education in British Columbia, operated on an eightfold division of the industry. These were:

- accommodation;
- food and beverage;
- transportation;
- attractions;
- ecotourism;
- conferences and events;
- travel trade;
- travel services.

The accommodation and food and beverage sectors in PRIT's classification equate to the 'hospitality' side of the industry, which in most countries represents the largest component by employment and revenue. The last two sectors represent the importance of information channels to this industry and reflect the information mission of PRIT. This aspect of the industry was divided into a private sector delivery via travel agencies, travel writers and tour wholesalers (travel trade) and public sector delivery via government departments and visitor information centres (travel services). Another feature of local significance in the PRIT interpretation of the industry was the inclusion of an ecotourism sector. This represents a major area of business in a province that promotes itself as 'SuperNatural BC'.

The above descriptive divisions of the industry represent just two ways to divide this expansive and interrelated business of tourism. Sectors of the tourism industry can be further described according to broad categories of ownership, including public, private, public-private partnerships and voluntary organisations. The important thing to note is that to plan this industry it is beneficial to divide it into component parts, and these components should make sense in both a business and local context.

People power

What keeps businesses focused on the customer and working together is people. Tourism is a people industry that needs to go beyond regular service if it is to understand its customers and deliver on their expectations. To provide for this growing industry and its need for professional service management there has been an explosion of college and university courses over the past 20 years. However, there has been little emphasis in this training and education on the engine-room of the industry, its dominant SMEs and their leaders – the entrepreneurs.

Entrepreneurship consists of three distinct yet interacting elements: creativity, risk-taking and business capabilities (Echtner, 1995: 122, cited in Shaw & Williams, 1998). Entrepreneurs tend to be seen as those who shake up the *status quo* by pushing ahead with their dreams, sometimes in unconvential ways, and they are growing in number as the tourism market fragments into a myriad of special interests and large corporations are cutting back on middle management personnel. In a review of why more people do not engage in entrepreneurial activities, the following three perceptual barriers to entrepreneurial behaviour have been identified by Mitchell (1997):

(1) Starting and running one's own business is too risky.
(2) Someone must be a 'born' entrepreneur to succeed in self-started ventures.
(3) Engaging in a single economic relationship, such as when one's

employed, is easier and preferable to multiple economic relationships, such as with suppliers, employees and customers.

However, Mitchell considers that all of these perceptions are flawed and stresses that in today's uncertain economic and employment environments, venturing out on one's own could become synonymous with personal economic security and job satisfaction, while at the same time promoting overall economic growth and prosperity for society.

The driving desires to be self-employed include independence, lifestyle change and the opportunity for greater financial rewards. But that does not mean everyone wishes to become another Conrad Hilton, Walt Disney or Richard Branson. Webster (1998: 207) drawing upon statistics from the US shows the majority of new businesses started by entrepreneurs are 'lifestyle' or 'marginal small firms' and that 'lifestyle firms are those which are privately held and usually achieve modest growth owing to the nature of the business'. Growth potential does not rank that highly for many small firms. Harkim (cited in Webster, 1998: 208) found in her research that 55% of small businesses did not want to grow while 35% aspired to modest growth.

Due to their propensity to break or change the rules, entrepreneurs often thrive in areas that are just beginning to realise their development potential and are therefore not highly regulated. The Gold Coast in Australia went through a boom period that lasted from the 1960s through to the 1980s, when a procession of remarkable individuals transformed this tropical beach area into a centre of night life, theme parks, high rise buildings and resort development (Russell & Faulkner, 1999). While the economy has thrived in the Gold Coast, the changes to the cultural and natural environments have been substantial and for some unacceptable. The spectacular successes and failures of local entrepreneurs, their strong personalities and abilities to transform communities can leave many observers to view entrepreneurs with either a combination of admiration and awe, or of ridicule and contempt. Entrepreneurs can be the bane of planners and regulators who seek to moderate and control change, but their energy and ideas can invigorate a destination.

Tourism entrepreneurs can be seen as 'brokers' between tourists and host communities in that they immerse themselves in the business side of tourism, while maintaining their ties with the host community (Jafari, cited in Shaw & Williams, 1998). While this ability to see tourism opportunities through the eyes of a business and of a citizen should enable entrepreneurs to respond more appropriately and decisively to issues and priorities arising from the business and community aspect of tourism, their performance results on these matters are mixed. Too often in the past many small owner-operated businesses have failed due to insufficient business acumen regarding the basic principles of management.

This is certainly the view of Gerber (1995) and his *E-Myth,* and is the *raison d'être* for many university business programmes that emphasise entrepreneurship. Gerber (1995: 19) considered that 'everybody who goes into business is actually three people-in-one: the entrepreneur, the manager and the technician'. Many people have a technical skill and some feel they can turn it into a successful business. A prime example of this in tourism is the professional or amateur chef who feels they could operate such a successful restaurant that people would be lining up to get in. They may well be first-rate technicians but do they have the entrepreneurial flair to deliver their product in a special way, and the management skills to pick the best location, hire the right staff, control costs, and listen to their customers? Unfortunately, the survival record of independent restaurants would suggest the answer is often, no!

To help the tourism industry plan for its future, both large and small businesses, and for them to develop the symbiotic relationships with the host communities that can assist their survival and success, several planning theories have been developed.

Planning Theories

One aspect of business development that has received some attention in management planning is that of product lifecycles (PLC). The PLC theory argues that products and the industries associated with them undergo an aging process, passing through several stages and leading to an eventual decline (Gordon *et al.*, 1990: 159–69). Typically many new products are 'introduced' to the market, but only a few take-off and 'grow' because that stage requires the support of opinion leaders (Figure 1.2, p. 32). After the product gains wider acceptance its sales 'mature', but growth starts to slow as it saturates its market. Its production either 'declines' to a replacement rate or terminates altogether as new or better products emerge to take its place. Examples of this process are legion, but some of the more recent include the disappearance of vinyl records, eight-track cassettes, and typewriters.

Destination lifecycle and adjustments

The most well-known 'stage' or 'step' model in tourism research is Butler's Destination Life-Cycle Model (DLC) (1980). This model sees destinations as passing through a number of stages of tourism development, whereby the number of tourists increases with time until a point is reached when either the destination renews itself or starts to deteriorate. Butler's model predicts that destinations will be drawn through a series of set stages in a predictable manner, with the ultimate fate of the destination being decided by local management practices.

Debate has arisen over the application and utility of this model. It has been argued that while the idea behind the model is intuitively appealing and frequently substantiated, it is hard to apply to any specific tourist situation. This is because it is difficult to assemble the required data (number of visitors) over an extensive period (30–50 years) to provide the necessary time frame for the evolution profile to occur (Foster and Murphy, 1991; Haywood, 1986). It is also difficult to determine the exact turning point between the various stages on the S-shaped evolution curve (Douglas, 1997; Grabler, 1997). In addition the model has been criticised for being descriptive rather than prescriptive, which limits its strategic planning relevance.

In one recent empirical test of the model Lundtorp and Wanhill (2001) examined the development of two resorts that they believed had the uniformity and replication necessary to empirically test its propositions. Their data were drawn from the case study areas of the Isle of Man in the UK from 1912–67 and the Danish island of Bornholm that spanned 1912–67, but excluded the duration of World War II. They found in the early years the case study areas followed the model quite well; however, over time so many other external factors influenced the evolution of tourism in these destinations that clear linkages to the DLC were no longer evident.

In most cases the DLC model is applied in a more general manner to destinations drawing heavily on limited data, anecdotal evidence and researcher observation. Given the difficulties in applying the DLC model using quantitative analysis, this model may be best suited as a general paradigm within which to view destinations, rather than as an empirical research method (Haywood, 1986; Lundtorp & Wanhill, 2001).

The value of attaching management styles and motivations to stage models like the DLC as one way of making them more relevant to management is an approach being undertaken by some. Churchill and Lewis (1983) apply management implications to each development stage for organisation. Their first stage 'existence' has an owner managing the firm with little need for an organisational structure, while their final stage 'resource maturity' predicates that a well-developed management structure should be in place to enable the firm to maximise its profits. Other researchers dispute the relevance of a linear stage model that progresses in a regular fashion from inception to maturity. Gray (1993), cited in Webster (1998: 210), notes that such models are too static and unrealistic given the small size and modest growth expectations of most new businesses. He also raises concerns that management's attitudes towards growth largely dictate the extent to which a company will develop and also need to be included in development models. Adopting a more inclusive and flexible view of business development incorporating personal motivations and external factors that allow for businesses to move up and down the development scale without necessarily going through a set number of stages is probably the most practical way of utilising stage and step models.

Schumpeter's theory

The importance of personal motivations as drivers in the development of tourist businesses and destinations is reflected in several theories and models. Schumpeter's theory of entrepreneurship highlights the essential role that innovation plays in business cycles. Given that radical innovations can open up new markets as well as disrupt existing business practices then businesses must respond to these changes (Schumpeter, 1934). The individual who is well placed to respond to such changes is the individual who is free of the incumbrances of large organisations and is willing to innovate. The tourism entrepreneur can be seen as agents of this 'creative destruction' in that their innovative efforts can transform existing conditions and can propel business and destinations in their development.

Chaos/complexity theory

A key aspect of chaos/complexity theory is that relationships are highly complex and unstable, which enables small factors to trigger substantial changes if the timing is right. This theory is now used widely as a way of explaining weather patterns since they are highly complex and interrelated. Consequently, unstable and dramatic changes can be triggered by numerous small factors, such as changes in moisture, temperature and wind flow. This theory can also be seen as relevant to tourism in that the factors affecting the industry are highly complex and often unstable and dramatic changes in the industry can be triggered by any number of factors, such as hurricanes, terrorist attacks or the fall of the Berlin Wall.

Russell and Faulkner (1999) have combined the principles of entrepreneurship and chaos/complexity theory with Butler's destination lifecycle as a way of providing an alternative framework within which to assess the dynamics of tourism development. In their study of the development of Queensland's Gold Coast, they found that entrepreneurs played a vital role in moving this destination along the development curve of its tourism industry, especially in its formative and rejuvenation stages. They propose that during the 'involvement stage' (stage 2), local entrepreneurs act as triggers to take destinations to the next level of intensification, while during the 'development stage' (stage 3) migrant entrepreneurs play a larger role. The entrepreneurs are seen to be attracted to opportunities that only present themselves when areas are ripe for change, such as either coming out of a difficult economic period, or when councils are seen to be pro-growth with the powers of regulators held in check. The role of entrepreneurs as 'triggers' enabling destinations to progress onwards from one stage to another is also supported by the research of Shaw and Williams (1998).

Russell and Faulkner (1999) consider an important explanation of the entrepreneurs' role in the development of a destination is their tendency to thrive in periods of change, or periods of chaos in the minds of regulators.

They demonstrate the contrasting decision-making styles of entrepreneurs as 'chaos makers', compared with government administrators as 'regulators'. These decision-making differences lead to the dual notions of 'edge of chaos' and 'phase shifts' in the development of a community. A situation reaches the edge of chaos when the existing community equilibrium state is on the verge of collapse and facing rapid change. When that happens the relative stability of the equilibrium phase can be jolted into a burst of activity by entrepreneurial or innovative actions, leading to an evolutionary change or phase shift. In this way entrepreneurs can be viewed as significant agents of the evolutionary shifts from stage to stage as predicted in tourism's destination lifecycle.

Value chain and beyond

All businesses, whether they are local SMEs operated by entrepreneurs or multi-national corporations, need to offer customers value if they are to succeed. It is value which drives the exchange process involved with any form of business, and if customers cannot see any value to them in the exchange they will move on to other alternatives and opportunities.

Porter 1990 has emphasised the importance of understanding each business' value chain in order to identify the 'add-on' opportunities that lie at each step of a manufacturing or service process. His 'generic value chain' consists of a business' primary activities such as assembling inbound materials, processing them and the outbound distribution of goods and services. Other front line primary activities that assist this process are the marketing and service departments. Also recognised are the important contributions of the behind-the-scenes support activities of the business' infrastructure, its purchasing department, the human resource department and the growing importance of the technology area. All of these activities make individual contributions to the overall value and profit margin. The generic model is shown in Figure 8.1A and hypothetical tourism example is offered in Figure 8.1B.

One of the strengths of this model is its applicability to service industries and its flexibility to take into account changing circumstances. For example, a travel agency's inbound materials will be information on the selected destinations, packages and companies the business has chosen to promote. Travel agency information operations are linked closely with marketing and service, in order to create the outbound product of satisfied customers. Behind the scenes, key areas include the human resource function of selecting the best travel consultants, those who have the required knowledge, personal and sales skills to service a customer and close a sale. In travel agencies it is important to keep up with technological advances such as the Internet and Web, and individual businesses will undoubtedly benefit from infrastructure arrangements such as association and franchise networks.

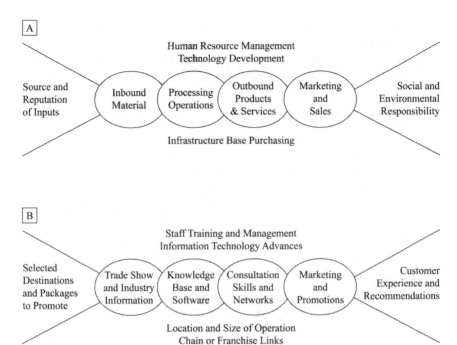

Figure 8.1 Modified value chain
Source: After Porter (1990) and Moore (1992)

Its flexibility can be seen in Moore's (1992) modifications to the basic model in Figure 8.1A. These reveal how the value chain can incorporate customer concerns over the origin of inbound materials, as has become important in terms of the 'sweat shop' origins for many tourism souvenirs or low-cost overseas trip options. At the other end of the chain there is growing concern over the disposal of packaging and old products like rusting cars and discarded fridges in the manufacturing sector, while in tourism there are increased expectations regarding visible community benefits from visitor expenditures. In terms of the travel agency example these are represented by the input reputation of the destinations and packages the agency wishes to promote and with which to be associated. At the end of the process will be the test of the customers' experiences and whether they will use the same travel agency again or recommend it to their friends.

As the modified value chain indicates businesses have to be aware of external factors and changing conditions, and Porter (1990) suggests five competitive forces always need to be considered in today's business environment. These he identifies as:

- *The threat of new entrants.* In the free market system of global tourism new entrants are appearing regularly.
- *The threat of substitute products and services.* New variations and models are a constant in consumer industries like tourism; witness the rise of snow boarding in 'ski' resorts.
- *The bargaining power of suppliers.* As tourism has grown, big multi-national corporations have developed and now have considerable clout in negotiating volume and price.
- *The bargaining power of buyers.* In tourism this has increased as a result of growing customer experience and raised expectations.
- *Rivalry among existing competitors.* This occurs in tourism as with other industries, but more businesses are approaching it as collaborative competition within their own destinations. This recognises that businesses must collaborate to first draw tourists to their destination and then compete to attract them to their particular business

But external conditions do not always represent threats, for under certain circumstances the presence of local competitors and rival interests can be turned into a locational advantage.

Cluster theory

Porter's (1998) cluster theory attempts to explain why certain industrial concentrations have maintained their dominance while their initial locational advantages have eroded with time. His answer is that during their existence they have built institutional advantages which more than make up for the competitive advantages of new firms and locations. The essential institutional advantage is the power of clusters, which take advantage of local collaboration, a growing international reputation, and government assistance. Clusters can be viewed as an extension of the economic and spatial features of industrial districts to incorporate organisational and social features such as business administration and leadership (Jackson & Murphy, 2002).

The changing nature of competition has been recognised by Porter (1998). He has shown how his earlier diamond model of competition can be modified to include the advantages of collaboration and clusters. Within the premises of this model tourism businesses can be expected to meet *demand* by working with government to streamline visa and other entry or access requirements. In terms of *inputs* they will work together to gather market information and provide attractive packages. They will work with local service providers to develop the appropriate human resource skills and management techniques, and will form local associations to limit their insurance liability exposure and to leverage their marketing funds. As indicated in this new approach to business operation the individual businesses' *strategic planning* and relationship to rival and *supporting industries* will change. It will consist of a combination of collaboration and competition. Tourism businesses will collaborate to bring the tourist to their destination and then compete to become the business of choice within that destination.

Clusters have become significant forces in tourism development, particularly where they have gelled into active destination associations. The main function of these associations is to market the local area and to provide cooperative marketing opportunities for their members, that will in effect give them greater market exposure and reach than would be possible within their individual marketing budgets. This is often aided by government encouragement in the form of partnership marketing, whereby the government provides matching marketing dollars. But many destination associations have moved beyond marketing to include research, training, services and product development under their umbrella.

A good example of an umbrella destination association is 'Tourism Victoria' in Victoria, BC Canada. This organisation grew out of a more focused visitor information centre to produce a broader and more open task structure, yet its principal focus remains on the marketing of Victoria (Figure 8.2). Its structure is open-ended to permit the entry of any

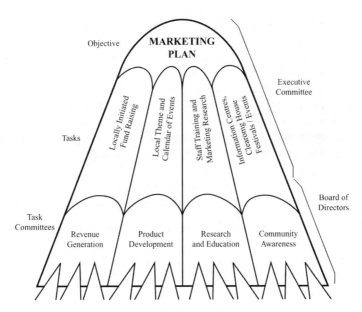

Interested groups join Task Committee(s) where they feel they can provide the greatest contribution.

Figure 8.2 Original task model for 'Tourism Victoria'
Source: Murphy (1985: 278)

interested parties to a variety of tasks, and the chairs of these task committees serve on the executive board. The local university and college serve the area of research and education, while a broad cross-section of the community serve on its product development and environment committees.

Such broad-based involvement in the marketing and improvement of a destination is being repeated around the world. In Victoria, Australia, the 'gold rush' town of Bendigo exemplifies the community cluster approach to marketing their city and region. In addition to its gold rush heritage Bendigo wants to remind visitors of its agricultural delights, and through a word play on being the central piece of the state's 'Jigsaw Campaign' and the well-known desert red centre of Australia, it promotes its excellent red wines (Figure 8.3). To put these and other ideas in front of the tourist and public the Bendigo Tourism Board has called upon a wide range of community members to assist its professional staff. These members include not only industry representatives, but council appointees that includes local citizens and the odd professor (Figure 8.4).

Organisation

Competition and limited resources are forcing all businesses to organise their internal operations and to explore any external collaboration that can help them become more efficient and effective in meeting their goals and objectives. The need for improved organisation is important everywhere, but is especially acute for businesses and communities beyond the major urban and resort destinations. In the UK it has been shown that many small coastal resorts are suffering since their attractions are too small to act as major destination draws and this lack of business is feeding a downward cycle of decreased investment in products, services and marketing (Shaw & Williams, 1997). Where internal operations lack the economies of scale or critical mass to operate efficiently and effectively external collaboration can assist survival and sustainability.

It has been suggested that external collaboration can take on three different forms (Jacobs & de Man cited in Vanhaverbeke, 2001: 99):

(1) Regional (i.e. geographical concentration of successful and related firms).
(2) Vertical relations (i.e. networking between companies).
(3) Aggregations of connected sectors (i.e. concentrations of complementary and mutually supportive businesses).

These organisational groups can be viewed as based primarily on place or on some form of strategic relationship. International examples of the former include the Pacific Asia Travel Association (PATA) which promotes travel and professionalism within the Asia-Pacific region. Examples of the

Figure 8.3 Bendigo's food and wine product with an emphasis on its red wine reputation

Figure 8.4 "Bendigo Toursim" Board 2003, representing a diversity of interests

Figure 8.4 'Bendigo Tourism' Board of 2003, representing a diversity of interests

latter include the World Travel and Tourism Council (WTTC) which is an international lobby group for the industry, and strategic airline alliances like 'One World' or 'Star Alliance' that permit individual airlines to offer global coverage via code-sharing and other business arrangements.

Given the focus of this book on tourism businesses of all sizes and their particular strategic management challenges in operating within destination communities, this section will focus on national and regional organisational structures.

Place based organisations

Convention and Visitor Bureaus (CVB) represent some of the oldest, most pervasive and best funded destination tourism organisations. Detroit, Michigan, is credited with being the birthplace of the first Convention and Visitor Bureau (CVB) in 1896 (Morrison *et al.*, 1998: 2). The International Association of Convention and Visitor Bureaus (IACVB), has grown from an initial 28 member cities in 1920 to over 900 members in the US alone. CVBs can represent towns, cities, regions and are the most common form of destination association.

While the traditional focus of CVBs was marketing their destination, increasingly they are becoming involved in product development, research, facilitation and tourism planning, as illustrated in the earlier discussion of 'Tourism Victoria' in Victoria, BC, Canada. CVBs are seen to represent four publics: members, local citizens, visitors and elected officials. In North America most CVBs fit into one of the following four categories (Morrison *et al.*, 1998: 3):

- independent (non-profit associations/business leagues);
- Chambers of Commerce (non-profit associations, or independent subsidiaries);
- local government agencies, department or public authority; or
- Special legal entity/authority.

Regardless of which category CVBs fit into, those CVBs that engage in active public–private partnerships outperform their counterparts, according to Morrison *et al.*, (1998).

Most of the IACVB members are independents (60%), the second single largest membership category is that of Chambers of Commerce (15%), and the remaining members are split between the last two categories and can be described as being 'public agencies' (25%) (IACVB cited in Morrison *et al.*, 1998: 3). Funding for CVBs can be extraordinary, sometimes exceeding the funds for government tourism offices at the state, national and international level. The budget for the CVB of Las Vegas continuously exceeded that of the past US Travel and Tourism Administration (Morrison *et al.*, 1998).

Common forms of funding for CVBs include bed or room taxes (often accounting for more than half of a CVB's budget), bonds, general tax dollars, membership dues, user fees and charges for information and other services. Of these the less argumentative are user fees for they are usually seen as legitimate service charges to both customers and local providers. But raising funds through a bed or room tax is far more contentious. This is because only one group, the accommodation sector, is targeted for funds that are used to assist every tourism sector in the local destination. While in most instances the accommodation sector is prepared to become the fund raiser for a common good it becomes problematic when this 'small' local tax is added to existing federal and state taxes, making the destination less competitive. For example, it is not unknown for some major destinations to be adding 20–25% of taxes to room rates, which makes them a very expensive option.

The benefits of combining resources at key locations, particularly expertise and skills from a cross-section of industries and sectors were demonstrated in the Local Enterprise and Development (LEAD) in tourism programme as initiated by the Wales Tourist Board. The LEAD concept is based on growth pole theory, in that is provides government grants and a supporting tourism framework for the development of 'lead' businesses in 'growth pole' areas, so that these areas can attract additional investments and generate sustainable tourism growth (Wanhill, 1996). LEAD areas were identified based on those areas with tourism proposals that were judged to be the most achievable, cost effective and offer the greatest package of well-rounded benefits. The LEAD approach draws upon extensive utilisation of available local knowledge regarding tourism opportunities and constraints, so that the return on tourism investments can be maximised. In the Wales example the LEAD approach was seen to provide 'an integrated approach to tourism development, stimulating local authority investment and offering a tourism framework for the allocation of resources' (Wanhill, 1996: 42).

Value constellations

The concept of 'value constellations' as developed by Normann and Ramirez (1993) builds upon the benefits of constructing strong ties between key businesses as a way to effectively stimulate economic development in specific sectors. This concept was developed in response to criticisms that the 'value chain' concept limits value to something that is accumulated as one moves along an internal chain of production, without due regard to the importance external relationships play in building value. 'Within the value constellation concept companies do not just add value but they reinvent it by means of a system. Within this logic, networking and inter-organizational relationships become central pieces of corporate strategy design' (Vanhaverbeke, 2001: 98).

According to Vanhaverbeke value constellations are seen as a useful way to view tourism services for three main reasons:

(1) Since value is created by relationships between companies and customers, cooperation between companies is necessary to ensure they provide the most attractive package of offerings to customers.
(2) As tourism offerings become more multi-dimensional, strategies that address the growing complexities of providing these offerings to consumers are needed.
(3) True competitive advantage can be realised by developing and implementing value-creating systems.

Since the tourism industry involves multiple sectors and interacts with a variety of other industries, such as resource development and manufacturing, it can be challenging to develop and implement value-creating systems that incorporate the needs, potential and constraints that affect many different sectors and industries.

One way to foster value constellations is to form strategic alliances. Strategic alliances have been defined as: 'voluntary arrangements between firms involving, sharing, or co-development of products, technologies or services. They can occur as a result of a wide range of motives and goals, take on a variety of forms, and occur across vertical and horizontal boundaries' (Gulati cited in Telfer, 2001: 21–2).

At their core all strategic alliances have a form of collaborative arrangement; and the businesses, organisations and individuals who are part of the alliance agree to share or divide managerial control (Starke & Sexty, cited in Telfer, 2001). Benefits of such alliances relate to power, in that group members can pool their resources and benefit from the expertise and skills of others in the association, while in turn the association can develop strategies to effectively address complex issues. An additional benefit is that working together as part of an alliance can reduce competitive rivalries between members.

This transformation from competitors to partners can be particularly striking in rural and regional areas when limited understanding of market conditions and marketing impacts can lead to misconceptions as to who the 'real competitors' for tourist dollars are and how to respond appropriately to out-perform these competitors. A recent study found that the performance of companies that were part of a strategic alliance out-performed their peers between 1983 and 1992 (Chan *et al.*, 1997). Strategic alliances can take a formal approach, by invoking codes of conduct and quality standards, or an informal approach, by providing networking opportunities, or a combination of these approaches. Strategic alliances can either function as vertical organisations, by forming a hierarchy of organisation within a particular sector; or as horizontal organisations by creating ties between sectors, as happens in destination marketing associations; or a combination of these organisational orientations as occurs with national lobby groups.

Roles

Developing a destination image requires a collective effort, as a broad array of public and private sector organisations are responsible for the goods, services, atmosphere and marketing of destinations. The interdependency of these organisations often leads to the creation of collaborative destination or industry associations. Many of these organisations revolve around marketing a destination, for through a pooling of resources a greater audience for the destination can be reached and a more comprehensive and compelling image of the destination can be created and sold to tourists. While there appear to be natural advantages to forming such organisations, the effectiveness of these organisations can vary markedly. Much of this variation depends on the effectiveness with which an association's multiple roles are conducted.

To help identify the multiple roles that need to be considered, Pearce *et al.* (1998: 351–2) have compiled a list of the top 10 roles for tourism organisations:

(1) *Pursuing standards.* Within destination (place) organisations this involves meeting customer expectations by demanding an acceptable base level of service and quality and building up from these to offer an accredited range of facilities that provide customers with a maximum choice.

(2) *Promoting training.* Within sector and destination organisations this places an emphasis on service quality, by providing the necessary staff training. A base level training system called 'Superhost' was developed by Tourism British Columbia in preparation for the Vancouver Exhibition in 1986. It proved so popular and successful it has since been franchised and sold around the world. In Australia it trades under the name 'Aussie Host'.

(3) *Developing codes.* One of the ways to ensure a quality product and travel experience is to operate in an environmentally sensitive manner. Increasingly more destinations and sectors are introducing some form of self-regulation codes of behaviour to ensure they do not overburden the physical and social environments of a destination. Examples of this are offered later under the heading of 'control'.

(4) *Professional organisation management.* To handle the complexity of modern business more organisations are turning to professional business managers. This team of educated and experienced managers generally operate key functional areas under the supervision of a CEO, and work alongside the numerous volunteer or appointed board members representing the industry and the community.

(5) *Supporting research.* To manage an organisation requires information and while some of this comes from government or industry sources these often do not address local issues because of their generic and large scale nature. Consequently, more organisations are striving to complement published data sources with their own surveys of members and customers. It is in this area that university links can be very helpful, by ensuring objective and professional analysis.

(6) *Partnerships with government groups.* Whether the organisation is a sector or destination association it will need to work with different levels of government and different government departments. Sector organisations find it useful to work with government before legislation is introduced on topics such as health and safety standards. Destination associations find such working relationships equally helpful, as they rely on government goodwill and the occasional government operating and infrastructure grants.

(7) *Enhanced networking.* No single organisation is solely responsible for local tourism activities given the ubiquitous nature of the industry and the mobility of its customers. Consequently, networking with other organisations is an essential ingredient to drawing visitors to a destination and ensuring they have plenty to do and see while they are there. Specific examples of this in tourism include packaging, where individual businesses and destinations combine to present tourists with an appealing combination of activities.

(8) *Expanding the view of tourism.* Despite tourism's size and significance its very ubiquitous nature makes it invisible to many. This means it is often an under-appreciated economic activity and that its potential to collaborate with other sectors goes unrecognised. To make people more aware of the industry and its benefits a prime function for organisation CEOs and presidents is to promote the industry and handle media relations.

This point was emphasised in Tourism Victoria's (Australia) Industry Strategic Plan for 2002–2006. Its first 'challenge' was recorded as being: 'Low community and government (specifically other departments) awareness of the value of tourism. There is a need to clearly articulate the economic, social and environmental benefits of tourism' (Tourism Victoria, 2002: 9).

(9) *Signature events.* One popular way to put tourism on the map for locals as well as tourists is to promote local events. Many communities have developed local festivals and events over time to celebrate and remember significant occurrences. Some of these have evolved naturally into signature tourism events, such as Munich's 'Oktoberfest', and New Orleans' 'Mardi Gras'. Others have required more artificial stimulation and management such as Melbourne's Grand Prix and the annual American Super Bowl.

(10) *Operation by delegation.* Given the size and complexity of the task of organising tourism at a destination level or via a sector, it is normal to
witness a great deal of responsibility delegation. Destination associations in particular are dependent on the collaboration of many
independent operators and at their visitor information centres and special events they rely heavily on volunteers. A growing trend around the
world is the appearance of 'local ambassadors' at key destinations.
These are generally volunteers who are trained to meet and greet visitors, assisting them with enquiries and directions. It is at this personal
and informal coalface that all the destination management and planning is being presented to the customer – truly operation by delegation.

Collaboration

A common thread to all organisations is the collaboration between
members. It is the willingness to assist others for a common good that
enables a group's output to exceed the sum of individual enterprise efforts.
In recognition of this fact there is growing research into what elements can
assist the collaboration process. Among the literature on this topic, with
respect to tourism organisations, is research into management styles, the
integration of volunteers, and the responsiveness to community interests.

The governance patterns of local tourism associations vary considerably, depending on the size of the community and relative importance of
tourism to the local community. Palmer's (1998) examination of the governance styles in tourism marketing associations found that key factors in the
success of such tourism organisations is a formal governance style, decisive
leadership and strong administrative support. Formal or 'tight' governance of these organisations is typified by following set rules and
procedures, as well as having formalised role functions and codes of
conduct for dealing with inter- and intra-organisational issues. He found
that 'incompatibility among members results in a more effective local association' (Palmer, 1998: 197), demonstrating that those destination
associations with a broad membership base can be expected to be more successful in reaching their objectives.

One area which destination associations need to embrace and integrate
into their organisation is the active support of local volunteers. The
multiple functions of tourism, especially local festivals and events, depend
on volunteers; but there is also a need for regular professional assistance
from the ranks of bankers, lawyers and accountants, and the enthusiasm of
special interest factions concerned with the environment and heritage.
Bringing these volunteers together helps to make the industry more aware
of community resources and potential, while allowing citizens to help plan
the level and type of future tourism development for their community.

Responding to community needs will be an important goal and function
for tourism organisations, but there is always a danger of becoming too

inward looking and failing to appreciate the full ramifications of tourism as an open system. Tourism involves customers who are mobile and this means any destination is only one of several options for their time and expenditure. Consequently all tourism organisations should look beyond their boundaries and extend collaboration to surrounding destinations and regions. This is particularly relevant to those smaller destinations that may not have sufficient attractions to hold tourists overnight, when the majority of tourist spending occurs. In some focus group research certain regional tourism boards have been criticised for being too insular. Berry and Ladkin (1997: 437) report how participants wanted to see a more regional focus with an 'integrated, hierarchical marketing structured with clear lines of responsibility and terms of reference'.

'Manager strength can influence the existence of competitive advantage by developing appropriate organisational competencies' (Dimmock, 1999: 323). Researchers suggest that developing positive interpersonal styles in organising, coordinating and controlling can make a firm more successful as such a style can improve productivity effectiveness and teamwork building (Blake & Mouton; Tomer cited in Dimmock, 1999). What works for individual businesses becomes a vital ingredient for an organisation representing a sector or destination, with all its various interests. Hence, leadership is becoming an essential factor in the successful development of individual businesses and destinations alike.

Leadership

As discussed in the earlier chapter on leadership this feature of management has taken on greater significance as business has become more competitive and uncertain. But since leadership involves a combination of technical and personal skills plus timing, it has proved difficult to isolate, analyse and prescribe the elements that create an effective leader. This is even more so in the area of tourism where so much depends on the collaboration of others and the political environment, as indicated in Russell and Faulkner's (1999) assessment of the Gold Coast's development.

Since there is little tourism-related leadership research that has led to specific hypotheses and guidelines we offer three examples of successful tourism leadership drawn from secondary sources and personal observation. These three cases represent three scales of operation, international/national, regional and local leadership with a focus on the leadership lessons that can be learned from each.

On the *international and national scale* is the example of Walt Disney and his personal drive to establish a theme park concept that has been emulated around the world. Disney's theme park concept was so innovative that despite his success as a film maker he struggled to raise the capital to open Disneyland. 'Walt raised the money through a variety of channels, of which the most frequently referred to are borrowing on his life insurance policies and forming a liaison with television' (Bryman, 1995: 12). In the end his concept of a fun, safe and clean fairground based on the theme of his movie characters proved to be so popular that it has spread around the world, and it helped the Disney company purchase its television 'banker' in 1995, to form one of the world's major entertainment conglomerates.

Among the entrepreneurship lessons that have emerged from Walt Disney's early theme park decisions and the company's later strategies one key factor has been the purchase of sufficient land. Mark Twain once recommended: 'Buy land, they're not making it anymore', and the Disney Company needs a lot of land for its theme parks. Walt Disney's early financial difficulties were caused in part by the large amount of land needed for his concept; and upon opening his theme park he wished he could have purchased more, as he saw other businesses feeding off his customers and turning the surrounding area into a strip development of hotels and restaurants. Walt Disney learned his lesson, and when he assembled the site for his second theme park near Orlando, Florida, he purchased 27,400 acres (11,088 hectares) – far more than was needed for one or two theme parks. The other land was to be developed for the financially beneficial accommodation sector; to provide other attractions such as golf courses and water parks to create a resort environment so there is little need for customers to leave the property; and to act as a buffer to the inevitable parasitical businesses drawn to the business opportunities presented by this major attraction.

Associated with the expense incurred with such large rural land purchases is the need to receive government assistance in its development. Walt Disney started negotiations with the State of Florida before committing to the Orlando site, and among the agreements he secured was the right to create his own local government jurisdiction. This enabled Disney to build according to his own high standards and to raise capital as a government authority, which translates into lower interest rates. Such political negotiations over the final purchase of land were continued in France when the Disney Company set up Euro Disneyland, which is now called Paris Disneyland.

In Europe the 'Disney company was able to assemble such a large amount of land (2,000 hectares) thanks to the assistance of the French government, which owned the land and had been leasing it to local farmers but was eager to see economic development in this part of rural France' (Murphy, 1997: 228). To entice Disney the French government offered the land at 1971 agricultural prices and guaranteed those prices for 20 years (Flower, 1991: 208). In addition it linked the site of the new theme park to Paris via a freeway and extension of the Metro subway system. Plus, it linked the theme park to the high speed rail system, which with the opening of the Channel Tunnel places Paris Disney within three and a half hours of London.

While one of the early reasons for such extensive land assembly was to protect the Disney investments from surrounding businesses, the presence of undeveloped land next to a successful and attractive resort has presented the opportunity to create greenfield residential complexes. This process has started in Disney World with the construction of Celebration, a state of the art residential community (Diski, 2000). It will continue in Europe, where the opportunity to build a satellite town both for Paris and within Europe's golden triangle of development makes a perfect complement to the clean air industry of a theme park resort.

As a consequence Disney's entrepreneurial experience has shown the importance of buying sufficient land for a tourism venture that is land intensive in its own right and can benefit from the control of adjacent land, either to protect the original investment or to create attractive spin-off investments. It also reveals the importance of negotiating from a position of strength, especially when tourism is bringing economic activity and amenity development to rural and depressed regions. However, land acquisition and negotiation is not a simple process, as the Disney experience in Virginia illustrates. This is discussed elsewhere in the book.

At the *regional scale* is the enterprise of Tim Smit, who is the visionary behind the Eden Project in Cornwall, England. The Eden Project is a living theatre of plants and people designed to link people with their global environment and is located in rural southwest England. It is situated in an old clay quarry near St Austell with two giant greenhouse biomes presenting a humid tropical environment and a warm temperate Mediterranean climatic zone (Figure 8.5). The rest of the 15 hectare site is in its early planting and development phase and will eventually contain native Cornish flora. This facility opened in March 2001 after a seven year capitalisation of £86 million (A\$235 million), with half the funding coming from the UK's millennium lottery grant. Since its opening it has exceeded projected visitor numbers, and now attracts around one million visitors a year.

The entrepreneur who put this project together was a successful Dutch-born record producer in London who moved to Cornwall for a change of lifestyle in 1987. Once there Smit's energy and drive drew him to his first horticultural project, the revival of the 'Lost Gardens of Heligan' which has become 'Britain's most visited private garden, attracting over 300,000 visitors a year' (*The Weekend Australian*, 2001: R5). Then his thoughts turned to the potential of this discarded quarry in the Cornish countryside.

Smit's vision was to create 'a futuristic botanical institute exploring the relationship between man and plants' that would combine education, research, conservation and entertainment (*Western Morning News*, 2001: 2 and 5). It was expected to become a major inland tourist attraction that would balance the coastal magnets of Devon and Cornwall, and bring a boost to the declining rural economy. His main task was to garner sufficient support and funding to turn this vision into action. He achieved this via his 'Tinkerbell theory':

> . . . if you believe in a great idea then it will exist. Also, if you don't go away you will irritate people so much that after a while they will give you whatever you want. Put those two things together, you've got a pretty immovable force. (*Western Morning News*, 2001: 5)

But there is obviously more to it than that. First, this entrepreneur had a good track record in business and horticulture-tourism. Second, he was able to see the big picture of Cornwall's inland potential and the prospects of combining research, education and entertainment into a tourist attraction. Third, he could convince various governments that his tourism vision could bring employment and investment to a rural backwater and he was able to secure their funding support as an investment in the future of this region.

The Eden Project has become a success in the short time it has been open and continues to exhibit innovative management. Not only has it exceeded its visitor projections, some days it has been overwhelmed with visitors – especially on wet days when holiday makers have fled inland in search of a wet weather attraction. 'Now, the project has taken out advertisements asking people to choose more carefully when they come – and not to visit at all on wet days' (McGinnes, 2001: 4). This 'de-marketing' may be viewed as an 'unusual step', but it really reflects good management. In attempting to control the flow of visitors the project is trying to provide an optimal experience and develop satisfied customers.

At the *local scale* is the baker, Tom O'Toole, who has converted his business into a multi-million dollar tourist attraction that has helped to convert Beechworth in rural northeast Victoria, Australia into a burgeoning regional tourism venue. The small town of Beechworth, with a current population of just over 3000, was a significant regional centre in the nineteenth century, but since then has been bypassed by economic and political developments. Over time it has become a small and sleepy rural community, blessed with significant history and heritage buildings, but steadily losing its few remaining public sector institutions as modernisation and economies of scale overtook them. Consequently, it has become a town that needed to reinvent itself and one of the leaders in this process was the local baker – Tom O'Toole.

O'Toole is a believer in 'the power of positive thinking' and on purchasing the small bakery in Beechworth converted it into a multi-million dollar business that depended on the growing tourism business as well as locals. His strategy was:

Figure 8.5 Eden Project in Cornwall, England

> I worked really hard and the bakery became successful. I did some creative marketing which really helped. I started getting wacky promotional ideas. And most important of all, I started to blend the bakery into the Beechworth local community through sponsorships and general community support. Then my business started to really grow. (O'Toole with Tarling, 2000: 161)

In the process he converted a peripheral tourism business into a major local attraction that worked with the community in developing its heritage tourism potential (Figure 8.6).

O'Toole created his successful tourism business by implementing and personalising some basic management concepts. Many of these are included in his book. *Breadwinner: A Fresh Approach to Rising to the Top* and are introduced as 'The Gospel of Thomas'. Among our favourites are:

- *Entrepreneurship*
  'Get out of your comfort zone! Take a risk – smile! Shock people! Enjoy your work! Have goals! Get famous! Beware of the dream-takers!' (The bankers who assess your business plan from an actuarial perspective only.)
- *Teamwork*
  'None of us is as strong as all of us. I know when we all work together, we all win together'.
- *Continuous Learning*
  'The more you learn, the more you earn'.
- *Recruitment*
  'Without good people, you're ratshit . . . My staff is my biggest asset, because without them I don't have a business. My staff are my biggest investors – they invest their time, their energy and their imagination . . . you can buy your milk and bread anywhere, why buy it from my place? It's because of them'.
- *Marketing*
  'If I can get them (customers) to Beechworth I've got a chance of getting a dollar out of their pockets – but first I've got to get them to Beechworth'.
- *Training*
  'I spend a lot of money training my staff. Some think I'm investing too much in my people and they say to me: "Tom, what if you train them and they leave?" To which I usually reply: "What if I don't train them and they stay".'
- *Personal Motivation*
  'Choose to be happy. The power of choice is incredible. We can choose to think great thoughts, we can choose enthusiasm, we can choose to bunge jump right out of our comfort zones'.

Figure 8.6 Beechworth Bakery
Source: Beechworth Bakery

- *Personal Philosophy*
  'It's got to be simple . . . all the customers want you to do is, look at them, greet them, talk to them, and thank them'.

It is not that simple of course, and none of this comes about without hard work, for to paraphrase Edison 'success is 1 percent inspiration and 99 percent perspiration', and entrepreneurs such as these put body and soul into their businesses.

Controlling

The need to ensure that private company and corporate destination objectives are being achieved and are appropriate for long-term sustainable relationships requires consideration of control measures. While this management function is widely recognised it is seldom operated to its fullest extent in tourism for a variety of reasons. First, the reliance on collaboration and the support of others means individual businesses and destinations are not in complete control of their own destiny. These external relationships make monitoring and measurement more challenging than normal, and leave corrective responses dependent in part on outside cooperation. Second, the seasonality of many tourism businesses and destination means there is a back-breaking and mind-numbing period of intense activity when it is difficult to stand back and assess how well the organisation is satisfying its customers and meeting its objectives. Third, given the dependence of tourism on a healthy social and physical environment it is frustrating how few dependable and simple impact indicators have been developed.

All three control issues for businesses and destinations are clearly illustrated in Lennon's (2001) report on Scotland's 'Visitor Attraction Monitor'. Like a growing number of monitoring procedures the Scottish Tourist Board has linked up with a university, in this case Glasgow Caledonian University, to monitor an aspect of the industry. This centrally funded collaborative research provides the type of data central agencies and individual businesses need in order to measure their own performance. The seasonality of the attractions, that can range from 'free entry' museums and galleries to entry fee castles and zoos, is concentrated in the high season of July to September, with a strong shoulder season between April and June. During these busy time periods most attractions can register the basic information relating to their number of visitors, but some (13%) depend on periodic samples or visitor books and 'honesty / donation' boxes.

Collaboration

A 'distribution channel is the path products take as they move from the producer to the ultimate consumer' (Richardson, 1996: 76). The producer is generally a separate business that operates within a destination community and the ultimate consumer can be a local resident, a domestic tourist or an international tourist from another country. In many destinations, especially where most of the businesses are small, the majority of sales are direct, with entry or bed nights sold directly to the passing customer. However, to reach more distant and targeted markets many tourism businesses utilise a variety of distribution channels to build inbound travel. These distribution channels in effect become control mechanisms for much of the tourism business because to use such marketing devices requires accreditation, monitoring and collaboration.

The first and least expensive distribution channel for most businesses is the local destination-marketing organisation. Membership in these organisations permits businesses to place their brochures at information centres, to be included in generic destination advertising and trade shows, and to participate in local booking services. Many businesses, especially those in the hospitality sector, link up with motoring organisations to be included in their travel directories. In addition, some businesses will use wholesale tour package operators to combine their product into packages that are of interest to distant target markets, while others will use additional distribution channel operators like high street travel agents. A good description of these distribution channel networks can be found in Heath and Wall (1992).

The distribution channels and associated businesses are facing a turbulent future. The Internet and e-commerce are providing customers with more information and purchasing options than ever before, but just as importantly they are providing individual businesses with more direct access to customers, near and far. This provides smaller businesses with the opportunity to match traditional distribution channels and to sell directly to customers, with the associated savings in commission and flexibility of pricing and individual control.

Financing

The financial health of any organisation determines its survival, although some airlines and other national institutions seem to be able to delay the inevitable result of continual losses through government subsidy. However, for the majority of businesses and organisations the crucial control factor is their financial position. While some lifestyle tourism businesses will feel this factor is not so crucial for them because 'the business' is simply supporting their chosen lifestyle and location, they will still find that financial concerns can undermine their management practices and personal relationships.

For small businesses in tourism a primary source of capital has been personal or family savings, and as a result two important control points can be missed. Many who rely on self-funding fail to prepare a disciplined and detailed business plan. Among the many calculation omissions this can lead to is a failure to assign a reasonable salary to the operator(s). Thus many end up paying themselves nothing and fail to consider forsaken opportunity costs.

Boer (cited in Thomas, 1998: 9) has identified several sources of small business failure that can contribute to a poor financial situation. These include 'poor operational management, high gearing, poor senior management and a weak local economy'. Taking these in reverse order, it is important for tourism entrepreneurs to enquire about the economic health of their local region and its tourism industry, rather than be guided by its tourism delights. The importance of an objective business plan from senior management cannot be over-emphasised, and such a cold and analytical document can be a sobering experience for the entrepreneur as well as the banker. An overenthusiastic assessment of business opportunities and a rush to get started can lead to an overcommitment.

Kuratko and Hodgetts (1998: 430–1) describe five common fund-raising dilemmas, and offer some sensible advice which has been paraphrased below:

(1) *What do you plan to do with the money?*
    If you can compartmentalise the business, seek funding support for the low-risk and therefore more secure components.
(2) *How much do you need?*
    Determine the exact amount you need for each component and prioritise those components. See if you can plan and expand the business in stages.
(3) *When do you need it?*
    Do not approach a banker without a business plan, and one that includes time-lines regarding loan(s) and repayments.
(4) *How long will you need it?*
    The shorter the requested loan period the better, as this indicates the business is likely to be in a profit-making position quickly and the banker's funds will not be committed for too long.
(5) *How will you repay the loan?*
    'This is the most important question', and can be answered with conviction if there are other sources of income or forms of collateral.

A common problem in terms of operational management is the question of cash flow, which can become crucial in seasonal businesses like tourism. One answer to this problem which is gaining in popularity in the UK is factoring. Factoring is a process whereby businesses send their invoices to a company that pays them most of their money upon receipt of the invoices and then collects the debt for the company, all for a small fee. This sort of debt-collection service can be of great benefit to small companies that regularly have to wait for one or more months for full payment of services from their clients. The UK has experienced a boom in factoring, fuelled by the growing number of small businesses. Most business owners are put in

touch with factors by banks. Factoring has been found to be primarily beneficial to companies with an annual turnover of more than £100,000
(A$300,000). The owner of one chauffeuring company in the UK credits
factoring with enabling him to expand his business from six cars and six
employees to a company valued over £1 million with 34 employees (*Daily
Express*, 2000: 56).

Customer expectations

To achieve financial success businesses must meet their customer
expectations, and if possible exceed them within their operational and
financial constraints. One problem is that the quality expectations of
customers are rising as they have experienced an ever-increasing array of
quality tourism options. It has been found in recreational research that
aggregate levels of visitor satisfaction tend to rise, and that it can be independent of changes in the types or amount of use (Lindberg *et al.*, 1997).
This phenomenon can be a reflection of 'succession and displacement'
process. This occurs when one group is first attracted to an area for certain
qualities, but as their satisfaction wanes due to the area becoming more
crowded the new and larger groups who visit the now 'accessible' and
popular recreational spots express increased satisfaction. The findings of
Lindberg *et al.* suggest concerns about customer satisfaction and quality
can be handled by managing the demand for tourism products and
services, such as targeting different markets, rather than managing the
supply of actual products or services. However, once a tourist destination
becomes degraded in the eyes of some, the market potential for its associated product and services can decline as negative word of mouth spreads
and the competition looks more attractive. Furthermore, once a service or
product is viewed as sub-standard it can no longer charge top prices,
which will create a downward spiral or reduced prices, profits, investment and demand.

The above customer expectation model has obvious parallels to the
product lifecycle model and Butler's associated destination evolution
model.

Ethics

Ethics refers to a system of morality. In practice ethics can refer to
ensuring that one's actions are just, fair and honourable. The extent to
which tourism businesses have a responsibility to act in an ethical manner,
beyond obeying the law, is debatable.

> As is well know, Friedman argues that ethics are not the province of
> business, while Davis insists that business must embrace social respon-
> sibility, not merely profitability. (Walle, 1995: 263)

Milton Friedman (cited in Walle, 1995) stresses that the only legitimate role for businesses is to pursue profits, while dwelling on ethical considerations for any reason other than generating profits is unsupportable. Others, including Davis, believe that businesses have an obligation to society to act ethically due to their profound and pervasive influence on society. Friedman and those who support him believe that businesses should act in an ethical way if it is part of their strategy, such as building goodwill or diversifying their product to improve their profits. Walle (1995: 264) suggests that there is a continuum of ethical behaviour, which is outlined below:

- *Social obligation.* Businesses are only required to obey the law (Friedman's approach).
- *Social responsibility.* Businesses are required to act in ethical and socially responsible ways (Davis' approach).
- *Social responsiveness.* Businesses build on their ethical role of 'social responsibility', with the added requirement to anticipate and respond in an ethical manner to potential future challenges.

The tourism industry has some key characteristics that need to be considered when determining its ethical responsibilities. First of all, progress in terms of appropriate development, investments and marketing can be a divisive issue in tourism as different stakeholders have different views of 'progress'; therefore, a careful balance needs to be achieved between what customers want, what other stakeholders want and what is profitable. Secondly, the industry can effectively destroy that which it relies upon, so even from just a profitability viewpoint, businesses need to be highly aware of the potential impact of their actions and help to ensure that 'their money makers' are preserved. Third, the needs of all stakeholders need to be identified and appropriately addressed in the interest of widespread support for the industry and its prolonged profitability, as well as its moral responsibilities to affected people and environments. Therefore, the domain of ethical behaviour for tourism businesses can be addressed from either a pragmatic perspective, based on pursuing actions that improve the bottom line, or on more philosophical lines, based on pursuing actions that are 'right', 'just' and 'for the betterment of society'. It is our contention that those perspectives are not necessarily mutually exclusive.

Stakeholder-community ethics

Engaging in ethical behaviour that meet stakeholders' needs can be good for business as indicated by Mitchell's (1997: 21) assertion: 'the ability to identify, prioritize, and respond to stakeholders is the ability to recognise opportunity'. In the interest of increasing their return on investments, businesses are discovering a range of potential benefits from taking a 'green approach'. This includes 'cost savings, increased efficiencies, early identification of potential environment liabilities, improved corporate image, marketing and sales benefits, enhanced visitor and regulatory confidence, and improved staff motivation' (Goodall, cited in McBoyle, 1996: 255). But others have pointed out the unethical approach of some companies, which brand their product as eco-sensitive or green, without any substantial effort to apply sustainable practices. To overcome this dilemma more tourism businesses are being encouraged to join an independently accreditation system, like the WTTC's Green Globe programme.

Even if a corporation endeavours to be ethical and responsible in its actions, imposing its ethics and practices on a community can cause problems, especially if these ethics and practices are not in keeping with those of the local community in which it operates. This situation can be exacerbated in isolated and underdeveloped communities, where there is a history of colonial activities that have threatened the culture and rights of local citizens. Baldacchino (1997) describes a situation that he refers to as 'small-scale labour syndrome', whereby incompatibilities arise between small island communities and multi-national operations that establish businesses in these communities. He found that a small-scale labour syndrome worked on the following levels:

- large corporations sending expatriates to exercise 'gunboat diplomacy', by imposing the corporate line on the locals; and
- local communities subverting the corporate rules and regulations in a manner that reflected their own culture, experience and values.

Baldacchino (1997: 176) sees this syndrome as representing 'a foray into forms of worker resistance to the global threat . . . [that shapes] the contested terrain of labour-management relations'. Examples of small-scale labour syndrome are found with regard to the acceptability of hiring friends and relatives, issues of confidentiality and responsibilities to the company. Baldacchino advocates that corporations recognise and plan for the small-scale labour syndrome. This planning involves achieving the right balance between creating strategies, procedures and policies that uphold corporate objectives and ensuring that the organisation is also responsible to local cultural conditions and requirements.

Others have suggested that the association between multi-national corporations and host communities, especially in developing countries, has been in favour of corporate values. Britton, S.C. (1982) and Lundgren (1972) have emphasised the dominance of core economies over the pleasure periphery nations, but over time these host nations have learned to be more demanding negotiators. It is now more common to find clauses in development agreements relating to the hiring of locals within the management ranks and the use of local suppliers, but the balance still remains in favour of the multi-national corporations which have more options than the individual communities or developing nations.

Now the emphasis is on community partnerships, so that as many stake holders as possible can benefit from tourism development. The community approach has emphasised the ethical and business benefits to be obtained through an industry-community business partnership. This can be seen at several levels of development. With international 'hallmark events' the industry can benefit not only from hosting the event, but thanks to the international exposure can expect subsequent years of higher international visitation. The community can benefit from an increased supply of infrastructure, amenities and in some cases housing. Some claim that this has hardly moved us beyond the Roman era of cake and circuses and that many of the infrastructure and amenity developments would have come eventually (Hall, 1992; Murphy, 1991); but it takes a community spirit to bring these things together in an event and it is that collaboration that is often a springboard to further community development. At the other extreme are the local museums and festivals that increasingly depend on tourist revenue to survive. Economic studies of community festivals continually reveal the importance of tourist revenue to the event and community at large (Carmichael & Murphy, 1996; Getz, 1991).

Codes of behaviour

Perhaps the most evident sign of the growth of ethics and a community approach in tourism is the rise in codes of behaviour. These codes have been introduced by different tourism organisations as pre-emptive management strategies to help ensure the industry remains in harmony with local environments and therefore sustainable. The most evident are those relating to the environment, as is the case of the 'Code of Conduct for Commercial Tour Operations in Gwaii Haanas/South Moresby' in British Columbia referred to elsewhere in this book. But there are less visible codes that are also changing the industry. The Australian Federation of Travel Agents has created a binding code of conduct for all of its members, which was developed to protect customer interest (Pearce *et al.*, 1998). A Global Code of Ethics for Tourism was prepared by the World Tourism Organisation (WTO) to recognise the role of tourism in the world and to outline the responsibilities of the industry to the people of the world (WTO, 1999).

Summary

This chapter outlines the wide variety of components within the industry and discusses the issue of its definition. It suggests the industry be viewed as a conglomerate industry with a service focus on its customers. It reveals there is a range of tourism products and industry types that can be expected to change in importance and emphasis depending on local resources and priorities, and over time.

To plan for this industry various management theories are explored and applied. The organising components examine various organisational types and their inter- and intrarelations. The leadership component of this chapter focuses on innovators and the importance of training and inspiring industry workers: the control component looks at the dynamics of product and service mix and how important it is for small businesses as well as large organisations to monitor and improve performance. The chapter closes with an overview of the growing importance of ethics and offers some guiding principles and examples for the tourism industry.

As an industry tourism holds much promise for the future, but like all industries this promise can only be realised through careful planning of inputs and outputs. Tourism, more than most industries, is acutely reliant on the goodwill of residents in that part of the product it sells is the community itself. It has been noted that successful communities involve a broad cross-section of residents in determining and planning for the future and this is certainly the case in tourism. The following chapter explores the needs, types and actions of residents as they relate to community tourism initiatives.

Chapter 9

Residents

The amount of research concerned with tourist destination residents has been extensive, especially with respect to the social science perspectives on resident–visitor relationships. Such research has revealed some consistent patterns concerning resident attitudes and opinions of local tourism. These appear to be related to factors such as the residents' proximity to and involvement in the industry, the volume of and type of tourism experience and the level of similarity between the visitor origin and destination cultures.

With the growth of tourism as a global industry and its more evident impacts on local communities planning for this activity has received more attention. Initially such planning research and practice focused on the physical and spatial issues, but more recently there has been a shift to incorporate the human and political dimensions. Included in this area of investigation has been the need to find processes that will facilitate the involvement of a wide range of stakeholders, including differing resident reactions.

What has been missing in much of the previous resident research and tourism management has been an exploration of resident involvement in the delivery and management of local tourism. This is beginning to change with some research exploring prospective models of resident-tourism industry collaboration and in certain destinations that are beginning to involve residents more proactively in the development and delivery of the local tourism product.

Objectives

Even though communities are made up of different individuals and group interests there are some common objectives that can be expected among local resident stakeholders. On an individual basis it is a very human trait to desire to 'have one's cake and to eat it too'. In terms of tourism this translates into wanting to live in a beautiful location, to have significant cultural icons and amenities, and to have the revenue to support a comfortable lifestyle that permits a person to enjoy the above. Then we want to keep all this to ourselves! In today's global village that is not likely; for modern communication and media attention will ensure that news about such communities spreads and the global tourism industry will endeavour to bring visitors to the residents' door.

Once tourists arrive at the community's door there are three general objectives that most residents will consider. First and foremost they will view tourism as a business and want to see a return to individuals and the community. The economic return can be in several forms. For many it will be employment, for some business revenue, and for all a substantial tax base – for tourism is one of the most taxed businesses in the world now that VAT and GST have become widespread. In most cases tourism will make an ideal supplementary community industry, because many tourists come to see a living community and its sense of place. They like to see people going to work, being prosperous and happy. If tourism is the only or major local industry a community will lose its variety and some vitality, which becomes very evident with the regular seasonal downturns of tourism or the aftermath of a terrorist act.

Many residents will be aware of the environmental resources and attractions in their local community and will be among the first detectors of stress and damage. They will appreciate the taxes that are used to support local parks, beaches and amenities such as toilets, parking and interpretation facilities. But they will become concerned if they cannot access these themselves or see them overrun to the extent that the site and recreation experience begin to deteriorate. It will often be the tourists who are blamed for such difficulties because they are highly visible, but they are only a portion of the users and their tax dollars will have contributed to the environment's care and protection.

The importance of human perception is paramount at the social level of host–tourist interaction. Residents have the right and expectation to go about their own business in their own home community, but this relationship will be seriously challenged by the arrival of tourists who have a different agenda and timetable. The management of these human expectations and flows within a community will be crucial to the success of tourism's local operations and image. Some of this management will involve physical planning to separate conflicting group interests, such as separating local traffic from tourist traffic wherever possible. Some will involve behavioural management. One of our favourite examples of this are the small signs at Cape Canaveral, Florida, which tell you to stick to the path because of snakes. No one wandered off the path while we were there. Who would risk it?

These three dimensions of resident objectives can be managed and brought into a sustainable development context through Elkington's 'triple bottom line'. His concept is:

> Sustainable development involves the simultaneous pursuit of economic prosperity, environmental quality, and social equity.

Companies aiming for sustainability need to perform not against a single, financial bottom line but against the triple bottom line. (Elkington, 1999: 397)

Since its introduction this concept has received increased attention and is beginning to appear in more government tourism planning, such as the Tourism Victoria (Australia) Industry Strategic Plan of 2002–2006 (Tourism Victoria, 2002). Its appeal is particularly strong for communities seeking a new direction as their traditional industries decline, and they desire to develop public–private sector partnerships to tap all remaining community resources and redefine their future. Rogers (2001: 136–139) in talking about this situation for Australia's country towns feels that using the triple bottom line audit along with community-based indicators and local leadership can lead such communities to more sustainable futures. This would involve a more proactive stance from local residents and planning methods to integrate these stakeholders more effectively into the decision-making process on the future of their communities.

Planning

The relationship between 'host' resident and 'guest' tourist has been examined in a variety of contexts and locations. A leader in this area is Valene Smith (Smith, 1989; Smith & Brent, 2001) who has explored the social and anthropological relationships between visitors and host populations in a variety of settings. Another concern of anthropologists is the effect of globalisation on established concepts such as 'culture' and 'society' (McGibbon, 2000), that in many cases will take the form of tourism and increase its capacity to change host environments. The imagery of a borderless world 'suggests states (and all communities) have been rendered impotent in the face of overwhelming global forces and that there is little they can do except adjust to the imperatives of the global market' argues Richardson (1997: 55). Yet it is remarkable how resilient communities have been in the past to economic and military imperialism. From such studies have emerged certain theories and stratagems that indicate possible ways to integrate resident concerns and viewpoints into a general strategic plan for community tourism.

One of the earliest theories of resident–tourist interrelationships was Doxey's 'irridex', which has been embellished into more comprehensive and practical models. As the title of Doxey's (1975) model indicates, he saw the relationship as undirectional and inevitably apocalyptic, with increased exposure to tourism leading to increased negative reactions from residents. He envisioned community–visitor relationships steadily progressing downward, from a state of euphoria to one of apathy, to annoyance and eventually antagonism. He provided evidence of such a pattern from his consultancy work and since then there have been incidents which unfortunately confirm rising tourist numbers are still an influential factor. However, this correlation is simplistic and begs the introduction of management techniques such as physical planning or behavioural management to reduce the impact of increasing numbers.

One of the earliest modifications to Doxey's approach was the recognition that not all residents would develop the same negative reactions, and that their attitudes to local tourism would be influenced by a variety of factors. Lankford and Howard (1994) in their development of a tourism impact attitudinal scale identify from the literature ten variables that could influence a resident's opinion about local tourism. These are presented below with our elaborations:

- *Length of residency*
  The longer people had lived in the community the more negative they are likely to become towards tourism because of the changes it brings. It appears that the perceived negative changes are often more noticeable than the positive changes.
- *Economic dependency on tourism*
  Residents who depend on tourism-based employment (directly or indirectly) have been found to be more favourable toward tourism and tourists.
- *Distance of tourism (activity) centre from resident's home*
  In general the 'out-of-sight out-of-mind' syndrome seems to work in tourism cases. Those living far from the industry have been found to be in favour of its development because they are not personally bothered by the associated congestion and other nuisances. Of course a resident's home location does not necessarily correlate with their exposure, especially when their place of work is close to the major tourism areas.
- *Resident involvement in tourism decision-making*
  When residents are involved with various local development decisions they appear to be more favourable to community change and this includes tourism.
- *Birthplace*
  Residents' origins appear to have an influence on their views. We have observed in various locations that newly arriving retirees from big cities sometimes wish to 'pull up the drawbridge' and see their retirement haven remain the quiet and beautiful retreat they had perceived it to be.
- *Level of knowledge*
  The general level of knowledge about tourism and its significance to the local economy has been shown to influence local attitudes regarding its development and tourists.

- *Level of contact with tourists*
  Although obviously related to the earlier employment and resident location factors it has been found that personal contact with tourists has an influence on residents' attitudes, both positive and negative.
- *Demographic characteristics*
  Related to many of the above factors is the influence of age and gender. A resident's personal profile will have an impact on how they perceive tourism's influence. While we have noted some negativity from certain retirees tourism is generally popular with local youth because of its employment and excitement prospects.
- *Perceived impacts on local outdoor recreation opportunities*
  When local residents have difficulty in accessing their favourite outdoor recreation activities because tourists got there first, the desire for further tourism development understandably weakens.
- *Rate of community growth*
  The rate of community growth or decline appears to influence residents' interest regarding further tourism development. When a community is losing its traditional industries some 'boosters' point to tourism as a potential saviour without due consideration of its implications. Such enthusiasts often fail to recognise that tourism is a very competitive industry; that it takes quality products with a critical mass of attractions to draw tourists overnight; and it depends on quality service to build up its reputation for value and excellence.

With this wide range of potential influences on resident attitudes to tourism and signs of correlation or overlap between some of the variables, Lankford and Howard (1994) conducted a factor analysis of these variables in data gathered from several small Oregon communities. They found two significant factors associated with resident attitudes in these towns. These were a 'concern for local tourism development' and the perceived 'personal and community benefits', which combine several of the listed variables into significant attitude motivations for these communities.

Given this multi-dimensional nature of resident attitudes toward local tourism, there have been several attempts to broaden the Doxey causation model. One early adjustment was Bjorklund and Philbrick's portfolio approach that took into consideration residents' involvement with the industry and the degree of similarity between host and tourist cultures (cited in Butler, 1975). From such a two-dimensional approach it is possible to incorporate Doxey's original observation into a broader context than one simply based on tourist numbers.

This multi-dimensional approach to modelling resident reactions to tourism and finding ways to incorporate them into the planning process has been developed as part of the Australian Cooperative Research Centre's Gold Coast Revisioning Project. Faulkner and Tideswell (1997)

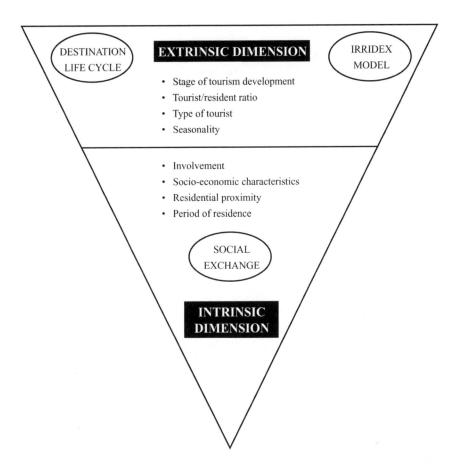

Figure 9.1 A framework for analysing the social impacts of tourism
Source: Faulkner and Tideswell (1997: 6)

have proposed a multi-dimensional model for analysing the community impacts of tourism (Figure 9.1). This model identifies extrinsic forces that include the tourist–resident ratio from the Doxey model and the stage of development from the Butler model of destination development. In addition they identify the potential impact of the type of tourist attracted and the influence of seasonality. These extrinsic forces represent the external influences of tourism impacting on a community, while the intrinsic forces are how residents of the community react to these external forces and attempt to integrate tourism into their general life. The major way residents are expected to respond to local tourism is through the sequence of social exchange, as outlined in Chapter 1. But they recognise individuals' intrinsic assessment of their personal trade-off between costs and benefits will be influenced by personal variables such as their level of involvement with the industry, their socio-economic standing, and their period of residence.

Faulkner and Tideswell (1997) examined the significance of the identified extrinsic and intrinsic variables in a survey of Gold Coast residents. The Gold Coast is a mature beach resort destination and a factor analysis of resident responses revealed the classical 'juxtaposition of an appreciation of the benefits of tourism (Factor 1) on the one hand and an acknowledgement of its costs on the other (Factor 2)' (Faulkner & Tideswell, 1997: 14).

On the whole, Gold Coast residents viewed tourism in a positive light, and the specific contribution of individual extrinsic and intrinsic forces varied relatively little from the predicted patterns. Such evidence led Faulkner and Tideswell (1997: 26) to conclude:

> The positive view of tourism among Gold Coast residents overall, and the marginal variation in opinion irrespective of such background variables as period of residence, place of residence and involvement, suggests that the altruistic surplus factor may apply to tourism.

This and other empirical studies support the existence of a complex yet stable pattern of relationships between resident perceptions of local tourism and their attitude toward its development. Jurowski *et al.* (1997) surveyed residents from the Mt Rogers National Recreation Area in Virginia to determine the interplay of factors that impact on residents' views of tourism. They use a path analysis model to track the link between what residents perceive to be tourism's economic, social and environmental impacts and their personal values, listed below:

- *Economic gain* – the potential for personal and community economic benefit from tourism.
- *Resource use* – the importance residents place on their use of tourism resources like parks and beaches.
- *Community attachment* – resident sentiments toward their town and surrounding region.
- *Ecocentric attitude* – ecological perspective of residents, particularly with respect to maintaining a balanced ecosystem.

They found the model helps to explain ambiguities in residents' views of tourism by demonstrating how residents' values and experiences shaped their perceptions of tourism impacts. Community attachment and potential economic gain were the strongest positive variables in shaping the residents' views of tourism's impacts, whereas resource use and an ecocentric attitude were negatively related. However, within these general relationships were certain sub-groupings that demonstrated it is not a simple linear relationship for any of the studied values. For example,

within the generally positive economic gain variable its most positive relationship for the residents occurred with social impacts, while it had little
effect on their environmental assessments. Similarly, while the resource
users were reticent to support development in natural settings they were
more positive elsewhere.

Gursoy *et al.* (2002) find support for local tourism is influenced primarily
by the state of the local economy, which in turn influences residents' perceptions of tourism's benefits and costs, thus confirming 'the usefulness of
exchange theory in explaining residents' attitudes toward tourism'
(Gursoy *et al.* 2002: 100). However, the authors point out that their study
like 'most research on residents' reactions toward tourism has been
confined to rural and small town populations' (Gursoy *et al.*, 2002: 100) and
needs to be extended to larger urban areas.

Following social exchange theory, one can see how residents' support
for tourism initiatives intended to benefit them will be influenced by their
values. Williams and Lawson (2001) found that differences between
residents grouped according to 'community interests' were more statistically significant than those grouped according to socio-demographic
factors. These researchers go on to suggest that 'value' measures of
residents can be a more accurate way of understanding residents' views of
tourism. Once the key values of stakeholder groups are understood then
decision-makers are in a better position for developing proposals on how
tourism generated funds and public funds raised to further tourism should
be spent.

In New Zealand, Horn and Simmons (2002) examine two very different
destinations. Rotorua in the North Island is a bustling rural regional centre
where tourism is based on their hot springs and Maori attractions and
accounts for 18% of local employment. Kaikoura in the South Island is a
small coastal town, where the key tourist attractions are the beach and local
fishing, especially crayfish. In this small town tourism accounts for 30% of
local employment. Their research shows the following five factors affect
local perceptions of tourism in Rotorua and Kaikoura.

- the relative economic importance of tourism;
- the visibility of tourists;
- the actions of the two local councils;
- the sense of control residents felt they had over local tourism development;
- the meaning of tourism in relation to local conditions and history.

They conclude that Rotorua residents view tourism as a source of stability,
supplementing other local economic activities and that they have control
over it, while Kaikoura residents associate tourism with rapid change and
feel they are reacting to change, not directing it.

These community perceptions and various models indicate that while a general pattern of explanatory variables links resident reactions to tourism, we can expect to see local variations and nuances. These local variations are to be expected as local conditions and opportunities vary from place to place. After all, variety and something different are principle tourism motivators! But throughout these studies there is an overwhelming pattern of residents wishing to have more input into local tourism development decisions.

Organising

Butler's model of destination evolution indicates that the early stages of tourism development are likely to be spontaneous responses to the demands of small numbers of inquisitive tourists. As tourist numbers grow, destinations need to develop more formal and commercial relationships to handle increased volumes and benefit from them. This calls for organisation on behalf of the community, as well as for the industry.

McGibbon's (2000) anthropological study of tourism development in the village of St Anton in the Tirolean Alps of Austria demonstrates many of the community issues facing smaller destinations around the world. She considers:

> the development of tourism in St Anton is neither 'a blessing nor a blight', but rather a complex process with diverse and uneven effects. While a few residents have been able to build up small local empires in the context of tourism, others struggle with the pressures of high debts . . . Local struggles focus on how much tourism (development) communities should permit, how the industry should be organised, and the nature of future tourism developments. (McGibbon, 2000: 218)

The organisation and regulation of tourism in St Anton involves the local council (*Gemeinderat*), the local tourist association that is run as a public corporation, where each business pays a 1% turnover tax on its tourism component, and a range of voluntary organisations that contribute to community life and local tourism activities.

Lewis (1998) developed a *Rural Tourism Development Model* as a way of explaining the stages of tourism development that he observed in four small rural communities in the US. Unlike Doxey's causation model, Lewis' model was developed as an organisational process to manage tourism at a slower and more manageable pace. The four stages of Lewis' model and the intervening transitionary stages are listed below.

- **Evolution**: Beginning stage of development; tourism growth is organic; home-grown tourism services and goods are provided; no planning or advertising, resources and word-of-mouth attract visitors.

> Transition No. 1: Beginnings of tourism infrastructure, businesses and organisations

- **Formation**:   Second stage of development; establishment of tourism infrastructure, businesses and organizations; provisional tourism planning.

> Transition No. 2: Beginnings of tourism events, attractions, programmes and marketing

- **Development**:   Third stage of development; establishment of special tourism events and attractions; increased promotion for individual businesses and events as well as the destination; beginning of scheduling conflicts.

> Transition No. 3:   Beginnings of tourist taxes, increased coordination of tourism providers and packaging of destination

- **Centralisation**:   Final stage of development; establishment of Convention and Visitors Committees; implementation of tourist taxes; co-ordinated tourism planning, promotion and advertising at the local, regional and national levels.

Lewis states that the ability of local residents to increase their control over the tourism process is one of the main features that differentiates his model from other models, such as those of Butler (1980) and Doxey (1975). In addition to a strong local desire to keep control of tourism development, perhaps the success that locals have in controlling the impacts of tourism in the rural case study areas of Indiana, used by Lewis, can be attributed also to limited development demands in these areas. One can postulate that the limited appeal of certain areas to tourists also limits the potential profits, and therefore the appeal of these areas to either outside tourism investors, or local entrepreneurs, would be limited. If this is so, Lewis' model holds more promise for rural communities being able to develop tourism at a modest pace, where they can maintain a larger degree of control over the industry.

One tourist destination that has attracted a great deal of interest from both internal and external investors is Australia's Gold Coast. This major coastal resort has been a popular urban destination for many years and has become both a popular international-national destination and retirement area. In the process its residents have seen a tremendous growth in population and the waxing and waning of individual businesses within the general record of tourism growth. Within this context Weaver (2000) has asked whether the stages of stagnation and decline within the Butler model are inevitable or whether some form of regulation and organisation can delay or prevent such deterioration.

Management model

Weaver (2000) proposes that regulation, which includes planning and organisation, can divert the inevitable decline of the Butler destination evolution model. His proposed model consists of four potential outcomes for destination tourism, conditioned by the volume of tourism business and degree of regulation or organisation (Figure 9.2A):

- *Circumstantial Alternative Tourism* (CAT)   This represents a non-regulated, small-scale tourism sector that resembles alternative tourism or early stages of the Butler model.
- *Unsustainable Mass Tourism* (UMT)   This represents the end result of the Butler model, where unchecked development has led to decline as a destination's tourism resources have become overwhelmed in the absence of restrictive regulation and appropriate organisation.
- *Deliberate Alternative Tourism* (DAT)   This outcome occurs when a destination deliberately caps its development at the small-scale development levels of CAT. Weaver provides examples of this happening in a growing number of locations around the world. But it is noticeable they are either located in distant developing countries or are well removed from the urban centres of developed economies, permitting the creation of exclusive up-market nature-based or culture-based attractions. This would support our previous comments regarding the suitability of the Lewis model to smaller and rural communities.
- *Sustainable Mass Tourism* (SMT)   This represents the coexistence of large volumes of visitors and a large-scale tourism sector operating within local carrying capacities and sustainable limits.

Given the acceptance of Butler's model and its predecessor the product lifecycle, some would consider this STM objective to be an oxymoron, an impossibility. But it does not have to be so, for regulation in the form of planning and organising can set parameters and development directions that ensure the two sides of the sustainable development coin can be

A. Destination Possibilities

B. Gold Coast Destination Development Scenarios

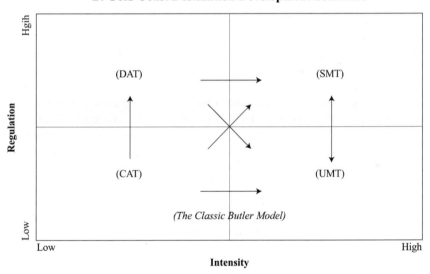

Figure 9.2 Potential influence of regulation and development intensity on destination evolution

Source: Weaver (2000: 218, 219)

achieved. Examples generally involve carefully planned resort destinations like Cancun in Mexico or Disney World in Florida. In the latter a marginal agricultural area was transformed into a global destination through water management, business planning and organisational control: a destination that now attracts millions of visitors to a site that includes a wilderness sanctuary which has restored the central Florida wetlands to something approaching their original state – a sanctuary that is easier to protect because it is in private ownership and thus does not face the public access pressures of national parks.

Weaver applied his model to Australia's Gold Coast resort and reported that all four outcomes were either apparent or emerging due to the size and different circumstances within the region (Figure 9.2B). Along the developed coastline he considers tourism is moving from its UMT to a SMT state due to the move toward more extensive planning and organising and the presence of high threshold sites such as the developed shoreline and beach environment. In comparison, the rural and tropical rain forest areas of the hinterland have smaller numbers of tourists and can be converted from their present CAT situation to a DAT status with the appropriate policy directives.

Moving from the theoretical approach to community organisation of tourism to real-life examples reveals residents are ready and willing to participate in the development of this community industry. Many community responses spring up around a particular issue, which is a feature of neighbourhood organisations. These grassroots groups tend to be spontaneous in their establishment, focus on a single or limited range of issues, are informal in practice, and have relatively short life-spans. More lasting and interactive with the industry are those groups that have been assigned to establish planning and advisory roles by government or the industry. These residents are selected or volunteer as representatives of community interests and participate in local tourism associations and planning as sounding boards. Between the dichotomy of grassroots and government/ industry appointments on local boards, there are a number of organisations that combine the features of both.

Examples of communities responding in an *ad-hoc* organisational style to tourism can be drawn from the sudden and unexpected influx of tourists when their location has been selected as the site for a popular television or film location. As Beeton (2000: 129) reports:

> An influx of visitors is not always welcome or advantageous, with many town unsuited to supporting the concomitant (film-induced) tourism growth because of limited infrastructure, facilities and services. In most cases the local community did not seek to be the site for the filming, yet they are left to cope with the consequences of increased traffic, crowding and pollution.

This situation has been experienced around the world, but especially in those small rural communities that exemplify the tranquil scenic atmosphere that some films and television programmes are trying to relate in their stories. Examples include the *Ballykissangel* television series based on the village of Avoca in Ireland (O'Connor & Flanagan, 2002) as illustrated in Figure 9.3; the English series *Heartbeat* based on the town of Goathland (Demetriadi, 1996); the Hollywood film *Roxanne* shot on location in Fort Nelson, British Columbia, Canada; and the television series *Sea Change* based on the fishing village of Barwon Heads in southern Australia (Beeton, 2000).

In Victoria, Canada, where a coal baron's 'castle' located in a prime residential area became a tourist attraction, because of its architectural and heritage appeal, tensions rose between its new commercial users and its residential neighbours. Local residents banded together around their concerns over the manner and magnitude of tourism development in their neighbourhood. These residents collectively opposed the development of bus-coach access and parking on its grounds because of the increased noise, pollution and perceived danger to local inhabitants, especially children and the elderly. So now coach tourists have to disembark a few blocks away on a major street and walk the remainder of the way to the castle. The residents surrounding the castle have no objection to walking tourists, because that style of visitation fits in with a quiet residential neighbourhood. They are also prepared to live with the increased car traffic associated with the castle and its FIT market. It is the intrusion and perceived danger of bus-coaches that caused the neighbourhood to protest and pressure city hall.

In Melbourne, Australia, an example of grassroots residential advocacy arose with the introduction of the Formula One Grand Prix. This international event with global television coverage was a coup for this event-oriented city and tourist destination, but its establishment in a public park within a wealthy suburb drew a great deal of opposition. The Albert Park Action Group was formed as a reaction to the anticipated negative impacts in terms of noise, safety, interruption of daily activities and a general threat to the overall quality of life. The actions of this group, which included large-scale protests and civil disobedience, received extensive media coverage. Although the group was able to persuade the state government to make some minor changes to their policies relating to the event and venue, they felt they were prevented from having a meaningful say in the running of this annual event. The state government passed special legislation – the F1 Act – that gave extra powers to the government and Grand Prix promoters to proceed with the event while curtailing opportunities for the public to prevent or otherwise impair the abilities for the mega-event to proceed as planned.

The more formal organising of resident input into tourism development

Figure 9.3 'Ballykissangel' image for the village of Avoca

has occurred mainly in established tourism destinations. An example of this is the Florida Keys, where residents have a formal role as advisers to district branches of the Tourism Development Council, an umbrella organisation that advises elected officials and markets the Keys as a destination from a bed tax funding source. Residents can also express their tourism views by contributing to the Comprehensive Plans that guide development in the Keys. They do this by voting for elected officials based on public stances on tourism development issues and attending public meetings to influence the creation and implementation of tourism-related policies and actions. Despite these established processes many residents felt their views were not being heard and were taking an increasingly pessimistic view towards tourists and tourism.

The Tourism Development Council (TDC) and the Board of County Commissioners (BOCC) – two organisations with a keen interest in tourism in the Keys – decided they needed to have a better understanding of residents' views on tourism so that they could incorporate these into their plans and policies (see case study at the end of Chapter 10). Their survey results indicated that the residents were at odds with the tourism industry and the organisations in place to guide its development on a range of important issues. Particular concerns were that they did not have enough of a direct say over tourism management and the allocations and priorities for spending tourism-generated funds. In response to the survey results and the public's views expressed at associated meetings, inclusive tourism planning was given a higher priority and more tourist dollars have been redirected to public works and infrastructure (Monroe County, Florida, 1999). More information on this example is provided in the case study at the end of this part of the book, pp. 328–335.

Leadership

A number of factors can impact on whether or not leaders in tourism development will emerge from communities. Community leaders can certainly stand out in all sorts of communities, as the earlier examples in this book of Tom O'Toole in Beechworth, Australia and Paul Miller, in Victoria, Canada, have shown. Community cohesion can encourage the formation of staunch support bases from which leaders can draw strength and resources. Governments also play an important role in creating environments that either encourage or stifle innovations, and encouraging the leaders responsible for the conceptions and spread of these innovations.

Leadership and resident relationships can be complex and multifunctional in nature, because while many leaders are also residents their success depends on the response from other residents including those who hold important local government roles. To simplify this natural mix of motives and behaviours we have focused on the individual business and government leaders as being a proactive force within the community. Local residents, with their own priorities and interests, are viewed largely as reactive agents to innovation. Local government is treated as an interpreter and facilitator, helping residents and voters appreciate the broader community implications and opportunities. However, it should be appreciated that individual roles and behaviours will not necessarily follow these artificially imposed categorisations.

Motivation

The motivation for taking on a leadership role tends to come from personal and community interests. These motivating factors can include beliefs, values, interests, abilities, resources, support, and relationships. However, Madrigal (1995: 87) points out that those motivations for taking on a leadership role in community politics can be far from altruistic.

> The political organisation of many communities is often dominated by individuals benefiting either directly from a specific development alternative (property owners, investors, speculators) or indirectly as a result of overall growth (realtors, bankers, owners of industries servicing the direct beneficiaries).

Although personal self-interest, either direct or indirect, may explain motivation as the driving force for many leaders, interest in a 'greater good' with respect to improving the community can also be a strong motivator. Furthermore, once leaders have started a crusade around a narrowly defined set of interests, they often grow to understand and advocate for a wider range of interests. Bono has used his rock star status as lead singer for the group U2 to advocate for a growing number of humanitarian issues. Bono's dedication to human rights has expanded from giving benefit concerts to meeting with top ranking political, religious and business representatives as he advocates for debt relief (Tyrangiel & Nugent, 2002). Government interest in addressing the issue of global debt relief created the opening needed to convert the dedication that individuals were showing to this cause by developing the policies necessary to put these ideas into action.

Many tourism leaders, who started out by promoting their enterprise, similarly go on to promote the destination and finally align themselves with quality of life issues for their communities. These community ambitions can be more easily realised if they are aligned with the aspirations that local governments have for their communities. In Bali, several of the top local surfers during the 1970s and who are now successful businessmen, have followed this pattern. While they initially focused on promoting their surfing businesses in the early 1980s, they went on to promote Bali as a destination and are now heavily involved in environmental issues aimed at preserving the spectacular natural resources of their island home (Australian Broadcasting Corporation, 2002).

Resident response

Community size can be a factor in how people respond to tourism and the ability for leaders to direct tourism's development. Mason and Cheyne (2000) studied residents' views regarding a cafe/bar development for use by tourists and locals in a small New Zealand village with minimal tourist visitations. They found that residents were concerned over the potential impacts of the bar/cafe on their community, even though they supported the development and 58% stated they would use it. This research confirms earlier findings that small communities are likely to express more concern over tourism developments and that the high visibility of such developments leads to heightened concerns (Capenerhurst, 1994).

Tourism leaders promoting public participation in tourism planning in small communities need to be aware of the challenges and opportunities such communities present. Small communities, such as rural areas or neighbourhoods within cities, tend to lack sufficient specialists or retired locals who can be identified as relevant stakeholders and active volunteers for community planning projects. However, even when communities are small a wide range of differing attitudes can be expressed regarding tourism developments (Allen *et al*,. 1988, Perdue *et al.*, 1990). Therefore, tourism leaders need to anticipate and respond appropriately to a range of opinions and values that exist even in small communities which in many other respects appear quite cohesive. Furthermore, a lack of adequate resources, especially funds, expertise, legislation and experience can make it harder for leaders in small communities to put into practice their ideas for change. This forces some to do a great number of additional tasks themselves, as well as bringing in necessary resources from outside the community. Community members' preference for local control may outweigh some or all of the benefits of outsourcing, which can hinder tourism leaders' options for developing and otherwise changing destinations.

The attitudes of elected representatives towards economic development, quality of life issues and tourism's desired role in their communities can make a big difference in how tourism develops and how the residents participate in its development. Elected officials and the government structures that support them often 'take the lead' in tourism development, in that their decisions create the legislative and functional context for tourism growth and controls. Richins (1997/98) assessed elected officials' attitudes towards various tourism development scenarios as a way to understand the direction in which they would lead tourism development in their communities. In Richins' study, 789 local government councillors in Queensland and New South Wales, Australia, were presented with 10 characteristics to describe a range of potential development scenarios. These are shown in Figure 9.4, and the councillors were asked to rate the scenarios in terms of what they would choose.

The councillors were then presented with the following five potential

Range of characteristics of various scenarios

Characteristic category for comparison

Expansionist extreme	↔	Contractionist extreme

---

1. Encouragement of tourism development – *Level of encouragement and development rate expected*

Maximum development encouragement and very high rate expected	↔	Minimal development encouragement and low or reduced rate expected

2. Restrictions on tourism development – *Level and enforcement of barriers and restrictions*

Little or no barriers and restrictions nor enforcement	↔	Comprehensive controls/restrictions which are strenuously enforced

3. Orientation of tourism development – *Focus regarding residential vs. tourism development*

Peripheral residential with substantial tourism and shopping development	↔	Residential orientation to the community with minimal tourism development

4. Degree and source of development – *Scale of tourism development and origin of investors*

Large-scale tourism development with multi-national investors	↔	Small scale, if any development with only local investors

5. Impact motivation for decision-making – *Economic, socio-cultural, environmental motivation*

Economic motivation in decision-making	↔	Sociocultural and environmental motivation

6. Growth of population – *Visitor population vs. residential growth rate*

Very high visitor population growth rate compared to residential	↔	Decreased visitor growth rate, moderate–low residential growth rate

7. Promotion of tourism from local government/community – *Encouragement level and funds available*

Very high visitor population growth rate compared to residential	↔	Decreased visitor growth rate, moderate–low residential growth rate

8. Visitor target market encouraged – *International, capital city, regional, local*

International and capital city visitor market	↔	Visitors not encouraged, but may have some local/regional and VFRs

9. Visitor facilities encouraged – *Priority of accommodation, attractions, activities encouraged*

Higher end accommodation, attractions activities encouraged	↔	Visitors not encouraged, but may have some local/regional and VFRs

10. Council priority regarding provision of services and facilities – *Visitor or resident focus of Council*

Primary visitor focus with lower resident priority	↔	Local residents as priority, visitors low priority

Figure 9.4 Continuum of tourism development in communities

Source: Richins (1997/98: 32)

development scenarios based on the continuum characteristics of Figure 9.4, and their associated political platforms (Richins, 1997/98).

- Expansionist   'Develop at any cost'
- Tempered Expansionist   'Develop but control it'
- Moderationist   'Be cautious regarding development'
- Preservationist   'Keep things as they are within the community'
- Contractionist   'Reduce development in the community'

The most desired scenario was that of the moderationist, followed by preservationist and tempered expansionist. These results indicated that many elected officials might be predisposed to be cautious in regards to supporting tourism development. It is important to note that the moderationist approach to tourism can also be a strong reflection of the middle-of-the road or centrist approach; whereby politicians opt for the safety of satisfying as many voters as possible by pursuing policies that offend as few people as possible. The obvious drawback of such a guarded approach is that rather than leading their constituents forward with development and conservation options, a moderationist approach can result in conventional, lack-lustre policies that fail to achieve remarkable results. As noted by Richins, the community tourism scenarios could serve as an excellent way to gauge political support for tourism development. Once the positions that elected officials take on tourism development are better understood, then stakeholder groups are in a better position to more effectively lobby their elected representatives on tourism issues. Therefore, once a community better understands its elected leaders' views of tourism, its non-elected leaders can more efficiently prepare their own tourism strategies.

On a larger scale, Honolulu in Hawaii, USA has benefited from the actions and ideas of a number of notable leaders. A recent example of a leader at this level is Jeremy Harris, who is currently the Mayor of the City and County of Honolulu and previously served as its managing director (City and County of Honolulu, 2002). The mayor was awarded the American Planning Associations' 2002 award for distinguished leadership by an elected public official in recognition of his substantial contributions to planning (APA, 2002). His notable achievements included the '21st Century Oahu: A Shared Vision for the Future'. This community based planning initiative involved thousands of members of the general public and stakeholder representatives in determining quality of life issues in a tourism dependent community. The mayor has devoted US$38 million in capital improvement funds to support this initiative, helping ensure that residents' ambitions for their communities are realised (APA, 2002: 17).

Tourism leaders promoting tourism development in large communities also need to be aware of the challenges and opportunities such communities present. Large communities, such as major cities or regional growth cores, tend to have sizeable populations in which a variety of stakeholder groups and other members of the public may exist and need to be included in community planning initiatives. Tourism leaders need to anticipate and respond appropriately to the wide range of opinions and values that exist in large and often disjointed communities, where people can be separated not only by socio-demographic, attitudinal and behavioural factors, but also by great distances. In large communities people can be isolated from other community members to such an extent that they may feel they have little if anything in common. Larger communities often, but not always, tend to have extensive resources in terms of funds, expertise, legislation and experience that tourism leaders can draw on when pursuing their goals. While these resources may be more plentiful in large communities, tourism leaders may find the competition with other community members for these resources is so fierce that a significant portion of their time is devoted to differentiating their proposals from other resource competitors.

Controlling

Understanding the range of tourism impacts requires careful analysis because of the many interrelationships and dimensions involved. To manage those impacts effectively, so the negative factors are ameliorated and the benefits are enhanced, requires community willpower and consensus. One advantage for tourism in this regard is that most people have been tourists at one time or another so they have first-hand experience with the industry, but associated with that is a mistaken belief that they know all about the industry. So to examine residents' participation in the control of tourism we start with an examination of their knowledge and education, before turning to questions regarding their involvement and authority.

Education

One of the key ingredients to enhancing resident input into the control over local tourism is to improve their knowledge of the industry through education. A knowledgeable resident will be in a far better position to understand the nuances of the industry and the necessary trade-offs that will need to take place if this industry is to complement other activities and contribute to the general quality of life. But few residents can develop such knowledge without some form of education and this is one area where tourism, an industry built on information and marketing, has so often fallen short. What business refers to as 'internal marketing', informing an organisation's employees what is happening and why, becomes essential when you are selling community resources and depending on local goodwill. Yet evidence of such internal marketing in community tourism is sparse.

Many studies show that with increased understanding of the tourism industry, residents demonstrate increased levels of support for the industry. However, opportunities to educate residents can digress into efforts to 'sell' residents on tourism development that does not meet their needs. Residents have expressed concern that the tourism information made available to them is often insufficient. They tend to question the sources of the pro-tourism educational information. Since this information usually comes from groups with a blatant tourism bias, such as local tourism marketing and promotional bodies, the reasons for their concern are understandable. Residents also have concerns about the depth and relevance of the data they receive in terms of understanding what the typical expenditure patterns of tourists are and how much they contribute in taxes and job creation compared to the costs incurred while servicing their needs. Simmons (1994: 103) found residents were unimpressed with the tourism information provided to them, as one-third rated it as either 'poor' or 'very poor'. These residents also ranked tourism, marketing and promotion as the lowest rated information source, indicating their dissatisfaction with the industry's ability to provide them with the information they wanted.

Psychology and experience tells us how we are more likely to take in and respond to messages in a positive manner if they are in keeping with our world view. Depending on how far removed pro-tourism messages are from a resident's perception of the industry, these messages will either be cynically received or rejected. Messages that are dramatically different from a person's existing beliefs can even cause a shift in attitude that is opposite to what was intended (Eagly & Chiken, cited in Lindberg & Johnson, 1997). If a tourism message presented to residents is seen to be a lie, then angered residents might become less hospitable to tourists and can turn on the industry. Tourism insiders and those with anti-tourism feelings will be more resistant to messages that overstate the benefits of tourism.

In their review of ways to increase the effectiveness of educating residents on tourism impacts, Lindberg and Johnson (1997) put forward several suggestions that are summarised below.

- Balanced: The message needs the right balance of scale (the attitude continuum from highly negative to highly positive) and weight (impact on residents' attitudes).

- Clear and unencumbered: The message needs to be easily understandable, succinct and disentangled from other issues. Linking tourism with a decline in other industries in the message can carry the impression that tourism is the cause of such declines.
- Fit 'world view':   The message needs to be in keeping with the world view of the community. If there is already a widely held negative perception of tourism then a message needs to address these concerns.
- Credible source: The message will be more readily accepted if it comes from a source that is either already trusted, or is seen to be impartial. In many cases an assessment from an outside source, such as a university, will be seen as less biased.

Destinations should not shy away from painting a realistic picture of tourism impacts to residents in their educational efforts. While the tourism industry may hope to minimise information on tourism's negative impacts, these impacts are generally well known (King *et al.*, cited in Lindberg & Johnson, 1997). In his article on tourism decision-making groups Murphy (1991a: 12) suggested that:

> ... an annual independent audit of the taxes paid and people employed by the tourism industry, published locally, would demonstrate to the public the industry's contribution to the local economy.

Knowing who pays for tourism research and analysis and who will be privy to the results can have a large impact on how well such information is received. Ideally such research should be funded and directed by more than just pro-tourism factions. If such partnerships are not possible then a great deal of transparency and impartiality needs to be demonstrated throughout the process. Part of this transparency should include providing reports that clearly layout in data tables, charts and graphs the numerous impacts of tourism. Providing stakeholder groups with complicated and unsorted data is as unacceptable as only providing them with one page 'good-news' fact sheets that try to make tourism seem as shiny as the glossy paper they are printed on. Only when governments, industry and businesses speak to residents in a language that they understand and in a manner that is convincing will their tourism educational messages achieve their desired effects.

Involvement

The potential for investing tourism dollars in initiatives that are roundly supported by the community can be realised only if the public has an opportunity to participate in tourism planning and management. Public participation in deciding tourism matters needs to involve the following (adapted from Sewell & Phillips, cited in Simmons, 1994):

(1) Decision-maker support.
(2) Extensive citizen involvement.
(3) Equity in participation.
(4) Efficiency in participation.
(5) Implementable results.

It is important to realise that a measure of flexibility is required when following these guidelines. Depending on decision maker support (factor 1), which can relate to available budget, time, professional assistance or delegated power, certain trade-offs between factors 2 to 4 will be necessary. Therefore, in the interests of hearing and then incorporating a wide range of opinions on a matter (factor 3), the efficiency of the process (factor 4) would likely be impaired. In practice public participation in tourism planning tends to include one or more of the following techniques: public meetings, special committees, workshops, interviews, surveys and focus group discussions.

Simmons (1994) utilised informal interviews, a postal survey and focus groups to create and evaluate a public participation programme for an area that had not undergone extensive tourism development – Huron County, Ontario. Simmons was interested in determining the extent to which integrating field and survey methods would help with understanding tourism planning issues and improve the validity of collected data. He found that this combined approach identified key issues and objectives (through the interviews), provided hard data to access broad public sentiment about the issues and objectives (through the surveys) and then enabled citizens to develop appropriate strategies to guide tourism development (through the focus groups). The outcome of the public participation initiative in the case study area was a commitment by the county to develop advisory committees to allow for further public input into tourism planning. The success of the overall process builds upon the outputs of each of the three steps. Simmons notes that 'meaningful participation' in tourism planning will be dependent on residents' abilities to contribute to the process as well as their perceptions of influence over final and related decisions. The abilities of residents to contribute in a meaningful manner to tourism planning are determined by their own commitment to the process as well as the support, guidance, resources and data that are made available to them.

Lankford and Howard (1994) developed a multiple item tourism impact attitude scale as a way of providing a standardised measure of residents' attitudes towards tourism and assessing the effects of independent variables on these attitudes. Using multiple regressions they found that the 'ability to influence tourism decision making' had the most significant impact on the category of 'perceived personal and community benefits of tourism' compared to the other independent variables presented in the analysis. They found their results supported earlier studies that demonstrated a strong connection between positive attitudes towards tourism and the residents' perceived abilities to participate in the tourism decision-making process. Lankford and Howard (1994: 135) go on to provide the following advice:

> If people feel they (a) have access to the planning/public review process *and* (b) that their concerns are being considered, they are inclined to support tourism. Local governments and tourism promoters should pay particular attention to these pre-conditions for public support.

One of the most visible and enduring impacts of tourism can be increased public investment in amenities like parks, museums, promenades and piazzas. The public's support of such investment can again be linked to the social exchange theory, in that if residents see a personal or community net gain from such investment they are more likely to support them. Many resident surveys show that the public is aware of the improvements to the appearance and functioning of their town that tourism can bring (Brunt & Courtney, 1999; Oakes, 1997). Thus, their support of the industry and its tax contribution can enable a community to enhance its infrastructure and amenity base.

Just as having guests over to your house can motivate you to make your house look its best, tourists can motivate communities to 'look and act their best'. In the Brunt and Courtney (1999) study, the influx of visitors is seen to help justify investments in the town centre of an old seaside resort, and overall tourism development is supported. Many resident surveys have shown support for new developments that will be used by locals and residents. Lindberg and Johnson (1997) found that while residents rank the economic benefits of tourism most highly, those that increase the number and variety of local facilities are also valued. Perdue *et al.* (1990: 597) found that more residents support the statement 'tourism development increases the number of recreational opportunities for local residents', than the statement 'tourism reduces the quality of outdoor recreation'.

The research of Mason and Cheyne (2000) confirms earlier findings that small communities are more likely to express concerns over tourism developments and that the high visibility of such developments leads to heightened concerns. Many residents prefer small-scale tourism developments (Prentice, 1993; Ritchie, 1988). Such residents are less likely to support sport stadiums and conference centres, even if these facilities would be used by locals and residents. Limited financial resources and concerns over rapid change generally encourage smaller and less intrusive investments. Simmons (1994: 104) found in his focus group discussions with rural residents in New Zealand that preferences for small and medium scale developments are linked to residents' 'fear of "loss of control" over their rural way of life, visual landscape and environment'.

Tourism-generated funds should be invested in community amenity enhancements that benefit tourists and residents. However, when tourist dollars are to be spent 'for the good of the public', it is essential that the public be consulted on how and where they want these funds spent. If such consultation is lacking then statements that tourism dollars are being spent to better the community can produce results that are disappointing to the community. Community consultation needs to reach as wide a range of stakeholders as possible to ensure that tourism's investments in a community are effective in meeting broadly supported community goals. Murphy (1983a) found in one study that a major point of contention between different stakeholder groups is facility development, with business representatives enthusiastically supporting additional leisure facilities, while other groups are more sceptical of such developments. To address divided opinions on appropriate tourism investments intended to benefit residents Murphy (1991a: 12) suggests that: '. . . facilities requiring public funds become truly multipurpose, designed and operated for local residents as well as visitors'.

A good example of this is the Royal British Columbia Museum's 'Futures Project', where widespread consultation revealed 'we needed to become more accessible, relevant and responsive to our public' (Barkley, 1997: 154), the public being both the residents of Victoria, the province of British Columbia, and the tourist industry, because the provincial museum is one of Victoria, BC's major attractions.

Power

To provide all residents a chance to control the development of tourism within their community requires an open system that permits real and effective participation. Some would consider this as either idealistic or impractical, but there is plenty of evidence to suggest it is feasible when there is trust and collaboration on all sides. In democratic societies it is not idealistic when all residents have the vote and exercise their rights freely. It is not impractical because experience has shown it is only a few opinion leaders who have the conviction and patience to become involved.

When residents believe they have the ability to personally influence tourism impacts in their area they are likely to have much more positive views of tourism than if they feel their views are not heard (Madrigal, cited in Lindberg & Johnson, 1997). More favourable attitudes towards tourism have been closely linked with high levels of community members' perceived control over tourism planning and development (Lankford & Howard, 1994). Low levels of perceived resident control of tourism have been linked to negative attitudes towards tourism, tourists' dissatisfaction with their vacation experience and the eventual decline of tourist destinations (Hernandez *et al.*, 1996; Potts & Harrill, 1998). Host communities often express strong preferences for local ownership (Simmons, 1994). A factor in this support can be that local residents feel they can understand and trust local people and their ideas to a greater extent than 'foreign people and ideas'. Local ownership can enable residents to keep tourism development in check with their priorities and set within a familiar context.

The abilities of destinations to control tourism development vary according to a range of factors noted by France (1998) who depicts the levels of public participation in tourism in the West Indies islands utilising Pretty's earlier model. The West Indies model of participation in tourism starts with the low level involvement of residents during the plantation era and progresses on to higher levels of local control demonstrated in the 'self-mobilisation' era. During the earlier stages the money earning tourism ventures are owned and controlled by individuals and companies with ties to traditional elites and overseas capital. The purpose of these ventures is to provide profits for the owners and little consideration is given to the impacts of these ventures on the local community or the means by which they could contribute beyond menial labour. As tourism ventures expand and endeavour to secure loans and other forms of financial backing the opportunities for public participation tend to increase.

The roles of local/residents builds slowly as the tourism industry expands, in that increasingly locals are asked to contribute ideas, resources and a wider range of services to the tourism sector (France, 1998). It is only in the final two stages of France's seven stage model that the public are seen to exercise real control over tourism development in terms of guiding planning, being in control of local decisions and being able to proceed successfully with independent initiatives. The author notes that the control local residents are able to demonstrate in the final stages of this model are tied strongly to their improved economic situation, stating that 'local people who have amassed capital from tourism strengthen and extend their activities and also use this capital to move into a wider range of economic activities' (France, 1998: 225). One can also extrapolate from this model that the locals' increased sophistication in dealing with tourism, coupled with their increased personal and community income, contributes greatly to their empowered position.

Summary

This chapter outlines the role of residents in community tourism. The chapter opens with an overview of residents' needs and ways of measuring these needs as a means of guiding tourism plans. Close attention is paid to the Irridex model and its relevance to resident perceptions and reactions to tourism in their communities; different types and functions of resident groups are reviewed in the organising component of the chapter; the value of community involvement in tourism planning initiatives and ensuring that tourism expenditures benefit visitors and locals are a focus of the leadership component; and finally, the control component looks at the scope and scale of tourist–resident benefits.

Residents bring life, vitality, history and services to their communities. Tourists are attracted to the types of places where residents want to live – areas that are beautiful, vibrant, prosperous, well serviced by infrastructure, accessible and shine as something special. Residents can have great enthusiasm, ideas and in many cases reservations about tourism development; however, without a proper conduit they can find that their contributions are largely ignored, or marginalised. The following chapter explores the roles that governments serve in creating mechanisms to realise the ambitions of their constituents. The growing importance of non-government agencies in providing a voice and a means by which community groups can share their views and help shape their communities are also explored throughout the next chapter.

Chapter 10

Government

Government involvement in tourism takes place to varying degrees at different levels as per a government's scope of powers, commitment to tourism management and available resources. Government involvement in tourism can include local councils, regional government, state, national and international bodies. Aboriginal government involvement in tourism also ranges from the local through to the international level and can help to reorientate the way Aboriginal and non-Aboriginal people regard and interact with tourism destinations. All levels of government in tourism typically focus on the economic aspects of tourism, with a strong focus on tourism promotion. Priorities for the types, locations and the magnitude of public sector financial support of tourism developments are established through a range of government policies; and this chapter will focus on the situation in countries with developed economies and democratic institutions.

Governments aim to serve the people they represent in a just and effective manner. A government's ability to make and enforce laws, including those relating to land uses and taxation, can enable it to wield great influence over tourism developments and subsequent management. In democratic societies government's extensive powers tend to be held in check by the 'separation of powers' approach to governing. This approach reserves law making authority for the executive, while the legislature administers these laws and the judiciary interprets them (Beazer, 1998). While democratic systems of government are primarily accountable to their constituents, their actions are directed largely by commitments made to other entities as well as regulations and requirements from other levels, or types of governments. Therefore, while a community might call on its local and state governments to invest in a tourism attraction, such as setting aside land for a new park, the local government might not be able to afford having this area taken off its tax rolls and paying for maintenance. Other factors that could work against a park designation could include state government commitments to other uses, or federal environmental regulations that severely limit the development of essential infrastructure, such as roads, necessary to open up the area's tourism potential. These various and sometimes conflicting commitments can make it difficult for governments to make the 'right' decisions in terms of deciding how and to what extent they will support and regulate tourism.

Tourism's complexities and heterogeneous nature challenge elected officials and policy makers alike, as they struggle to understand and manage the industry. Most countries in the world recognise tourism as a way to diversify their economies and create corresponding tourism programmes and strategies to support the industry. Tourism can provide a multitude of economic benefits for governments, including attracting outside investors, creating jobs and earning foreign currency to help with a country's trade balance. As a service industry tourism has become a principal source of employment and tax revenue. Governments also benefit when tourism enhances an area's international, national and regional reputation, which in turn can attract additional investment while fostering a sense of pride of place, culture and history among their citizenry.

Typical tourism challenges that governments face include determining the appropriate physical areas for tourism development, the types of tourism products and services that they will support, the level of funding for these tourism initiatives and how to integrate them with other government priorities. Since tourism is a relatively new industry and one that is dominated by small businesses, it can be especially difficult for governments to predict the potential impacts of their tourism efforts.

An underlying factor in the long-term success of tourism in any destination is the perceived legitimacy of the industry by the general public, which is related to its overall costs and benefits and the extent to which they are distributed. Another factor of legitimacy that governments must address is whether or not their investments in tourism and other industries are perceived to be in the best interests of the community. Governments can control tourists directly by limiting who is allowed to travel and where they are allowed to travel. Governments can also limit lengths of stay for tourists and the types of uses and visitation numbers to specified areas through visa controls and other associated measures.

This chapter outlines the pivotal role that governments play as facilitators in creating situations that are either conducive or inauspicious for tourism. The planning component of the chapter examines the roles of different levels of government, including Aboriginal groups, in tourism developments. The change in orientation of governments as they move from a welfare or social responsibility approach to take on more of an entrepreneurial or business approach is also discussed in detail. The organising component of the chapter looks at tourism infrastructure and financing. The issue of financing is discussed at length with particular regard given to raising funds to support tourism-related expenditures and ways to realise revenue from tourists and the tourism industry. The leadership component of the chapter focuses on how governments are re-evaluating and transforming their roles as 'leaders' as they embark on a number of different approaches in their efforts to fulfil their mandates. The increasing leadership shown by non-government organisations (NGOs) in terms of delivering community services and watching out for the interests of stakeholder groups is also discussed. The control component of the chapter focuses on how government actions shape community growth and development through legislation, policies and politics. The courts in turn play an important role in interpreting the tourism-related laws created by government and ensuring that the intent and purpose of such laws are upheld.

Objectives

In order for governments to act in the best interest of the people they serve they need to meet several prime objectives, the first of which is to identify and appropriately respond to the potential that tourism has for meeting stakeholder requirements. Governments need to be aware of their legal obligations when considering what these groups want and how these things can be provided to them. For example, there are often restrictions on what revenues from 'tourist taxes', such as bed taxes, can be spent on, which in turn limits governments' options for financing tourism proposals. Another objective for governments is to create a balanced approach to the development of resources and provision of services and other deliverables to their communities. This involves going beyond the 'highest and best use' criteria based on short-term economic return, such as zoning land for high density commercial uses, to look at potential social, environmental and 'spin-off economic returns'. This can occur when devoting land to passive recreation increases the property values and subsequent taxes for surrounding properties. Governments need to be cognisant of stakeholder priorities and resources to find the right balance, given that complex negotiations and detailed problem solving can be required to satisfy the demands of their constituents and the other stakeholders. Such a balance needs to be considered when deciding on allocating resources to worthy tourism proposals, while honouring existing financial commitments.

An additional objective of government is to ensure that a balanced approach is actually implemented and maintained. While investing in discretionary developments, such as conference centres, can bring many benefits to communities, there are many other essential services, such as education, that must be adequately resourced. Governments need to find the right mix between investing in projects that have the potential to stimulate further economic development and community enhancement, while ensuring that they devote enough resources to provide the core services upon which both residents and tourists depend.

Policy needs to be guided by information so an important objective of any government should be to gather the best intelligence possible about the tourism industry. To use an accounting dictum, something 'never measured is never managed'. Therefore, there has been more effort put into obtaining more tourism data, either directly through primary research or indirectly through satellite accounts. There is great potential for more efficient and economical information gathering through partnering. For example, Canada, Mexico and the US have funded a series of reports on the characteristics of potential overseas travel from specific travel markets around the world (Coopers & Lybrand Consulting, 1995, 1996). The highly detailed data bases created from this research were then made available to major universities from these countries, which allowed for even more refined information searches, such as looking at the characteristics of potential Japanese and German travellers to rural destinations in Canada (Murphy & Williams, 1999).

Finding the right balance between investing in tourism and adequately addressing other government commitments and priorities requires integrity, expertise and information. The use of triple bottom line assessments where the environmental, social and economic impacts of proposals are all considered is an important starting point for finding this balance. The potential impacts of tourism options must be effectively appraised and audited so that the appropriate community balance for tourism can be achieved. The effectiveness of such assessment will be dependent largely on the following factors:

- political context (time, money and support for the processes);
- who conducts these assessments (in-house, or impartial outside observers);
- assessment criteria (most important factors and their weighting);
- feedback loop (necessary adjustments need to be highlighted and then implemented).

Government priorities and their corresponding regulations and policies impact greatly on the success of tourism industries at different locations. Establishing community tourism goals and objectives can be an emotionally charged and openly challenged act. In many ways the final decisions on tourism planning are political decisions.

Planning

Tourism depends heavily on scarce and finite physical resources, ranging from pristine and uncrowded wildernesses to primate cities with the world's best cultural and sporting attractions. Such exceptional places represent an inherently unequal distribution of resources and keeping these places exceptional is a result of largely political decisions. These decisions are political in that governments consistently favour particular stakeholder interests over those of other groups when making decisions in the 'public's interests'. Huffman (1994) notes that competing groups, such as environmentalists and land developers, will often claim that they are acting in the best interests of the public as they assert their views. Environmentalists' desire for a healthy environment that is preserved for the world's inhabitants belies the fact that it is primarily the world's elites who have the resources to visit environmental reserves and partake in ecotourism activities. At the same time the desire of developers to ensure that a strong and diversified economy is maintained must also be seen in the context of the personal financial risks and gains facing individuals associated with such developments.

If governments shared their tourism resources equally among all their constituent groups and areas, they could effectively water-down the attractiveness of any single location and the tourist drawing potential of their overall area since the nexus of a 'must see destination' would be lost. Governments select certain areas where they will concentrate their tourism activities and which public interests they will favour over others. Around the world we see governments strongly market and invest in their main cities as destinations and gateways for tourists, who are subsequently encouraged to explore beyond those centres and enjoy regional areas.

The attempts of governments to attract and then dispense visitors can be seen in operation globally. In Australia, Victoria is an example of how a state government focuses on its main city, Melbourne, to draw people in and once they have arrived tries to tempt them to take short trips out into regional areas (Tourism Victoria, 2002: 30–1). Regional areas in Victoria, Australia still have reason to be concerned about their secondary tourism status, especially given that many of their targeted 'hero' destinations (primary regional tourist areas) identified in the strategic plan are only a few hours drive from Melbourne.

Making large cities the base for rural tourism excursions does not necessarily encourage the types of extended or overnight stays, which bring in the maximum financial returns. However, in some cases there are insufficient attractions to hold tourists overnight and the hero strategy provides a start in raising the profile of local tourism. Likewise, the international icon of London, England, is very successful at drawing international visitors but less so in dispensing them to the tourist attractions of its suburbs or home counties (Murphy, 1982). Victoria, as the capital city of British Columbia in Canada, dominates the tourist market of Vancouver Island and continues to do so despite marketing and transport developments to facilitate its growth elsewhere on the island (Keller & Murphy, 1990). In China, the tourism dominance of its coastal provinces is encouraging the central government to select certain inland growth centres to encourage more international visitors to explore its eastern and highland provinces (Zhang, 2001).

Government roles are largely shaped by the level at which they occur. These levels can be divided into the following categories:

- national;
- state;
- regional/local.

As the impacts, both positive and negative of tourism, become better understood and the competition for tourists increases, so too many governments are creating tourism strategies and plans to direct the manner and direction of tourism growth in their communities. Different levels of government have different levels of resources as well as different primary goals and objectives, all of which impact on their tourism regulations and spending. At the various government levels tourism planning policies address issues of product development, security and protection of natural, historic and cultural resources along with tourism marketing, promotion and related economic incentives.

National

While tourism is being integrated increasingly into national policies (Edgell, 1993, cited in Butler, 1999; Gunn, 1997), the main focus in many of these policies is marketing, as opposed to tourism education and product development. In the United States the *National Tourism Policy Act (1981)* built upon the *US International Travel Act (1961),* and promoted increased visitation as well as reducing barriers to tourism and increasing awareness of the tourism industry. The *United States Travel and Tourism Administration* (USTTA) was established under the 1981 Act to take on the role of a national office for tourism. The USTTA's established policies were to promote travel to and within the US and reduce the country's travel deficit. The USTTA was replaced by *US National Tourism Organisation* (USNTO) in 1996 which had a much more restrained mission, focusing on international promotion and budget matters (Goeldner *et al.,* 2000). The United States also has a *Tourism Industries Office,* a *Tourism Policy Council* and a *Rural Tourism Development Foundation* that are responsible for creating and implementing plans that will increase travel and tourism revenues by attracting foreign markets (US Code, 2001a,b). The chaotic aftermath of September 11 promoted a flurry of new bills, such as the *Travel America Act (2001)* that provides tax and other travel incentives to support the travel and tourism industry (US Senate, 2001). In light of the lack of consistent, adequately funded tourism management guidance at the national level, Goeldner *et al.* (2000: 109) consider 'the United States (policy making) is an example of how not to develop tourism'.

There are some better examples of national tourism management from the UK and Australia. The English Tourism Council (ETC) is committed to partnering with industry and other stakeholders in implementing *Tomorrow's Tourism*, a comprehensive document that provides 'leadership and direction to England's fragmented tourism industry in the implementation of the government's strategy' (ETC, 2002: 1). The national *Tomorrow's Tourism* strategy aims to exceed a 12% growth rate for British tourism by the end of 2010 (Tourism Forum [UK], ND: 1).

The 15 action points that make up the core of this strategy include the following: a blueprint for sustainable tourism, incentives to increase access, increased funds for promotion, new information and reservation technologies. In the wake of September 11 and the outbreaks of foot and mouth disease, the Scottish Tourism Board (STB) developed a *Tourism Framework for Action: 2002–2005* (STB, ND). This action plan is built around partnerships, as it provides detailed recommendations and assigns responsibilities for these actions to different tourism stakeholder groups. This collaborative approach is working, according to Eccles from the Monarch of the Glen Project (STB, ND: 18):

> Led by the private sector and with the support of all the public agencies, the success of the Monarch Country initiative has been twofold. The availability of the same advertising material to all businesses throughout the Strath has increased visitor awareness and drawn us all together in an area which has suffered from in-fighting for many years.

The Australian Tourist Commission (ATC) was established in 1967 to attract overseas visitors to Australia and continues to work towards this aim in partnership with the tourism industry and other agencies (ATC, 2003). The ATC receives approximately $123 million a year in funding from the Australian government and the tourist industry to help it achieve its objectives. The result has been some very successful promotional campaigns involving Paul Hogan, Elle McPherson, Ian Thorpe and others, and a steady increase in international visitor arrivals.

Nations that fully access their tourism potential, develop comprehensive tourism plans with realistic targets, and provide the funds to implement these plans create a solid foundation upon which many other tourist initiatives can develop.

National parks and World Heritage Sites

National parks serve the needs of numerous stakeholders and it is the domain of national governments to manage the parks to meet various stakeholder requirements. National park customers are those who visit the parks for reasons as diverse as relaxation, recreation, education, spirituality and sightseeing. However, tourism is not the only stakeholder in national parks. Different industry groups from mining, forestry and farming lobby the government for different usage and access rights to national parks.

In most national parks people are not allowed to live within park boundaries; however, there are some notable exceptions. Aboriginal people can have special rights to reside in national parks that were traditionally their lands, as is the case with the Smoky Mountains National Park in the US. In Canada's Banff National Park people reside permanently within the boundaries of the national parks in designated areas, such as the Banff township that grew up with the early railway development and the Banff Springs Hotel. In the UK the crowded nature of the countryside meant that areas of outstanding beauty and cultural significance had to be preserved by superimposing park status on living communities, creating national parks that allow the coexistence of the past with the economic and cultural structures of the present.

Residential and tourist communities within parks tend to be highly regulated with strict caps on the number of units and maximum occupancy of these units, plus they are constrained by specific architectural and development guidelines. Even with these restrictions it can be difficult to contain the pressures to live in or adjacent to such desirable areas. The strict development restrictions on national parks tend to encourage robust development just outside the park boundaries, as is evident with the rapid growth of Canmore, just outside of Banff National Park in Canada, and Gatlinburg, which serves as a gateway community to the Great Smoky Mountains National Park in the US.

Various federal laws protect the natural, cultural and agricultural resources in national parks. In the US there are detailed federal laws that prohibit possessing or damaging living or dead wildlife, plants, geological features and other aspects of these environments (US Code, 2001, c). Similar laws can be found in many countries; however, it can be exceedingly difficult for developing countries to enforce these requirements if they are beleaguered with inadequate funds, corruption and other factors contributing to negligence in management.

The lack of a strong legal system that balances environmental, commercial and community rights is just one of the substantial challenges to sustainable tourism management in the developing world. According to (Tosun 2000: 626) there are many obstacles to collaborative planning in developing countries which lead to:

> political instability, patron–client relationships, low level of literacy, unfair and unequal distribution of income, severe macro-economic problems, lack of services of the welfare state, lack of democratic institutions, lack of democratic understanding among state elites, unwillingness of the elite to share the fruits of development with the majority in society in the developing world.

The tourism challenges facing developing countries need to be addressed in a manner appropriate to the economic and political development of these countries. Problems of tourism mismanagement in developing countries can be exacerbated when it goes against cultural practices to challenge established decision-makers. In countries where traditionally power is placed in the hands of a few and challenging their rights of leadership is seen as an affront to unity, citizens may not be prepared to hold their governments accountable for their actions (Timothy, 1999). Rather than grafting tourism planning ideas onto other countries Tosun and Jenkins (1998: 111) suggested that:

> perhaps the most appropriate way to address these needs is to train and develop indigenous planning expertise. This is already happening in a number of developing countries where tourism is an important sector in the economy.

Once governments are aware of their tourism opportunities and constraints they can direct their tourism growth in a manner that they feel is appropriate.

International recognition and planning has transformed some sites into major world destinations. World Heritage Site status has been a boon for conserving areas of exceptional beauty and cultural significance around the world for projects as diverse as colonial slave trading complexes in Africa, ancient cities in Asia and wilderness reserves in the Americas (UNESCO, 1993). The historic city of Sukhothai in Thailand has benefited from its world heritage designation through aid in developing a Master Plan, funds of over US$500,000 for implementation of the plan and an associated campaign to raise awareness and enable significant restoration works (UNESCO, 1993: 17). Africa's wildlife parks represent an effective partnership between international agencies and national governments that has conserved the distinctive flora and fauna of this region of the world and turned them into world-class tourist attractions. By 2002 there were 730 world heritage sites and 'nations lobby hard to get their glorious buildings, wilderness, and historic ruins on the list, a stamp of approval that brings prestige, tourist income, public awareness, and, most important, a commitment to save the irreplaceable' (O'Neill, 2002: 60).

Indigenous

Indigenous people around the world are asserting their rights to control their culture, lands and economic development. Indigenous people are recognised in certain countries, such as Canada and the US, as sovereign people who have rights attributed to their state within a state. In certain African and European countries, the rights of indigenous people relate primarily to the lands and other resources that they own or traditionally use, rather than being recognised rights to establish and maintain their own system of laws.

In Kenya wildlife tourism is one of the country's most profitable industries, yet until recently the Massai, the indigenous people, have not had a significant role in its tourism management, or benefits (Berger, 1996). The Massai are now bringing their skills to park management, as well as leasing their land to tourism operators by establishing some of their own tourism businesses and attractions (Berger, 1996).

Wildlife tourism is also of great importance in Zimbabwe, yet the successes of tourism there have brought many hardships to indigenous people in terms of denying them access to their traditional resources. The Zimbabwe government developed the CAMPFIRE programme that encourages local decision-making through consensus and directs tourism proceeds towards community development, as a way of sharing tourism management and its benefits with local people (Potts *et al.*, 1996).

The Sampi are indigenous people who are now primarily found in the northern part of Norway, in an area commonly referred to as Lapland. The rights of the Sampi, such as free access to the countryside, have been largely usurped by Norway's citizens and through default by the tourists (Pedersen & Viken, 1996).

> This has resulted in a race for the best fishing areas and hunting grounds, and pressure on, or even suppression of, the old Sampi rights to harvest according to kin-group (siida) agreements. Sampi protests against this encroachment of their old rights were not heard, and as a minority, they had no power to defend their old common rights. (Pavel, 1979 cited in Pedersen & Viken, 1996: 80)

This marginalisation of the role of indigenous people and the threats that increased tourist visitations bring to their environment and traditional ways of life is found around the world. The best way to ensure that the rights of indigenous people are protected is to enshrine these rights in law, with sovereign rights providing the highest level of indigenous independence and opportunities.

Extensive sovereign rights of the Inuit people of Northern Canada were recognised in 1993 with the creation of Nunavut – a territory three times the size of France – as a semi-autonomous nation (Smith, 1996). These land, resource and governing rights combine to provide the Inuit people with unique tourism development opportunities. The primary attractions to this area are its pristine environment and cultural resources, yet its tourism potential remains underdeveloped. It has been suggested that the indigenous people in Nunavut take a self-assessment of their tourism potential, using the four H's of tourism (Smith, 1996: 42):

- *Habitat*: access options, costs, distinguishing features, partnering opportunities.
- *Heritage*: what aspects are appropriate to share and how, monitoring, social issues, such as whether or not to allow alcohol.

- *History*: what events occurred, landmarks, who will be involved and how.
- *Handicrafts*: distinctive, availability, distribution, special events and marketing.

Applying the 'Four H's' to indigenous tourism ventures can be particularly useful given its focus on traditional values and attributes. With each of these steps the potential impacts of the proposals on the indigenous community are examined by its members, which allows for greater self-determination in tourism management.

In the US indigenous people are working towards managing the tourism resources of their own land, within the confines of limited sovereign rights recognised by the federal government. In the US the *1934 Indian Reorganisation Act (1934)* restored what remained of Indian lands to tribal ownership and established a process that enabled tribes to organise for the purposes of self-government under the supervision of the federal government (Minnesota Indian Gaming Association (MGA), 2002). The classification of 'what remained of Indian lands' in 1934 was controversial then and is even more so now.

Hawaii was officially recognised as a sovereign nation by the US as early as 1826, however, the nation's government was overthrown and subsequently annexed by the US in 1893 (Masten, 2002: 2). Native Hawaiians are petitioning the federal government *(see bills S. 2899 and H.R. 4904)* to formally apologise for the overthrow of the Hawaiian government and to recognise the sovereignty of Native Hawaiians. These measures are seen by many people to be essential to protecting Hawaiian culture and lands. The culture and natural resources of Hawaii are the foundations of the rich tourism industry that has flourished there for over half a century and if they are degraded the appeal of Hawaii will diminish greatly. Therefore, the potential ramifications of Native Hawaiian sovereign rights on the tourism industry are immense.

Another landmark statute relating to indigenous sovereignty in the US that has particular relevance to tourism is the *Indian Gaming Regulatory Act (1988)* (MIGA, 2002: 1). This Act allows sovereign governments to choose to allow gaming on their lands. The Act recognises that gaming and gambling on Indian lands can assist with the economic development and self-determination of indigenous people. Since areas recognised as Native American lands tend to be isolated, stripped of natural resources, poorly served by infrastructure and community services, economically depressed and battling immense social problems, gambling and gaming represent one of the few viable options for economic development on Native Indian reservations in the US. In a recent review of developments Thompson (2003) notes the money generated by gaming has been used to benefit social capital and other enterprises on many reservations, but it also exposes the indigenous people to exploitation and criminal activity. But he also comments that some tribes are using gaming revenue for lobbying and campaign funds as they recognise the importance of influencing policy makers.

The limitations of gambling and gaming as a means of economic development and its potential negative social consequences have been recognised by indigenous and non-indigenous people around the world. In fact most indigenous nations in the US do not engage in gaming and where gaming does occur on native reservations it makes up less than 10% of the entire gaming industries in the US (MIGA, 2002). However, the development of these islands of gambling in areas where it is illegal to operate casinos outside of the reservations/reserves has created local tensions (Carmichael *et al.* 1996). Hsu (2003: 229) argues the 'debate continues about the costs and benefits of Native American gaming within tribes, and about the legitimacy of gambling as a Native American enterprise'.

In the US a number of indigenous groups have come together as 'tribal nations' to promote their tourism products. Comprehensive tourism development policies have been developed by the Pueblos at Taos, New Mexico, the Navajos of Arizona and the Cherokees of North Carolina (Smith, cited in Gunn, 1997: 15). The residents of the Acoma pueblo, which is close to Alburquerque, New Mexico, and well serviced by freeways, established their own tourism policies to preserve and promote their native heritage and have developed into a major tourist destination that includes a casino. The *Alliance of Tribal Tourism Advocates* (ATTA), which was established in 1993 by a number of tribes in the South Dakota region of the US, is an example of a tourism association created and run by Aboriginal people (ATTA, 2002). The goals of this organisation are to enhance tourism development opportunities for tribes by bringing economic and employment benefits to Indian communities. The beliefs and priorities of this indigenous tourism organisation include the following (ATTA, 2002):

- Support cultural integrity and traditional values in the development of tribal tourism.
- Acknowledge the sovereignty of tribes.
- Preserve the sanctity of sites, artefacts, rituals and ceremonies considered sacred by tribes.
- Protect the natural environment of tribal homelands.
- Assist in tourism code and policy development.
- Publish and distribute intertribal tourism material.
- Host tribal tourism workshops and training.
- Provide technical assistance to members in developing publicity materials and tour packages.

- Sponsor national and international marketing efforts and trade missions.
- Develop inter-tribal tour packages.
- Broker the sale of tours for ATTA members.

In Australia the *Native Title Act of* 1993 enshrines in law the rights and interests of Aboriginal and Torres Strait Islander peoples to lands over which their title is recognised (National Native Title Tribunal, 2003). Unfortunately, it is exceedingly difficult under this legislation to establish native title, which greatly curtails the powers of Aboriginal and Torres Strait Islanders peoples to control their traditional lands. Ayers Rock, now known as Uluru, in Uluru-Kata Tjuta National Park is now managed under the guidance of the Uluru-Kata Tjuta Board of Management. This board consists of six indigenous people, the Director of National Parks and Wildlife, a scientist and representative from the Ministry of Environment and the Ministry for Tourism (Parks Australia, 2000). At the state level there are some promising developments, such as the *South Australia's Department of Environment and Planning's* 1987 management framework that incorporates indigenous skills and knowledge in the management of its parks (ParksWeb, 2003).

State

At the national level, legislation can be too broad and complex to influence key factors for tourism's success, while at a local level the resources necessary for preparing and enforcing effective tourism management policies can be lacking. Therefore, the state level can be a practical and effective way of influencing the development and management of tourism, as it benefits from a larger share of financial, technical and professional resources than local government, while being close enough to the issues to properly understand and respond to them. The *Alaska Community Tourism Handbook* offers expert guidance on assessing the potential impacts of tourism on communities and how to invest resources so they will have their desired impacts (State of Alaska, ND). State agencies can use handbooks and other information sources to highlight key issues that destinations should consider in developing their own approaches to tourism management.

In many countries each state is responsible for preparing an official state plan to guide development that in turn serves as a set of standards that all local governments must adhere to in preparing their own official plans. In regard to land use or town planning, state plans set general goals and objectives that municipal governments must support in their detailed planning goals and objectives and related land development regulations. Land use or town planning can have as great an impact on the development and management of tourism enterprises as tourism specific legislation. Land use or town planning requirements are the primary means by which governments establish and maintain standards for developing and managing resources in developed areas. A state planning directive to increase the use of coastal resources by residents and visitors could be supported by a municipal planning objective to encourage the development of marinas and by specific land use regulations, such as those relating to zoning that allow for the development of these marinas.

Specific tourism planning legislation is still a rarity and often serves more as a marketing flourish than as a detailed guide of what is required by the industry and how it is to be achieved. However, a good example of comprehensive state guidance in tourism planning can be drawn from the state of Queensland in Australia, which has created a 'whole-of-government strategy' to integrate and coordinate tourism policies throughout State legislation and general government practices (Tourism Queensland, 2002). Under the state's goal to 'increase Queensland's visitor market share while ensuring its sustainability in the long term' the state has committed to 'initiating cooperative research on yield management issues' (Tourism Queensland, 2000). An example of the state of Victoria's approach to tourism management is offered elsewhere in this book as a case study.

State resource management and service requirements can be relied upon to a lesser or greater degree by local governments depending on their motivations and capabilities to guide their tourism development. When departing from state standards the onus is on local governments to show that such departures will still enable to them to meet state goals and objectives. If a local government does not have the resources to develop its own tourism strategies, it can draw on those of the state, thereby ensuring a consistent base-line standard in developmental and environmental practices relating to tourism. However, local government provides one of the best opportunities for residents to directly participate in tourism decision-making within developed and democratic countries.

Local

Local government areas with well-established tourism industries tend to have detailed plans and strategies to guide their tourism development. The *1992 General Plan for the City and County of Honolulu* shows a strong commitment to combining local quality of life issues with tourism development. Throughout this document the needs of visitors are discussed alongside those of residents creating an almost seamless approach to managing the natural, physical and cultural environments of Honolulu for current and future inhabitants of this area. A main objective of this plan is, 'to maintain the viability of Oahu's visitor industry' (City and County of Honolulu, 1992: 15), for the resort area of Waikiki comes under the county jurisdiction. Policies supporting this objective include the following:

- designating Waikiki as Oahu's main resort destination and directing public expenditures to this area to support this role;
- placing caps on accommodation units and densities;
- managing the development of new resort areas to minimise adverse impacts on the environment and the cost of providing public services to these areas.

The *1992 General Plan for the City and County of Honolulu* encourages extensive public participation in the planning process, as evident from the following extract (City and County of Honolulu, 1992: 9–10):

> To provide the residents of the City and County of Honolulu with the opportunity to democratically and meaningfully participate in the determination of the direction and quality of future growth of Oahu, a citizen participation process which focuses on citizen advisory boards as called for in the City Charter has been established.... Members of the advisory boards can provide valuable assistance by soliciting the input of other neighbourhood groups and residents and identifying the concerns of the areas they represent. By monitoring conditions they can also help to make sure the policies of the General Plan are implemented.

The commitment of the City and County of Honolulu to public participation in tourism planning is further evident in their community visioning programmes, special areas plans and sustainable community plans (City and County of Honolulu, DPP, 2002).

The need to integrate tourism with other economic and social activities becomes paramount at the local level (Butler, 1999). The growing interest in heritage and cultural tourism attractions means that more tourists wish to learn about the past and present workings of the host community – its sense of place. This has resulted not only in a growing link with museums and festivals but a tourism interest in 'industrial tourism', where visitors learn about current industrial practices (Frew & Shaw, 1998). To facilitate such an interface more local jurisdictions are engaging in planning and management policies that will permit the leisure interests of tourists to operate alongside the commercial interests of various industrial sectors. An example of this can be seen in the earlier description of Canterbury's planning for its historic shopping district (Laws & Le Pelley, 2000).

Entrepreneurial approaches

The characteristics of governments and governing, especially at the local level, are widely viewed as going through an evolutionary change. One of the most notable changes is that many governments are moving from a welfare state orientation to a business or entrepreneurial orientation. The welfare state approach focuses on issues regarding the re-distribution of available resources, 'from each according to his ability to each according to his need', whereby the larger society is seen as being responsible for the well-being of all its citizens. In contrast, taking a business approach to government operations involves a number of entrepreneurial characteristics such as innovation, profit focus, risk-taking and promotion (Hall & Hubbard, 1998). The objectives of entrepreneurial governments are intrinsically tied to growth and minimal regulation of the 'free market' environment. These objectives include the following:

- job creation;
- expanded tax base;
- support for small firm development;
- attract new investment;
- simpler tax regulations;
- streamline development process;
- privatisation of utilities and transport sectors.

Increasing global competition fuels the need to take an entrepreneurial approach, as those governments that are not perceived as being innovative and business focused risk a net drain of resources. As noted by Hall and Hubbard (1998: 6):

> The idea of the internationalisation of economic activity, the increased geographic mobility of production and investment and the rising power of transnational corporations appears to have instilled an edgy insecurity at all levels of the urban hierarchy.

Unlike many other industries, tourism is less threatened by the unbridled competitive impacts of globalisation in that it has never been a tariff protected industry and the sense of place qualities intrinsic to a destination, can make it 'unique' and still desirable. However, investing in 'mega projects' that appeal to mass tourism and global markets as well as residents, such as sport stadiums, waterfront activity areas and entertainment districts is more susceptible to global competition and investment pressures, and can lead to a sense of 'placenesses'. The proliferation of colourful banners, royal palms, neo-classical architecture and transnational chain establishments in the retail, food and beverage and entertainment sectors can blur the differences between destinations. Environments can increasingly be replicated through artificial means. The large bio-domes in Cornwall, England, enable visitors to feel like they have had a 'tropical experience' while the indoor ski facilities in Japan enable users to enjoy outdoor recreation experiences, without travelling far or facing the elements.

Taking an entrepreneurial approach translates into engaging in proactive strategies to create partnerships with the private sector to provide services and to stimulate overall economic development. While an entrepreneurial approach is seen to raise the standards of what a destination has to offer, these offerings tend to be championed by elite groups and to largely serve their interests. New sports stadiums and arts performance centres can draw heavily on public funds, while the admission charges for these venues can be beyond the means of many members of the public. The potential trickle-down effect of spending public funds on improving the look and level of discretionary services offered by a jurisdiction are often used to justify diverting public funds from basic public services. Spending on 'big ticket' entrepreneurial projects, however, can divert public funds from less glamorous, but highly necessary areas of public investment in schooling, transport, housing and medical care.

A successful example of the entrepreneurial approach is the 'Glasgow's Miles Better' campaign with its prominent placement of Mr. Happy from the Mr. Men cartoon, exuding a sense of fun, optimism and opportunity at a time when Glasgow was suffering from numerous economic and social challenges (Ward, 1998). A campaign of related policies to invest in the city's cultural and service assets is credited with encouraging local businesses and entrepreneurial activity as well as attracting investment to Glasgow. The increase in civic pride from a successful promotion and investment in a city can invigorate local economies and encourage residents, tourists and outside backers to invest their time and money in these special places. Another example of this was Vancouver's successful international *Expo'86* which helped to raise international awareness of this Pacific Rim city and left behind tourist infrastructure like its new cruise ship terminal, that has been an important part of the 'Inside Passage' to Alaska cruise market growth (Figure 10.1).

Organising

Government processes and procedures relating to financing and infrastructure have particular relevance to the ability of government to set into motion the goals and objectives established through the planning process. It needs to balance the priorities of its residents and voters with those of specific interest groups, such as the tourism industry. It does this by organising its powers and resources according to its administrative philosophy. Government organisation can involve minimal assistance through the development of a basic infrastructure or take a more proactive approach via the creation of government departments and an investment in major attractions and events. An important part of governments' approach to tourism is how they organise their financial and taxation structure with respect to this industry.

Figure 10.1 Vancouver's cruise ship terminal and cruise ship

Financing

Governments can put in place regulations and incentives to bolster tourism development given they have sufficient funds to support these efforts. However, governments may be reluctant to make the necessary financial commitment to tourism given the complexities of the industry, varying levels of public support for the industry and limited available funds and funding options for tourism. The financial management of governments is under increased scrutiny, as evident by the number of external audits of government departments that are being demanded by the public and various interest groups. The financial management of governments is also increasingly restricted due to balanced budget laws that require governments and their departments to achieve a balanced budget each financial year and to caps placed on the taxation burden that governments can levy on their citizens. As governments try to 'do more with less', they are utilising different forms of financial analysis to help them determine how best to spend their money.

All methods of financial analysis involve varying degrees of forecasting, in that they all try to predict the future using imperfect information. However, they are still required to give a strong indication of appropriate budgeting and auditing practices. Given that tourism is a service based industry made up primarily of small businesses, it can be very difficult to track the return on tourism investments and to make future predictions. An over-reliance on such forms of analysis can favour investments that are more conventional and easy to track, which can disadvantage tourism. Of all the available financial analysis options, cost–benefit analysis, shift–share analysis and input–output modelling are among the most applicable for predicting the impacts of tourism investments.

Cost–benefit analysis endeavours to assign numerical values to all potential costs and benefits associated with a proposed project, and rates proposals with a ratio higher than one as providing more benefits than costs (Davis, 1993). Applying this form of analysis to potential tourism expenditures takes into account many of the factors, such as those relating to quality of life, that are missed by less inclusive forms of analysis. Shift–share analysis is useful for understanding how well an area, or region is doing in terms of tourism development compared to the nation. This form of analysis can be useful for studying competitive advantage between regions and nations, and for determining growth potential in regard to larger trends, such as with a national tourism industry that is either expanding or retracting. Input–output modelling addresses secondary impacts and is adept at showing how changes in different industry sectors create impacts that reverberate throughout the economy (Davis, 1993). Given that tourism is highly interdependent on the rest of the economy, this form of modelling provides a more comprehensive picture of how changes in tourism will impact on the economy, as well as how changes in non-tourism sectors will impact on tourism.

Funding options

When properly managed, tourism can improve the quality of life for communities; however, when mismanaged the reverse can occur. Governments address tourism costs through a variety of methods. These include making developers and users pay fees and charges aimed at capturing the direct and indirect costs of development and use. Governments also fund tourism programmes and pay for tourism costs through dedicated funds, tourist related taxes, sales taxes, lottery funds, grants, loans, tax exempt bonds and loan guarantees.

Typically, governments attempt to place the financial costs of tourism development, including the cost of development and use of infrastructure and services, on developers. These developers, in turn, pass the costs along to business owners who pass the costs along to their customers. The actual costs of tourism growth and development can be difficult to calculate in a proactive manner, especially given that many tourism impacts indirectly affect communities and that it can take years for signs of its impacts to become evident. Therefore, calculating the costs of growth for communities and sorting out who currently pays for this growth and who should pay is difficult.

Development and impact fees Tourism developers and business owners pay for tourism growth through a system of development charges and impact fees. These sources of government revenue can include permitting fees, infrastructure costs, utilities levies, real estate transfer taxes and contributions to government programmes for community enhancement, such as affordable housing and parks programmes. These 'contributions' can raise difficult issues for governments if they are seen to be 'exaction', whereby cost burdens are inappropriately placed on individuals or businesses. In the US while the issue of 'exactions' is dealt with differently by different states, the main responsibility of governments is to show that all their development charges and fees are warranted and that funds collected by these fees are not spent in unrelated areas. The scope of governments' abilities to fund projects and services linked to tourism, such as subsidising affordable housing to offset increased prices spurred on by tourism, or investing in road improvements and buying new lands for preservation, can be hampered by legal and government restrictions relating to 'exactions'.

Dedicated funds Capital Improvement Funds, transfer taxes and bonds can be useful sources of funding for projects that serve the interests of both residents and visitors. The bike trail linking Ohio's major cities, recreation areas and parks has received widespread government support and $2 million of the state's Capital Improvement Funds (Thompson, 2001: 6). A transfer tax on the sale of properties in Vail, Colorado, that was approved by referendum in 1980 generates over $2 million a year for open space acquisitions that are used for natural, park and recreation areas (Howe *et al.*, 1997: 76). In America a series of bills that would provide between $20 to $70 billion dollars in tax-exempt bonds and loan guarantees have been proposed to help save Amtrak (Eisenberg *et al.*, 2001: 69). In Canada there is a long history of the government providing funds to assist communities in developing tourism plans. In Alberta a partnership programme between the public and private sector provides funds for the development of community tourism action plans that includes goal setting, identification of local priority projects and programmes to support tourism development (Gunn, 1997).

Tourist taxes Tourists' taxes are commonly imposed as a minor tax on accommodation to help offset some of the costs of tourism – particularly marketing. Such taxes are quite popular amongst residents as the people who vote for these taxes do not have to pay for them. However, industry groups are concerned that tourists should not be over-taxed, and argue that when prices are raised by increasing taxes tourism businesses have to reduce their costs to compensate for the price increase to stay competitive with other destinations. The tourist industry is also opposed to tourists taxes, such as those on accommodation, airports, parks, transportation and other facilities and utilities being used to fund items that are not related to tourism, as can be the case if these monies go towards general government funds.

A 'tourist impact tax' was approved by Florida Keys voters in 1988 to help to offset some of the costs of providing services to tourists and to improve the area (Howe *et al.*, 1997: 78). Half of the funds raised by the 1% tax on hotels and motels goes towards the county's general fund, while the rest is used to pay for the acquisition of lands for purposes that include land preservation and affordable housing. A 2% bed tax has been in existence in Victoria, BC, for a decade or more. Half of the money raised, generally over C$4 million a year, goes to supporting the city's conference centre. The rest supports the marketing and community efforts of Tourism Victoria, the local destination's marketing association.

Public support
It is politically astute to fund projects that are seen to serve the greater public good, strike the right balance between public and private sector funding and do not jeopardise funding for other community priorities. Funding for parks, historical restorations and highway improvements can be viewed as more equitable uses of the public coffers than offering tax breaks, reducing user fees and subsidising land prices for tourism businesses. An example of public spending that was seen by some to go beyond

acceptable levels is the £331 million that the Birmingham City Council invested in its 'city-centre prestige projects'. These included a convention centre, indoor arena, hotel complex and aquarium, between 1986/87 and 1991/92, and were clearly oriented toward increasing tourism (Loftman & Nevin, 1998: 137–9). While many residents were supportive initially of the improvements, over time the real cost associated with these projects, in terms of drastic cuts in spending on health, education and housing were seen to be too high. Another point of contention was that more than half of the total cost for these capital improvements was subsidised by the local council while the council also underwrote private sector funds, which in effect was a double contribution if things went wrong. Therefore, the use of 'public-private partnerships' to finance these improvements became viewed by many as over-dependent on government funds. The pro-growth council was replaced by a new council with 'back to basics' priorities and led to dramatic changes in budgeting.

More recently, Manchester served as the host city for the *2002 Common-wealth Games* and attracted worldwide praise for its excellent facilities, vibrant urban centre and friendly and welcoming citizens. The Manchester example underlies the impact that local government's successive fiscal policies can have on the overall social, economic and physical environment of destinations. But it is a continuous struggle between competing interests and views as to how best address these community needs, and in turn their impact on the attractiveness of a city to residents and tourists.

Infrastructure

The potential monetary gains from tourism can only be realised if infra-structure that meets the needs of both tourists and residents is available and in good condition. This physical manifestation of organisation becomes an essential building block for tourism business. The infrastructure for tourists goes beyond the provision of airports, roads and other facilities and includes tourist services and needs like safe food and water, sewerage systems, hospitals and policing. In the Great Ocean Road region of Victoria, Australia, which is home to the world famous Bells Beach surfing area, the local council estimates that is has spent close to a million dollars on building and maintaining basic tourist infrastructure, such as toilet and changing room facilities over a 10-year period (DOI, 2001: 8). This is a significant expense for a small community. As the state and local governments work on preparing a comprehensive management plan for the region they recognise that 'funding the necessary infrastructure to support tourism growth will be a major challenge' (DOI, 2001: 8).

Transportation

Transportation is a key component of tourism, as it can either facilitate or hinder the safe, efficient and cost-effective means of access for visitors and goods. The dominant forms of transportation that are regulated and funded by federal and state governments are airlines, trains and roads. The problem with most forms of travel infrastructure is that they are very expensive to build and maintain, while the public baulks at paying the full price for using the infrastructure. The high costs are tied to the technical expertise, expensive materials and high number of employees needed to build and maintain transportation infrastructure. Health and safety concerns, especially with regard to the potential for disruption of services, injury and death, greatly increase both the liabilities of governments and the associated funds that governments must pour into the infrastructure to make it as safe and reliable as possible.

One common problem for all infrastructure is its periodic use. Whether it be roads, water or electricity systems each has its peak periods, which means the system is under pressure for certain limited time periods, but in excess of requirements for much of the time. This peaking inefficiency can be exacerbated by tourism seasons. When a community's roads that are designed for the permanent population are put under pressure by the inflow of thousands of tourists, special management is required. Some of the government organisation that takes place under these circumstances includes temporary adjustments such as additional traffic lanes and parking spaces, or park and ride schemes. At times tourism business has to be diverted elsewhere because the community is full to capacity, as has happened occasionally in Venice.

Airports and airlines

Many nations of the world have established their own airlines, also referred to as 'national flag-carriers', as a way of providing a network of internal flights as well as transportation to international destinations. The prestige factor of having a national airline, the economic opportunities associated with a well integrated national airline service, the high employment potential of these airlines, and the internal dependency on air service to regional and out-of-the way destinations all contribute to nations supporting flag-carriers. Unfortunately, many of these flag-carriers have struggled to stay out of debt, both as public and private sector businesses. Deregulation has been blamed for increased flight delays and overcrowding as privatised airlines struggle to make profits in a highly competitive environment. In a study of the 31 busiest airports in the US the *Federal Aviation Administration* (FAA) found there were eight airports with significant passenger delays: New York La Guardia, Newark, New York Kennedy, Chicago O'Hare, San Francisco, Philadelphia, Atlanta and Boston (FAA, 2001: 2). It is also predicted that the first six of these airports along with Los Angeles will continue to have significant delays over the next 10 years. As these airports are all major national hubs and several are world hubs, significant delays at these airports cause service problems on a much larger scale, as delayed flights can lead to missed connections and loss of bookings for other tourism services.

The costs associated with offering a range of services on all flights and travelling to marginal destinations, along with high employee costs have left many national airlines struggling to make a profit. The last few years have seen the loss of a number of major airlines including Canadian (Canada), Ansett (Australia), Swiss Air (Switzerland) and Sabena (Belgium), with many others in desperate situations. Sabena airlines made a profit only twice during the 75 years it was in operation (*The Economist*, 2001d). The second largest airline in the US, United Airlines has recently sought the protection of Chapter 11 status. Chapter 11 is a 'time out' lifeline that allows companies on the verge of insolvency to restructure and get their business in order, to hopefully avoid a complete and irreversible declaration of bankruptcy. At the same time that many major airlines are struggling, discount carriers, such as Ryanair, Easy Jet and Virgin, are making profits by cutting costs, and customising their service. They provide minimal on-flight services, limit flights to popular destinations, use less expensive second tier airports wherever possible, vary prices according to time of day, and provide inclusive packages and other traveller incentives to tempt passengers.

The loss of national carriers can be devastating for tourist destinations more than a few hours from international airports. Many smaller regional areas are unable to attract a high and continual flow of tourists and therefore are primarily ignored by airlines that do not have a mandate to serve these areas, as is usually only the case with national carriers. Some regional centres have been able to adjust by working with the discount carriers, who are able to offer a point-to-point service using smaller planes.

Rail

Railways hold an important tourism role in some nations, while in others they are sliding into obscurity. India's rail service has the highest capacity of any in the world and dominates the movement of people and goods in that country. Romantic notions of touring the continent or more practical considerations can draw tourists to riding the rails as part of their experience of India. However, India's rail system suffers from one of the world's worst safety records, so tourists need to take that into account. The UK is famous for its train travel, its magnificent old stations and the grand expanses of countryside that can be viewed while riding the rails. The pleasantries of the rail experience in the UK have become corroded, however, by chronic under-investment that has contributed to endless train delays and a number of tragic accidents (*The Economist*, 2001d).

Public transportation around the world, particularly passenger railways, receives substantial government subsidies, as it represents not only an essential government service but also an emotionally charged indication of political power. A well-run railway network is in a nation's interest as it allows for the effective and efficient movement of goods and people and generates a sense of pride. It is noticeable that some publicly operated passenger systems which have received substantial public investment, as in France and Japan, can offer a service that rivals domestic airlines for speed and efficiency. America's national rail system, Amtrack, however is chronically under-funded. In America passenger trains receive US$0.5 million in federal subsidies compared with the US$13 billion received by airports, while highways receive annual federal subsidies of over US$30 billion a year (Eisenberg *et al.*, 2001: 68). America dedicates federal funding to airlines and highways, through gasoline and ticket taxes, while rail services have no such source of federal funding.

Highways and roads

Road and highway services are important to tourism, as they tend to be the least expensive and most convenient way of 'touring'; so it comes as no surprise that tourist surveys often indicate 80% of tourists use car or bus travel to get around. In the developed world most countries have elaborate highway systems that connect regional areas with hub cities. A recent study of the Newell Highway in Australia, which links Melbourne and Brisbane, revealed the creation of a route promotions committee to take advantage of such linear regional travel. Their communal brochure promoted 478 local tourism operators, 53 towns and 31 local governments over its 1100 kilometre length, and 35% of surveyed highway travellers were using the brochure (Houghton *et al.*, 2002).

The joint levels of funding and responsibilities for a nation's highways are well demonstrated by the creation of the interstate highway system in the US. In 1944 the *Federal-Aid Highway Act* authorised the designation of a 65,000 mile 'National System of Interstate Highways' that was to be a cooperative effort between national and state highway departments (Public Roads On Line, 1996: 4). In 1952 the *Federal-Aid Highway Act* authorised only US$25 million for this system on a 50:50 matching funds basis; however, by the mid-1950s it was estimated that state and national investments in the highway system would require over a hundred billion dollars (Public Roads on Line, 1996: 11). The highway system was financed subsequently through dedicated funds, bonds, gas taxes and various highway user charges. The current annual budget for America's Federal Highways Administration exceeds US$30 billion (FHA, 2001: 1). In Australia, during the late 1990s the federal government provided A$750 million to upgrade the Pacific Highway, which assisted several coastal tourism destinations and provided a more efficient transportation for Australia's east coast economy (Houghton *et al.*, 2002).

There can be mixed results with regard to the impacts of major highway improvements for tourism. One of the most famous highways in the US is

'Route 66', which for a time served as the primary means of connecting the northeast and southwest corners of the country. The Chicago-to-Los Angeles route connected the main streets of many rural and urban communities and brought these areas the benefits of access to a major national east-west artery from the 1930s to the 1960s (NHR66F, 1995: 2–6). A number of tourist innovations came to life along Route 66, including motels, service stations and fast food outlets. Most of the original sections of Route 66 were replaced by a four-lane highway in the 1970s, which has left many of the towns along this once bustling trade route struggling to survive. When super highways with limited access, via select entry/exit points, are installed the resulting impact is that towns without access lose business, as people bypass these areas in their quest to arrive at their destinations quickly. However, there are tourism advantages to be gained when the loss of highway traffic is treated as an opportunity to make towns less car focused by creating environments where travellers want to walk around, shop and enjoy a quieter ambience. The tourism success of small rural towns that have been bypassed by major highway, such as Ross Village in Tasmania and West Bury in Victoria, Australia, is testament to how some communities can weather the storms of organisational change that government infrastructure priorities can create (Kelly & Spark, 2001).

Leadership

The very nature of the tourism industry makes it a challenge for governments to understand and manage in that tourism is service based, dominated by small businesses and difficult to separate from larger community services. The diversity of tourism industry membership can create real difficulties in producing a united vision and then effectively conveying this vision through leaders. Most lobby groups for tourism are neither as well organised, nor as powerful as entrenched interest groups, which can lead to them being overlooked by government agencies. When governments make a firm commitment to tourism they can help unite this diverse industry and motivate others to work towards a clear tourism vision, but this requires leadership.

Leadership in government on behalf of tourism can take many forms. It can come directly from elected officials, as part of their mandate. It can emerge from the initiative and tenacity of senior government service personnel. It can arise from the efforts of NGOs which often depend on government funding and support in order to be effective. It can emerge from the efforts of individuals in the private sector who have caught the imagination of government and have been facilitated in the pursuit of their dreams.

An example of the first has occurred in Tasmania, where unlike the normal situation of tourism being the responsibility of a junior minister the past Premier, the Right Honourable Jim Bacon, took responsibility for this portfolio. This fortunate combination brought strong leadership and much appreciated political commitment and resources to tourism development in Tasmania. Further leadership is provided through *Tourism Tasmania Corporate*, a statutory agency established in 1997 and guided by a diverse group of high-level tourism experts, including the co-founder of Lonely Planet (Tourism Tasmania, 2002: 1). Tourism Tasmania Corporate organises its business across four key areas: tourism marketing, retail, wholesale and tourism development. This business approach enables it to function as a leader to the industry across many diverse sectors. Part of this organisation's leadership comes from its active Market Research Unit that engages in extensive data collection and the sharing of numerous surveys to its tourism stakeholders.

Even when elected politicians take on the responsibility for tourism they often have other responsibilities, and tourism is usually incorporated as part of a joint ministry. Consequently these busy ministers become heavily dependent on the advice and vision of their senior bureaucrats. The authors have lived in a variety of locations around the world and have been impressed with the knowledge, commitment and initiative of these individuals. They genuinely want to see the industry succeed but have a tough assignment obtaining the funding they require and the unified support of a very disparate industry. But overall they are slowly gaining the respect and support of other government departments and senior politicians.

In a growing number of cases the leadership from government has come indirectly through NGOs or partnerships with private individuals. Unfortunately, the poor performance of many governments as leaders in tourism development has led certain researchers to believe that the public sector is not the best leader for directing tourism development, given governments' strong role as regulators and limited experience and success in creating new and viable opportunities for community development. While a government's role as regulator is valuable for setting standards of acceptable conduct, its limitations are noted by Howe *et al.* (1997: 71) who state that:

> By themselves, however, regulations will not bring out the best in a community or protect what people value most about their town. Because they focus on prevention regulations cannot offer a positive vision of how things should be. Without other approaches, communities might well experience indistinguishable look-alike development that simply follows the letter of the law.

The 'other approaches' as advocated by Howe *et al.* (1997) and Ritchie (2001), can include a shift in focus from a primary role as a regulator towards that of being a 'facilitator'. Governments can act as 'facilitators' in helping communities find and nurture their own leaders and in turn develop appropriate tourism plans and environments to encourage individual innovations. Governments can also help communities see their local issues in broader governing, economic, social, environmental and legal contexts.

Godschalk *et al.* (1994) note that as governments are being forced to do more with less, in terms of answering to a wider range of interest groups with less direct taxation dollars, they have to change their ways of doing business. Decreases in government funds are tied to the public reluctance for increases in taxes, especially in the US, along with their scepticism that the public sector can provide quality goods and services on budget and on time. Changing government priorities and decreasing levels of government funding are spurring governments to re-think their roles and form new relationships with private industry, different levels of government and interest groups, to receive the financial and moral support to move forward with proposed projects. The rise in the power and prominence of NGOs can be attributed directly to the changing, and in many cases weakening, role of governments.

The traditional government approach is a top-down approach whereby the leaders are seen to both know what is best and have the means to ensure that their decrees are followed. Haywood (1994) details a number of approaches to community development of leisure and recreation opportunities that can be applied also to tourism development. Several of these approaches are outlined below, sorted under the categories of *Top-Down, Client Led* and *Partnerships*.

Top-down

Direct provision

Governments can prescribe certain actions if they have the authority to do so and believe their requirements are in the best interests of those they represent. An example of direct provisions for tourism-related issues is the 'concurrency' requirements in Chapter 9J–5 of Florida's Administrative Code (Florida Dept. of State, 2002). The state of Florida mandates all of its local jurisdictions ensure that an 'acceptable' level of service standards is provided before allowing additional development to occur. This concurrency provision helps to ensure that the booming development that typifies this large tourist drawing state does not exceed the abilities of local jurisdictions to provide an adequate level of public facilities such as roads, potable water and parks. Given the unrelenting pressures to build new tourist facilities, including resorts, hotels, restaurants and amusement parks in Florida, this legislation has helped to slow down and in some cases prevent developments that would otherwise overwhelm local communities.

Facilitating approach

Governments can be seen to apply facilitating approaches when they provide resources to a different governing body or non-government organisation as a means of furthering a goal that involved parties mutually support. One of the most common forms of government assistance in this manner is the government grant. It is interesting to note that many NGOs that are referred to as 'grass roots' organisations, owe much of their existence and power to government funding making them the offspring of 'top-down' support. Tourism-oriented government grants are evident in downtown revitalisation schemes, heritage restoration works, upgrading existing parks and purchasing public recreational lands. Government assistance that follows the facilitating approach is also evident in tourist-related investments, such as the provision of affordable housing. Such housing is often needed for an industry located in desirable and high price locations, and where many of its positions are front-line service positions paying low or minimum wages. In regard to affordable housing in the US, the agency of *Housing and Urban Development* (HUD) sets the definition of categories of affordability throughout the US each year. These categories then serve as parameters to guide the standards for evaluating and funding affordable housing initiatives by the various levels of government, as well as the NGOs that work in the affordable housing field.

Outreach work

The outreach approach is a way of expanding opportunities for groups and individuals who are in need of government assistance yet have difficulty accessing available services. A great deal of outreach work is accomplished by new arms of government services and by NGOs, since the outreach effort is necessitated by an inability of traditional government services to reach certain people. *The Community Futures Development Corporations* is a government-funded organisation that has offices throughout regional Canada. The mission statement of one of these offices in Alberta is as follows (West Central Community Futures Development Corporation, 2002: 1):

> To assist individuals within the West Central Community Futures region with their business goals and objectives, thereby significantly improving local employment, sustainable development, and the economic well-being of communities.

The *Community Futures* office in Cowichan, BC, Canada, has been involved in re-training unemployed forestry workers for work in the service industry, with much of this work relating to tourism enterprises in this scenic rural region. Through the innovative use of government funds, organisations such as *Community Futures* can establish and run business assistance centres in rural regional centres. These centres provide a 'one stop shopping' approach to support small business and local economies in communities that might otherwise miss out on these opportunities as they are outside of major metropolitan areas.

Client led

Community development groups

Community development groups can be described as those groups that form in a spontaneous manner due to a shared sense of purpose. These groups tend to have medium- to long-term goals and as such their pace of action can be relatively moderate. Tourism examples can include 'friends of' groups, such as the *1000 Friends of Florida* who work to improve the quality of life in their community. These groups tend to show a great deal of creativity in drawing upon local resources including their members to achieve most of their aims (One Thousand Friends, 2002). NGOs that promote festivals, environmental protection or any of the many enriching aspects of community life can be seen to fit into this sub-category.

Community action groups

Community action groups tend to form around a particular cause that is pursued in the short to medium term. They tend to be more focused than community development groups and can be typified by bursts of intense activity in output as they strive to achieve their goals. Following the loss of the World Trade Centre due to terrorist activities, there was a spontaneous and unstoppable public outpouring of offers by citizens to help in any way they could. One of the top priorities for many people was to be involved in charting the course for how the World Trade Centre site should be redeveloped. Under this cause a number of organisations formed, including *New Visions: Coalition for the Rebuilding of Lower Manhattan* and *The Civic Alliance*, each of which consists of hundreds of volunteers who are forming committees and working groups to put together ideas on how to rebuild after this tragedy (Langdon, 2001).

Social groups

Social groups tend to form primarily for the purpose of social interaction and have an orientation that includes the short term through to the long term. The benefits to the larger community can be subtle in terms of adding to the overall colour and flavour of an area, or they can be readily apparent. Many tourists are drawn to visiting 'artists' quarters', be they along the River Seine in Paris or in Soho in Manhattan, or artist communities in rural areas, where they hope to soak up the atmosphere and buy some pieces. The rising prominence of noted 'gay areas' such as the 'Boys Town' neighbourhood in Chicago and the West End of Vancouver present spectacles and social attitudes that have a widening appeal. Certain cities, such as Key West, Florida, are now well known for their gay culture and draw huge crowds of gays and straights to public art exhibits, drag shows and gay pride parade days. The fashion and trend sensibilities of gay culture has led to gay groups often being in the forefront of identifying, visiting and enriching 'must see' destinations, such as South Beach, Florida, and San Francisco, California.

Partnerships

Tourism's low integration with other areas of government can leave it at cross-purposes with other government departments and agencies. This need for greater integration, especially when there are multitudes of involved stakeholder and decision-making groups, spurs on the creation of partnerships. A principle objective of the recent *Strategic Tourism Plan* in the State of Victoria, Australia, is to raise the awareness of tourism's impor-tance to other government departments (Tourism Victoria, 2002). This objective recognises that a high level of understanding and cooperation between government bodies is necessary to achieve efficiency and effec-tiveness in the creation and implementation of all government policies, not just in the tourism area. For example, tourism development impacts areas like roads and transport, major industries like forestry, fishing and agricul-ture, and is having a growing influence on a variety of revenue and finance issues.

The planning process associated with the Great Ocean Road Region in Victoria, Australia, cuts across five local council areas and contains numerous national parks and other conservation areas, yet this region relies heavily on tourism as well as traditional resource extraction indus-tries and farming for its economic well-being. The Great Ocean Road Region receives more visitors than any other area of Victoria, outside of Melbourne, attracting 2.7 million overnight visitors and 5.4 million day-trip visitors, which places great developmental pressure on this region (Department of Infrastructure, 2001: 7). The state's Department of Infra-structure is taking the lead in coordinating this planning process as it endeavours to work in partnership with the local councils, the Department of Natural Resources and Environment, VicRoads, Tourism Victoria and the Victorian Coastal Council, along with numerous community and development groups and infrastructure authorities (DOI, 2001: 5). The con-sultation process has included a number of stakeholder/community workshops to examine issues and concepts. The draft strategy has been widely available for public comment, which included allowing for written public submissions, as well as feedback provided on line. It is intended to be an inclusive planning process that permits tourism to work with other industries and the various communities within the region.

Just as NGOs can benefit from the financial, technical and political support of governments, governments can benefit from their associations with NGOs. A strong advantage to partnering is that it allows for a level of experimentation and risk in exploring new tourism options that govern-ment agencies would be unwilling to explore by themselves, due to concerns of incurring long-term financial obligations that carry with them some unpredictable outcomes. Another advantage of partnering is that it is seen by the wider community as bringing more democracy to the running of public affairs, in that a cross-section of community stakeholder groups and individuals are provided with an opportunity to guide and possibly conceive community initiatives. The advantages of partnerships encourage governments to shift from direct providers to 'enablers' of tourism products and services.

Close connections between the public and private sector can help highlight areas where either the public or the private sector is more appropriate to take the lead. The *Alberta Tourism Partnership Corporation* was founded in 1996 as a way of transferring marketing responsibilities from the state to the business sector (Gunn, 1997). In British Columbia, Canada, tourism marketing and research has been separated out from the provincial ministries. These services are now undertaken by *Tourism BC*, which was recast as a crown corporation with a strong businesses focus and its own budget and money earning capabilities.

The *Cooperative Research Centre* (CRC) initiative in Australia is an example of a government supported body acting as a facilitator of industry led tourism research and development strategies. The CRC for Sustainable Tourism was started in 1997 and was renewed in 2002 with an A$26.7 million grant from the federal government for its second iteration (CRC, 2002). A variety of CRCs have been created in Australia to bring industry and universities together through central funding to tackle identified issues and opportunities in their respective fields. While there is only one tourism CRC there are 13 related to agriculture, but they all leverage the initial federal contribution with either in-kind or additional funding support from their respective industry and university partners.

Transborder tourism partnerships may be required in order to manage tourism in a sustainable manner. In a study of managing parks along the US-Canada border it was found that making progress on joint management issues can be both costly and time-consuming (Timothy, 2000). Despite the inefficiencies and frustrations that can accompany cross-boundary management these partnering endeavours are often the only way of ensuring that joint tourism resources are properly managed and promoted.

Cross-border partnerships can benefit from treaty agreements, where the roles and responsibilities of each party to the agreement are clearly stated. Not all transboundary agreements need to be legally binding or to address joint management issues, as is evident from the numerous regional tourism promotion partnerships that have formed between different levels of government and various stakeholder groups. Timothy (1998) reports on how the New England states have formed a cooperative marketing policy to promote themselves as part of a tourism region.

Tourism partnerships ebb and flow as they progress from early to advanced stages of development. Different levels of activity, end-products and motivation can be expected from tourism partnerships as they pass through what Caffyn (2000) refers to as the 'tourism partnership lifecycle'. The tourism partnership lifecycle draws upon Butler's (1980) tourist area lifecycle to illustrate the various challenges and opportunities that arise as tourism partnerships mature. This lifecycle is useful for breaking down the steps of tourism partnerships into discrete and easily understood components. Arduous tasks relating to the prepartnership, take-off and growth phases must be completed as pre-requisites to tourism partnerships before they can reach their peak level of utility. Caffyn (2000) finds the primary factors to successful tourism partnerships are adequate financial and social capital, with the skills of project managers featuring strongly. The fact that many tourism umbrella organisations and other forms of tourism partnerships go through frequent shuffles of top level management, can be seen as a reflection of the different skills, such as consensus building or revenue raising, required by project managers at each partnering phase.

Controlling

Control for government is achieved through regulation, persuasion and education. Governments have a responsibility to regulate on behalf of the common good, to ensure health and safety standards are met and that development proceeds within legal and statutorial limits. This role is present in all areas of public responsibility and for many is the *raison d'être* for governments. However, with tourism's ubiquitous and interrelated nature it is often difficult for government to determine exact causes and impacts, or to monitor every transaction and transgression. Therefore it is difficult to comprehend let alone 'prove' tourism's impact which raises difficult issues for governments as they struggle to monitor tourism and make the necessary changes to keep the industry on track. While the available data can serve as useful reference points in setting limits on prices and access, the numbers cannot speak for themselves. This opens up great room for debate about what the numbers mean and interpretation of their meaning can vary according to which stakeholder group one belongs to and the interests that one represents.

Tourism standards

Standards for tourism development can only be assured if they are formalised and enforced. Standards that are firmly established in law, through legislation and associated policies and then upheld through legal challenges, are robust. Tourism standards developed under less rigorous conditions can falter more easily. It shows real political commitment to create a comprehensive legislative and policy framework for tourism development at the national, state and local level. Examples of state legislation affecting tourism development can be drawn from *Environmental*

Impact Assessments (EIAs) or *Statements* (EISs) that are required for medium to large-scale developments around much of the world. In their study of the impacts of EIAs on coastal tourism developments in Australia, Warnken and Buckley (1996) found that while EIAs placed additional restrictions on development proposals they were not actually barriers to tourism development.

Court findings can greatly impact on the extent to which governments can uphold the standards they establish through the political process. Lake Tahoe, a popular US tourist destination, has been embroiled in law-suit over government's rights to control development that has made it all the way to the US Supreme Court. The case of *Tahoe-Sierra Preservation Council Inc. v. Tahoe Regional Planning Agency* looked at the question of whether or not temporary development moratoriums are legal (Lucero & Soule, 2002). The court upheld the government's rights to create temporary development moratoriums, literally stopping the development clock, if such moratoriums are used to provide communities with time to work on preparing citizen-based plans for their communities. While the land rights of private citizens in the US are particularly strong, this court case highlights legal and political challenges that government agencies around the world are faced with as they try to provide a balanced system for development in their communities.

It can be very difficult for governments to find the time, resources and political support necessary to consult with and explore the needs of all stakeholders so they can develop appropriate and popular tourism plans and strategies. Threats of legal challenge heighten the perceived risks that governments take when trying to be progressive in their planning. However, inaction is not a real alternative given that governments are also legally required to meet numerous regulations, such as those relating to environmental integrity and service provision, as well as facing the wrath of their constituents if they fail to prepare for the future.

Even when tourism development standards, such as those relating to environmental impacts, public consultation and allowable uses are established in law, the ability of governments to pass amending or new legislation can alter the playing field of what is allowable. Queensland initiated fast track legislation, such as the *Sanctuary Cove Development Act 1985* and the *Integrated Resort Development Act 1987* that exempted a number of large resorts from formal EIA procedures, effectively removing the public's consultation rights, while putting in place other requirements, as a means of encouraging tourism growth (Warnken & Buckley, 1996: 242). Therefore tourism standards need to be backed by ongoing political and industry support, as well as community vigilance to ensure that these standards are not only put in place, but are able to work effectively over the long term.

Tourism's low level of integration with other areas of government is problematic when it is kept out of important discussions on resource use and other government policies that are profoundly interrelated with a healthy tourism sector. The lack of communication between various government departments can not only cause tourism to lose opportunities, it can also lead to a less than optimal return on government investment and policy. An excellent example of where government has recognised the importance of developing an inclusive and coordinated approach to managing its tourism industry comes from the US. The *Tourism Policy Council* (TPC) was established in 1996 to 'ensure that the United States' national interest in tourism is fully considered in Federal decision making' (US Code, 2001b). The members of this senior council include the following:

(1) The Secretary of Commerce, who serves as the Chair.
(2) The Under-Secretary of Commerce for International Trade.
(3) The Director of the Office of Management and Budget.
(4) The Secretary of State.
(5) The Secretary of the Interior.
(6) The Secretary of Labour.
(7) The Secretary of Transportation
(8) The Commissioner of the United States Customs Service.
(9) The President of the United States National Tourism Organisation.
(10) The Commissioner of the Immigration and Naturalisation Service.
(11) Representatives of other Federal agencies which have affected interests at each meeting, as deemed appropriate and invited by the Chairman.

The members of this council meet at least twice a year in order to discuss and coordinate the activities of their respective agencies in regard to tourism impacts and other national interests. 'The council shall coordinate national policies and programmes relating to international travel and tourism, recreation, and national heritage resources which involve federal agencies' (US Code, 2001b: 1–2). The council also works with private sector interests and other levels of government to further the coordination of interests and actions.

At the other end of the spectrum state and local governments set and apply basic health and safety standards. For many small tourism businesses their most common interaction with government control comes in the form of health inspectors and other local government compliance officials. These are important ways for government to ensure standards are being met and to gauge the effectiveness of current policy as society and technology changes. Perhaps one of the biggest changes to occur at this level around the world has been the growing legislation banning smoking in public places. This has certainly affected leisure behaviour and has been resisted by certain businesses like pubs and casinos, but in general the predicted business catastrophes have not occurred and everyone can breathe easier.

Regulating tourist flows

Nations can engage in various practices to either encourage or restrict the travel patterns of tourists. Countries restrict the number and type of tourists that visit them through their customs and immigration procedures. Countries can require visas for some or all international visitors as a way of conducting cursory background checks on potential visitors and as a way of controlling the number of visitors by limiting the numbers of visas granted. Visa quotas can be set for certain countries, while routinely denied for others. Some borders are quite open and allow for drive-through custom checks, as is the case between Canada and the US, while crossing other borders can be a long and complicated procedure. Trade blocks, such as NAFTA and the EU, encourage much freer movement of people and goods between member countries, which saves costs and encourages travel.

While most citizens of Western countries are allowed to travel freely around the world, there are still controls on travel. It is still illegal for most Americans to travel to Cuba, although they still slip in via flights from countries outside the US and by boat. Nations also post travel advisories to warn their citizens of those countries they consider risky to visit, which unfortunately has been the fate for many African countries and became an issue in South East Asia after the Bali bombings. Health concerns, such as SARS, have led to the issuance of a WHO travel warning advising tourists not to travel to Beijing and Toronto, which has greatly hurt their tourism trade and convention business (*The Economist*, 2003b). Certain Islamic countries, such as Iran, Egypt and Saudi Arabia, restrict the ability of women to freely travel within and outside their borders (Beyer, 2001). Nations can also 'recall' tourists and foreign nationals at times of pending crisis, as has happened in Indonesia repeatedly over the past 10 years, with the East Timor drive to independence and more recently with the Bali bombings of 2002. In addition to government policies relating to freedom of movement within and between countries, foreign exchange policies and restrictions to the amount and types of goods that can be brought back into a country impact on tourism growth and patterns.

Education

Governments endeavour to educate residents and visitors in tourism matters as a means to accomplishing various ends. In Wales tourism education has been aimed at both residents and travellers as a way of building and strengthening positive images of the country. Tourism's educative role in this process is to 'promote and protect Welsh culture, to consciously and deliberately craft its messages about Wales that are sent through the medium of tourism' (Berger (1980) cited in Morgan & Pritchard, 1998: 154). Despite the long historic efforts of the English to assimilate the Welsh, since the 1990s Wales has made great strides in promoting its unique 'Welshness', by using a number of strategies including those relating to tourism promotion and education. Another example of tourism education aimed primarily at residents is Indonesia's national 'Seven Charms' programme (Timothy, 1999). This programme uses advertisements in print and the electronic media to increase national pride and encourage actions that will increase safety, beauty, environmental protection and hospitable behaviours.

Dispersing tourism impacts

Governments often try to spread the impacts of tourism around their jurisdictional areas in an attempt to prevent patchy tourism development that presents a pattern of 'tourism haves and have-nots'. The tourism development offices of the government of British Columbia have been working for years to spread tourism development around the province beyond the Victoria-Vancouver-Whistler areas that are known as the 'golden triangle' of tourism in BC. Regional tourism development policies pursued by the provincial government in BC include the following:

- increased advertising for attractions in outlying areas;
- staging large events in these areas;
- encouraging package tours that include city and rural tourism experiences;
- providing better access to these areas;
- improving the infrastructure in outlying areas and investing in the development of tourism products and services outside of major tourism centres.

A recent study by Zhang (2001) of regional tourism development for the international tourist market shows the concern for spreading tourism's positive aspects is global. In a comparison of Australian and Chinese experiences she notes how the state of Victoria has tried to encourage international visitors to travel beyond Melbourne and explore the delights of country Australia. Likewise, China has attempted to spread international visitors from its eastern provinces into the more rural regions of the mountainous western provinces. To achieve this China has identified certain tourism growth poles and it is focusing on those with the development of quality attractions and good transport links to major regional airports.

Given that the economies of most developing countries are neither as diverse, nor as robust, as those in developed countries, the impacts of either transnational companies or national government decisions in developing countries can be monolithic. Brohman (1996: 54) notes that 'if provisions are not made to increase local economic participation, this greatly increases the likelihood of the domination of Third World tourism sectors by transnational capitals from the metropolitan core'. In developing countries uneven tourism development can be exasperated by centralised political decisions, as demonstrated in Oakes' (1997) study of tourism development in rural China.

Oakes finds that tourism opportunities in the rural communities of Gaozeng and Zhaoxing in the province of Guizhou are greatly impacted by government policy and funding decisions. Gaozeng was designated as historically important by the government in 1982 which made it eligible for a number of government grants for repairing and enhancing the cultural heritage features of the village (Oakes, 1997: 58). By 1988 a large number of tourists, including 20 tour groups a year, were visiting Gaozeng and the economic and social benefits of tourism were widely shared throughout the village. Unfortunately, when a fire destroyed much of the village later that year, the government withdrew its special historical status along with all related funds and did not provide funds to restore the village as it was felt restored features would 'have no value as traditional antiques' (Oakes, 1997: 58). Government focus and funds then shifted to the village of Zhaoxing, which is now seen by government officials and tourism operators as the principal cultural heritage tourism destination in the region.

Gaozeng has seen its tourism opportunities dry up as tourism entrepreneurs either leave the village or focus their efforts in other areas and remaining policies supporting tourism growth and protecting cultural heritage have been revoked as the tourism potential of the village was seen to be 'ruined' (Oakes, 1997: 59). This example shows that government decisions in terms of granting or withdrawing support for tourism development can have a profound impact on the development of tourism in developing countries.

Conflicting roles and interests

Government needs to balance not only different regional opportunities but different interests if it is to control tourism for the public benefit. However, it is important to note that substantial power imbalances between parties can leave certain groups and local administrations largely out of the loop when it comes to determining tourism policies. Mitchell and Reid (2001) observe that the well-balanced and integrated nature of community based tourism in the Taquile islands of Peru has been threatened by a change in national policies. The federal government of Peru passed a series of anti-monopolisation laws that challenged the traditional ways local people operate their tourism ventures and share the benefits. Under the new legislation outsiders won the right to use docking and other tourism facilities that had previously been the sole domain of the islanders. Mitchell and Reid caution that the new federal laws bring in outsiders who not only compete based on the price of their services, but also bring different values with them that threaten the traditional communal ways of the islanders.

In free market economies it is challenging for governments to control tourism for the benefit of the community, when they are philosophically committed to free enterprise. The dilemma becomes one of setting standards and numbers that will ensure a sustainable industry while denying certain business interests and citizens from participating in the industry. A common example of this dilemma and the balancing act it requires occurs with the issue of taxi licences. The number and cost of such licences is generally based on anticipated demand and the estimated revenue needed to keep the vehicle in good order and to provide a reasonable living. Once this 'imperfect' calculation has been made and all the licences issued no further licences are available until a major change in the supply–demand equation occurs. As such it favours the first mover and established businesses, which in places has encouraged illegal operations and fringe operators.

The same dilemma and balancing act is now required with sustainable nature tourism strategies. In some locations governments are being pressured to add to the early first mover whale watcher or ecolodge operator because of increased demand, but they do not know what the exact carrying capacity is in terms of the environment or economic sustainability. Under these circumstances it is safest to act with caution and to expand slowly, if at all. This of course exposes government to accusations of favouritism, but it also rewards the first mover – the original risk taker.

The diversity of tourism industry membership can create real difficulties in producing a united vision and then effectively conveying this vision to governments. Therefore, governments can find themselves trying to forge effective tourism policies with the cooperation of warring interest groups. In her study of community-based tourism planning in Squamish, BC, Canada, Reed (1997) found a great deal of dissension among and between stakeholders led to the development of an unsatisfactory planning strategy, and that in the end was not implemented. The public participation process was prompted by the provincial government's refusal to approve a major resort in the area unless the municipal government could show that the proposal had the support of the people of Squamish. A tourism coordinating committee was established by the municipality to make tourism planning recommendations to the municipal council. There were concerns that the committee was not representative of all stakeholders groups, that the scope of the planning was too closely tied to the proposed ski resort and that the recommendations were made without due regard to available funding sources. These concerns and associated divergent views split the committee and led to the creation of a rival committee that also put forward recommendations and added to the confusion and concerns about the validity of the process.

Best practice

Factors and processes that enhance a destination's ability to adequately access and then change elements of the tourism industry so that its goals and objectives are met are worthy of study. Howe *et al.* (1997) looked at a number of areas throughout the US, many of which are prime tourist destinations, to determine the 'secrets of successful communities'. They found that most of the successful communities had engaged in several of the following controlling activities (1997: 47):

- develop a widely shared vision;
- create an inventory of local resources;
- build on local assets;
- minimise the need for regulations;
- meet the needs of both landowner and community;
- team up with public land managers;
- recognize the role of non-governmental organisations;
- provide opportunities for leaders to step forward;
- pay attention to the aesthetics.

The benefit of creating a shared vision is that such a vision is much more likely to be supported than one that is perceived to meet only the needs of certain groups. Howe *et al.* (1997) recommend that inventories of local resources should include extensive public participation and result in the creation of maps of ownership, historical land use, current land use, current and pending zoning and potential future uses. In terms of building on assets, it is advisable that communities look to those characteristics that make them unique and attractive to tourists. The unique features could relate to environmental conditions, local history and culture, price competitiveness or convenient access. Since regulations are used to restrict options, often with the intent of achieving a greater good, they can have the less desirable effect of stifling creativity, innovation and fun.

Governments need to be careful that in their efforts to regulate they do not 'dull down' their communities. Increased stakeholder involvement in creating regulations allows for a greater understanding of divergent needs and views along with the flexibility to accommodate these differences. Governments should not only work diligently on establishing overall development plans for their communities, but they should also 'court reputable developers who are willing to do more than what's mandated by law and who work closely with the entire community, not just elected officials, throughout the development process (Howe *et al.* 1997: 83). Teaming up with managers of public lands, such as parks and wildlife reserves, as well as representatives of NGOs and other community leaders can allow for the sharing of resources and ideas in terms of joint planning, management and marketing initiatives. Developments that are aesthetically pleasing as well as functional help to make destination areas more enjoyable places in which to live and work.

Summary

Tourism's complexities and heterogeneous nature challenge elected officials and policy makers alike as they struggle to understand and manage the industry. Most countries in the world recognise tourism as a way to diversify their economies and create corresponding tourism programmes and strategies to support the industry. Tourism can provide a multitude of economic benefits for governments, including attracting outside investors, creating jobs and earning foreign currency to help with a country's trade balance. Governments also benefit when tourism enhances an area's international, national and regional reputation, which in turn can attract additional investment while fostering a sense of pride of place, culture and history amongst their citizenry. Some of the biggest tourism challenges that governments face is determining the appropriate physical areas, types of products and services and levels of funding for tourism. Given that tourism is a relatively new industry and one that is dominated by small businesses, governments can find themselves perplexed if not dumbfounded in terms of understanding the potential impacts of their policies and spending on tourism development.

The processes outlined in this section will never be straightforward and easy to implement in the real world of tourism strategic planning. To demonstrate this point we have included an appraisal of the efforts undertaken in one of the world's most treasured locations – the Florida Keys. The case study by Theresa Szymanis, an experienced regional and town planner who has worked in the Keys, illustrates that many of the processes advocated in this book are underway. But in the real world of personal greed, political expediency, uncertain data and analysis, appropriate and acceptable management will require considerable goodwill to be achieved.

Case Study: Tourism Management in the Florida Keys, USA

(Theresa A. Szymanis, AICP)

Ensuring that a high quality tourism product remains viable for future generations is a challenge which local governments in the Florida Keys are addressing. Connected by Highway US 1 to the Florida mainland south of Miami and Everglades National Park, this fragile chain of 46 bridged keys

Figure 10.2 The Florida Keys

(coral islands), situated on the third largest barrier reef ecosystem in the world, curves 170 kilometres from Key Largo to its southernmost point, Key West (Figure 10.2). The scenic Overseas Highway, in addition to scheduled airlines and a growing cruise ship industry, transport more than three million visitors to the Keys annually (Leeworthy & Wiley, 1996: 7). Visits are concentrated during the cooler months of December to April, and then subside as hurricane season accelerates to an October tourism low (English *et al.*, 1996: 3). On peak season nights up to 65,800 visitors, close in number to the Keys 80,000 permanent population, are estimated to sleep over (Leeworthy & Wiley, 1996: 8). The whole region falls under the jurisdiction of Monroe County, with the county seat being located in the central town/key of Marathon.

Tourism, the main employment industry in the Keys, in 1995/96 directly and indirectly engaged 21,848 local 'Conchs' in daily economic activities and generated $506.01 million, or 45% of official reported income (English *et al.*, 1996: 6). In spite of this success, in a 1999 Monroe County Tourist Development Council (TDC) survey to which 24.2% of Monroe County registered voters responded, 52.3% agreed that the negative impacts of tourism outweighed the positive economic benefits when it came to community needs and quality of life issues. Furthermore, 51.7% felt that the county should attract fewer visitors, 80.3% identified traffic as the major disadvantage of tourism, followed by environmental degradation (57.2%) and overcrowding (52.6%) (Shivlani, 2000: 13–17). This pivotal survey garnered much media attention, as the results challenged the common philosophy that economic growth is beneficial at any cost, and called for a reorganisation of available resources to counterbalance the perceived negative effects of tourism, to make the industry more locally acceptable.

Planning

While the 1999 TDC tourism survey gathered and collated qualitative data regarding voters' perceptions and reactions to tourism, *planning studies* conducted by state and county governments in the Keys confirmed that improvements to community quality of life, the foundation on which tourism is based, are indeed necessitated. Notably, issues of concern include: overtaxed infrastructure (highways; water supply; wastewater treatment; stormwater treatment; and hurricane evacuation) with capacity stretched to or exceeding acceptable limits (Monroe County, 1998–2002; URS Greiner, 1999–2002; Miller Consulting, Inc., 2001); planning policies and land development regulations which deter real estate investment, resulting in urban blight and decay; and resident dissatisfaction with service delivery from Monroe County resulting from disproportionate spending directed towards the county seat in Key West (Florida Legislative Committee on Intergovernmental Relations, 2001: 40). Remedies fall within the non-market realm and require changes to public policy and capital expenditures, which can be brought about through effective regional planning.

Organising

In combination, these and other concerns helped shape resident attitudes towards tourism and also towards the responsible government bodies, prompting a grassroots movement of citizens groups to lead the *re-organization* of the political structure from a county-wide government with a five-member Board of County Commissioners (BOCC) into more cohesive local government units. Incorporation into smaller communities allows citizens better access to decision-making processes and representation to senior governments, plus more fiscal control over local affairs. With an emphasis on citizen input for the planning and prioritising of budgetary items, solutions can be tailor-made for each community reflecting the specific values and goals of its residents and property owners.

Between 1997 and 2000, four separate municipal incorporation votes were held for small groupings of keys oriented around local commercial centres within Monroe County. Two of the votes were successful resulting in the incorporation of Islamorada, Village of Islands on 31 December 1997, and of the City of Marathon on 30 November 1999. Votes to incorporate Key Largo in November 1999 and to amalgamate Paradise Islands, Village of the Lower Keys in November 2000 failed. The new political structure of the Florida Keys is shown in Table 10.1. Citizen representation is increased dramatically through new Advisory Committees and Task Forces on local development issues, with 47 representatives in Islamorada and 26 in Marathon alone. This community autonomy is a far cry from the previous BOCC with its jurisdiction previously covering the 106 mile chain, except Key West, Layton and Key Colony Beach.

Community planning

The break away municipalities launched immediately into the task of drafting Comprehensive Plans to guide their redevelopment, required by Florida Statute to be adopted within three years of municipal incorporation. Comprehensive Plans consolidate data for analysis, used to formulate government policy, programmes and strategies addressing: future land use; transportation; housing; public infrastructure; coastal management; conservation; recreation and open space; intergovernmental coordination; and capital improvements, projected 20 years into the future. Simultaneously, in 1999 the Monroe County Planning Department initiated the Liveable CommuniKeys Master Plan Programme, with community planning focused on Big Pine/No Name Keys and Key Largo, where incorporation votes failed.

Award winning growth management rules from the Monroe County

Table 10.1 New political structure of the Florida Keys

Jurisdiction	Location by mile marker on US 1	Permanent population projection (2000)
City of Key West (Inc. 8 Jan. 1828)	MM 0–6	26,102
City of Marathon (Inc. 30 Nov. 1999)	MM 47 to 60	11,272
City of Key Colony Beach (Inc. 24 Sept. 1957)	MM 55	1,101
City of Layton (Inc. 18 Sept. 1963)	MM 68	208
Islamorada, Village of Islands (Inc. 31 Dec. 1997)	MM 72.5 to 91	7,665
Monroe County (Est. 2 July 1823)	Remaining Keys	39,274
Total		85,622

Data source: Monroe County Public Facilities Capacity Analysis, 2002

Year 2010 Comprehensive Plan (1992), approved by the Florida Department of Community Affairs (DCA) under Area of Critical State Concern legislation in 1997, provide a starting point for new planning efforts. Through the 2010 Plan policy the county slowed the real estate boom to the maximum extent of the law, protecting both the rare native ecology and private property rights. However, with a strong focus on conservation, this plan failed to adequately address the built environment, community character and citizen quality of life (Monroe County, 1999: 4). Now in the Keys, *community planning* with and for residents and property owners has ascended as a priority, with many secondary benefits arising from local improvements to accrue to the tourism industry. Revised Land Development Regulations are being drafted by both new municipalities and Monroe County to guide land developers in synchronisation with Comprehensive Plan policy and government investment.

In addition to plan-making the new governments embarked upon fulfilment of election promises, projects for which consensus was immediately clear. Budgets were allocated for a dream field of community enhancements including: public land acquisition; wastewater and stormwater planning; development of parks, Olympic swimming pools and recreation complexes; redevelopment of beaches and harbours; streetscape and highway beautification; construction of a linked cyclist/pedestrian network paralleling US 1; support for a Keys-wide Monroe-Dade Express bus service; and ecological rehabilitation. Using extensive community visioning and consultation, local identities are being defined and further improvements prioritised. Re-allocated Tourist Development Council bed tax dollars have been channelled through its five District Advisory

Committees (DACs) for many of these projects, but bank loans, intergovernmental transfers, fund balance transfers from Monroe County, grants and private-public partnerships are all in vogue to creatively address the latent demand for quality of life improvements.

Leadership

While local enhancement projects improve the liveability and attractiveness of Keys communities, such projects only partly mitigate the quandaries identified by the 1999 TDC tourism survey. By magnifying the attractiveness of the Keys as a prized destination, the larger growth management issues of population and tourism pressures on infrastructure and the environment may be exacerbated.

In the search for solutions, the fragmentation of Monroe County into multiple jurisdictions presents a new challenge – how to organise all of these disparate political units now that the independent municipalities are asserting their differences? At present, there is no agency, group or mechanism in place to resolve disputes over issues that transcend local boundaries, arising from articulated visions and clashing development policies. In a 2001 presentation to the Florida Legislature, the Legislative Committee on Intergovernmental Relations (LCIR) warned that there is increasing concern about such matters:

> The DCA continues to have conflicting jurisdictional issues arise, and the many *programs* for which it is responsible are not always easy to integrate. Communities in the Keys have not been strong adherents to intergovernmental coordination, thus leaving the area at risk to potentially serious problems concerning emergency management [hurricane evacuation, etc.] and water related matters. (Florida Legislative Committee on Intergovernmental Relations, 2001: 41)

Consider the pressing question, 'How many more residents and tourists can the Florida Keys reasonably manage?'; given the impacts to the marine environment from inadequate wastewater and stormwater treatment facilities, a finite supply of piped-in potable water being shared by all Keys jurisdictions, and the US 1 artery already bursting on peak season days. Acknowledging the impacts of new development, Islamorada's Comprehensive Plan (2001) caps growth at 14 residential units and 1340 sq. ft. of commercial space annually, with strict conditions limiting new tourist facilities. The new City of Marathon, on the other hand, encourages redevelopment through its draft Comprehensive Plan by allowing developers to build out to the maximum densities and intensities possible (City of Marathon, 2002: 1). Any traffic increase associated with new development downstream of Islamorada will exert pressure for a generally unwanted highway widening from three to five lanes throughout the Village (Miller Consulting, Inc., 2001) with impacts most severe in the Village Centre where the displacement of business parking, access and some commercial buildings is likely (Islamorada, Village of Islands, 2001: 2–7). With no mandated dispute resolution body in place, all jurisdictions independently push onward with their individual plan implementation, regardless of regional implications.

Florida Keys Carrying Capacity Study

It is hoped that the Florida Keys Carrying Capacity Study (FKCCS), ordered in 1996 by the Florida Administration Commission and the Governor, under the *leadership* of the US Army Corps of Engineers (USACE) and Florida DCA, will address these broader growth management concerns. The purpose of the $6 million dollar study and computer model is to ' . . . determine the ability of the Florida Keys ecosystem and infrastructure to withstand all impacts of additional land development activities and associated population growth' (US Army Corps of Engineers, 2002). Outcomes of the study will be used to modify the growth management policies within the separate Comprehensive Plans consistent with the study findings, thus promoting compatibility between the development goals of the county and municipalities.

However, when presented with the study and resulting draft Carrying Capacity Analysis Model (CCAM) for peer review, the National Academy of Sciences National Research Council (NRC) March 2002 report found that the fundamental problems remain. According to the NRC, the computer model does not adequately account for the impact of tourism on the islands; makes unrealistic assumptions about hurricane evacuation; fails to evaluate how shifts in population would affect the Keys; and does not address the effects of growth and tourism on water quality and the coastal marine environment (National Academy of Sciences, 2002: 1–4). Further modifications are now being made to revise the computer model to enable it to resolve crucial questions facing growth managers in the Florida Keys. A second independent peer review has been completed.

Control

The Monroe County Board of County Commissioners and Tourist Development Council took a step forward with the 1999 tourism survey, for the first time linking tourism planning with growth management concerns. These agencies heeded public opinion to guide their actions resulting in re-allocated funding and a higher quality tourism product throughout the Keys, enjoyed by local residents and tourists alike. While residents may feel that some of the problems associated with tourism in the late 1990s are now less critical due to the many new community facilities and enhancements, the real issues remain unresolved, and will be amplified as more visitors are attracted to the region.

Resolution of growth management issues has driven planning in the

Florida Keys since designation by the Florida government as an Area of Critical State Concern in 1974. The Department of Community Affairs, once responsible for consistency review and oversight of all plans and ordinances for Monroe County and Key West only, is now inundated with jurisdictional files, without a regional template to guide their decisions. Being economically reliant on tourism, there is a pressing need to strike the right balance between the number of people living in and attracted to the Florida Keys, in line with the ability of the Keys' infrastructure to accommodate their needs, and the fragile environmental resources to absorb their impacts. The carrying capacity model offers promise as a tool to help grasp changes to public policy and the capital expenditures needed to achieve this balance. More important than having the tool, however, is how the tool is to be used. Currently, the political will to initiate stakeholder discussion about conflicting regional issues is lacking. Still in the early stages of establishing a balanced tourism and growth management approach, Florida's Keys communities have accomplished much with independence, but have yet to discover the full benefits of a region melded together under ONE shared vision of sustainable development.

Part 4

A New Paradigm

New Approach

Up to this point we have analysed the major components of business management and stakeholder groups within a community tourism framework. To do so we have separated and dissected what is, in reality, a continual and fluid process of management. It is hoped that the discourse has demonstrated the need to link tourism management with the four functions of business and how these relate to the interests of all stakeholder groups.

It is necessary to combine management principles with community decision-making to develop local tourism that is in harmony with community aspirations and business realities. In tourism destinations there is considerable common interest and potential synergy between various stakeholder groups. Yet the identified business functions and groups tend to operate in a rather haphazard manner, and generally in response to crisis rather than as a result of deliberate forethought and planning.

What is needed is some way to pull the functions and stakeholders involved in community tourism together, to offer a process that will permit the relevant factors and players to come together. It requires a framework that will channel all pertinent elements and viewpoints along a realistic course. To be effective it will need to consider how to facilitate discussion that leads to constructive outcomes. These are challenging goals in themselves, but there is plenty of evidence in the previous pages that there is both a means and will in many communities to achieve a more strategic tourism management approach.

Part Outline

This part demonstrates methods to assist in decision-making and offers a model to ensure all relevant functions and stakeholders become involved. Chapter 11 reviews some of the components of conflict and how various individuals and organisations have developed techniques to harness the positive aspects of conflict. Chapter 12 describes a conceptual model that can help to ensure all relevant components and stakeholders are considered by presenting them as a bridge between tourism's potential and its reality. The bridge analogy is particularly relevant as a physical and widely recognised way of bringing essential tourism elements together.

Chapter 11

Working Together

Strategic community tourism management grows out of stakeholder cooperation. Tourism is an area where the public has a good grasp of basic facts and needs based on their own travel encounters. Tourism stakeholders have the knowledge and experiences necessary for providing a well-rounded view of issues. These groups are also empowered by increased access to information and favourable changes to legal and governance systems. The options for collaborative decision-making outlined in this chapter focus on non-emergency situations in a developed and democratic country where there is both the opportunity and the necessity to work with tourism stakeholders over a sustained period.

While collaborative decision-making processes have many merits, they are not appropriate for all situations. If there is an emergency or if essential elements of fruitful collaborative efforts are absent, then more centralised decision-making, such as through a state or national tourism body, might be the best way of ensuring that tourism will be sustainable. An emergency situation is an isolated occurrence for which abrupt, highly controlled and centralised measures are necessary. This can translate to an area responding to a sudden and dramatic plummet in visitor numbers, or an environmental catastrophe.

Objectives

This chapter looks briefly at some examples of challenges to collaborative planning in developing areas dealing with emergency situations and endemic under-resourcing. Collaborative tourism planning efforts are highly appropriate when there are long-standing disagreements in communities over how tourism resources should be managed and resources are available to support alternative proposals. As tourism impacts become more apparent and more options open up in relation to how tourism growth can be managed, stakeholders push for a larger role in directing the growth of the industry. The collaborative decision-making options outlined in this chapter focus in the main on non-emergency situations, where there are sufficient financial, environmental and social resources to enable stakeholders to work together over a sustained period.

The chapter examines ways to bring stakeholder groups together to

340

create fair, effective and efficient tourism development decisions using the four business management functions approach of earlier chapters. It opens with an examination of conflict and problems using traditional methods of decision-making. Planning issues and options are then explored from the vantage points of the various levels of citizen participation. In the organising portion of the chapter appropriate levels of public participation based on particular circumstances are detailed. Promising leadership options for tourism management arise from emerging collaborative decision-making methods, which draw upon principled negotiation techniques. Ways of controlling group-decision-making processes so they can fulfil their potential are then explored. Particular attention is given to ensuring that all stakeholders can participate in tourism decision-making processes in a manner that strengthens their individual power as well as enhancing the decision-making capabilities of the larger group.

Tourism conflicts

Tourism development in any community is bound to generate some conflict given that it modifies landscapes and changes community dynamics. Tourism conflicts are costly in terms of loss of trust, legal fees, financial overruns, project delays and lost opportunities. As the Urban Land Institute (1994: 15) notes, 'whether the result of greater racial, ethnic or economic diversity or an altered landscape, change generates tremendous uncertainty, that may lead to greater community conflict and political instability'. Conflict is described as a 'process that begins when one party perceives that the other has frustrated, or is about to frustrate, some concern of [theirs]' (Gordon, *et al.*, 1990: 532). These definitions can be expanded to include disagreements between individuals and within stakeholder groups and communities.

Once a community or a significant segment of it sours on tourism, reactions against tourists can damage its image and economic prospects. Public reaction against tourism activities can be as pointed as direct legal action, picketing, boycotting, blocking proposals for further development or removing from power those who are tied to the controversial matters. The terrorist attacks on tourists to Egypt led to a drop of 21.9% in the number of tourists and a 42.5% decline in tourism receipts between 1992 and 1993 (Aziz, 1995: 92). More recently, 'the tragic events of September 11 affected tourism in every region of the world' (WTO, 2002: 1). Certain groups are exploiting the fact that tourism is a soft and effective target for terrorist action, as shown with the Bali bombings of 2002. As these acts of terrorism show, the results of political concerns fuelled by anger can be devastating.

Anger

Anger is primarily a reaction against a real or perceived threat that gives rise to conflict. Susskind and Field (1996: 16) in their book *Dealing with an*

Angry Public: The Mutual Gains Approach to Resolving Disputes list three circumstances when anger is likely to flare up:

- people have been hurt;
- they feel threatened by risks not of their own making; or
- they believe that their fundamental beliefs are being challenged.

Susskind and Field (1996) found anger can be magnified by any number of related factors, most of which are tied to issues of power. These factors include people feeling weak against a much stronger adversary, such as when a group has limited financial and technical resources and is fighting a well-funded corporation or government agency. The anger of resident groups can become ferocious if they believe their views are not being taken seriously. Another anger factor is when people feel they have been treated unfairly, or with disrespect. Anger and conflict can create hostile tourism environments that make things unpleasant if not unbearable for all concerned, but it can lead also to benefits.

Anger in a tourism context can be fuelled by any number of injustices and imbalances in power relationships. Tensions between visitors and residents can arise if a destination is treated as a mere 'playground' for privileged outsiders who act disparagingly towards the people and environments they visit. The anger and disappointment expressed by locals towards tourists can stem from deep social issues, such as those arising from developing colonies being 'recolonised' by tourism firms and visitors who transform these countries into something that meets their needs, rather than those of the country's sovereign people. Morgan and Pritchard (1998: 242) are greatly concerned with the power imbalances that can be reflected in and propagated by tourism, as they note:

> This misrepresentation of historical relationships [between former colonies and the new colonisers] is just one facet of a much more complex, multi-dimensional power reality in which powerful white worlds dominate and define black worlds; in which male dominates female; and a dynamic First World contrasts itself with a static, timeless and unchanging Third World. This is not power confined to international politics and global players – this is the power and politics of everyday life.

Tourism management carries with it a moral responsibility to recognise inherent power imbalances and to develop practical and just ways to work with tourism stakeholders in pursuing more sustainable and equitable options.

Conflict can create both negative and positive outcomes for destinations, as 'within organisations, conflict can prevent stagnation, encourage the search for new solutions and developments and foster better understanding'

(Montgomery, 1986). This is certainly the view of Sumner Redstone, an American media magnate, who says 'It may sound strange but I invite confrontation, confrontation leads to truth' (*The Economist*, 2003a: 59). Potential negative and positive impacts of conflict from a business perspective are detailed below (Gordon *et al.* 1990: 537):

Negative

(1) Participants feel demeaned or defeated.
(2) Creates distance and hostility amongst participants.
(3) Creates a climate of mistrust.
(4) Participants focus on furthering their own best interests.
(5) Teamwork is eroded and resistance rises.
(6) Turnover of staff and customers increase.

Positive

(1) Creates better ideas.
(2) Identify and resolve long standing-issues.
(3) Clarify individual views.
(4) Raise interest and creativity.
(5) Explore new approaches.

Due to the high probability for conflict with many tourism issues, viewing conflict as an inevitable yet manageable occurrence and planning for it is the most sensible course of action. Organisational ways of addressing conflict include legal advisers, human resources advice, ombudspersons and other systems designed to deal with these conflicts. Organisations lacking a formal system for managing conflicts and disputes are likely to have informal ones. These informal systems are more *ad hoc* and dependent on the actions of key individuals as well as organisation norms and the pervading culture's ways of resolving issues (Stitt, 1998). When a conflict becomes so large that it includes multiple organisations as well as many different factions of stakeholder groups, a more elaborate technique for dealing with the conflict is required.

Problems with traditional methods

As stated earlier, tourism development is often an agent of change. Local governments are widely perceived as not being able to adequately address the threats that change brings to communities (Urban Land Institute, 1994). Concerns over local government's inabilities to manage factors of great community importance are expressed widely in Australia's country towns (Collits, 2001). Reasons for questioning the abilities of established decision-makers to make the right decisions are explored by Susskind and Cruikshank in their book *Breaking the Impasse: Consensual Approaches to Resolving Public Disputes* (1987). They identify a series of problems with traditional public dispute resolution methods that prevent effective decision-making on major public issues. These findings are summarised below and presented in a tourism context.

- *Tyranny of the Majority*
  When the option that is most acceptable to the largest group is the measure by which a decision is judged, innovative ideas can be ignored. Under these circumstances, a watered-down proposal not requiring extensive discussion or revision can be chosen rather than working through issues surrounding new ideas. Since tourism destinations need to offer something 'special' that will help differentiate them from their competitors, communities that will commit only to conservative measures, may find their return on tourism investments to be disappointing or even negligible.

- *Lack of long-term commitment*
  Pressures to perform well in the short term can override concerns and responsibilities for the long-term implications of actions. This is especially true for politicians with limited terms of office. Heads of businesses must give priority to their financial backers, be it their shareholders or bankers. Often destinations and tourism businesses are assessed on the basis of 'last season's results', rather than in terms of general trends and the results from similar businesses and destinations.

- *Limitations of voting*
  Voting does not encourage a building of options – it limits them. Voting tends to cause a polarisation of 'us' and 'them' views rather than a cross-fertilisation of ideas and motivations. When questions are put to a vote, such as referendums on tourist taxes, they should be simple and straightforward, so that people are clear on what options they are being asked to consider.

- *Complexity*
  There can be a range of technical issues and scientific uncertainties regarding the impacts of proposed options. Lack of clarity makes it difficult, if not impossible, to make the most appropriate decision. Therefore, when considering tourism development options, it is important to realise that to a certain degree the outcome will be unpredictable. As such, a degree of flexibility and responsiveness to change needs to be built into implementing these options.

- *Pre-disposition to win/lose conclusions*
  When there are identified 'losers' then the public interest has not been served. The losers may not only be the developers, but also larger segments of the community that could have benefited from the economic opportunities and job creation that a development could have created. If those opposed to a proposal work with its supporters, to-

gether they can develop options that may mitigate negative impacts. By working together they might agree upon certain flaws in the initial proposal and then move forward, creating opportunities for mutual gain.

More people are questioning the abilities and rights of established decision-makers to decide on their own what is best for communities. While past actions may be valiant, automatically deferring to the 'way things have always been done', can be symptomatic of rigidity, laziness and fear of the unknown (Montgomery, 1986). Studies show that public trust in government and organisations has plummeted, as the shortcomings of the people and policies associated with these groups are exposed and acted against (Klein, 2000; Roddick, 2000).

Prior to the political activism of the 1960s many Western societies were seen to be more cohesive. However, such cohesiveness masked a range of social, economic and environmental problems that were perpetuated by exclusionary practices. Diversity is becoming a more recognised component of today's society. This recognition is based on changing public perceptions and court interpretations of civil rights, resource allocations and government's role in society. Paradoxically, just as the public is increasingly questioning the abilities of elected officials to make the right decisions, many people in power have little confidence or trust in the public's abilities to understand and appropriately respond to pressing issues (Renn & Levine, 1990, cited in Dienel & Renn, 1995).

One of the best ways of dealing with conflict is to ensure that issues are dealt with as soon as possible. Conflict prevention can include educational measures, such as cultural awareness training, and the establishment of procedures to appropriately address issues before they progress into conflict. Partnering is a conflict prevention process used widely in the construction industry (Stitt, 1998). Before a construction project begins, all of the operators working on the job agree on how disputes will be resolved if they arise, with the underlying premise that dispute resolution will not stop construction activities (Stitt, 1998). This approach brings operators together as 'partners', creating an environment of understanding and mutual responsibility and reward. Destinations, like major construction operations, rely on many different parties to provide quality products. Therefore, it is advisable for tourism management strategies to include conflict prevention measures similar to partnering, that enable stakeholders to create strategies for dealing with issues before they mutate into problems.

Planning

Early planning can go a long way towards preventing, or at least mitigating, tourism conflicts. The public's ability to block tourism proposals should not be underestimated. The public has become more capable of stopping developments believed to be wrong. Advocates for citizen and environmental rights have helped to transform the way much of the world now looks at these issues. Dotson *et al.* (1989: A–6) list the following factors as contributing to increased public concern and action over contemporary planning issues:

- more active interest groups;
- greater legal scrutiny of public actions;
- increased scarcity of government resources;
- higher public awareness of planning impacts;
- more complex planning problems.

Governments endeavour to incorporate degrees of public participation in their decision-making processes. However, in their attempts to include public participation in their deliberations elected officials are often criticised for pandering to the most vocal interest groups, at the expense of the greater public good and for producing insipid appeasement packages.

Each stage of the tourism planning process is ripe for controversy and conflict. A brief description of these stages, drawing from Dotson *et al.* (1989), is provided below:

(1) Identifying goals and objectives, which involves gathering a wide range of opinions from effected stakeholders.
(2) Policy formation, which involves working with stakeholders' representatives to develop potential regulations that are responsive to the needs and objectives of the entire community.
(3) Plan preparation and adoption, which involves working with stakeholders to debate and formulate a specific strategy.
(4) Plan and programme implementation, which involves community debate at public hearings that can involve enabling language, budgets and council approval.
(5) Regulatory administration, which tends to involve stakeholders battling over the approval of specific private development projects.

At each of these stages differences and misunderstandings between stakeholders can intensify tensions and erode options. Different tourism stakeholders are bound to have different ideas and different levels of power in regards to determining what is best for them and the community. While a great deal of power is invested in the elites of society, operating from a top-down perspective, power also circulates through society at various levels like a web (Foucault, 1990, cited in Morgan & Pritchard, 1998). Therefore, certain stakeholders, such as charismatic and well-known environmental leaders, can have more power than other stakeholders.

Regardless of their positions and attributes, many stakeholders may be unsure of tourism's full impacts and potential for their community.

Government can assist in bringing members of stakeholder groups together to share their views and develop options in a manner that is sensitive and responsive to their differences. Providing adequate information on tourism's effects builds trust and empowers stakeholder groups to make informed suggestions. Planning departments are well positioned to assist destinations in developing tourism plans due to their experience and expertise in creating plans that account for a diverse range of impacts on an area's economic, social and environmental elements. While traditional decision-makers, such as elected officials and tourism boards, have the ultimate authority in most tourism decisions, there are various levels of public participation that can influence these decisions.

Levels of participation

The level of stakeholder participation in tourism issues can vary considerably, ranging from outside agitators to actual decision-makers. The eight steps of Sherry Arnstein's classic *A ladder of citizen participation* (1969) and our views of how these steps can apply to tourism stakeholders involved with a resort development proposal, are outlined below.

(1) *Manipulation* – Non-participatory
- 'Decide-announce-defend' approach, where the public cannot change what has been pre-determined.
- Educate the public as to what will be done, often through a set presentation to local government and through supportive stories in the media.

  Sell the public a finished package for a proposed resort development.

(2) *Therapy* – Very low level of participation
- Provide an opportunity for the public to share its frustrations and concerns, often through a 'special meeting' at the local government level.
- Focus on identifying and managing 'problem people' or types.

  Present a resort development's supposed benefits to members of the public and provide them with an opportunity to 'have their say' on the issue, without providing feedback mechanisms for modifying the proposal.

(3) *Informing* – Low level of participation
- First legitimate step in participation.
- Public concern over a pending decision can lead to minor alterations to the decision, the scope of these changes is limited.

Inform members of the public of a resort development concept and provide limited opportunities for them to suggest small changes, such as those relating to the appearance of the resort.

(4) *Consultation* – Minor level of participation
- Special forums for the public to share its views through mechanisms, such as surveys and workshops, designed to draw out the public's goals, ideas and concerns in relation to the pending decision.

    Control the extent of public discussion on tourism and use these discussions as a means of assessing community support for the proposed resort and other pending tourism decisions. While some changes to the proposal will be considered in response to the public's expressed views, whether it should be built will not be questioned.

(5) *Placation* – Moderate level of participation
- Public influences the decision in a broad-based manner, while certain individuals or groups have the opportunity to more closely advise the decision-making body(ies).
- Create taskforces, committees or other groups that are seen to represent the broader interests of the community and these groups advise the decision-making body(ies).

    A public advisory group with members hand-picked by elected representatives could be created to make recommendations for significant changes to the resort proposal. However, depending on the level of legitimacy that the decision-making body(ies) give to this group only politically palatable recommendations will be adopted, while more radical recommendations are deferred for 'further study'.

(6) *Partnership* – High level of participation
- Actual decision-making shared with members of the public.
- Redistribution of power through negotiations between the established decision-making body(ies) and members of the public through the establishment of joint committees.

    A joint committee made up of members from established decision-making body(ies) and the public reviews issues and makes recommendations that the decision-making body(ies) adopt, as long as these recommendations are supported by all committee members.

(7) *Delegated power* –Very high level of participation
- High level of participation in terms of actual decision-making being led by members of the public.

- The balance of power is weighted in favour of members of the public through the establishment of joint committees.

A joint committee made up of members from established decision-making body(ies) and the public, where members of the public are in the majority, review the issues and make recommendations that the decision-making body(ies) will adopt as long as these recommendations are supported by a majority of the committee members.

(8) *Citizen control* – Top level of participation
  - Highest level of public participation, in the sense that the general public holds all decision-making power.
  - Create cooperatives that are responsible for planning, policies and decisions that affect community members.

Certain ecotourism groups establish cooperative tourism boards, to plan and operate local tourism ventures, including resorts. The political success of such a process will be determined by the extent to which the public's representatives in this process are seen to legitimately represent their community and be in a position to make the best possible decisions for their community.

Power

It can be argued that much of the public's involvement in tourism decision-making processes ranges from 'manipulation' to 'placation' (Hall, 1995). Governments typically ask citizens to share their views on issues once the relevant decisions on these issues have already been made (Webler, 1995). Reasons given for minimising the role and importance of public participation in deciding community issues include concerns over the effectiveness of such participation and its costs. Concerns about diminishing returns, in terms of the overall value of increasing public participation are understandable. What is needed are practical ways of providing the right level of public participation for a given situation to produce practical, effective and fair decisions.

While elected representatives and heads of organisations are accountable for their actions and are subject to either elections or some form of vote of confidence, the general public has no such accountability (Dienel & Renn, 1995). This lack of accountability combined with limited expertise can lead to citizens advocating options that are not politically, financially or physically possible, especially over the long term. Furthermore, removing entrenched decision-making abilities from traditional decision-makers can be illegal, unconstitutional or otherwise unacceptable. If elected representatives or the heads of organisations are to respond to the 'public's general will' when making decisions they need to enter into a form of public discourse to understand how the public views the issues at hand, so they can respond appropriately (Webler, 1995). Therefore, the rights and responsibilities of appointed decision-makers need to be balanced with those of the public.

The level of participation that the public obtains is a direct reflection of local power dynamics. Power in decision-making processes can be defined as 'the potential or actual ability to influence others in a desired direction' (Gordon *et al.*, 1990: 589). Power begets power, in that if a particular stakeholder group shows itself to be powerful before, during and after negotiations, they are in a much stronger position to ensure that their contributions are meaningful. Power is a reflection of resources, including money, intellect, experiences, negotiation and leadership skills, as well as the ability to inspire. Those without substantial resources can increase their power by making strategic alliances, rallying support for their views and conducting themselves well in the collaborative decision-making process (Susskind & Field, 1996). Laws, institutions, cultural norms and language all profoundly influence power situations, thereby largely determining the extent to which the views of various stakeholder groups will be incorporated into tourism management strategies and approaches.

The final steps in Arnstein's model may be unachievable for political and economic reasons. Yet there are still strong arguments for the earlier steps, such as partnership, as a way of complementing existing systems (Webler, 1995). Tourism advisory groups, such as boards or committees, with representatives from industry, government and residents are a common way to include the public in tourism management decisions. These advisory groups are often used as a reference base for decision-making, but they can also serve on the boards that make the actual decisions. *Tourism Victoria*, the destination marketing association of Victoria, BC in Canada, has a general membership and executive made up of local citizens as well as industry and government representatives. Therefore, residents have an opportunity to influence the actions of this organisation in an advisory capacity, by serving as general members, or as decision-maker on its executive board. The abilities of citizens to influence tourism advisory groups are a function of their proportional representation in the general membership and executive of these groups, as well as the extent to which the other stakeholders support their views and are willing to work with them.

Processes

There are a number of processes for increasing the public's role in tourism management strategies. Public meetings, taskforces, small group workshops and shuttle diplomacy are all described in the control component of this chapter. Three processes that can be particularly useful in the planning stage of destination management are focus groups, the

Delphi technique and the nominal group technique. These techniques allow for a high level of analysis, the results of which can be used to enrich subsequent discussions and decision-making.

Focus groups tend to consist of eight to 10 participants who are brought together to discuss a narrow range of topics with guidance from a third party (La Page, 1994). These participants are chosen according to their abilities to provide insight into the views of particular stakeholder groups, or segments of these groups. Benefits of focus groups are that their members can explore issues and develop options together. The group dynamic of this approach can strengthen the relationships between stakeholder groups and lead to more comprehensive findings. The propensity for strong personalities to dominate these groups and problems with representativeness – especially given the low number of participants – are drawbacks to using focus groups.

The Delphi technique synthesises expert opinions on current issues and events to gain greater insight into likely future outcomes (Moeller & Shafer, 1994). This technique involves providing participants with rounds of questionnaires, the results of which are tabulated and fed back to participants for their consideration and refinement. The median responses drawn from these questionnaires are interpreted as the most likely future outcomes. Benefits of this approach are that group dynamics do not need to be managed, nor do schedules have to be coordinated, as the individual participants work in isolation and in fact usually remain anonymous. Also experts tend to be highly aware of opportunities and constraints in their field, which enhances the accuracy of their predictions. Challenges with this approach include missed opportunities for improving understanding between stakeholders and that the directors of these processes can easily influence process outcomes, due to their pervasive role in directing the process.

The nominal group technique (NGT) 'provides two specific types of output: first, it provides a list of ideas relevant to the topic in question; and second, the technique provides qualified individual and aggregate measures of the relative desirability of the ideas raised in the session' (Ritchie, 1994: 494). This highly structured technique uses a third party facilitator to guide the groups of experts through the processes. NGT starts with initial statements or topics being put to group participants who then reflect on them individually and share their views with the group. Options are expressed in written form, such as on a flip chart, and reviewed and ranked by all present. The facilitator compiles the results using voting preferences to indicate group priorities. The main benefit of using this approach is that it brings various stakeholder groups together in a constructive forum, where facilitators ensure negative views are subsumed by positive consensus. The largest challenge with NGT is to convert the declared priorities into action.

Peter Murphy used a particular NGT technique – the Delbecq technique (Delbecq *et al.*, 1975; Runyan, 1977) to pull together the ideas and opinions of 54 groups in Victoria, BC, Canada, regarding local tourism development and directions. He developed a three-stage workshop. At the opening session all representatives expressed their concerns about local tourism; these views were written on flip charts and then posted around the large assembly room. The second stage was a simulation exercise, where individuals were placed in unfamiliar roles and asked to locate a high rise commercial development in a sensitive environmental area of a 'sim-city'. The objective of this exercise was to encourage stakeholders to think of other viewpoints and to be prepared to make compromises. They needed to do that to construct the partnerships necessary to 'win the game' and achieve their preferred development option. The third and crucial last stage was to use the Delbecq technique (Murphy *et al.*, 1985).

The Delbecq technique necessitates the division of the whole group into several small mixed interest groups that separate to think about ways to solve the problems and concerns identified in the first session. With the help of a facilitator each small group thinks of 'solutions' individually and in silence. Then they share their thoughts, without any group comment allowed, which are placed on a flip chart. Once all thoughts are on the board the small group is allowed to comment on the preferred solutions, but *only* in a positive and constructive manner. For example, certain similarities may be observed with respect to some of the proffered solutions, enabling the construction of a joint solution. The final step at this stage is for the small group to rank their solutions. The top three to five small group ideas are then brought before the total assembly by the facilitator, with no reference to whose ideas they were. The total group is then invited to discuss the proposed solutions, again in a positive and constructive manner only, before voting on their individual favourites. In a variety of settings this approach has produced one to three dominant suggestions, which can be used to direct future community decision-making.

A key challenge is to move from the 'group-hug' atmosphere of the workshop to actual action. In the case of the Victoria, BC workshop a 'blue-ribbon' committee was created to develop an action plan to implement the leading and dominant recommendation. In this case it was to create a structure that would coordinate all the industry and community energy that was evident throughout the workshop. This committee, under the chair of a neutral representative – Professor Peter Murphy – reported back to the total group within the specified time period and presented a proposed umbrella organisation to guide the city's future tourism development. The proposal was accepted and *Tourism Victoria* was born as the capital region's destination marketing association.

Organising

Organising requires an understanding of what is needed to get the job done. Group decision-making can require significant resources (Tiegerman-Farber & Radziewicz, 1998). When putting a plan into action there should be a good fit between the matters of concern and the level of public participation necessary to solve them. It is also advisable to provide pertinent background information to participants before meetings and to brief them on issues on an 'as needed basis' (Dotson *et al.*, 1989). These processes are aided by structuring meetings in a prudent fashion and establishing ambitious, yet realistic deadlines for a deliverable outcome from the collaborative group.

Scale and scope

When organising resources to manage tourism development, the likely levels of potential conflict and corresponding public interest need to be anticipated. Dotson *et al.* (1989: A11) identify three types of conflict – issues, disputes and impasses – that they rank according to their level of intensity. Drawing upon Dotson *et al.*'s (1989) work, these conflict types are illustrated within the context of a proposal to develop a marina in an isolated location, as discussed below.

(1) **Issues**

- *Conflict level* Low to moderate and contained level of disagreement.

  The marina proposal is of a modest scale, it would be owned and run by local people and would not be in an environmentally sensitive area.

- *Negotiation required* Informal discussions by affected stakeholders.

  People interested in the proposal have the opportunity to meet and discuss the matter with its proponents in an *ad hoc* manner.

- *Third party involvement* Not usually required, often resolved at the staff level.

  The small number of people interested in the proposal and their low level of concern negate the need for outside assistance. The proponents with the possible assistance of affected government agencies are able to manage consultative processes to the general satisfaction of those involved.

- *Participation techniques* Public meetings to frame issues, examine alternatives, and help build consensus.

The general public can participate in the decision-making process by attending regularly scheduled meetings, such as those of local councils. At these meetings potential modifications to the proposal can be discussed.

(2) **Disputes**

- *Conflict level*   High and more public displays of concern.

The proposal is for a large-scale marina, owned by outside investors, operated by local people and would not be in an environmentally sensitive area.

- *Negotiation required*   Formal discussions by affected stakeholders.

More people are interested in the proposal than would have the opportunity individually and informally to discuss the matter with either its proponents or governing agencies. Therefore, particular forums, such as open houses and workshops, need to be set up so that information can be shared with a large number of people within a relatively short period of time.

- *Third party involvement*   Usually required, in the form of direct negotiations or the mediation of stakeholders' interests through a neutral third party.

The range of people directly involved in the proposal and a growing and diverse range of people interested in the proposal and its impacts make negotiations with stakeholders more difficult. Therefore, outside assistance in establishing and running a consultation process is advisable.

- *Participation techniques*   Disputes involving only a few parties are well suited for direct negotiation, while others will likely need to hold a series of facilitated group meetings.

An advisory group consisting of the parties involved with the proposal (local government representatives, developers, management company) as well as representatives from other interested parties (local residents, environmentalists, business and tourist associations) should hold a series of meetings that are open to the public. Input from other forums, such as council meetings and open houses, should be used to inform the discussions of the advisory council seeking viable options.

(3) **Impasses**

- *Conflict level*   Extreme and entrenched positions on areas of contention.

  The marina proposal is of a large scale, owned and operated by people from outside the community and is in an environmentally sensitive area.

- *Negotiation required*   Formal, often judicial.

  The complexities of finding a solution acceptable to all parties and an inability of the negotiation options to meet the needs of stakeholders, can lead parties to initiate legal proceedings. Alternatively potential environmental impacts or public outcry might be so great as to trigger formal review mechanisms, such as an environmental impact assessment (EIS), or a special government commission to review the issues.

- *Third party involvement*   Arbitration or litigation.

  Arbitration or mediation prior to, or in place of, court proceedings would be advisable.

- *Participation techniques*   Typically adversarial, though there are still opportunities to examine alternatives and help build consensus.

  Formal court and governmental hearings to decide on the fate of a proposal provide a more limited range of options for public participation. Stakeholder groups can become a party to these proceedings, which can include hiring legal representation and expert witnesses. Stakeholders can also submit petitions, reports and other forms of written responses as a way of conveying their views. If affected and interested parties are able to work together to find areas of agreement that they present to court or government hearings, these efforts will likely be viewed favourably and influence the final decision on the matter.

The marina example illustrates how contributing factors to increased tension and the corresponding process demands related to increasing the scale of the development, the degree of outside ownership and anticipated environmental impacts. This escalation of interests, costs and uncertainty could also be caused if public anger is triggered by concerns that the public is being deceived, cheated or otherwise excluded from having its rightful say. This example highlights the importance of planning a public participation process based on the level of need for increased public participation.

While some tourism development processes only require minimal resources for public participation, the greater the potential for conflict the more important it becomes to plan and invest in a negotiation process so that it can function as intended.

Assessment techniques

Once the decision has been made to work together with various stakeholders on a tourism project, the challenges of identifying and including the appropriate representatives from these groups must be confronted. Gray (1985), a renowned author in the area of collaborative decision-making, sees 'legitimate stakeholders' as having the ability and right to engage in the decision-making process. Their ability to participate is tied to available resources, including time, skills and a belief in the joint decision-making process. Their right to participate is tied to their being impacted by the outcome of the decision-making process and their capacity to accurately convey the views of both their interest group and the negotiation group.

Questions of legitimacy are often raised in determining who will represent tourism stakeholder groups (Blank, 1989) and ensuring that these decision-making processes are inclusive and effective (Haywood, 1988). As resources are not equitably distributed throughout societies, there can be great discrepancies at a negotiation table between the different members of a collaborative decision-making process. Given the interrelatedness of economic, social and environmental actions, we are all somewhat affected by these actions. Therefore, someone's right to participate in a decision-making process is usually related to perceptions of level of impact. Those living next to a proposed development can be seen as having a right to participate, as can the larger community to a lesser degree. As noted by Webler (1995) those with more at stake or more power may have a greater ability to undermine the decision-making process, either during implementation or through subsequent revisions if they feel they are not properly represented in the process.

Determining early in the process the level of potential public interest and conflict that a tourism proposal is likely to raise is highly advisable. However, sometimes it can be unclear as to the level of public interest in a tourism matter and the correspondingly appropriate planning response. Factors indicative of a highly contentious tourism proposal include, but are not limited to, the following situations:

- *Stakeholders* Large numbers, diverse, disjointed, uncertainties relating to representation and legitimacy or hostile relations between parties.
- *Proposal* Large scale, reliant on substantial government assistance,

does not fit in with current standards or could be a threat to other businesses.

- *Community* Potentially significant environmental, social and economic impacts.

If the potential for conflict is great it can be highly advantageous to engage in some exploratory assessment of issues in the preplanning stage of a tourism proposal. One method to consider is the *Conflict Assessment Technique* that has been used constructively many times in various countries as a way of identifying the potential to use mediation in resolving conflicts (Susskind, 2001). The basis of this technique is to identify a range of stakeholders and the issues underlying the conflict. While this technique might be too elaborate and resource intensive for most tourist destinations, it contains excellent ideas that could be adapted to suit an area's specific needs and capabilities.

The *Conflict Assessment Technique* begins with an assessment team approaching obvious 'players' concerned about a certain issue and interviewing them. These interviews are confidential as the views participants share are not attributed to them, but rather are noted in relation to general concerns and ideas relating to the issue. The first group of interviewees is asked to recommend additional people to contact in regards to the issue in question. The second group of potential stakeholders is interviewed in the same manner. Pending negotiations on the pressing issue are then announced publicly and more interviews are conducted of those parties that respond to the announcement.

The assessment team maps out the issues and sends this map back to all participants to see if they feel their input has been accurately represented. After making the necessary adjustments and responding to feedback from the survey participants, the assessment team makes a list of potential stakeholders to invite to the process and a potential negotiating procedure. The next steps involve drafting a 'suggested' agenda, budget for the process, allocation of fiscal responsibilities and ground rules for the mediation process. The assessment team then reports back to the lead agency with its opinion as to whether or not key stakeholders will participate in process and if such a process has the potential of being a viable means of resolving the issues.

The *Conflict Assessment Technique* advocates the use of an impartial third party to conduct this process. However, based on resources and the level of conflict this entire process or parts of it could be done in-house. Government is particularly well positioned for approaching other stakeholder groups and in cases act as an acceptable mediator given its mandate of protecting community interests. Government can act as a leader in moving forward the possibilities for different stakeholder groups to work as allies in tourism management.

Leadership

Leadership in tourism management can be by the few or it can be by the many. Conventional problem solving looks to the leadership of the few, where individuals make decisions with little input from outside sources. If 'a problem is easily defined, money is not an issue, the level of public concern is low, conventional problem solving works well' (Urban Land Institute, 1994: 16). When this is not the case, as is often true with tourism issues, the ranks of leaders need to be expanded and the cooperation between leaders and stakeholders must increase. A more inclusive approach to leadership should be considered under the following circumstances:

- complex issue;
- high level of public concern;
- wide range of affected stakeholders;
- emergency action is not required;
- long-term issue;
- no one agency has sole jurisdiction;
- the issues are negotiable and the parties are willing to negotiate.

Of all the above listed circumstances 'willing to negotiate' can be the key factor in whether a more collective leadership approach to tourism management will succeed.

There are different types of negotiation whose applicability and effectiveness can vary according to situational factors. Lewicki and Litterer (1985) divide negotiation processes into two types: distributive and integrative. Distributive bargaining revolves around trying to get the best possible personal outcome without regard to the other parties, while integrative bargaining revolves around creating a solution that is beneficial and acceptable to all of the negotiating parties. When there is little trust between parties and the willingness to working together is low then distributive negotiations might be the only option that parties are willing to pursue. When relations between groups are not openly hostile and there is a belief that by working together a better outcome can be achieved then integrative bargaining can be promising.

Principled negotiations

Leading with integrity is essential to ensuring that negotiations fulfil their higher potential, and those involved need to commit to a process of fair and effective negotiations. Fisher *et al.* (1991) developed a four-step process for *Principled Negotiations* that is highly effective in leading negotiations. These principles create an environment of trust and productivity and can result in innovative, widely supported and timely outcomes. Fisher *et al.* (1991: 15–81) principles are presented below with tourism examples added for the purposes of this book.

(1) *Separate the people from the problem*
Personal differences and tensions can cloud issues being negotiated. Therefore, it takes vigilance to be aware of when concerns are drifting over to personal issues and away from those being negotiated and to ensure that these are acknowledged and dealt with separately. A tourism example could involve members at the negotiation table who have clashed publicly and who are inclined to carry past grievances and personal problems with each other into the current negotiations. If a ground rule is made to forbid personal attacks, then participants who break this rule are quickly identified and effectively dealt with as per the rules of the process.

(2) *Focus on interests not positions*
When a hard line approach is taken on a position, then a tug-of-war between positions can ensue. Basic human interests relate to one's physical, emotional and economic well-being, which can include issues of protection, recognition, self-destiny and social connections. Positions, which are adopted stances, tend to complicate and undermine group negotiations. Positions represent set ways of doing things and are a form of prejudice in that they are believed to be the best and often only way of meeting one's interests. During tourism management meetings many interests are shared and they are a good starting place for discussion. Many tourism stakeholders' interests are similar, such as maintaining a high quality of life, while their positions meeting these interests can be manifestly divergent. Once shared interests are identified and documented then all negotiators can see they are working together towards certain common goals.

(3) *Invent options for mutual gain*
This step involves working together to generate ideas, analyse these ideas and then determine which ones will work best for the group. People need to feel comfortable in putting forward their ideas and collaborating with others, to create something that is better for the larger group. Unfortunately, this step does not often come naturally to a group made up of diverse participants. The role of a well-trained third party is to guide such groups through the negotiating process especially in regard to developing new ways of addressing lingering problems. It is essential that negotiation members treat each other respectfully to ensure that each person shares their input and does not stifle their ideas or bottle up complaints. If a tourism negotiation team is looking for ways to increase tourism revenues while not damaging the overall community well-being, they will need a well-

rounded understanding of the issues and the possibilities for work-able solutions. Economic realities play a substantial role in determining the feasibility of options, as do the availability of the organisational structures and qualified people to put proposed actions in motion.

(4) *Insist on using objective criteria*

Objective criteria only work if all of those negotiating feel comfortable that they are in fact 'objective'. Such criteria can be drawn from existing sources of information and the input of experts, when they are acceptable to all parties. If they are not acceptable to all parties, then practices of joint fact finding and the hiring of impartial experts chosen by the group can create new and broadly acceptable information. Tourism impact surveys and studies, designed and endorsed by a negotiation team is seen as relevant to the negotiators and the larger stakeholder groups that they represent.

These principles help to create an environment that is conducive to problem solving. Collective decisions are decided by either arguing, bargaining, voting or a combination of these techniques (Elster, 1998); and ground rules for behaviour coupled with a commitment to approach a problem based on principled negotiations are highly advisable. Ground rules, such as not allowing personal attacks, interruptions, or other signs of disrespect, let negotiating parties know what is expected of them and of others. Even if the relationships between the parties are poor, such principles and ground rules can discipline and enhance the actions and interactions of the negotiating parties.

Aspects of Fisher *et al.*'s 'Principled Negotiations' were incorporated into the Banff-Bow Valley Study that took a consensus building approach towards developing a tourism management strategy. 'Interest Based Negotiations' (the second principle) serves as the founding principle for this study that was directed by a Task Force of the Canadian government (Ritchie, 2000). The Task Force recommended that stakeholders should drive the process within the format of Round Table discussions of 14 interest sectors facilitated by a technical expert. The facilitator helped the different sectors reach consensus on a series of statements that they developed by moving beyond their initial positions to sharing their interests and looking for common ground. The study was deemed a well-rounded success in terms of participant satisfaction, the development and implementation of recommendations with broad-based support, greater understanding and cooperation between stakeholders, and improved management practices in the study area. The success of this study was aided by its generous budget ($2.4 million), time-frame (two years), and process support by the main stakeholder groups (Ritchie, 2000: 46).

Control

Even under the guidance of processes that have been designed to include stakeholders in a fair and effective manner there is still a need to monitor and control the system to achieve the desired results. Many local elites are predisposed to strongly promote economic growth, which can bias discussions on appropriate development strategies and initiatives for these communities (Little & Krannich, 1982: Reed, 1997). As noted by Jamal and Getz (1995) a collaborative decision-making process for tourism issues can be complicated by the need to attract outside assistance in terms of financiers, entrepreneurs and developers to help a community reach its tourism objectives. To convince outside investors of the viability of tourism proposals requires regular monitoring and controlled decision-making.

The challenges inherent in creating more equitable environments and processes for the collaborative decision-making process can be immense. Larissa Behrendt, an Aboriginal solicitor who obtained her doctorate at Harvard University, details the entrenched barriers to the just treatment of Aboriginal people in land disputes and proposes radical changes to address these injustices. Behrendt (1995) developed a conceptual model for dispute resolution within Aboriginal and Torres Strait Islander communities. This model encourages public participation by having a group of elders, with decision-making authority, preside over a series of public meetings, which take place in an informal way within the affected community. Such an approach could counteract biases against indigenous people in traditional tourism negotiations, as non-indigenous groups, such as major hoteliers, would be required to conform and operate within an indigenous way of doing things. This work with indigenous communities shows how culture plays a large role in determining appropriate ways of incorporating community views into community leadership.

Collaborative decision-making

Collaborative decision-making can be viewed as a mutual gains approach, where the ideas generated by a diverse range of people create more effective and inclusive decisions than those formulated from a single point of view. Taking a collaborative approach to tourism management strengthens the abilities of diverse people to work together and to create something greater than they can produce on their own. A collaborative approach can also motivate destinations to take a comprehensive look at the diverse factors that impact on their tourism developments and proposals, thereby enabling them to make better management decisions. Collaborative-decision making can only take place if it supported by established decision-makers as well as key stakeholder groups. Decisions that arise from collaborative processes supplement, rather than supplant those of established decision-makers, such as local councils and heads of industry.

Collaborative decision-making is an interactive process that empowers stakeholders to create innovative solutions for problems that are mutually defined by the participants in the process. Tiegerman-Farber and Radziewicz (1998), who have studied the application of collaborative decision-making in the educational system, find 'sharing' as the key to successful collaboration. They see mutual goals and shared participation, resources, respect and accountabilities as the foundation of an effective collaborative decision-making process.

Mediation and facilitation

Mediation and facilitation are two methods widely used to help with collaborative decision-making. Mediation refers to negotiations between parties that are assisted by a neutral third party who helps the parties arrive at solutions themselves (Boulle, 1996). Facilitation is similar to mediation in that it also refers to negotiations between parties that are assisted by a neutral third party. However, the role of the third party in running the process and finding solutions is much more active in facilitation (Stitt, 1998). A trained facilitator can be viewed like an excellent host who makes everyone feel comfortable, provides everyone with an opportunity to speak, keeps conversations moving in a constructive fashion and helps ensure that the event is viewed as worthwhile by all who attend. Facilitation can be the preferred option for multi-party disputes, especially when there are problems with power imbalances, communication difficulties, issue identification and cultural differences. Mediation and facilitation need not be seen as threats, but rather as methods of getting better results than by using traditional methods, such as political representation and legal challenges.

Skilled mediators and facilitators guide negotiations through the difficult periods of collaborative decision-making processes. When engaged in a conflict people are predisposed to believe their views and actions are 'right', while those that do not correspond to their views are 'wrong'. Facilitators and mediators can keep such feelings in check by drawing attention to actions or views that spring forth from misguided perspectives. This can be as simple as asking pointed questions as to why a meeting participant responded in a particular manner, or talking the group through the likely impacts of different proposals. Other methods include having participants engage in a series of role-playing exercises so that they understand other's values more clearly and are less judgemental and more empathetic when dealing with differences.

Consensus

It can be impractical to hold out for an agreement that all tourism stakeholder groups 'whole heartedly support'. An essential part of negotiation, facilitation and mediation processes is predetermining what level of consensus will be acceptable to all parties. Susskind (2001) categorises levels of consensus that move from the highest level of support (level 1) to the lowest level of mutual support acceptable to the group (level 3):

(1) Participants strongly support the solution.
(2) Participants can 'live with' the solution.
(3) Some participants do not support the solution, but they agree not to veto it.

These levels of support can be seen as degrees of enthusiasm for proposed options. It is advisable to strive for the solutions that stakeholder groups can 'live with' rather than holding onto an idealised outcome (Susskind, 2001). If the group accepts the lowest level of consensus at the beginning of the process, even those stakeholders who are upset with the settlement will not have the power to kill it.

Providing a voting mechanism within group negotiations can hold groups hostage to unreasonable demands. Disproportionate bargaining power can be provided to individual parties if their single vote has the power to swing the vote. This power is often used in the interests of the single party rather than larger group. Susskind strives to identify, activate and meet the needs of the 'constructive middle', rather than meeting the demands of the outer extremes that are often in the minority. Once the group collectively agrees on key issues and a good effort has been made to address any concerns that group members have of the proposal, then consensus is reached by 'overwhelming agreement', rather than by unanimous decision (Susskind, 2001).

Forums

There are various ways to build consensus over tourism issues in response to a destination's needs and resources (Creighton, 1980: Smith & Hester, 1982) several of which are discussed briefly below.

Public meetings

- Public meetings tend to be low cost ventures that provide good opportunities for providing information to the public and receiving a cross-section of opinions. However, they are not conducive to developing new options and assertive and organised groups can literally drown out other stakeholders.

Task forces

- Task forces are established on a temporary basis to carry out a specific function within a set period of time. Task forces tend to be well structured and run in an efficient manner. However, their disadvantages include a lack of representation of all stakeholder groups and a tightly constrained scope of action.

Small group workshops

- Small group workshops tend to consist of less than 50 participants and have an assigned task to be completed during one or more workshops. Although these groups can benefit from their diversity of opinions in generating options and the ability to build productive and lasting relationship, they can have limited participation and once again strong personalities can dominate the group.

Shuttle diplomacy

- If relations between stakeholder groups are openly hostile then shuttle diplomacy is worth considering. In this process a neutral third party sends messages between stakeholder groups, so that ideas can be considered without the added complexities of caustic personal relations. Shuttle diplomacy carries the disadvantage of being somewhat covert and more susceptible to manipulation by powerful stakeholders. While these techniques are primarily used by government agencies, they can also be utilised by the business sector and other tourism entities.

The appropriate form of consensus building will be determined largely by community support for the process and the nature of the issue. It is essential that affected stakeholders believe they have a key role in the decision-making process. Listening to stakeholders as early as possible and using their input as a way of setting up the decision-making process, lays the foundation for a solid and lasting agreement between diverse interest groups.

Tourism applications

Different forms and levels of collaboration in tourism management are achieved through a variety of processes. Three distinct examples of public participation in tourism initiatives are provided to highlight how these methods are used, as well as their strengths and limitations. The first example outlines collaborative tourism planning requirements that were developed by Canadian researchers. The last two examples, one from America and the other from Australia, are illustrations of what can go wrong when appropriate levels of public participation are not incorporated into the planning and development of tourism proposals.

Jamal and Getz (1995: 188) define collaboration for community-based tourism planning as 'a process of joint decision-making among autonomous, key stakeholders of an inter-organizational, community tourism domain to resolve planning problems of the domain and/or to manage issues related to the planning and development of the domain'. Upon reviewing theories and applications of collaborative decision-making in a tourism context, Jamal and Getz (1995: 195–200) developed six propositions for the application of collaborative tourism planning, which are summarised below.

(1) Recognise the high level of interdependence in planning and managing tourism products and services.
(2) Recognise the individual benefits as well as joint benefits derived from the collaborative process.
(3) Produce results that are implementable, otherwise participation in the process will be stymied and the process can lose its validity and effectiveness.
(4) Include representatives from the following key stakeholder groups: local government, tourism industry associations, resident groups, regional tourism organisations, social agencies and special interest groups.
(5) A mediator or facilitator who is experienced and acceptable to all parties is required to initiate and run the community based decision-making process.
(6) The following elements are necessary for collaborative strategic tourism planning: a vision statement for tourism development; jointly developed goals and objectives; self-regulation of the industry through the establishment of a collaborative organisation, or an oversight committee to monitor and make the necessary adjustment to the tourism plan's implementation.

Tourism is dependent upon continually meeting the expectations of residents and host communities in order to create and maintain environments that support the industry. Understanding the opportunities and costs of a potential tourism proposal involves an appreciation of market, political, economic, environmental and social conditions. Integrating public participation into tourism planning can be an essential step in understanding these conditions. However, as the following two examples show, there are a number of areas where public participation in tourism planning can become derailed. The first example looks at the proposal to build a historical theme park in Virginia, USA, while the second example looks at a proposal to build a Club Med Resort in Byron Bay, Australia.

Disney's America (Manassas, Virginia, USA)

In 1993 the Walt Disney Company unexpectedly announced its intention to open a historic theme park, 'Disney's America', in northern Virginia on 3000 acres of rural countryside (Zenzen, 1998: 166–7). Disney acquired the land and planned the Disney's America theme park in secrecy, which prevented the company from including local politicians and other stakeholders in the planning process. This lack of local participation during the early stages led to a loss of legitimacy for the theme park and is seen as one of the 'key mistakes' in the proposal (Eisner with Schwartz, 1998: 323). The Disney site in Virginia had the advantages of being easily accessible via Interstate 66 to Washington DC's large population and its 19 million annual visitors, many of whom are interested in the nation's history (Eisner with Schwartz, 1998: 320).

Although the chosen site was not designated as historically significant, it was within five miles of a Civil War battlefield in Manassas, which concerned a number of locals and historians (Zenzen, 1989: 166–7). There were concerns about scrutinising the ways of the South and making painful historical events 'entertaining'. There were also concerns that traditional ways of life would be challenged and potentially lost if there was the usual surge in developmental activity triggered by the theme park. Associated environmental concerns also were raised relating to the potential impacts of increased development on this largely undeveloped, rural corner of Virginia.

Disney's America was intending to highlight a cross-section of American history in an accurate, yet entertaining way, with a strong focus on the Civil War. Disney was 'committed to bringing history alive by telling emotionally compelling stories in dramatic ways' (Eisner with Schwartz, 1998: 325). The proposal's potential benefits included $680 million in tax revenue over 30 years, 2700 new jobs, a boom in visitation to historic sites in the area and a strengthened economy. These were all attractive to a county that had listed job creation and economic development as its top goals (Zenzen, 1998: 169–70).

After being widely criticised for excluding stakeholders from the early planning stages of the proposal, Disney showed itself willing to work with stakeholders by meeting with a range of community members, historians and government agencies. Disney offered to invest in local improvements, set aside extensive green space, promote surrounding historical sites and sell local products as part of its theme park proposal. In February 1994, several independently conducted polls indicated that Virginians supported the Disney proposal by margins averaging 3 to 1 (Eisner with Schwartz, 1998: 327). Despite well-financed opposition from prominent Southern families, including the Duponts and the owners of the *Washington Post*, Disney's America was fully approved at the state level. However, the theme park was shelved after extensive national media coverage ridiculed the proposal and due to the continual resistance from some local power-brokers. Losing this ambitious development caused substantial losses for the community in terms of jobs, economic opportunities and a forum to openly debate the legacy and future of the South.

Club Med Resort (Byron Bay, NSW, Australia)

Please note that the details on this case are drawn from Roger Brooks's (2000) article 'The collaborative approach to resolving tourist related conflict', in the *Australian Planner,* unless sourced otherwise.

Byron Bay is well loved for its tropical beauty, colourful locals and relaxed way of life. It has become a popular surfing destination, and has attracted many retirees (Figure 11.1). Byron Shire, which is 800 km north of Sydney and 180 km south of Brisbane, has a population of close to 30,000 and attracts approximately 1.7 million tourists a year (Byron Shire Council, 2003: 1). 'Byron has a reputation for fierce vigilantism against development' (Kinninment, 2003: 13). This reputation was earned from fighting large development proposals, with the battle over Club Med being one of the most notable examples.

The proposed Club Med resort was to consist of bungalow style units with a capacity for 641 beds, four restaurants and assorted conference and recreational facilities (bulletin cited in Brooks, 2000: 189). In response to the submissions, Club Med made some minor design and siting amendments and the proposal was approved subject to a substantial number of conditions. There was fierce opposition to the proposal, as evident by an anti-development petition with over 7000 signatures and a legal challenge to the proposal (*Echo,* cited in Brooks, 2000: 189). Residents rallied against the proposal with '"No Club Med" T-shirts, stickers and banners, and even TV advertisements' (Kinninment, 2003: 13). In response to this opposition Club Med scaled down its original proposal by half in terms of size and two-thirds in terms of its capacity.

The supporters of the proposal felt the resort would greatly boost tourism, provide a large market for local goods and services, infuse $16 million a year into the local economy and provide 200 jobs (*Australian Tourism Monitor,* cited in Brooks, 2000: 189). Opponents felt the potential negative impacts of the resort would exceed any economic benefits. There were also concerns that it would set a precedent for large-scale resorts and draw in multi-national companies – threatening the local environment and way of life. The Byron Shire Council tried to address community concerns by providing public meetings, group discussions and an extended display period to review the proposal. The developer initiated dialogue with community groups, modified the proposal and offered to enter into a community contract to resolve community concerns.

Club Med used an out-of-town consulting firm to run its community negotiations. These collaboration endeavours opened up dialogue between stakeholder groups and led to some compromises. However, process participants were critical of Club Med for not fulfilling its promise to invite all stakeholders to participate in the negotiation process and to enter into a 'community contract' to address key issues. Since Club Med hired the leaders of the negotiation team many residents felt that Club Med

Figure 11.1 Byron Bay, Australia

was primarily promoting its views, rather than listening and responding to what they said. The processes established by council and the developer were seen to lack legitimacy and fairness by a number of stakeholder groups. Club Med's inability to resolve key issues with stakeholders resulted in prolonged community opposition to the proposal and to legal actions. The *Land and Environment Court* overturned council approval to build the resort in 1996 and three years later Club Med pulled out of the area (Kinninment, 2003).

Analysis

If Disney and Club Med had included more meaningful input from stakeholder groups along the lines advanced in the first example, they could possibly have realised their ambitions as well as many of those of other affected parties. Perhaps a more collaborative approach was not taken in part because these companies did not want to let their competition know what was planned. However, a clandestine approach can be counter-productive when you need the support of a wide range of stakeholders, including at times your competition, to successfully complete a development.

Large development proposals create opportunities to work with developers to gain advantages for the community, such as increasing green space or investing in local priorities. These concessions to a community can be formalised with local governments in terms of community contracts, memorandums of understanding, or in certain cases development approvals. When large developments are consistently blocked they are often superseded by patchwork development whose impacts are harder to control. In Byron Bay it has been noted that 'the incremental creep has probably had as much effect as a couple of Club Meds . . . it's been a war of attrition' (Kinninment, 2003: 13). Due to the substantial positive and negative impacts that large developments can wield, approval for such proposals can be removed from local authorities and made the preserve of state or federal entities. In New South Wales the state government has usurped the right to make decisions on major coastal developments, as part of its new coastal protection regulations (Patterson, 2003).

Summary

Working together creates a larger pool of resources in terms of experiences, skills, funds and ideas. As individuals and communities become more empowered through education, sharing of information, organisation and the legal system they are in a stronger position to influence issues that affect them. Emerging ways to deal with conflict, such as mediation and facilitation, offer great promise for addressing community tourism issues. Tourism proposals that include meaningful public participation from the start are in a better position to build a climate of trust and cooperation. By working with broader community interests in a cost appropriate manner elected officials, government agencies and businesses can create innovative, responsive and effective tourism proposals. While not all stakeholders will embrace collaborative decision-making processes, as long as concerted efforts are made to address their interests and they can live with the final outcomes, then these processes can be considered a success. Despite the inherent challenges associated with collaborative tourism processes, they bring more legitimacy to decision-making processes. Broad-based community support for tourism initiatives can be both established and maintained in communities through the use of collaborative tourism processes.

Chapter 12

Bridging Tourism Gaps Through Strategic Management

Closing the distance between what stakeholders want and expect with what they experience increases their satisfaction. Tourist destinations need efficient and effective tools to help evaluate the levels of satisfaction that they achieve with various stakeholder groups, on both the demand and supply sides. Assessing satisfaction with services can be perplexing since the components of a 'service experience' can be difficult to isolate and measure. However, gap analysis has become a widely used technique for measuring service quality, and has strong potential for use in tourism management (Murphy, A., 2003).

Gap analysis can be used as a tool to draw attention to 'services and/or functions that have been accidentally left out, deliberately eliminated, or are yet to be developed or procured' (Open Group, 2002: 1). Gap analysis can be an impetus for ensuring data on the 'moments of truth' for various tourism stakeholder groups is relevant, disciplined and up-to-date. However, it is a indicator, not a management template. Gap analysis does not provide answers regarding why a gap occurs, whether or not the gap should be addressed, and if it is to be addressed the best way for doing so. These answers can only be found by considering the key business management functions and stakeholders' views through a collaborative decision-making approach. The *Bridging Tourism Gaps Model* presented in this chapter presents a framework for comprehensive tourism management that combines the indicative features of gap analysis with a business focused collaborative decision-making process.

Objectives

Understanding the needs and expectations of tourism stakeholders creates the opportunity for sound tourism management. The inability of many destinations to realise their tourism potential can be tied to a lack of any of the following:

- Adequate information, which can be drawn from an inventory of tourism resources, competitors' tourism offerings and stakeholder groups.
- Awareness of key variables, with particular regards to the core requirements of the stakeholder groups, compatibility of tourism with other sectors of the destination's economy and global economic, social and environmental trends.
- Ability to successfully act on available information, which relies on a tourism plan, funding, management tools and the political, financial and personal commitments necessary for ensuring that the goals and objectives of the tourism plan are achieved.

Tourist destinations must engage in realistic assessments of their abilities to meet the needs and expectations of tourism stakeholders and then act on these assessments so their goals and objectives can be achieved. While moving towards the successful implementation of a tourism plan, destinations can falter in a number of areas, often without realising the extent to which they are slipping, or that they are slipping at all. These tourism errors or omissions can be seen as gaps between what is required and what is achieved. The *Bridging Tourism Gaps Model* is intended to keep destinations focused on the most important factors in developing and maintaining tourism as a beneficial and vital part of their communities.

Planning

Difficulties in understanding what stakeholders want from tourism are exacerbated by the fact that the initial stages of tourism development are rarely informed by a community vision for the industry (Mitchell & Reid, 2001). As outlined earlier, the impetus for tourism development tends to be entrepreneurs. However, the personal motivations of entrepreneurs may not necessarily reflect what is best for the overall community. Tourism planning should take place before stakeholders become entrenched in positions and community commitments are made (McIntyre, 1993). Tourism development in communities can evolve quickly, in a manner that is relatively un-answerable to community views of appropriate tourism development. The drawback of the 'wait and see' approach is that it allows problems between stakeholders to grow and can turn into a 'wait for a crisis and react' approach. Identifying and working to enhance those factors that underpin the success or otherwise of tourism destinations during the planning stages, helps to ensure that development retains the right focus.

Tourism success stories are built on service quality, as we have illustrated throughout this book. While planning for quality products and services might seem like an obvious priority, understanding what quality means to different stakeholder groups and planning for its appropriate level can be perplexing. Quality is an important component of value, which many consider to be the key choice determinant in a competitive market-place. Value itself is consistently cited as a prime impetus for tourism demand (Murphy & Pritchard, 1997; Nagel, 1987). Quality is generally tied to notions of 'goodness' and 'luxury' (Takeuchi & Quelch, 1983). Quality can be defined as 'the ability of a service or product to perform its specified tasks' (Ennew *et al.*, 1993: 59) and should be at the core of all tourism management strategies.

Stakeholders' expectations as well as the performance of service providers guide their evaluations of quality and overall satisfaction. LeBlanc (1992) found that potential tourists strongly associated perceptions of 'quality services' with their level of satisfaction for the travel agency services they received. Customer satisfaction is also related to providing extra options or better values as well as the absence of deficiencies (Juran, cited in Flynn *et al.*, 1994). A tour company that offers an array of day trip options can be judged as being of higher quality than one who's tours are of the same excellent standard, yet does not provide as extensive a range of tours as its competition. However, a negative experience, such as a service-delivery failure, can overshadow otherwise positive views and lower customer perceptions of quality. The personal side of quality perceptions underlies how important it is for stakeholders to form realistic expectations of their tourism options.

'Service quality is the foundation for services marketing because the core product being marketed is a performance', according to Berry and Parasuraman (1991: 5), and performance permeates tourism. Parasuraman *et al.* (1985) suggest there are 10 criteria that consumers use regularly in developing their service perceptions. These factors are worth considering when planning for tourism development and management due to their impact on user satisfaction. Parasuraman *et al.*'s (1985) original service quality characteristics are listed below and placed in the context of quality elements for which Disney's theme parks are famous:

Service quality characteristics

(1) *Tangibles* Ensuring all public areas of the theme park, from rides, to walkways and rest facilities, are attractive, safe and clean.
(2) *Reliability* Maintaining an enticing, family-friendly and fun atmosphere at all times and at all Disney facilities.
(3) *Responsiveness* Catering to customer service demands, such as providing alcohol in the European theme park and training street cleaners to be on-the-spot guides and counsellors.
(4) *Communication* Providing information in various languages and formats, and informing customers how much longer they need to wait before reaching the end of a queue.

(5) *Credibility* Taking a conservative and measured approach that builds on Disney's legacy.

(6) *Security* Offering exciting but safe experiences for guests, while ensuring that they are not subjected to unruly behaviour or other threats

(7) *Competence* Training for all levels of staff is provided on site and through Disney University.

(8) *Courtesy* Careful staff selection and training of staff by Disney before they meet the public.

(9) *Understanding* Extensive customer research is conducted by and for Disney.

(10) *Access* Accessibility of the more modern Disney facilities is enhanced by freeway and railway agreements with local governments, while park and ride operations within all Disney theme parks allow guests to leave their cars and hop onto monorails, carriages and trams

Although knowing what stakeholders want is an indispensable part of the planning process, the resulting information is only valuable to the extent that it informs decisions on priority issues. Tourism plans need to consider where to invest resources and why. Another 80:20 rule of business is when 80% of business sales can be attributed to 20% of customers, with some industries, such as airlines and retail, consistently relying on a minority of their customers to provide them with most of their profits (Eckhouse, 2002: 2). Applying this rule to tourism suggests that trying to attract and satisfy a wide range of tourists and interests dilutes the impacts of these investments. Many destinations segment tourists based on their area of origin, demographic profile, length of stay, the amount they spend, and repeat visitations. Segmenting tourist markets according to their value and then focusing investments on attracting and satisfying these 'desired tourists' can result in greater potential returns or yield.

Determining which tourists are desirable to a destination is a reflection of a destination's tourism resources as well as the views and capabilities of its other tourism stakeholders. Up-to-date data on industry, residents and government should be collected, stored and analysed. This data needs to go beyond basic inventories of existing tourism businesses and tourism employment, so that an accurate picture of these stakeholder groups and the ways in which they interact with each other can be understood. A deeper level of understanding of all stakeholder groups helps to gain a realistic understanding of how tourism priorities can be achieved.

Process design

The processes established to enable collaborative decision-making are very powerful in directing likely outcomes. Even when a particular tourism management model has been selected as a means of addressing a tourism issue, a detailed process must be established that meets local conditions and stakeholder requirements. The process involves many aspects that may seem mundane, such as setting ground rules for how stakeholders will treat each other in negotiations, yet all these procedural items shape the environment within which decisions will be made. For example, the Canmore Growth Management Committee was established as part of a community round table tourism planning process. The committee consisted of 40 interest group representatives from the community of Canmore, just outside of Banff National Park, in Alberta Canada (Jamal & Getz, 2000).

Key process design features were seen to encourage consensus but often at the expense of the less powerful members of the group, who felt pressured to conform. In particular the 'shotgun rule', by which if any representative left the table then the process would collapse, was seen by several participants to be a coercive measure. One of the participants noted that:

> there were on numerous occasions groups who said I can't buy into this, whatever point was being made. And the: *rest of the group, they became a single force, telling this group they couldn't leave* . . . and so we literally had to debate *issues until we got everybody to a position* where it wasn't a deal breaker issue anymore. Lots of deal breakers. That was a very, very fundamentally important point without which we would never have succeeded. (Business-participant interview cited in Jamal & Getz, 2000: 172 – their emphases)

By the very nature of group decision-making extreme opinions are discouraged as they deviate from the opinions of the majority and therefore do not represent viable options to the group. Through discussion within the framework of the process design, the group works to treat each member respectfully as an individual, while working towards a decision that each group member can support for the good of the group. The level of group pressure in consensus decision-making is a product of process design as well as power imbalances, the intensity of the conflict, the issues and the available resources. Therefore, the process needs to be defined to fit the context.

Another contextual item influencing process design is the varying amounts of time that specific stakeholders will be prepared to devote to the process. The Costa Dourada collaborative tourism planning process in Alagoas Brazil involved a broad range of stakeholders, yet there were disparities in representation (de Araujo and Bramwell, 2000). Government officials and workers were over-represented, while industry leaders NGOs and community organisations were seen by many to be under-represented. The inequality in stakeholder representation was caused in part by cultural

and historical factors, given that emerging from a dictatorship the participants were used to government having unchecked power. Process issues in
this case related also to concerns that involvement in the process would be
too time consuming and would not produce worthwhile results. Some
stakeholders indicated they felt it would be better to wait and see how the
process evolved before becoming involved, especially since the time spent
on such processes would translate into time away from their jobs and other
pressing responsibilities.

Our own experiences with public participation planning processes in
developed countries show similar trends in stakeholder participation.
Government workers, whose attendance at these meetings is often part of
their job, tend to be over-represented at these meetings. Those who are
working full time in the private sector usually cannot afford to take much
time off from work to attend daytime or early evening meetings, that tend
to be set up by and for the convenience of the public sector. Industry leaders
can contribute greatly to developing plans that appeal to the private sector.
However, their time can be so valuable that they cannot justify participating in lengthy tourism planning processes. Therefore, with the exception of
development proponents, industry tends to be chronically under-
represented at these processes. Some of the ways processes can be designed
to better accommodate varying stakeholder needs include the following:

- clear goals and objectives;
- adequate resourcing;
- concise time frame;
- clear component parts to the process;
- meetings scheduled at various times – preferably evenings;
- options for participation – written submissions, attend open, houses,
  public meetings, interview, questionnaires and web applications.

A well-designed process enables various stakeholders to make informed
decisions regarding the amount of their time and effort they will need to
devote to a process to reach a successful outcome.

Organising

Putting a tourism plan into action requires a comprehensive, straightforward and adaptable approach. Finding the right approach can be difficult
given the complexities of the tourism industry and that the organisational
options for destinations are confined by limited budgets, staff and political
support. Weiermair (1997) supports the use of the gap model for managing
tourism's service quality based on two propositions: (1) that service quality
is of great importance to tourism due to the highly competitive nature of the
industry; and that (2) quality control systems need to be sufficiently
detailed to be effective. Strengths and weaknesses in the provision of

tourism services can inform decisions on the allocation of resources and assignment of tasks.

Parasuraman *et al.* (1985) developed *Gap Analysis* as a way to conceptualise service quality requirements. It compares how service performance measures up to customer expectations. Gap analysis used in relation to their concurrent *Gap Model* (Parasuraman, *et al.*, 1990) measures both tangible and intangible service elements. If there is a discrepancy between what is expected and what is provided, this represents a 'gap'.

Gap analysis can serve as a highly flexible and broadly applied assessment tool, as is evident from its application to the health care, education, environmental and tourism and hospitality sectors. Gap analysis is widely used as 'a scientific method for identifying the degree to which native animal species and natural communities are represented in our present-day mix of conservation lands' (Iowa Gap, 1997: 1). Some organisations specialise in preparing gap analysis processes designed to meet the particular needs of individual companies and governments (Alamo, 2002); however, the main focus of these ready-made gap processes tends to be accounting and inventory issues. Gap analysis has been used to measure perceived service quality in several tourism sectors, including airlines, hotels, restaurants and ski resorts (Fick & Ritchie 1991; Weiermair, 1997) and as a tourism planning tool (Murphy, 2003).

Gap model

Parasuraman *et al.* (1985) introduced the gap analysis model as a way to conceptualise service quality in terms of meeting customer expectations. This model moves the analysis of service provision from the overall picture of whether or not customers were satisfied with their service experience to one that breaks down the customer–business interaction into its individual components. It enables us to ask where and how businesses are not meeting customer expectations.

Five key service interfaces between customers and businesses have been identified. At these points gaps can occur between what is provided and what is expected. Such gaps can result in service failure and loss of business (Parasuraman *et al.*, 1985, 1990). Using the gap model as a base we illustrate this process using the example of a small rural community trying to attract stopover visits through the provision of basic services, like public toilets. While toilets may seem mundane they have considerable appeal to the motoring public, which is often the principal source of visitors to rural destinations (Strong, 2002; van Tiggelen, 2001).

The tourist on a motoring tour through the countryside expects to find a certain level of amenities, including toilets, at each potential stop. The community destination is aware of this expectation on behalf of the tourist, as well as of its own residents, so it constructs a public toilet facility in the centre of town close to the shops and other attractions of the main street.

Gap 1 can occur when the destination misunderstands what the tourists' specific needs are with respect to a toilet facility. Over and above the general desire for a clean facility they require adequate signage, because they may be unfamiliar with the destination, and convenient parking, because they are driving.

Gap 2 can occur when the destination's perception of the tourists' toilet expectations are not met by the service specifications for the facility. For example, failing to provide sufficient cleaning and maintenance throughout the day can turn a modern facility into a disaster area.

Gap 3 can occur when the local authority has the correct specifications to keep the toilet block clean and well stocked, but is unable to deliver to the necessary standard. For example, scheduling regular maintenance but lacking the staff or will to fulfil this requirement.

Gap 4 can arise when the destination fails to adequately inform the tourists of the toilet facility. In this case appropriate information in travel maps and brochures will alert tourists to the presence of such an amenity. Once in the town, visual cues such as signage and an attractive building will encourage people to stop.

Gap 5 occurs when there is a discrepancy between what the tourists expect and what they receive at the toilet block.

In this tourism gap example if the toilet block is easy to access, is clean and stocked with the appropriate supplies, tourists will have their expectations met and may well extend their stop to look around the town. If tourists' expectations are not met, their impression of the town will be tainted and they may need to continue onto the next opportunity immediately. However, as in all business situations there has to be a balance between what the tourists can reasonably expect and the community's ability and willingness to invest in a corresponding facility.

There are various ways of measuring service quality gaps when conducting a gap analysis. Parasuraman *et al.* (1988) developed the SERVQUAL scale to measure precisely ratings of service expectations and perceptions for service quality characteristics. This method can be described as a two-column technique, in that gaps are measured by subtracting rankings of service quality characteristics from those of service expectations. In the field there have been difficulties associated with using the SERVQUAL scale with regards to its consistency and the validity of results (Grapentine, 1994; Teas, 1993: Yoon and Ekinci, 2001). Literature review and research showed that the generic use of service quality characteristics (please refer back to the Disney example in the planning section of this chapter) and the use of 'ideals' as a standard of assessment were major limitations of SERVQUAL.

A more basic and conceptual approach to gap analysis shows much promise in tourism and hospitality. Instead of using 10 or five service quality dimensions as recommended by Parasuraman *et al.* (1988, 1991), service quality in tourism can be attributable to just a few key characteristics. Mei *et al.* (1999) cite three service quality characteristics – the behaviour of employees, tangibles and reliability – as the best predictors of service quality evaluations in the hospitality industry. These researchers also found that a simplified one-column survey provided a valid, reliable and user-friendly survey. The one-column approach ranks services from one to seven, with one representing total failure in meeting service expectations and seven representing greatly exceeded expectations (Mei *et al.*, 1999: 138).

Ennew *et al.* (1993) recommend creating 'an index of service quality' in which respondents' rank service characteristics as per their importance and then these rankings are compared with their quality perceptions. Oppermann (1995) used a gap analysis to explore the relationship between guests and operators of rural bed and breakfast (B&Bs) in Germany. The minimal gaps in the perceptions and expectations of these groups reflected the high level of understanding between the groups, which in turn is attributable to their shared culture, preferences and language, and the generally close and congenial contact between the B&B hosts and guests. Drawing from these findings destinations that wish to minimise gaps and corresponding disappointments between the expectations of their tourism stakeholders need to create opportunities for these groups to get to know each other.

Augustyn and Ho's (1998) application of the *Gap Model* to travel agencies revealed a number of service gaps which are summarised below.

Gap 1: Management does not know what customers expect
Travel agencies hardly ever conduct research on their customers, yet they presume to know their customers' expectations and design vacation packages based on their presumptions of what their customers want.

Gap 2: Service specifications work against fulfilling customers' expectations
Management's inaccurate perceptions of customers' service expectations become ingrained in the running of the business. Travel agencies generally pitch their efforts to profiles of what they believe to be typical customers and design their service delivery systems accordingly. This approach neglects differences in travel abilities and preferences and leaves large gaps between what is needed and the systems developed to address these needs. Service standards that consist of sweeping statements, such as 'the customer is always right', that fail to provide clear and easy steps for implementation are not helpful.

Gap 3: Management service specifications are on target, but staff cannot meet them
In travel agencies there is often a discrepancy between the level of professionalism and knowledge that management wants to provide and the capabilities of their staff. Agencies that function as general travel consultants rather than specialising, such as focusing on particular countries or activities, are especially prone to this gap.

Gap 4: Management promises too much
Types and quality of services advertised for travel agencies do not match what is available to customers. Many customers expect all-inclusive service from their travel agencies and are annoyed when they find that many of the responsibilities, such as arranging ground transportation, are left for them to sort out. The growing array of travel options can make it difficult for travel agents to know what is available while the widespread use of the Internet can serve to raise unrealistic expectations of travel services and vacation bargains. A lack of two-way communication between travel agencies and customers can exacerbate this gap.

Gap 5: Customers believe their service expectations have not been met
Gaps one to four all contribute to customers' perceptions of services, so problems with gaps at these earlier stages will feed into the final gap between customers' expectations of travel agencies and the way they perceive these businesses. There are also a number of personal factors, such as customers' world views, and external factors, such as the friendliness of hosts, that impact on customers' overall evaluation of whether a travel agency did a good job.

In stressful tourism environments, such as travel agencies and popular destinations, customer expectations are high. Yet often management does not truly understand its customers and front-line staff lack the resources and guidance necessary to close gaps between expectations and reality. These same challenges constrict the abilities of stakeholder groups to understand each other and to find solutions. However, these challenges should not be interpreted as 'fatal flaws'. Rather, they point to the value in identifying where differences in opinions and capabilities lie and the extent of these differences so that appropriate actions can be taken. True leadership is necessary to ensure that destinations take a hard look at what they have to offer, what their stakeholders want and then use this information to guide their development.

Leadership

Realising the tourism potential of destinations requires adept and responsive leadership. Leadership is capable of inspiring widespread support when it is seen to further the aspirations of the larger group in a way that people can relate to and actively support. Models are a useful way of conceptualising the steps communities need to take to achieve their tourism aspirations and lead communities in the right direction. Numerous models of tourism development have been created as a way to help guide communities, as discussed in earlier chapters, but they all have limitations.

Limitations of existing models

Models are helpful in drawing attention to many of the potential dimensions and impacts of tourism, yet their applicability as management tools for communities has been limited. Butler's evolutionary cycle of tourism development (1980) uses a bell curve to illustrate tourism's rising and then falling fortunes, yet offers little in the way of practical advice on how communities can avoid tourism's pitfalls. Murphy's community approach model to tourism development has been criticised as not recognising fundamental power inequalities that undermine the democratic principles and for not having more fully developed theoretical underpinnings (Reed, 1997). Some factors that limit the applicability of tourism models to real world situations are summarised below:

Economic

- difficult to quantify the benefits and costs of tourism;
- strong social science approach that neglects to consider proven business practices.

Social

- limited awareness of tourism impacts and low political commitment;
- difficult to find broadly acceptable solutions, given the conflicting needs and priorities of stakeholder groups.

Environmental

- undervalue the role of the environment in destination attractiveness;
- difficult to measure carrying capacities and stress levels;
- neglect political, social and economic factors that ultimately determine the extent to which sustainable environmental practices can be developed and maintained.

A new model and framework is necessary to address the limitations of earlier models. The proposed model is offered as a practical alternative, as it is based on demonstrated business techniques and is responsive to the interplay of elements that affect the fortunes of tourist destinations. Flexibility in tourism planning is essential. The endless array of variables that define a particular destination make the implementation of blanket and rigid requirements unworkable. Guidance on this matter is provided by Martin *et al.* (1998: 50) who found that:

- models that embrace and include differences may be more effective than models that attempt to achieve unanimity.

Tourism models need to go beyond advocating a collaborative approach to provide the comprehensive guidance necessary for turning tourism ambitions into reality (Reed, 2000). Structural and procedural elements, that include understanding power dynamics, business principles, stakeholder requirements, available resources and legislative and legal aspects all set the context within which workable tourism proposals can be forged.

While researchers strive to make their findings helpful to tourism practitioners, some feel 'a major gap still exists between the users and the procedures of research' Taylor *et al.* (1994: 9). Such gaps lead to unacceptable inefficiencies within the industry and the authors suggest some key elements to 'bridge' the research gap between industry and researchers. Among their suggestions are:

- develop a meaningful dialogue between tourism researchers and the industry;
- glean as much information from existing data sources as possible;
- develop regular and customised customer and operator surveys to supplement published data;
- provide big picture trend analysis as well as small picture and business specific information.

These suggestions are incorporated in the following model.

Other useful suggestions for tourism development approaches come from MacEochaidh (1994), who draws on planning experience in disadvantaged areas of rural Ireland. MacEochaidh suggests the following steps are essential for successful tourism development where the resources for change are limited (1994: 186):

- tourist agencies gain local support for tourism development on a range of tourism development issues, including financing;
- educate and train locals so they can make informed tourism decisions;
- support locals so they can identify their own tourism opportunities;
- establish networks and encourage partnerships so tourism information and resources can be shared – especially for marketing and product development;
- help communities develop comprehensive strategies for the long term.

These suggestions are incorporated in the following model.

Bridging tourism gaps model

The challenges that prevent tourism from meeting its potential can seem insurmountable at times. In tourism management, as in life, a bridge can be used to take you from where you are to where you want to be. The *Bridging tourism gaps model* shows how destinations can bridge the gap between tourism's promise and its reality by uniting the four business functions and major stakeholder groups into a community focused strategic management process (Figure 12.1). This model uses the analogy of a bridge to explain the necessary components and linkages of tourism management. Its structure is as follows:

- Business management functions: Footings
- Stakeholders: Pilings
- Collaboration: Cross-beams
- Gap analysis Surface

If we view the *business management functions* as the footings for the bridge and the *stakeholders* as bridge pilings, it is evident that additional elements are necessary to realise a community's overarching tourism objectives and goals. *Collaboration* functions as cross-beams for strength and connectivity, while *Gap analysis* functions as the bridge road surface and responds to changing conditions. All of these elements in the model come together, creating a bridge between what is envisioned and what is achievable for a tourist destination.

Business management functions: Footings

Tourism strategies, like bridges, need firm footings in their environments. A sound business foundation is the reliable base from which sustainable tourism developments grow. The business management functions can act as cornerstones for successful tourism ventures. In this case we start with the need for leadership.

Leadership Visualising the building of an actual bridge, one can see leadership as the starting point in construction. Leadership, rather than planning, often is the first step in developing a tourism management system, as it can take the push of strong leader to kick-start these processes. Leadership is also an important element in each of the other three business management functions. Leaders need to understand and make the most out of local conditions. An understanding of the current situation combined with a vision for what is possible and the ability to motivate others to adopt and move towards this vision are hallmarks of an effective leader. Local environmental, social and economic factors and the way that these factors interact with external elements create unique situations that need to be understood and incorporated into management plans. Customers, industry, residents and

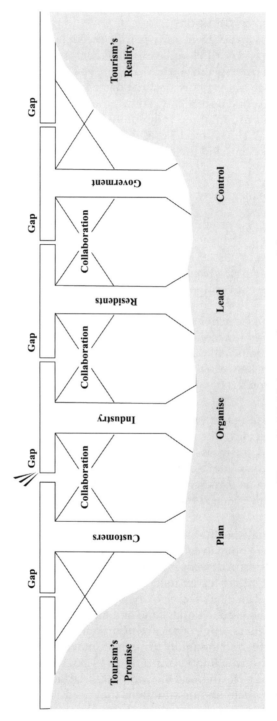

Figure 12.1 Bridging tourism gaps model

customers all impact upon the fortunes of tourism development, so adept leadership will acknowledge and work with these groups in developing tourism strategies.

Planning Planning, like the foundation stone of a bridge, is a logical and necessary starting point from which the actual development can occur. Planning grounds tourism's potential within the context of community goals and objectives. Planning explores the aspirations and abilities of tourism stakeholder groups, which are then incorporated into the larger vision of destination management. A community destination's tourism planning involves four steps:

Step 1:
Clarify or otherwise establish a community's general tourism goals and objectives.

Step 2:
Collect information on stakeholders, resources and other factors that serve as opportunities or constraints to tourism development.

Step 3:
Create forums in which community members can discuss tourism goals and objectives drawing on available information.

Step 4:
Assess the extent to which tourism can help or hinder a community's efforts to achieve its general and wider goals and objectives. Tourism strategies should be created and supported to the extent that they further tourism and overall community goals.

Organising Organising for strategic community tourism management means putting a process in place so that a community can achieve its goals and objectives. Tasks need to be assigned and resources allocated so that responsible parties, such as government departments and destination associations, can administer and respond to the impacts of their programmes in a timely and effectual manner. This does not have to be an excessively bureaucratic process for, as Porter's (1998) cluster theory advocates, simply creating a positive and entrepreneurial environment may be the best facilitation process any government can provide.

Controlling Control for community tourism development is concerned with the implementation, monitoring and adjustment of tourism initiatives that support community tourism goals and objectives. Just as the foundations of a bridge construction are soon overshadowed by the structure that arises from them, subsequent stages of tourism management can become the focus of attention while the importance of control is undervalued. Even though control is one of the more tedious aspects of tourism management, its role in understanding and responding to tourism's impacts needs to be recognised and resourced accordingly.

Stakeholder groups: Pilings

Stakeholders can be conceptualised as bridge pilings supported by the four business management functions foundation. Stakeholders, like bridge pilings, rise up with the promise of what is possible. Different stakeholder groups might not appear to complement each other, or even serve any useful purpose on their own. However, they are the elements upon which tourism management rests.

Strategic tourism management examines the strengths and weaknesses of its stakeholder groups, in terms of their abilities to help a destination realise its tourism vision. A destination's primary stakeholders are indicative of and responsive to local conditions. Bringing in outside tourism experts, focusing on desirable, yet hard to reach markets and adopting proposals that have worked under very different conditions carry with them great expense and often disappointing results. Communities should focus on the needs and abilities of their established customer bases and industries, while working within the guidelines of what is acceptable to their residents and proven funding sources. Imported ideas and new markets can make a valuable contribution to an area's tourism potential if the resources devoted to bringing them in are proportion to their net benefits.

Collaboration: Cross-beams

The pilings of a bridge, like stakeholder groups, are isolated, so additional resources are needed to bind them together to support tourism's potential. Collaborative decision-making processes can be seen as cross-beams that bring together the four stakeholder pillars. A combined strategic management approach that draws upon the opinions and views of all four stakeholder groups creates strong and durable decisions. Whereas, an approach that neglects any of the major stakeholder groups will be unbalanced and less likely to hold up over time.

At regular intervals tourism issues should be discussed in public forums, such as local council meetings. These forums provide a quick and relatively low cost way of gauging the community's tourism opinions and options. Quantitative tourism research, such as phone or postal surveys, can provide more detailed information on stakeholders' views and provide a more representative picture of stakeholders' opinions and likely actions. Once tourism issues have been identified, advisory groups can work on addressing these issues. Advisory groups should have representatives from the tourism industry, resident groups, administrators and elected officials. Advisory groups need adequate financial, political, administrative and technical support to working collaboratively in developing

tourism management recommendations that meet stakeholders' requirements (Lynn & Kartez, 1995).

Gap analysis: Surface

Just as laying down cross-beams makes it possible to sustain a bridge
surface, collaborative processes pave the way for making informed
decisions on how a community should invest its tourism resources. A
bridge's surface contains a number of gaps that provide the necessary flexibility in responding to changing conditions, such as freeze-thaw cycles in
colder climates, and load conditions. If these gaps are for the most part
small, then they allow for the safe, reliable, timely, smooth and inexpensive
transportation of goods and people. Larger gaps can be expected and
planned for at certain key junctures, such as where the bridge surface
transfers from land to the bridge supports. Gaps in a bridge's surface may
be too large to allow for a pleasant and easy crossing by all vehicles, which
can deter or prevent certain people from using the bridge. If the expected
traffic volumes are high the surface and its underlying components need to
be strengthened in readiness for heavy (mass) use.

Similarly, a tourism management strategy should recognise and incorporate gaps between tourism stakeholders' expectations and what a
destination provides. Accommodating such gaps allows a destination to be
flexible in the face of changing conditions. These changes can be in relation
to stakeholders' preferences as well as the tourism resources of a destination. If these gaps are kept small then the range of people who will be
satisfied with a tourism destination is large. If differences between what is
desired and what a destination can deliver are too incongruent then certain
stakeholder groups will be unwilling or unable to enjoy a destination. A
destination may want to attract high spending overnight visitors who
travel as singles or couples. However, if a destination does not offer what
these market segments expect, such as gourmet dining and areas of exceptional cultural significance, then it may have to focus on budget tourists.

Gap analysis results can be part of a clear-headed assessment of tourism
development options, ranging from the structural plan through to the
availability of resource. The extent to which stakeholders' tourism expectations are being met can be assessed using gap analysis. Potential questions
to explore using gap analysis include the following:

- Residents' expectations for tourism in their community/
  Residents perceptions of tourism's impacts on their community.
- Residents' expectations for tourism in their community/
  Desirable markets' tourism expectations.
- Desirable markets' tourism expectations/
  Abilities of a destination to meet these expectations.

The discrepancies between different groups that are revealed by these questions need to be evaluated within the context of a destination's general and tourism specific goals and objectives.

Controlling

The *Bridging tourism gaps model* can only function as a relevant and adaptive strategic management tool if appropriate control mechanisms are established and maintained. The tourism potential of a destination evolves as the cumulative effects of the industry become more apparent over time and limitations to development are addressed. Control mechanisms should be involved in this process. They should be both straightforward and adaptive so they can be applied by tourism's various stakeholders in different and changing environments.

Model limitations

There are a number of limits on citizen participation and collaboration in tourism planning, especially in destinations that are struggling to develop and maintain their tourism industry as a way of improving the overall quality of life for their constituents. Potential limitations to the applicability of the *Bridging tourism gaps model* can occur due to operational, structural and cultural factors. For example, Tosun's (2000: 613–33) study of tourism processes in developing nations identifies the following challenges to community participation in tourism management:

Operational

- centralised tourism administration;
- poor coordination within and between industry and government;
- insufficient information on industry resources, trends and impacts.

Structural

- professionals undervalue the contributions of the public;
- low levels of expertise among 'professionals';
- elites largely control tourism and enjoy its benefits;
- insufficient legal support in regards to legislation, case law and appeal processes;
- poor training of industry workers;
- potentially high cost of public participation;
- insufficient financial resources;

Cultural

- poor people struggling to meet basic needs have a limited capacity to participate;
- low levels of public awareness and interest

All of these factors identified by Tosun can be seen to be at work in developed countries also to varying degrees, especially in disadvantaged areas in the rural hinterlands of predominently wealthy countries. The balance point between the benefits of taking an inclusive planning approach, such as that advocated by the *Bridging Tourism Gaps Model*, and taking a more traditional tourism management approach hinges on the availability of resources to a community. Communities with a robust enabling environment (ample and sustained political, social, legal, economic and environmental resources) are in a strong position to empower their citizens' participation in the guidance of tourism develop-ment. Therefore, destinations need to undergo a thorough assessment of the enabling environment so they can adapt the *Bridging Tourism Gaps Model* to meet their particular circumstances.

As noted by a government official in Indonesia 'if a neighbourhood is being improved physically for tourism, it is unnecessary to involve the local people' (Timothy, 1999: 384). While this statement contradicts emerging Western ways of viewing citizen power, it speaks to the impor-tance of not sacrificing desired end states (improved quality of life for residents) for the sake of well-meaning processes. This model can be a valuable tool to help communities; however the destinations need resources to utilise this model to the best of its abilities. Communities that are in an emergency situation, such as responding to sudden and debilitat-ing losses in tourism revenues, or are severely under-resourced, might find traditional methods of centralised decision-making are their only viable options, at least in the short term. However, such circumstances can be prepared for to some extent under the controlling function, with regular reviews of progress and the inclusion of a crisis management component.

The impact of an enabling environment on a tourist destination's abilities to successfully take a collaborative approach to tourism planning is illustrated by comparing two destinations facing similar challenges. In the 1990s the Florida Keys and Bonaire, two Caribbean tourist destinations, were investigating ways to sustain their tourism industries in the face of mounting environmental damage and citizen discontent. Of particular concern for both areas was the damage being caused to their waters and coral reefs by the lack of a central sewerage system and the corresponding threat to tourism revenues caused by a degraded environment.

Both of these destinations engaged in collaborative tourism planning endeavours involving various levels of government, industry and resident groups. In Bonaire, these processes were *ad hoc*, lacked financial support and drew primarily upon existing networks and partnerships between industry, government and other established organisations (Parker, 2000). In Bonaire the limits noted by Tosun (2000) all eroded the abilities of this area to come to a successful solution using collaborative efforts (Parker, 2000). A bizarre situation arose where in order to keep Bonaire's stake-holders working together planning discussions centred around unrealistic 'best case' scenarios despite the area's limited resources and options. Even with 50% of their 1000 rooms unoccupied it was projected that by greatly increasing room numbers Bonaire would attract more flights (Parker, 2000: 91). This was expected to bring more tourists and then allow the cost of a sewerage system to be more manageable by spreading the funding over a greater number of rooms. Unfortunately, by the late 1990s tourist numbers to Bonaire failed to meet projected growth and 'no coordinated progress has been made on hotel construction, the treatment plant or the question of airline capacity since 1997' (Parker, 2000: 94). Bonaire can be seen as an example where an under-resourced planning environment thwarted local aspirations for a successful collaborative approach to tourism management.

In contrast, at this time the Florida Keys made great strides in its collabora-tive tourism efforts. The Florida Keys drew upon its wealth of economic, political and social resources in ensuring that these processes were forma-lised, well-financed and included extensive community outreach programmes to supplement the contributions of existing networks (please see earlier discussions on planning processes in the Keys). The Florida Keys obtained millions of dollars of financial assistance from various levels of gov-ernment to address its sewerage problems. These funds were obtained through the hard work, dedication and political skills of elected officials as well as members of industry, environmental and resident groups. Although tourism development in general and waste-water projects in particular are highly contentious (see www.Florida.Keynoter.com), efforts to take a collab-orative approach have been fruitful. The Florida Keys can be seen as an example where a non-emergency situation and an enabling planning envi-ronment created a situation where collaborative approaches to tourism development, such as those advanced by the *Bridging Tourism Gaps Model*, can aid in the development of a sustainable tourism destination.

Appropriate scale

Some problems in operating the *Bridging Tourism Gaps Model* can be overcome by adjusting the scale and scope of operations to suit local condi-tions and resources and starting with small and manageable tasks. Applying the model to a discrete and well-defined aspect of a destination's tourism offerings, will allow communities to learn how to use the model and evaluate its effectiveness as a tourism management tool. Timothy's

(1999) exploration of participatory planning in rural Indonesia can be seen as an example of how the model can be applied at a small scale. Rural residents' recognition of the tourism potential of their region's unique fruit and their grassroots approach to developing its tourism potential incorporate the main features of this model namely: business management, stakeholders, collaboration and gap analysis. The four business management principles are all evident in the community developing its own tourism goals and strategies.

Timothy notes that leaders in the community presented the fruit promotion idea to the local council, which supported the idea and successfully petitioned other levels of government and industry to support this local tourism initiative. Stakeholder involvement started with residents, who devised the idea. Government supported the idea through actions that included hiring private consultants to study its tourism potential. Industry involvement included promotion, while domestic, Japanese and Dutch travellers were targeted as customers.

Collaborative efforts were evident in residents, government and industry working together to develop the area's tourism potential, which culminated in a fruit agrotourism project which commenced in 1992 (Timothy, 1999: 380). Elements of gap analysis can be observed when looking at the strategy to develop the area's tourism potential. Specific tourism products and services were developed, in relation to fruit production, leaving other tourism needs such as accommodation to other suppliers. Half-day tours were developed linking the area to more established tourist destinations to allow for the specialisation of local tourism offerings, according to the needs and capabilities of the host destination. Communities can therefore start small, by looking at a particular tourism product they want to develop and progress through the stages of the model, building on what they learn.

Measuring performance

It is essential that the relevant data inform the planning and implementation of the *Bridging Tourism Gaps Model*, from its inception through its implementation and maintenance. Since the quality of decisions depends heavily on the quality of available information, gathering information in an efficient and effective manner is important to the fortunes of tourist destinations.

Enthusiasm for knowing as much as possible about a situation can run high as typified by this quote from a management consulting firm that sells its gap analysis services to other companies, 'In God, we trust ... All others bring data' (Adams Six Sigma, 2002). The relevance of data is a function of its usefulness, cost, quality, timeliness and focus. The high cost of collecting, storing and updating databases is a reflection of the reluctance of many organisations to commit substantial resources to this matter. But for tourism operators and destinations data collection and management can be made less onerous if they work with state governments and local tertiary education institutions on these matters.

Since the expectations of customers can be measured with reasonable accuracy and are relatively stable over time (Clow & Vorhies, 1993), customers' satisfaction and views on quality can help inform community tourism planning. Berry (1995: 34–5) and Eckhouse (2002: 4–6) suggest that to understand customers the following guidelines would be helpful:

(1) Randomly check on customers at regular intervals and where possible include these check-ups as part of the regular service delivery.
(2) Use a website as a two-way communication device (provide a comment section and customer surveys), and track what items on the website are the most popular.
(3) Provide comment cards at customer interfaces.
(4) Conduct representative surveys of stakeholder groups and where practical hire outside firms or tertiary education institutions to conduct these surveys.
(5) Coordinate and regularly update all data sources. This can be aided by linking with national and state data banks and drawing from other sources of published data.

While it seems natural that service industries should collect and use data on service quality, research in this area has produced surprising results. A recent study of 150 business-technology professionals found that most of their companies did not regularly track customer satisfaction and the customer data they had was neither readily available nor effectively used to guide management decisions (Eckhouse, 2002: 3–4). These results are surprising and disappointing, given that service firms are so dependent on customer satisfaction as a way of differentiating themselves from the competition and ensuring that they stay in business.

There are numerous government and non-government organisations that provide excellent data on broad tourism trends, such as numbers of visitors, top visitor activities and attractions, and the revenue and jobs generated by tourism. These sources are an excellent first stop for information. Researchers at Oklahoma State University have been exploring ways that communities can use existing databases to assist them in conducting gap analysis as a tool for community economic development. Barta and Woods (2002) recommended that communities use data from the state's tax commission data, which is reported according to Standard Industrial Classification (SIC) codes, along with data from the Bureau of the Census on local and county population and per capita income to identify gaps in retail sales. Gap analysis of retail sales identifies the supply and demand of retail items in relation to local and non-local customers, which in turn can provide an indication of the importance of tourist spending in an area.

More specific tourism information may require detailed searches and a measure of original primary research. Government and industry grants are sources of potential funding for tourism research. Since many universities include tourism and hospitality in their curriculum there are excellent opportunities to work with these universities on tourism research. Such partnering efforts can greatly lower costs, as well as providing a cross-fertilisation of ideas between academics, students and practitioners. This is the fundamental philosophy behind Australia's successful Cooperative Research Centre for Sustainable Tourism.

Prior to engaging in new research it is important to check on how related data has been collected and stored and to replicate these conditions where possible. This can involve asking the same questions in the same manner and using the same statistical methods to analyse the data. Another useful data management approach is to keep copies of raw data. This allows data to be segmented and re-analysed according to different needs, while a comprehensive set of the overall results remains intact. If such precautions are not taken then research opportunities are restricted. For example, researchers at the Chugach (Alaska) National Forest could not compare findings across different study periods due to significant changes in data collection and computation methods within the parks database (Brooks & Haynes, 2001).

An ongoing concern with customer surveys is when they are only developed for tourists, neglecting the views of other stakeholders – industry, resident and government. The ability to compare the views of stakeholder groups can be hampered by inconsistencies between different types of data, and the methods used to collect and store data. Since community tourism involves local stakeholders it is important to extend data collection beyond customer considerations. Strategic community tourism management should incorporate regular assessments of community impacts and reactions. Ideally this could be incorporated into the stakeholder involvement processes outlined above. If tourism is to be treated as a community industry, destinations should also produce an annual tourism progress report along the lines of corporate annual reports.

Summary

Bridging tourism gaps pulls together elements essential to identifying and making the most of tourism opportunities. This approach is responsive to the requirements and resources of tourism stakeholders and the community at large. The *Bridging Tourism Gaps Model* unites many of the assessment and management approaches that are currently being used in business, community and tourism settings. The model brings these approaches together to create a coherent and manageable context for understanding and directing tourism developments.

To illustrate the type of comprehensive management process the proposed model would provide, we offer a final case study. The case has used several of the techniques and approaches recommended in this book, but it was not set up as a complete bridging exercise. This case is provided because it reveals the importance of stakeholder consultation, the relevance of the four business functions, and the benefits of combining these two aspects, rather than because of its outcome.

The outcome was to resist development. Since that decision was made many feel, with the advantage of hindsight, that it was the correct one; given that the Australian ski resorts have been struggling with declining snowfalls and interest over the past few years. Some feel the collaborative decision-making process was wasteful because of the time and money spent on simply maintaining the *status quo* (Michael & Plowman, 2002). However, it is the ability of the process to produce effective and inclusive decisions that matters most. This example reveals how different stakeholder groups analyse a situation collectively to create a community response.

Case Study: Bridging the Gaps at Mt Stirling

(Robin Saunders, Principal, Robin Saunders Environmental Solutions Pty Ltd)

Overview

The processes and issues that surrounded the proposal to develop downhill skiing at a largely undeveloped area in Australian Alps show how the components of the *Bridging Tourism Gaps Model* can come together to provide clearer guidance on the appropriate course of action. This case study draws upon the tourism planning process surrounding a major development proposal for Mount Stirling in Victoria, Australia.

Background

Tasmania, Victoria and New South Wales are the only states in Australia with conditions conducive to snow skiing and snowboarding. Mt Stirling, with its peak elevation of 1746m, is one of Victoria's six designated alpine resorts. Mt Stirling is about a three-hour drive from Melbourne, which at four million people is Australia's second largest city and a state capital. Mt Stirling is located next to Victoria's most popular ski resort, Mt Buller (Figure 12.2). Mt Buller is the closest and most accessible alpine resort to Melbourne with reliable snow, and attracts a variety of downhill skiers and day-trippers, with an annual visitation of approximately 500,000 persons during the period 1982 to 1995 (Saunders & Stephens, 1998: 10). The neighbouring Mt Stirling snowfields have poor road access, and are used for cross-country skiing in the winter months.

In 1979 the Land Conservation Council, which was appointed by the

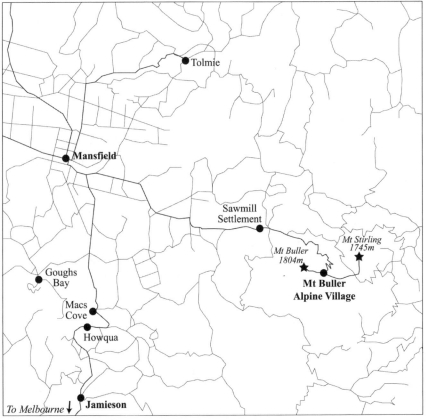

Figure 12.2 Mt Buller and Mt Stirling

state government to advise on the use of public lands, recommended that Mt Stirling be developed for downhill and cross-country skiing to address the anticipated boom in demand for such facilities (Saunders & Stephens, 1998: 4). In 1983 the Forests Commission prepared plans for developing the downhill skiing potential of Mt Stirling; however, lacking private sector interests these plans languished. In 1989 the Alpine Resorts Commission prepared a draft strategy for developing a resort facility to service both Mt Buller and Mt Stirling. This ambitious proposal included a high-speed gondola that would link the two mountains to a new base station as well as building 14 ski lifts with a capacity for 12,500 skiers on Mt. Stirling (Saunders & Stephens, 1998: 4). This proposal was so controversial that the government of the day decided not to endorse it. A change in government and renewed private sector interest in Mt Stirling prompted the Minster for Natural Resources to announce new plans to offer a lease to Buller Ski Lifts Ltd that upon acceptance would act as a trigger for an Environmental Impact Statement (EIS), which would carry with it opportunities for public input. The reaction to this proposal was swift and volatile, leading to a Supreme Court injunction blocking the proposal on procedural grounds.

In response, the government required the preparation of an EIS to investigate a range of possible developments for Mt Stirling. As there was little confidence in the independence of the Alpine Resorts Commission, and it was subsequently dissolved, in April 1994 the government required the Environment Assessment Branch within the Department of Planning and Development to manage and prepare the EIS. This branch had the responsibility of managing the EIS legislation in Victoria, and providing advice on the Environment Effects Act (1978) to the Minister for Planning. In the following analysis, the Environment Assessment Branch will be referred to as the proponent of the EIS for the future planning for Mt Stirling. The analysis will apply the *Bridging Tourism Gaps Model* to the decision-making process that took place with Mt Stirling's tourism management.

Business management functions

The widespread public interest in how Mt Stirling should be developed, the uncertainty over the potential impacts of different uses on the mountain, and the high level of public mistrust over the general handling of previous development proposals, put pressure on the government to address the issue in a more open and comprehensive way. Given that Mt Stirling is on public land there is an extra level of responsibility on government to show that it is acting in the public's best interests when deciding on how these lands should be managed. There were also concerns that development of this primarily undeveloped mountain would rely too much on the public purse in terms of establishing the necessary infrastructure. In view of the controversy surrounding the Buller Ski Lifts Ltd proposal, the government was compelled to look at ways to open up the planning process to greater public involvement. In reviewing the processes that were established to determine appropriate uses of Mt Stirling, one can see how the four key business management functions all played important roles in this major community land use decision.

Leadership

The *1978 Environment Effects Act* provided the then Minister of Planning with the authority to administer this Act with a great deal of discretion over assessment processes, including the determination of whether an EIS would be required on a case-by-case basis, and direction of the proponent on the scope of the EIS, the alternatives considered, and the degree of public consultation. The practice of the Minister appointing a Consultative Committee, with all major stakeholders and the community represented, to guide the preparation of the EIS, was established in the later 1980s. The Minister showed leadership in requiring an EIS, and appointing such a committee for the EIS, inviting the participation of interest groups both favouring and opposed to downhill ski development at Mt Stirling. The members appointed to the Consultative Committee included the following: '5 government agencies; the local council; various tourism operators; and community groups representing downhill skiing, nordic [cross-country] skiing, the local community and environmental interests' (Saunders & Stephens, 1998: 7).

The proponent met with representatives of the major interest groups involved, and assured them of the commitment to an open, consultative process. The EIS was then managed in a manner that kept faith with the assurances given, building the commitment of the stakeholders to the process.

Planning

Principal steps in developing and assessing the EIS are listed below in point form:

- Appointment of the Consultative Committee.
- Developing a consensus within the Committee to the objectives of the study.
- Preparing a study brief that detailed the issues that needed to be addressed and the alternatives to be considered.
- Engaging a consulting firm to undertake the work of preparing the EIS.
- Seeking public submissions on the EIS.
- Referring the EIS and the submissions to an independent Inquiry Panel for a report.
- The panel make recommendations to the Minister, the Minister mak-

ing an assessment of the EIS, as required by the Act, and providing it to the decision maker (government) as advice. Government to make a subsequent decision.

The community goals and objectives for developing Mt Stirling related to issues of equity, fairness, accountability and sound financial as well as economic management. Early in the study process the Minister made two important rulings. The first was that for the purpose of the study, earlier government policy decisions on the future of Mt Stirling were to be disregarded. The second was that the EIS would not include a preferred option, so that all alternatives would be considered equally on their merits during the exhibition period. Often when a proponent designates a preferred option, other options attract little consideration in public submissions.

Had the Buller Ski Lifts Ltd agreement been completed, the EIS would have focused on their proposal, while other options might not even have been considered. Stakeholder groups are often predisposed to fight against those decisions that they had no role in formulating, and where their only role is to offer their opinions on whether to accept or reject proposals. The mechanisms for the public to express their view on the development of Mt Stirling included serving on (or being represented on) the consultative committee, responding to invitations to respond to the initial study scope, attending forums and displays during the preparation of the EIS, making written submissions after the EIS was put on public display, and making a presentation to the independent inquiry panel that would make recommendations to government on the EIS.

Organising

The organising principles for the Mt Stirling decision-making processes were expressed in the objectives developed for the study, the assessment criteria developed for evaluating the alternatives, and the management of time and the limited money available to the proponent. The scoping process assisted in focusing on the key environmental, social and economic parameters that needed study, and developing alternatives that ranged from virtually a 'do nothing' alternative, through low-scale recreation and cross-country skiing alternatives, to full downhill skiing development.

The consultant brief was drafted by the proponent, and was subject to exhaustive discussion at the Consultative Committee, over several committee meetings. In the end it was amended to meet the reasonable expectations of all members of the committee. The rigour with which the brief was vetted proved a key factor in managing the consultant process, and controlling costs. Late in the study process it became apparent that a further alternative would be useful in drawing out the implications of a variation of one of the existing alternatives. Additional funds were sought therefore to expand the study brief to include the additional alternative.

Preparing the Mt Stirling EIS involved the following four steps:

- Identifying current and potential future uses of Mt Stirling.
- Developing a range of options for the mountain.
- Assessing the potential social, environmental and economic impacts of the options.
- Evaluating the options based on EIS criteria established at the beginning of the process.

The assessment criteria looked at potential environmental, social and economic impacts from both quantitative and qualitative perspectives. Environmental criteria included the potential impacts of global warming and issues relating to water quality and soil stability. Social criteria included considering the impacts development would have on Aboriginal and European heritage, and impacts development would have on residents in nearby towns and current and potential users of the mountain. The economic criteria looked at the potential financial impacts of the options and how they impacted on the viability of these options.

The established procedures for the preparation and assessment of an EIS reflect the political, administrative and economic realities that underlie available options as a state government endeavours to identify and support proposals that will help the state achieve its overall goals and objectives, as well as those that it specifically sets for tourism related initiatives. The elected government retains the legal responsibility and right to decide how best to manage public funds and lands in relation to a tourism and recreation development proposal, while creating opportunities for public review and participation in the process.

Control

Control for the Mt Stirling proposal related to ensuring that effective and fair decision-making processes would be implemented, monitored and adjusted to support overall state goals and objectives. The consultative committee played an important role in holding the government and other involved stakeholder groups accountable for their review processes and recommendations. Enabling other interested groups to participate in the process by acting as observers, commentators and presenters to the committee furthered this accountability. The level of transparency that was provided through the open consultative meetings and the ready access to the materials that they drew upon and produced helped to build confidence in the process. Furthermore, by providing the consultative committee with the responsibility for reviewing key issues that would need to be addressed, the range of potential alternatives and the criteria that would be used to assess them, a large measure of control was delegated. Thus the stakeholders who represented a diversity of ideas and views relating to how Mt Stirling should be managed had a strong degree of public control over 'setting the agenda'. In turn this created an atmosphere more conducive to trusting the established decision-makers to make the right decision for the larger community.

Stakeholder groups

The stakeholder groups interested in the management of Mt Stirling represented the resources that could be used to either facilitate or block proposals for the mountain. Their resources included monetary funds, as well as expertise, experience, community contacts and an understanding of the issues from a wide range of perspectives. The stakeholder groups involved in the Mt Stirling proposal can be divided into the categories of customers, industry, residents and government used in this book, and their contributions to the EIS development included the following:

Customers

- Knowledge of how they would like to use the area, what they currently value about the area, and what they would like to see happen.
- Knowledge about the environmental and social attributes of the mountain and its environs.
- Networking with local and regional contacts to raise awareness about the process and the issues.

Industry
- Detailed knowledge of the industry and its requirements was provided by the Mt Buller Committee of Management.
- Knowledge, ideas and critical comments were provided by other groups using the mountain, such as the cross-country ski industry and nature-based and educational tourism operators.

Residents

- Environmental groups with a particular interest in nature conservation ensured that natural values were appropriately addressed.
- Residents in the immediate vicinity of Mt Stirling, and beyond, contributed their knowledge of potential social impacts, and concern about regional impacts on water quality and accessibility.

Government

- The Alpine Resorts Commission championed the downhill ski development, and subsequently was an advocate for this alternative.
- The Environment Assessment Branch, Department of Planning and

Development acted as the proponent for the EIS, and managed the EIS process.

- The Mansfield Shire Council provided local government knowledge to the Consultative Committee.
- State Government Departments responsible for nature conservation, water resources, tourism, heritage protection and pollution control contributed to the development of the EIS.
- The Minister of Planning initiated the EIS, appointed the Independent Inquiry Panel, and made the final assessment of the EIS (as a recommendation to government).

Collaboration

As detailed earlier in the paper, the approach taken to the preparation of the EIS was a collaborative one, where all stakeholders were involved in the shaping of the study, and wide opportunities for public input and comment were provided during the EIS preparation.

In addition to the public's opportunities to participate in earlier stages of the decision-making processes, the completion of the EIR opened up the process for even wider public review and comment. The EIS was exhibited to the public from the end of June until the end of August in 1996 (Saunders & Stephens, 1998: 10). Information on the EIS findings relating to Mt Stirling was displayed at over 30 locations in urban and rural areas throughout Victoria. More than 600 submissions were received during the public exhibition period of the EIS and over 60 stakeholder groups and individuals made presentations to the planning panel charged with making recommendations on the management of Mt Stirling to the Minister of Planning (Saunders & Stephens, 1998: 11).

After completing the public hearings the panel put forth its recommendations to the Minister, which the Minister accepted. The panel had found that the overall economic and environment costs associated with developing downhill skiing at Mt Stirling could not be offset by the potential benefits that such as development could bring to the state. The Victorian government promptly announced that Mt Stirling was to be retained as 'an all season, nature-based recreational and educational destination' (ibid: 11) and ruled out the development of downhill skiing facilities. Saunders and Stephens note that the reactions of stakeholder groups to the government's announcement were overwhelmingly positive as environmental groups, nature based tourism groups and even the public sector proponent for downhill skiing publicly supported the government's handling of the issues and final decision.

The continual involvement of the public from the early stages of proposing options and setting the criteria, against which their options would be evaluated, to the final stages of widespread public exhibition and feedback on the options, enabled the government to make a wise decision. The consultative committee and the public interest groups that observed and communicated their views to the committee during the important preliminary stages of the EIS consisted of a cross-section of affected stakeholders. The stakeholder group representatives were drawn from various segments of the tourism industry, residents, environmental groups and administrators. The key stakeholders publicly supported the EIS process and outcome.

The Victorian National Parks Association (an environmental group) described the Mount Stirling EIS as an 'exemplary process' and 'a major watershed in the alpine resort development debate . . .. It is by far the most comprehensive planning study ever conducted into a proposed alpine resort development in Victoria and has important implications for future alpine development and planning'.

The Mount Stirling Development Task Force (a community group supporting nature-based tourism) stated; 'There can be no doubt that this process succeeded for its impartiality in that no one was excluded and all were given the fullest of opportunities to be heard'.

Buller Ski Lifts Ltd (which initially favoured downhill skiing development on Mount Stirling) welcomed the government decision and said: 'We are looking forward to working with the government and the community to ensure Mount Stirling is well looked after and preserved for future generations of Australians' (Saunders & Stephens, 1998: 11).

Although the public was not able to have the final say on how Mt Stirling should be developed, their pervasive and formalised involvement in the process ensured that the right questions were asked throughout the process, which in turn clearly illuminated for government the right decision. Indeed the openness of all stages of the process, and the strong conclusions of the Inquiry Panel, would have made any other decision by Government open to public scorn.

Gap analysis

The key budgeting issue was to ensure that the limited funds available for the study (some A$250,000) were allocated to the investigation of critical gaps in information and analysis. At the beginning of the study, all available baseline data was assembled, and key issues were highlighted through the public scoping phase. The study brief reflected areas where further data needed to be collected, and listed the key issues. The brief required six alternatives to be prepared and analysed, but left it up to the consultants to frame each of these alternatives.

Independent consultants who were acceptable to both the Department of Planning and Development and the consultative committee representatives conducted the EIS. The consultants drew upon their professional expertise when evaluating the alternatives, using the committee's assessment criteria. The consultants presented the likely impacts of each alternative without ranking the options, so as not to be seen as favouring one option over another. Saunders and Stephens (1998: 9) note that the following revelations arose from the EIS:

- Earlier studies had not adequately addressed the potential of the mountain for education and nature based tourism.
- Skiing was not growing as expected in Victoria, or worldwide, as the baby-boomers became too old to ski and their children decided to spend their money on other types of activities and vacations.
- Mt Stirling had significant native vegetation and rare species that could be adversely affected by the development of downhill skiing facilities.
- The greenhouse effect could have particularly dire consequences for ski resorts in Australia given the low altitudes of the country's mountain ranges.
- Developing downhill skiing facilities at Mt Stirling would not be commercially viable, due to the extensive infrastructure costs that would be incurred as a direct result of developing the facility and the limited demand for more skiing facilities in Victoria.

While a formal gap analysis was not a part of the Mt Stirling EIS process, elements of a gap analysis approach are apparent. Foremost among these was the gathering of a wide range of applicable data relating to stakeholders' expectations and resources and then looking at the costs and benefits of developing the mountain under the different scenarios. This comparison of what is desired to what is required to meet these desires is also a key principle of budgeting, as one considers how to best allocate resources. These resources can be financial, such as the costs of building new roads, as well as nature based, such as the potential impacts that road development would have on the integrity of an area's ecosystem. When all the relevant resources, expectations, costs and benefits for the six options were considered it became evident that developing downhill skiing facilities on the mountain raised significant concerns, while other options held more promise.

Management implications

The processes involved in deciding how to develop and manage Mt Stirling in the best interests of stakeholder groups and the general public went beyond a typical Environmental Impact Statement or Analysis to include a greater range of opinions and resources. These processes were still streamlined and carried out in a prompt and effective manner without costing the government or other stakeholders groups an unacceptable amount of money, or time. Had a private sector proponent implemented the original concept for a downhill ski resort, the costs documented in the EIS included likely financial failure of the resort through lack of suitable snow conditions, high impacts on the fragile ecosystem of the mountain, and significant public funds required for road infrastructure upgrading. These costs can be compared to the very considerable benefits of supporting low-impact tourist and recreational uses on the mountain.

Epilogue

The purpose of this book is to advocate strategic business management as a practical way to convert a community's interest in tourism into the most appropriate and competitive position for today's tough global tourism market. It is based on the premise that tourism at the community level should be viewed as a business first and foremost, that should incorporate the host community as a major stakeholder. The book uses the expanding business management literature, that is built on the four functions of management, and has demonstrated how business can be more socially responsible, and its tenets applied to small business and entrepreneurial situations. It makes extensive use of the tourism literature that has been moving toward Jafari's (1990) knowledge platform, in advocating a multi-disciplinary approach to tourism management that will embrace the findings of many disciplines to address the broad and complex task of developing the most appropriate tourism product for a host community.

In drawing these management and tourism threads together the book takes a prescriptive role, to guide the tourism development process for a wide range of community sizes and types. It focuses on communities as living organisms, where tourism is but one economic activity that needs to be considered along with other activities and options. Communities are the coalface of this industry, where tourists come to gaze and 'the production of many services is *context* dependent, they depend for their successful production upon aspects of the social and physical setting within which they occur' (Urry, 1990: 72). Such communities as destination settings, providers of attractions and labour, and political support are fundamental to the success of this industry.

After setting the scene for community tourism management the book has divided the complex and continuous strategic management process for tourism communities into three major sections, to facilitate its comprehension. The first is to emphasise how well the four basic functions of business management fit the community's need for an objective assessment of tourism's local potential, and how to plan and organise for its development. These functions also emphasise the need to monitor and control this industry, so that it does not bolt and drag the community into undesirable directions and consequences. While much of the management literature defers to corporate situations there is a growing appreciation of its relevance, with appropriate modifications, to the small business environment and entrepreneurship. Last, but certainly not least, the management function of leadership becomes vital to small business within tourism when it is viewed as a community industry. To pull the various industry and community components together to form an approved and competitive community tourism product will be fundamental to the success of a destination, and this whole process calls for leadership to come from some quarter. As we have shown, such leadership can come from a variety of stakeholders.

The second emphasis has been on understanding the views of major stakeholder groups with respect to tourism development in the destination community. We have chosen to analyse four major groups that cover the total spectrum, but the actual division is not sacrosanct and should vary according to local circumstances. One group we feel should always be identified and analysed is the customer, for this industry and its community investment is nothing if it cannot attract tourists. Tourists are now experienced and demanding, compared to the early post-World War II era, and have split into a multitude of special travel interests. This variety of interests provides many communities with a tourism development opportunity, but given the sophistication of modern tourists and the global competition for their business an aspiring community must develop a quality product and experience.

The final section attempts to show a way in which the business functions and interests of stakeholders can and should be linked. It offers a bridging model that shows the importance of collaborative decision-making and the significance of identifying gaps that may exist between the anticipated and actual experiences with this industry. Using the growing literature on conflict resolution we recommend some tried and tested techniques that can or have been used in tourism management, and we relate these to the service industry's interest in gap analysis. While this type of analysis has focused on potential gaps between providers' and customers' perceptions it has equal relevance to the different perspectives of various stakeholders. The various collaborative decision-making models in planning offer the chance for many of these perceptual gaps to be explored and minimised.

Conclusion

The *Bridging Tourism Gaps Model* is offered as a framework for communities to consider in the management of their tourism products and experience. Its main purpose is to ensure that communities consider all the pertinent facts and players, but from a pro-active business perspective. Such an approach will encourage a more complete assessment of development opportunities and current business activities, and as illustrated in the final case study, can produce a development freeze as well as a new product and image. Either way, if a community has applied the four functions of management, consulted the relevant stakeholders, and done so in an open partnership process, it will be in a better position to develop its tourism potential and take its place in the global marketplace.

Appendix

Strategic Tourism Planning Resources

International Organisations

World Tourism Organization

http://www.world-tourism.org/

This site is full of excellent quantitative measures of the global tourism industry. Analyses of tourism impacts are provided at multiple-levels, from international to national.

From this main page try the following links:

- Facts and figures and statistics and economic measures of tourism
- Sustainable development of tourism – links to Code of Ethics
- Regional activities

Accessed on 14/11/03

World Travel and Tourism Council

http://www.wttc.org/

This industry lobby group site provides an overview of global tourism trends and issues. The website emphasises the positive economic and employment impacts of tourism drawing on quantitative research.

From this main page try the following links:

- TSA Research
- Regional Initiatives
- Media & Resource Centre

Accessed on 16/11/03

Regional Organisations

European Travel Commission

http://www.etc-corporate.org/

The European Travel Commission is made up of the 33 National Tourism Organisations of Europe. There are two websites for the ETC – one with a corporate focus and the other with a traveller focus. This site provides a myriad of information on the impacts and potential of tourism in Europe. The site is a rich resource of tourism date.

From this main page try the following links:

- Statistics
- European Tourism News
- New Media Review

Accessed on 16/11/03

Pacific Asia Travel Association

http://www.pata.org

This website focuses on the activities of the Pacific Asia Travel Association and its members. The website has many interesting links and features, including annual reports that abound with tourism data. The website also has a members only component containing information and data searches that are free to PATA members.

From this main page try the following links:

- Events
- Publications
- Destinations – direct links to government tourism offices and other travel-related services throughout Asia and the Pacific.

Accessed on 16/11/03

National Organisations

Office of Travel and Tourism Industries (USA)

http://tinet.ita.doc.gov/

This site provides quantitative information on the tourism industry in the USA.

From this main page try the following links:

- About OTTI – links to tourism development and tourism policy
- Research Programmes – links to basic and monthly statistics
- Latest statistics/outreach – links to inbound and outbound figures
- TI News – summary of impacts, forecasts for arrivals and updates on tourism policy

Accessed on 14/11/03

ATC Online – tourism industry essential (Australia)

http://www.atc.net.au/

This site provides a wide array of information on the status of Australia's tourism industry. There are numerous links presented as overviews and in more detailed forms.

From this main page try the following links:

- Daily News Service
- Latest Statistics / outreach – links to visitor arrivals and tourist profiles
- Quick Find – annual report, FAQ, marketing advice and visitor arrivals

Accessed on 14/11/03

Scottish Tourism Organisation
http:/ / www.world-tourism.org /
This site is tailored to travellers and is an excellent example of the how a website can convey the 'must see' aspects of a destination. The site is accessible in a number of languages and is customised for the needs of different international travellers. There is also a newsletter service that can be subscribed to along with numerous value and special interest packages.
From this main page try the following links:

- Short Breaks
- Festive Breaks
- Customised international links

Accessed on 17/11/03

Japan Travel Bureau
http:/ / www.jtb.co.jp / eng /
This site is aimed primarily at travellers with a wide array of information on opportunities for exploring and enjoying Japan. There are useful links to tourism service providers, with the connections to train service proving especially helpful.
From this main page try the following links:

- Japan Now
- Location Focus
- In-depth Guide to the Regions

Accessed on 17/11/03

Switzerland Tourism
http:/ / www.myswitzerland.com /
This site provides a comprehensive overview of tourism opportunities fro travellers in several different languages. There are useful links to tourism service providers, with plenty of maps and web cams to give a real feel for the country. The website customises its information to the area from which a request is made.
From this main page try the following links:

- Services
- Experiences
- Swiss Travel System

Accessed on 17/11/03

Indigenous Organisations

Alliance of Tribal Tourism
http://www.attatribal.com/attatribal/
The alliance of Tribal Tourism Advocates is an association of Tribes, Indians, and Non-Indian individuals, agencies and organisations that are concerned about responsible tourism development on the reservation and in off-reservation communities. This is an important site for tourism planners and others interested in sustainability issues, especially with respect to cultural issues.

From this main page try the following links:

- Mission
- Board
- Goals

Accessed on 17/11/03

Centre for World Indigenous Studies
http://www.cwis.org/
This site provides extensive information on indigenous issues around the world. While not tourism specific, it does provide background on many facets of indigenous life that need to be considered in regard to tourism's potential and limitations. From this main page try searching for 'tourism' to see relevant documents.
Accessed on 16/11/03

State and Local Organisations

Welcome to Victoria (Australia)
This site, which is aimed at travellers, offers many interesting links and has sites specifically created for visitors from key target markets.

From this main page try the following links:

- Experience Victoria – see Travel Planner
- Special Interest
- Related Links – customised fro specific target markets

Accessed on 16/11/03

Tourism BC (Canada)

This site is the official travel and accommodation site for British Columbia and advertises the 1800HELLOBC travel information hotline. While this site is aimed at travellers, it has useful links to tourism data as well.

From this main page try the following links:

- Travel Articles
- Tourism BC Corporate Website – see tourism research, plans and reports

Accessed on 16/11/03

The City and County of Honolulu, Hawaii

http://www.co.Honolulu.hi.us/

While this site is not tourism specific, searching by 'tourism' provides excellent quantitative measures of the tourism industry. Honolulu has integrated tourism into its strategic planning, thereby linking the well-being of tourism to that of the city.

From this main page try search by the keyword tourism for access to the following:

- Hawaii Tourism Authority County Product Enrichment Program
- Economic development opportunities relating to tourism
- Tourism education and training
- Council bills and resolutions relating to tourism

Accessed on 18/11/03

Florida Keys

http://www.co.Monroe.fl.us/

http://www.fla-keys.com

While The Monroe County site is not tourism specific, tourism is a cornerstone of the planning, development and management of the Keys. The website offers translation options, and a direct link to the Tourism Development Council, which is primarily a marketing body, is provided.

From this main page it is also useful to look at the following government websites of the other municipalities of the Florida Keys:

- Marathon
- Islamorada
- Key Colony Beach
- Key West

Accessed on 18/11/03

Bibliography

Aaker, D.A. (1992) *Developing Business Strategies* (3rd edn). New York: John Wiley.

Aaker, D.A. and Shansby, J. (1982) Positioning your product. *Business Horizons* (May–June), 56–62.

Abbot, J. (1995) Community participation and its relationship to community development. *Community Development Journal* 30 (2), 164.

Adams Six Sigma (2002) Gap analysis through data analysis turns data into information. *Adams Six Sigma.* http://www.adamsixsigma.com/Newsletters/data_analysis.htm. Accessed on 19 December 2002.

Alamo (2002) Gap analysis. *Alamo Learning Systems.* http://www.alamols.com/consulting/gap.htm. Accessed on 19 December 2002.

Alberta Tourism (1988) *Community Tourism Action Plan Manual.* Edmonton, Alberta: Alberta Tourism.

Alford, P. (1998) Positioning the destination product – can regional tourist boards learn from private sector practice? *Journal of Travel and Tourism Marketing* 7 (2), 53–68.

Allen, L.R., Long, P.T., Perdue, R.R. and Kieselbach, S. (1988) The impact of tourism development on residents' perceptions of community life. *Journal of Travel Research* 27 (1), 16–21.

Alliance of Tribal Tourism Advocates (ATTA) (2002) *ATTA.* http://atta.indian.com. Accessed on 15 January 2002.

American Planning Association (1999) *Study Guide for the Comprehensive AICP Exam.* Memphis, TN: University of Memphis.

American Planning Association (2000) Development moratoria, not a property taking. *APA Public Information: For the Press.* www.planning.org. Accessed on 5 December 2001.

American Planning Association (2001) Land-use planners cautious about Supreme Court decision rejecting taking claim but expanding future claim standards. *APA Public Information: For the Press.* www.planning.org. Accessed on 5 December 2001.

American Planning Association (2002) Leaders. *APA Planning: Special Awards Issue* 68 (3), 16–18.

Anderson, A.R. and Jack, S.L. (2002) The articulation of social capital in entrepreneurial networks: A glue or a lubricant? *Entrepreneurship and Regional Development* 14 (3), 193–210.

Ap, J. (1992) Residents' perceptions of tourism impacts. *Annals of Tourism Research* 19 (4), 665–90.

Archer, D., Griffin, T. and Hayes, A-L. (2001) Managing people by understanding people: A review of current visitor monitoring practices by Australian parks agencies. In C. Pforr and B. Janeczko (eds) *Capitalising on Research.* Proceedings of the Council of Australian University Tourism and Hospitality Education (CAUTHE) Conference, Canberra, 1–16.

413

Arnstein, S. (1969) A ladder of citizen participation. *Journal of the American Planning Association* 35 (4), 216–24.

Athiyaman, A. (1995) The interface of tourism and strategy research: An analysis. *Tourism Management* 16 (6), 447–53.

Augustyn, M. and Ho, S.K. (1998) Service quality and tourism. *Journal of Travel Research* 37 (1), 71–5.

Australia (2002) *The 10 Year Plan for Tourism: A Discussion Paper*. Canberra: Industry Tourism Resources.

Australian Broadcasting Corporation (ABC-TV) (2002) *True Stories: A Balinese Adventure*. Directed and produced by Bill Leimbach. Thursday, 21 February 2002 (10:00–11:00 p.m.).

Australian Heritage Commission (1999) *Protecting Local Heritage Places: A Guide for Communities*. Canberra, ACT: Commonwealth of Australia.

Australian Tourist Commission (2003) About the ATC. *ATC Online*. http://www.atc.australia.com/. Accessed on 28 January 2003.

Axelrod, J. (1968) Attitude measures that predict purchase. *Journal of Advertising Research* 8, 3–17.

Ayala, H. (1995) From quality product to eco-product: Will Fiji set a precedent? *Tourism Management* 16 (1), 39–47.

Aziz, H. (1995) Understanding attacks on tourists in Egypt. *Tourism Management* 16 (2), 91–5.

Bacrach, S. and Lawler, E. (1981) *Bargaining: Power, Tactics and Outcomes*. San Franciso: Jossey-Bass Publishers.

Badger, A., Barnett, P., Corbyn, L. and Keefe, J. (1996) *Trading Places: Tourism as Trade*. London: Tourism Concern.

Baker, J.E. (1997) Development of a model system for touristic hunting revenue collection and allocation. *Tourism Management* 18 (5), 273–86.

Baldacchino, G. (1997) *Global Tourism and Informal Labour Relations: The Small-Scale Syndrome at Work*. London: Mansell.

Barbalace, R. (2000) Environmental justice and the NIMBY principle. http://EnvironmentalChemistry.com. Accessed on 17 November 2000.

Barkham, J.P. (1973) Recreational carrying capacity: A problem of perception. *Area* 5, 218–22.

Barkley, B. (1997) An institution in transition: The Royal British Columbia Museum's Futures Project. In P.E. Murphy (ed.) *Quality Management in Urban Tourism* (pp. 149–56). Chichester: Wiley.

Barta, S.D. and Woods, M.D. (2002) Gap analysis as a tool for community economic development. *Oklahoma State University (OSU) Extension Facts*. (WF–917). www.agweb.okstate.edu. Accessed on 19 December 2002.

Bartunek, J.M. (1981) Why did you do that? Attribution theory in organizations. *Business Horizons* 24 (Sept.–Oct.), 66–71.

Baum, T. (1996) Tourism and the host community: A cautionary tale. *Tourism Management* 17 (2), 149–50.

BC Ferries (2002) *Inside Passage and Queen Charlotte Islands Schedules*. http://www.bcferries.bc.ca. Accessed on 31 December 2002.

Beazer, M. (1998) *Access and Justice: Legal Studies for Units 1 and 2* (3rd edn). Sale, Victoria: Beazer Publishing Co.

Becker, B. (1999) Visioning. In *Study Guide for the Comprehensive AICP Exam* (p. 66). Memphis, TN: University of Memphis.

Beeton, S. (2000) 'It's a wrap'. But what happens after the film crew leaves? An examination of community responses to film-induced tourism. In *Lights, Camera, Action:*

Spotlight on Tourism in the New Millennium (pp. 127–36). 31st Annual Proceedings of the Travel and Tourism Research Association, San Fernando Valley, California.

Behrendt, L. (1995) *Aboriginal Dispute Resolution*. Sydney: Federation Press.

Bellamy, D. (1992) The grand tour: A force for good or evil? *Traveller* 22 (3), 46–7.

Benson, J.K. (1975) The interorganizational network as political economy. *Administrative Science Quarterly* 20 (2), 229–49.

Berger, D.J. (1996) The challenge of integrating Maasai tradition with tourism. In M.F. Price (ed.) *People and Tourism in Fragile Environments* (pp. 175–98). Chichester, UK: John Wiley and Sons.

Berry, L.L. (1995) *On Great Service: A Framework for Action*. New York: Free Press.

Berry, L.L. and Clark, T. (1986) Four ways to make services more tangible. *Business*. (October–December), 53–4.

Berry, L.L. and Parasuraman, A. (1991) *Marketing Services: Competing Through Quality*. New York: Free Press.

Berry, S. and Ladkin, A. (1997) Sustainable tourism: A regional perspective. *Tourism Management* 18 (7), 433–40.

Bertsch (1999) Budgeting. In *Study Guide for the Comprehensive AICP Exam* (pp. 199–205). Memphis, TN: University of Memphis.

Beyer, H. and Bunbury, C.M. (1993) *The Chemainus Murals*. Chemainus, BC: Chemainus Festival of Murals Society.

Beyer, L. (2001) The women of Islam. *Time International: Special Report*. 3 December, 50–5.

Bhide, A. (1999) The questions every entrepreneur must answer. In the *Harvard Business Review on Entrepreneurship*. Boston, MA: Harvard Business School Press, 1–28.

Bitner, M.J. (1992) Servicescapes: The impact of physical surroundings on customers and employees. *Journal of Marketing* 56 (2), 57–71.

Blake, R.R. and Mouton, J.S. (1985) *The New Managerial Grid*. Houston: Gulf Publishing.

Blank, U. (1989) *The Community Tourism Imperative: The Necessity, the Opportunities, its Potential*. State College, PA: Venture Publishing.

Boothroyd, P. and Davis, C.H. (1993) Community economic development. *Journal of Planning Education and Research* 12 (3), 230–9.

Bosselman, F.P., Peterson, C.A. and McCarthy, C. (1999) *Managing Tourism Growth: Issues and Applications*. Washington, DC: Island Press.

Boulle, L. (1996) *Mediation: Principles, Process, Practice*. Sydney: Butterworths.

Boyd, S.W. and Butler, R.W. (1996) Managing ecotourism: An opportunity spectrum approach. *Tourism Management* 17 (8), 557–66.

Bramwell, B. (1994) Rural tourism and sustainable rural tourism. In B. Bramwell and B. Lane (eds) *Rural Tourism and Sustainable Rural Development* (pp. 1–6). Proceedings of the 2nd International School on Rural Development, 28 June–9 July 1993, University College Galway, Ireland 2 (1&2).

Bramwell, B. and Rawding, L. (1996) Tourism marketing images of industrial cities. *Annals of Tourism Research* 23 (1), 201–21.

Branson, R. (1998) *Losing my Virginity*. London: Virgin Publishing.

Britton, R.A. (1979) The image of the third world in tourism marketing. *Annals of Tourism Research* 6 (3), 318–29.

Britton, S.C. (1982) The political economy of tourism in the Third World. *Annals of Tourism Research* 9 (3), 331–58.

Britton, S. (1991) Tourism, capital and place: Towards a critical geography of tourism. *Environment and Planning, Society and Space* 9, 451–78.

Britton, S. and Clarke, W.C. (1987) *Ambiguous Alternative: Tourism in Small Developing Countries*, Suva, Fiji: University of Fiji.

Brohman, J. (1996) New directions in tourism for third world development. *Annals of Tourism Research* 23 (1), 48–70.

Bronner, F. and de Hoog, R. (1985) A recipe for mixing decision ingredients. *European Research* 13, 109–15.

Brook, R. (2000) The collaborative approach to resolving tourist related conflict. *Australian Planner* 37 (4), 186–94.

Brooks, D.J. and Haynes, R.W. (2001) *Recreation Tourism in South-Central Alaska: Synthesis of Recent Trends and Prospects*. United States Forest Service.

Brougham, J.E. and Butler, R.W. (1981) A segmentation analysis of resident attitudes to the social impact of tourism. *Annals of Tourism Research* 8 (4) 569–90.

Brown, F. (1998) *Tourism Reassessed: Blight or Blessing?* Oxford: Butterworth-Heinemann.

Brundtland, G.H. (1987) The Brundtland Report – *Our Common Future*. World Commission on Environment and Development. Oxford: Oxford University Press.

Brunt, P. and Courtney, P. (1999) Host perceptions of sociocultural impacts. *Annals of Tourism Research* 26 (3), 493–515.

Bryman, A. (1995) *Disney and his Worlds*. London: Routledge.

Buck, R.C. (1977) Making good business better: a second look at staged tourist attractions. *Journal of Travel Research* 15 (3), 30–2.

Buhalis, D. (2000) Tourism in an era of information technology. In B. Faulkner, G. Moscardo and E. Laws (eds) *Tourism in the 21st Century: Lessons from Experience* (pp. 163–80). London: Continuum.

Burke, J.F. and Gitelson, R. (1990) Conversion studies: assumptions, applications, accuracy and abuse. *Journal of Travel Research* 26 (3), 46–51.

Burnett, P. (1980) Spatial constraints-oriented approaches to movement, micro-economic theory and urban policy. *Urban Geography* 1, 53–67.

Burns, R. (1996) *Robert Burns Selected Poems*. London, England: Penguin Books.

Burr, S.W. (1991) Review and evaluation of the theoretical approaches to community as employed in travel and tourism impact research on rural community organisation and change. In A.J. Veal , P. Johnson and G. Cushman (eds) *Leisure and Tourism: Social and Environmental Changes* (pp. 540–53). Proceedings of the World Leisure and Recreation Association Congress, Sydney, Australia.

Butler, R.W. (1975) Tourism as an agent of social change. *Tourism as a Factor in National and Regional Development* (pp. 85–90). Occasional Paper 4, Peterborough, Ontario: Department of Geography, Trent University.

Butler, R.W. (1980) The concept of a tourist area cycle of evolution: implications for management of resources. *The Canadian Geographer* 24 (1), 5–12.

Butler, R.W. (1990) Alternative tourism: Pious hope or Trojan horse? *Journal of Travel Research* 28 (3): 40–6.

Butler, R.W. (1999) Problems and issues of integrating tourism development. In D.G. Pearce and R.W. Butler (eds) *Contemporary Issues in Tourism Development* (pp. 46–80). London and New York: Routledge.

Butler, R.W. and Walbrook, L.A. (1991) A new planning tool: The tourism opportunity spectrum. *The Journal of Tourism Studies* 2 (1), 2–14.

Byron Shire Council (2003) *Byron Bay Council – Concepts*. www.byron.nsw.gov.au. Accessed on 19 January 2003.

Cabinet Office (1999) *Rural Economics: A Performance and Innovation Unit Report*. London: Cabinet Office.

Caffyn, A. (2000) Is there a tourism partnership life cycle? In B. Bramwell and B. Lane (eds) *Tourism Collaboration and Partnerships: Politics, Practice and Sustainability* (pp. 200–29). Clevedon, UK: Channel View Publications.

Calantone, R.J. and Mazanec, J.A. (1991) Marketing management and tourism. *Annals of Tourism Research* 18 (1), 101–19.

Callenbach, E., Capra, F., Goldman, L., Lutz, R. and Marburg, S. (1993) *EcoManagement*. San Francisco: Berrett-Koehler.

Cameron, B. (1992) Creative destinations: Marketing and packaging: Who wants what and why? An overview of the Canadian Pleasure Market Study. In *Tourism Partnerships and Strategies: Merging Vision with New Realities* (pp. 154–67). TTRA 23rd Annual Conference Proceedings. June, Minneapolis.

Campbell, K. and Lapierre, J. (1991) Developing a satellite account for tourism and information system for tourism. In *Tourism Building Credibility for a Credible Industry* (pp. 7–17). Proceedings of the 22nd Annual Conference of the Travel and Tourism Research Association, Long Beach, California.

Campfens, H. (1997) International review of community development. In H. Campfens (ed.) *Community Development Around the World: Practice, Theory, Research, Training* (pp. 13–46). Toronto: University of Toronto Press.

Canada (1990) *Tourism on the Threshold*. Ottawa: Industry, Science and Technology Canada.

Canan, P. and Hennessy, M. (1989) The growth machine, tourism, and the selling of culture. *Sociological Perspectives* 22 (2), 227–43.

Canestrelli, E. and Costa, P. (1991) Tourist carrying capacity: a fuzzy approach. *Annals of Tourism Research* 18 (2), 295–311.

Capenerhurst, J. (1994) Community tourism. In L. Haywood (ed.) *Community, Leisure and Recreation* (pp. 144–71). Oxford: Butterworth-Heinemann.

Capodagli, B. and Jackson, L. (1999) *The Disney Way*. New York: McGraw-Hill.

Carlzon, J. (1987) *Moments of Truth: New Strategies for Today's Customer-Driven Economy*. New York: Harper & Row.

Carmichael, B. and Murphy, P.E. (1996) Tourism economic impact of a rotating sports event: The case of the British Columbia Games. *Festival Management and Event Tourism* 4, 127–38.

Carmichael, B.A., Peppard, D. and Boudreau, F. (1996) Mega resort on my doorstep: Local resident attitudes towards Foxwoods Casino and casino gambling on nearby Indian Reservation land. *Journal of Travel Research* 34 (3), 9–16.

Carnegie, R. and Butlin, M. (1993) *Managing the Innovating Enterprise: Australian Companies Competing with the World's Best*. Canberra: Business Council of Australia.

Carpenter, S.L. (1990) *Solving Community Problems by Consensus*. Washington, DC. Program for Community Problem Solving.

Chacko, H. (1996) Personal communications with authors, June 10. Cited in Pizam *et al.* (1997) Making tourists feel safe: whose responsibility is it? *Journal of Travel Research* 36 (1), 23–8.

Chan, S.H., Kensinger, J.W., Keown, A.J. and Martin, J.D. (1997) Do strategic alliances create value? *Journal of Financial Economics* 46, 199–221.

Chon, K-S. and Olsen, M.D. (1990) Applying the strategic management process in the management of tourism organizations. *Tourism Management* 11 (3), 206–13.

Choy, D.J.L. (1995) The quality of tourism employment. *Tourism Management* 16 (2), 129–37.

Christopher, M., Payne, A. and Ballantyne, D. (1991) *Relationship Marketing: Bringing Quality, Customer Service and Marketing Together*. Oxford, UK: Butterworth-Heinemann.

Church, N. (1989) Promoting rural tourist regions in Canada and the United States: Characteristics of successful regional marketing campaigns. In F. Dykeman (ed.) *Rural Tourism Opportunity Recognition: Insightful Marketing and Development Concepts* (pp. 1–13). Rural and Small Town Research and Studies Programme. New Brunswick: Mount Allison University.

Churchill, N. and Lewis, V. (1983) The five stages of business growth. *Harvard Business Review.* May/June, 30–50.

City and County of Honolulu (1992) *General Plan: Objectives and Policies.* Honolulu: City and County of Honolulu, Department of General Planning.

City and County of Honolulu, Department of Planning and Permitting (DPP) (2002) *Planning Information.* www.co.honoluludpp.org/Planning/. Accessed on 31 December 2002.

City and County of Honolulu (2002) *Biography of Mayor Jeremy Harris.* www.co. honolulu.hi.us/mayor/major.htm. Accessed on 31 December 2002.

City of Marathon, Florida (2002). *City of Marathon Comprehensive Plan Draft Elements,* Marathon, FL.

Clancy, D. and Webber, R. (1995) *Roses and Rust: Redefining the Essence of Leadership in a New Age.* Sydney: Business and Professional Publishing.

Clegg, S.R., Hardy, C. and Nord, W.R. (eds) (1997) *Handbook of Organisation Studies.* London: Sage Publications.

Cloutier, K.R. (2000) *Legal Liability and Risk Management for Adventure Businesses.* Kamloops, BC: Bhudak Consultants Ltd.

Clow, K.E. and Vorhies, D.W. (1993) Building a competitive advantage for service firms. *Journal of Services Marketing* 7 (1), 22–33.

Coccossis, H. (1996) Tourism and sustainability: Perspectives and implications. In G. Priestly, J.A. Edwards and H. Coccossis (eds) *Sustainable Tourism? European Experiences.* Oxford: CAB International.

Cock, P.H. and Pfueller, S. (2000) *Australian Ecotourism: Contributing to Ecological and Community Sustainability.* Monash Publications in Geography and Environmental Science Number 54, Melbourne: Monash University.

Cohen, E. (1988) Authenticity and commoditization. *Annals of Tourism Research* 15 (3), 371–86.

Collits, P. (2001) Small town decline and survival: Trends, causes and policy issues. In R. Rogers and Y. Collins (eds) *The Future of Australia's Country Towns* (pp. 32–56). Centre for Sustainable Regional Communities, La Trobe University, Bendigo, Victoria: Australia.

Coopers and Lybrand Consulting (1995) *The Canadian Tourism Commission, US Tourism Industries/International Trade Administration and the Secretarial de Tursimo (Mexico) Pleasure Travel Markets to North America: Japan Travel Trade Report.* Toronto, Ont.: Canadian Tourism Commission.

Coopers and Lybrand Consulting (1996) *The Canadian Tourism Commission, US Tourism Industries/International Trade Administration and the Secretarial de Tursimo (Mexico) Pleasure Travel Markets to North America: German Travel Trade Report.* Toronto, Ont.: Canadian Tourism Commission.

Court, B. and Lupton, R. (1997) Customer portfolio development: Modeling destination adopters, inactives, and rejecters. *Journal of Travel Research* 36 (1), 35–43.

Covey, S.R. (1989) *The Seven Habits of Highly Effective People.* Melbourne: Business Library.

CRC (2002) Media Release: Record Funding for Cooperative Research Centres. The Honourable Peter McGauran, Minister for Science, 10 December.

Creighton, J.L. (1980) *Public Involvement Manual.* Washington, DC: US Department of the Interior.

Cressy, R. and Cowling, M. (1996) Small business finance. In M. Warner (ed.) *International Encyclopaedia of Business and Management*. London: Routledge.

Crompton, J. (1979) An assessment of image of Mexico as a vacation destination and the influence of geographical location upon that image. *Journal of Travel Research* 17 (Spring), 18–23.

Crotts, J.C., Buhalis, D. and March, R. (2000) Global alliances in tourism and hospitality management. *International Journal of Hospitality and Tourism Administration* 1 (1), 1–10.

Daft, R.L., Fitzgerald, P.A. and Rock, M.E. (1992) *Management* (First Canadian Edition). Toronto: Dryden Canada.

Dahles, H. (2000) Tourism, small enterprises and community development. In G. Richards and D. Hall (eds) *Tourism and Sustainable Community Development* (pp. 154–69). London: Routledge.

Daily Express (2000) Payment upfront put me on the road to success. *Enterprise Express-Daily Express*, 11 September 2000, 56.

Dallen, J.T. and White, K. (1999) Community-based ecotourism development on the periphery of Belize. *Current Issues in Tourism* 2 (2&3), 226–42.

Dalton and Dalton (1975) *Community and its Relevance to Australian Society*. Canberra: Department of Tourism and Recreation.

D'Amore, L.J. (1983) Guidelines to planning in harmony with the host community. In P.E. Murphy (ed.) *Tourism in Canada: Selected Issues and Options* (pp. 135–59). *Western Geographical Series* 21, Victoria: University of Victoria.

Davidson, T.L. (1985) Strategic planning: a competitive necessity. *The Battle for Market Share: Strategies in Research and Marketing* (pp. 103–8). Travel and Tourism Research Association, Salt Lake City: Graduate School of Business, University of Utah.

Davidsson, P. (2000) Where do they come from? Prevalence and characteristics of nascent entrepreneurs. *Entrepreneurship and Regional Development* 12 (1), 1–23.

Davies, J. (1994) Less Mickey Mouse, more Dirty Harry: Property, policing and the modern metropolis. *Polemic* 5 (2), 63–9.

Davis, C.H. (1993) *Regional Economic Impact Analysis and Project Evaluation*. Vancouver, BC: UBC Press.

Davis, D., Allen, J. and Cosenza, R.M. (1988) Segmenting local residents by their attitudes, interests and opinions toward tourism. *Journal of Travel Research* 27 (2), 2–8.

Davis, T.R.V. (1984) The influence of the physical environment in offices. *Academy of Management Review* 9 (2), 271–83.

Day, G.S. (1981) The product life cycle: Analysis and applications issues. *Journal of Marketing* 45 (4), 60–7.

Day, G.C. (1990) *Market Driven Strategy: Processes for Creating Value*. New York: Free Press.

de Araujo, L.M and Bramwell, B. (2000) Stakeholder assessment and collaborative tourism planning: The case of Brazil's Costa Dourada project. In B. Bramwell and B. Lane (eds) *Tourism Collaboration and Partnerships: Politics, Practice and Sustainability* (pp. 272–74). Clevedon, UK: Channel View Publications.

Decrop, A. (1999) Personal aspects of vacationers' decision making processes: An interpretivist approach. *Journal of Travel and Tourism Marketing* 8 (4), 59–68.

De Filippis, J. (2001) The myth of social capital in community development. *Housing Policy Debate* 12 (4), 781–806.

Deery, M. and Jago, L. (2001) Paid staff or volunteers? The dilemma facing tourism organisations. In C. Pforr and B. Janecko (eds) *Capitalising on Research* (pp. 57–68). Proceedings of the Council of Australian Tourism and Hospitality Education (CAUTHE) Conference Canberra.

De Kadt, E. (ed.) (1979) *Tourism: Passport to Development?* Oxford: Oxford University Press.

Delbecq, A.L., Van de Ven, A.H. and Gustafson, D.H. (1975) *Group Techniques for Program Planning*. Glenview, IL: Scott, Foresmen & Co.

Delbridge, A. and Bernard, J.R.L. (eds) (1988) *The Macquarie Concise Dictionary* (2nd edn). New South Wales: Macquarie University.

Demetriadi, J. (1996) The tele-tourists. *Hospitality*, October/November: 14–15.

Department of Infrastructure & Sinclair Knight Merz (1996). *Mount Stirling Environment Effects Statement*. Melbourne: Victoria Government.

Department of Infrastructure (DOI) (2001) *Great Ocean Road: Towards a Vision for the Future (Discussion Paper)*. Melbourne: DOI.

Department of Infrastructure (DOI) (2002) *Planning Panel Reports and Hearings*. www.doi.vic.gov.au/doi. Accessed on 31 December 2002.

Dienel, P.C. and Renn, O. (1995) Planning cells: A gate to 'fractal' mediation. In O. Renn, T. Webler and P. Wiedemann (eds) *Fairness and Competence in Citizen Participation: Evaluating Models for Environmental Discourse* (pp. 117–40). The Netherlands: Kluwer Academic Press.

Dietvorst, A. (1993) Planning for tourism and recreation: A market-oriented approach. In H.N. van Lier and P.D. Taylor (eds) *New Challenges in Recreation and Tourism Planning* (pp. 87–124). Amsterdam/London: Elsevier.

Digance, J. (1997) Life cycle model. *Annals of Tourism Research* 24 (2), 452–5.

Dimmock, K. (1999) Management style and competitive strategies among tourism firms in the Northern Rivers. *Tourism Management* 20 (3), 323–39.

Ding, P. and Pigram, J. (1995) Environmental audits: An emerging concept in sustainable tourism development. *Journal of Tourism Studies* 6 (2), 2–10.

Diski, J. (2000) What a Mickey Mouse Scheme. *The Scotsman*. 26 August S2 Weekend, 1–5.

Dotson, B.A., Godschalk, D. and Kaufman, J. (1989) *The Planner as Dispute Resolver: Concepts and Teaching Materials*. NIDR Teaching Material Series. National Institute for Dispute Resolution (NIDR).

Douglas, N. (1997) Applying the life cycle model to Melanesia. *Annals of Tourism Research* 24 (1), 1–22.

Doxey, G.V. (1975) A causation theory of visitor-resident irritants: methodology and research inferences. In *The Impact of Tourism* (pp. 195–98). Sixth Annual Conference Proceedings of the Travel Research Association, San Diego, California.

Driver, B. and Tocher, S.R. (1979) Towards a behavioral interpretation of recreational engagements with implications for planning. In C.S. Van Doren, G.B. Priddle and J.E. Lewis (eds) *Land and Leisure: Concepts and Methods in Outdoor Recreation* (pp. 86–104). London: Methuen.

Drucker, P.F. (1985) *Innovation and Entrepreneurship*. New York: Harper Business.

Drucker, P.F. (1993) *Managing for the Future*. New York: Plume/Penguin Books.

Drucker, P.F. (1994) The age of social transformation. *The Atlantic Monthly* 294 (5), 53–71.

Dunn, K.D. and Brooks, D.E. (1990) Profit analysis: Beyond yield management. *Cornell Hotel and Restaurant Administration Quarterly* 31 (3), 80–91.

Echtner, C.M. (1995) Entrepreneurial training in developing countries. *Annals of Tourism Research* 22 (1),119–34.

Eckhouse, J. (2002) Customer strategy: Think your customers are just names in a database? Think again – your survival may depend on a more human touch. In Gap Analysis. *Optimize: Ideas. Action. Results.* (February). http://optimizemag.com/issue/oo4/pr_gap.fhtml. 1–12. Accessed on 19 December 2002.

Edgell, D.L. (1993) *World Tourism at the Millennium*. Washington, DC: US Travel and Tourism Administration.

Eisenberg, D., Coady, E., Kher, U. and Ressner, J. (2001) Is this any way to run a railroad? *Time International: Special Report* (pp. 68–9). 3 December.

Eisner, M. with Schwartz, T. (1998) *Work in Progress*. London: Penguin Books.

Elkington, J. (1999) *Cannibals with Forks: The Triple Bottom Line of 21st Century Business*, Oxford: Capstone Publishing.

Elster, J. (1998) Introduction. In J. Elster (ed.) *Deliberative Democracy* (pp. 1–18). Cambridge: Cambridge University Press.

Emerson, R. (1972) Exchange theory. Part 1: A psychological basis for social exchange. In J. Berger, M. Zelditch and B. Anderson (eds) *Sociological Theories in Progress* (pp. 38–87). New York: Houghton-Mifflin.

English Tourism Board (ND) *Tomorrow's Tourism: A Growth Industry for the New Millennium*. Department for Culture, Media and Sport.

English Tourism Council (ETC) (2002) Building partnerships. ETC. www.englishtourism.org.uk/default.asp?id-2226. Accessed on 28 January 2002.

English, D.B.K., Kriesel, W., Leeworthy, V.R. and Wiley, P.C. (1996) *Economic Contribution of Recreating Visitors to the Florida Keys*. Key West: Consulting Report.

Ennew, C.T., Reed, G.V. and Binks, M.R. (1993) Importance-performance analysis and the measurement of service quality. *European Journal of Marketing* 27 (2), 59–70.

Falconer, B. (1991) Tourism and sustainability: The dream realised. In L.J. Reid (ed.) *Tourism – Environment – Sustainability Development: An Agenda for Research* (pp. 21–6). Conference Proceedings of the Travel and Tourism Association of Canada.

Faulkner, B. and Tideswell, C. (1997) A framework for monitoring community impacts of tourism. *Journal of Sustainable Tourism* 5 (1), 3–28.

Federal Aviation Administration (FAA) (2001) *Airport Benchmark Report: Executive Summary*. FAA. www.faa.gov/events/benchmarks/download.htm. Accessed on 3 December 2001.

Federal Highways Administration (FHA). (2001) *Funding for Highways and Disposition of Highway User Revenues, All Units of Government*. FHA. www.fhw.dot.gov/ohim/hs00/hf1.htm. Accessed on 5 December 2001.

Feizkhah, E. (2002) She's not right mate: A big damages award for a surf accident adds to concerns about the future of the Aussie lifestyle. *Time International* 27 (May 46).

Fick, G.R. and Ritchie, J.R.B. (1991) Measuring service quality in the travel and tourism industry. *Journal of Travel Research* 30 (2), 2–9.

Fishbein, M. and Raven, B.H. (1967) The AB scales: An operational definition of belief and attitude. In Fishbein, M. (ed.) *Readings in Attitude Theory and Measurement* (pp. 183–9). New York: John Wiley.

Fisher, R. and Ury, W. (1981) *Getting to Yes: Negotiating Agreement Without Giving In*. Boston: Houghton Mifflin.

Fisher, R., Ury, W. and Patton, B. (eds) (1991) *Getting to Yes: Negotiating Agreement Without Giving In* (2nd edn). New York: Penguin Group.

Fleischer, A. and Felsenstein, D. (2000) Support for rural tourism: Does it make a difference? *Annals of Tourism Research* 27 (4), 1007–24.

Flood, R.L. (1993) *Beyond TQM*. Chichester: John Wiley.

Florida Department of State, Division of Elections (2002) *Florida Administrative Code*. http://fac.dos.state.fl.us/fac. Accessed on 31 January 2002.

Florida Statute. Chapter 163.3164. Local Government and Comprehensive Planning and Land Development Regulation Act.

Florida Statute. Chapter 380. Land and Water Management.

Flower, J. (1991) *Prince of the Magic Kingdom: Michael Eisner and the Re-Making of Disney*. New York: John Wiley.

Flynn, B.B., Schroeder, R.G. and Sakakibara, S. (1994) A framework for quality management research and an associated measurement instrument. *Journal of Operations Management* 11 (4), 339–66.

Foley, M. (1994) Managing the tourist gaze: Visitor services at Edinburgh Castle. In A.V. Seaton (ed.) *Tourism: The State of the Art* (pp. 792–98). Chichester: John Wiley.

Font, X. (2002) Environmental certification in tourism and hospitality: Progress, process and prospects. *Tourism Management* 23 (3), 197–205.

Foster, D. and Murphy, P.E. (1991) The resort cycle and retirement: A reappraisal of the Butler model. *Annals of Tourism Research* 18 (4), 553–67.

France, L. (1998) Local participation in tourism in the West Indian Islands. In E. Laws, B. Faulkner and G. Moscardo (eds) *Embracing and Managing Change in Tourism: International Case Studies* (pp. 222–34). London: Routledge.

French, C.N., Craig-Smith, S.J. and Collier, A. (1999) *Principles of Tourism*. Melbourne: Addison Wesley Longman Australia.

Frew, E.A. and Shaw, R.N. (1998) An empirical study of industrial tourism attractions. In B.J. Gray and K.R. Deans (eds) *Marketing Connections: Proceedings of the Australian New Zealand Marketing Academy Conference* (pp. 772–85), Dunedin, NZ.

Funnel, B. and Ainsworth, P. (1996) The nature of the tourism market as an occupational field and the place of small businesses and training within it. In J. Stevenson (ed.) *Learning in the Workplace: Tourism and Hospitality* (pp. 245–89). Centre for Learning and Work Research, Griffith University, Queensland.

Gee, C.Y. (1996) *Resort Development and Management* (2nd edn). East Lansing, Michigan: Educational Institute of the American Hotel and Motel Association.

Gerber, M.E. (1995) *The E-Myth Revisited*. New York: Harper Business.

Gershuny, J. and Miles, I. (1983) *The New Service Economy: The Transformation of Employment in Industrial Societies*. London: Frances Printer.

Getz, D. (1983) A research agenda for municipal and community-based tourism in Canada. Paper presented at the Fourteenth Annual Conference of the Travel and Tourism Research Association, Banff, Alberta.

Getz, D. (1987) Tourism planning and research: Traditions, models and futures. Paper presented at The Australian Travel Research Workshop, Bunbury, Western Australia, 5–6 November.

Getz, D. (1991) *Festivals, Special Events and Tourism*. New York: Van Nostrand Reinhold.

Ghiselli, E. (1971) *Explorations in Managerial Talent*. Pacific Palisades, California: Goodyear.

Gibbons, M., Limoges, C., Nowotny, H., Schwartzman, S., Scott, P. and Trow, M. (1994) *The New Production of Knowledge*. London: Sage.

Gilbert, J. (1982) Rural theory: the ground of rural sociology. *Rural Sociology* 47 (4), 609–33.

Gilbert, D. (1990) Strategic marketing planning for national tourism. *The Tourist Review* 1, 18–27.

Gill, A.M. (1997) Competition and the resort community: Towards an understanding of residents' needs. In P.E. Murphy (ed.) *Quality Management in Urban Tourism* (pp. 55–65). Chichester: John Wiley.

Glasson, J., Godfrey, K. and Goodey, B. (1995) *Towards Visitor Impact Management*. Avebury: Ashgate Publishing.

Godschalk, D., Parham, D., Porter, D., Potapchuk, W., Schukraft, S. (1994) *Pulling Together: A Planning Development Consensus-Building Manual.* Washington, DC: Urban Land Institute.

Goeldner, C.R., Ritchie, J.R.B. and McIntosh, R.W. (2000) *Tourism: Principles, Practices, Philosophies* (8th edn). New York: John Wiley.

Goleman, D. (1998) What makes a leader? *Harvard Business Review* 76 (6), 93–102.

Goodall, B. and Stabler, M. (2000) Environmental standards and performance measurement in tourism destination development. In G. Prichard and D. Hall (eds) *Tourism and Sustainable Community Development* (pp. 63–82). London: Routledge.

Google.com. (2002) http://www.google.com/search?q=Gap+Analysis. Accessed on 19 December 2002.

Gordon, J.R., Mondy, R.W., Sharplin, A. and Premeaux, S.R. (1990) *Management and Organizational Behavior.* Boston: Allyn & Bacon.

Grabler, K. (1997) Cities and the destination life cycle. In A.J. Mazanec (ed.) *International City Tourism.* London: Pinter.

Graefe, A.R., Kuss, F.R. and Vaske, J.J. (1990) *Visitor Impact Management: The Planning Framework.* Washington, DC: National Parks and Conservation Asssociation.

Graham, R., Nilsen, P. and Payne, R.J. (1988) Visitor management in Canadian National Parks. *Tourism Management* 9 (1), 44–62.

Grapentine, T. (1994) Problematic scales. *Marketing Research* 6 (4), 8–21.

Gray, B. (1985) Conditions facilitating interorganizational collaboration. *Human Relations* 38 (10), 911–37.

Griffen, D.W. and Ross, L. (1991) Subjective construal, social interference, and human misunderstanding. *Advances in Experimental Social Psychology* 23, 319–59.

Grinder, B. (1992) Dance carries on traditions. *Windspeaker* 10 (6), 10–14.

Gunn, C. (1972) *Vacationscape.* TX: University of Texas Press.

Gunn, C.A. (1979) *Tourism Planning.* New York: Crane Russak.

Gunn, C.A. (1994) *Tourism Planning* (3rd edn). Washington, DC: Taylor & Francis.

Gunn, C.A. (1997) *Vacationscape: Developing Tourist Areas* (3rd edn). Washington, DC: Taylor & Francis.

Gursoy, D., Jurowski, C. and Uysal, M. (2002) Residents attitudes: A structural modelling approach. *Annals of Tourism Research* 29 (1), 79–105.

Hall, C.M. (1992) *Hallmark Tourist Events.* London: Belhaven Press.

Hall, C.M. (1995) *Introduction to Tourism in Australia: Impacts, Planning and Development.* Melbourne, Australia: Longman.

Hall, C.M. (1998) The politics of decision-making and top-down planning: Darling Harbour, Sydney. In D. Tyler, Y. Guerrier and M. Robertson (eds) *Managing Tourism in Cities* (pp. 9–24). Chichester: John Wiley.

Hall, R.H., Clark, J.P., Giordano, P.C., Johnson, P.V. and Roekel, M. (1977) Patterns of interorganizational relationships. *Administrative Science Quarterly* 22 (3), 457–72.

Hamilton, S. (2002) Marketing Mt Buller Ski Resort. Workshop Presentation, La Trobe University Campus, Mt Buller.

Hansen, D.J. and Walker, R.H. (1997) *Ecologically Based Macro-Marketing and Management of Tasmania as a Tourism Destination.* Working Paper Series 97–05. Hobart: Department of Management, University of Tasmania.

Hanson, S. and Hanson, P. (1981) The travel-activity patterns of urban residents: dimensions and relationships to socio-demographic characteristics. *Economic Geography* 57 (4), 332–47.

Hardin, G. (1969) The tragedy of the commons. *Science* 162, 1243–8.

Hart, C. and Bogan, C. (1992) *The Baldridge.* New York: McGraw-Hill.

Harvey, D. (1989) From managerialism to entrepreneurialism: The transformation in urban governance in late capitalism. *Geografisk Annaler* 71, 3–17.

Haspeslagh, P. (1982) Portfolio planning; uses and limits. *Harvard Business Review*, 60 (1), 58–73.

Hawkes, S. and Williams, P. (eds) (1993) *The Greening of Tourism*. Centre for Tourism Policy and Research, Simon Fraser University, Vancouver, Canada.

Hawkins, G. and Backman, K.F. (1998) An exploration of sense of place as a possible explanatory concept in nature-based traveler conflict. *Tourism Analysis* 3, 89–102.

Haywood, K.M. (1986) Can the tourist-area life cycle be made operational? *Tourism Management* 7 (3), 154–67.

Haywood, K.M. (1988) Responsible and responsive tourism planning in the community. *Tourism Management* 9 (2), 105–18.

Haywood, K.M. (1990) Revising and implementing the marketing concept as it is applied to tourism. *Tourism Management* 11 (3), 195–205.

Haywood, K.M. (1997) Creating value for visitors to urban destinations. In P.E. Murphy (ed.) *Quality Management in Urban Tourism* (pp. 169–82). Chichester: John Wiley.

Haywood, L. (ed.) (1994) *Community Leisure and Recreation: Theory and Practice*. Oxford: Butterworth-Heinemann.

Heath, E. and Wall, G. (1992) *Marketing Tourism Destinations*. New York: John Wiley.

Hemphill, J.K. and Coons, A.E. (1957) Development of the leader behavior description questionnaire. In R.M. Stogdill and E.A. Coons (eds) *Leader Behavior: Its Description and Measurement*. Columbus, OH: Ohio State University, Bureau of Business Research.

Hernandez, S.A., Cohen, J. and Garcia, H.L. (1996) Resident attitudes towards an instant enclave resort. *Annals of Tourism Research* 23 (4), 755–9.

Hersey, P. and Blanchard, K. (1974) So you want to know your leadership style? *Training and Development Journal* (February), 22–32.

Heskett, J.L., Sasser, Jr W.E., Schlesinger, L.A. (1997) *The Service Profit Chain*. New York: Free Press.

Heung, V.C.S. and Leung, K.P. (1998) Co-operative approach to marketing: Implications for hotel and tourism industry in Indo China. *Journal of Travel and Tourism Marketing* 7 (2), 105–18.

Hiaasen, C. (1986) *Tourist Season*. New York: Warner Books.

Hjalager, A-M. (1997) Innovation patterns in sustainable tourism. *Tourism Management* 18 (1), 35–41.

Ho, S.K. (1995) *TQM: An Integrated Approach – Implementation through Japanese 5-S and ISO 9000*. London: Kogan Page.

Hof, M., Hammett, J., Rees, M., Beinap, J., Poe, N., Lime, D. and Manning, B. (1994) Getting a handle on visitor carrying capacity – a pilot project at Arches National Park. *Park Science*, Winter, 11–13.

Holder, J.S. (1993) The Caribbean Tourism Organization's role in Caribbean tourism development towards the year 2000. In D.J. Gayle and J.N. Goodrich (eds) *Tourism Marketing and Management in the Caribbean* (pp. 205–19). London: Routledge.

Horn, C. and Simmons, D. (2002) Community adaption to tourism: Comparisons between Rotorua and Kaikoura, New Zealand. *Tourism Management* 23 (2), 133–43.

Houghton, M., Jackson, J. and Ritchie, M. (2002) The long road to . . . a study of Newell Highway visiting patterns. Unpublished paper, School of Tourism and Hospitality, La Trobe University, Melbourne, Australia.

Hovinen, G.R. (1995) Heritage issues in urban tourism: An assessment of new trends in Lancaster County. *Tourism Management* 16 (5), 381–8.

Howatson, A.C. (1990) *Toward Proactive Environmental Management: Lessons from Canadian Corporate Experience*. Ottawa: The Conference Board of Canada.

Howe, J., McMahon, E. and Propst, L. (1997) *Balancing Nature and Commerce in Gateway Communities*. Washington, DC: Island Press.

Hsu, C.H.C. (2003) Social impacts of Native American Casino Gaming. In C.H.C. Hsu (ed.) *Legalised Casino Gaming in the United States* (pp. 221–32). New York: Haworth Hospitality Press.

Hubbard, P. and Hall, T. (1998) The Entrepreneurial City and the 'New Urban Politics'. In T. Hall and P. Hubbard (eds) *The Entrepreneurial City: Geographies of Politics, Regime and Representation* (pp. 1–23). New York, NY: John Wiley.

Hudson, S. (2000) Consumer behaviour related to tourism. In A. Pizam and Y. Mansfeld (eds) *Consumer Behaviour in Travel and Tourism* (pp. 7–32). Binghampton, NY: The Haworth Hospitality Press.

Huffman, J.L. (1994) The inevitability of private rights in public lands. *University of Colorado Law Review* 65, 241–77.

Hughes, G. (1995) The cultural construction of sustainable tourism. *Tourism Management* 16 (1), 49–59.

Hunt, J.D. (1975) Image as a factor in tourist development. *Journal of Travel Research.* 13 (Winter) 1–7.

Husock, H. (1998) Let's break up the big cities. *City Journal* 8 (1), 71–87.

Hutchison, J. (1997) *Tourism: Getting it Right for the Millennium*. Sydney: Sydney Convention and Visitors Bureau.

Inskeep, E. (1988) Tourism planning: An emerging specialization. *American Planning Association Journal* 54 (3), 360–72.

Inskeep, E. (1991) *Tourism Planning: An Integrated and Sustainable Development Approach*. New York: Van Nostrand Reinhold.

Inskeep, E. (1994) *National and Regional Tourism Planning*. A World Tourism Organisation Publication. London: Routledge.

Iowa Gap (1997) What is Gap Analysis? *Iowa Gap.* http://www.ag.iastate/edu/denters/cfwru/iowagap/whatisit. Accessed on 18 December 2002.

Islamorada, Village of Islands (2001) Islamorada, Village of Islands Comprehensive Plan: Reclaiming the Keys. Florida: Islamorada Municipality.

Jackson, T. (2002) Major sporting and leisure investments in the 'contested countryside': golf tourism and sustainable rural development in Scotland. In N. Andrews, F. Convery, S. Flanagan and J. Ruddy (eds) *Tourism and the Environment: Developing Sustainable Tourism* (pp. 189–208). Dublin: Dublin Institute of Technology.

Jackson, J. and Murphy, P.E. (2002) Tourism destinations as clusters: Analytical experiences from the New World. *Tourism and Hospitality Research* 4 (1), 36–52.

Jacobs, J. (1962) *The Death and Life of Great American Cities*. London: Jonathan Cape.

Jacobs, J. (1984). *Cities and the Wealth of Nations: Principles of Economic Life*. New York: Random House.

Jacobs, T.O. (1970) *Leadership and Exchange in Formal Organizations*. Alexandria, VA: Human Resources Research Organization.

Jafari, J. (1990) Research and scholarship: The basis of tourism education. *Journal of Tourism Studies* 1 (1), 33–41.

Jamal, T.B. and Getz, D. (1995) Collaboration theory and community tourism planning. *Annals of Tourism Research* 22 (1), 186–204.

Jamal, T.B. and Getz, D. (1997) Visioning for sustainable tourism development community-based collaborations. In P.E. Murphy (ed.) *Quality Management in Urban Tourism* (pp. 199–220). Chichester: John Wiley.

Jamal, T. and Getz, D. (2000) Community roundtables for tourism-related conflicts: The dialectics of consensus and process structures. In B. Bramwell and B. Lane (eds) *Tourism Collaboration and Partnerships* (pp. 159–82). Clevedon, UK: Channel View Publications.

Jansen-Verbeke, M. (1994) *Tourism: Quo Vadis? From Business as Usual to Crisis Management*. Rotterdam: Centre for Tourism Management, Erasmus University.

Jenkins, C.L. (1997) Impacts of the development of international tourism in the Asian region. In F.M. Go and C.L. Jenkins (eds) *Tourism and Economic Development in Asia and Australasia* (pp. 48–64). London: Pinter.

Jenshel, L. (1994) Of mice and men: There's turmoil in Disney's Magic Kingdom. Can America's fantasy maker find a happy ending? *Newsweek* 41–7.

Johanson, J., Lars, H. and Nazeem, S.M. (1991) Interfirm adaptation in business relationships. *Journal of Marketing* 55 (2), 29–37.

Johnston, R.J., Gregory, D. and Smith, D.M. (1988) *The Dictionary of Human Geography* (2nd edn). Oxford: Blackwell Reference.

Jones, K. and Simmons, J. (1987) *Location, Location, Location: Analyzing the Retail Environment*. Toronto: Methuen.

Joppe, M. (1996) Sustainable community tourism development revisited. *Tourism Management* 17 (7), 475–9.

Judd, D.R. (1995) Promoting tourism in US cities. *Tourism Management* 16 (3) 175–87.

Jurowski, C., Uysal, M. and Williams, D.R. (1997) A theoretical analysis of host community resident reactions to tourism. *Journal of Travel Research* 36 (2), 3–11.

Kariel, H.G. (1989) Socio-cultural impacts of tourism in the Austrian Alps. *Mountain Research and Development* 9 (1), 59–70.

Kaufman, D. (2000) Running on empty: Building the online economy. *The Age* Tuesday, 7 November I.T.2.

Keller, P. and Murphy, P. (1990) Destination travel patterns: An examination and modelling of tourist patterns on Vancouver Island, British Columbia. *Leisure Sciences* 12 (1), 49–65.

Kelly, K. (2000) Blood in the boardroom. *Time International* 6 November, 58.

Kelly, I. and Spark, M. (2001) Tourism as a strategy for bypassed towns. Paper presented at the Council for Australian University Tourism and Hospitality Education (CAUTHE) Conference, Canberra, February.

Kent, N. (1977) A new kind of sugar. In B.R. Finney and K.A. Watson (eds) *A New Kind of Sugar: Tourism in the Pacific* (pp. 169–98). Santa Cruz, California: Center for South Pacific Studies, University of California, Santa Cruz.

King, B., McVey, M. and Simmons, D. (2000) A societal marketing approach to national tourism planning: evidence from the South Pacific. *Tourism Management* 21 (4), 407–16.

King, J. (2001) The Vision. *Welcome to Eden* 1 (1), 4–5.

Kinninment, M. (2003) Stopping paradise from being lost. *The Age* (Melbourne): Perspective. Wednesday 15 January 2003, 13.

Klein, N. (2000) *No Logo, No Space, No Choice, No Jobs: Taking Aim at the Brand Bullies*. London: Flamingo.

Klemm, M. (1996) Langeudoc Roussillon: adapting the strategy. *Tourism Management* 17 (2), 133–9.

Koh, K.Y. (2000) Understanding community tourism entrepreneurism. In G. Richard and D. Hall (eds) *Tourism and Sustainable Community Development* (pp. 205–17). London: Routledge.

Koh, K.Y. and Combs, C.S. (2000) The tourism entrepreneurial process: A qualitative study. In *Lights, Camera, Action: Spotlight on Tourism in the New Millennium* (pp. 164–72). 31st Annual Conference Proceedings of the Travel and Tourism Research Association, San Fernando Valley, California, June.

Korca, P. (1996) Resident attitudes toward tourism impacts. *Annals of Tourism Research* 23 (3), 695–726.

Kotler, P. (1997) *Marketing Management* (9th edn). Upper Saddle River, NJ: Prentice-Hall.

Kotler, P. (2001) *Kotler on Marketing: How to Create, Win and Dominate Markets.* London: Simon & Schuster.

Kotler, P. and Armstrong, G. (1989) *Principles of Marketing* (4th edn). Englewood Cliffs, NJ: Prentice-Hall.

Kotler, P., Fennell, O.C. and Lamb, C. (1987) *Strategic Marketing for Non-profit Organisations* (3rd edn). Englewood Cliffs, NJ: Prentice-Hall.

Kotler, P., Haider, D.H. and Rein, I. (1993) *Marketing Places.* New York: Free Press.

Kotter, J.P. (1990) What leaders really do. *Harvard Business Review on Leadership* (pp. 37–60). Boston, MA: Harvard Business Review Press.

Krippendorf, J. (1982) Towards new tourism policies. *Tourism Management* 3, 135–48.

Krippendorf, J. (1987) *The Holiday Makers.* London: Heinemann.

Kuratko, D.F. and Hodgetts, R.M. (1995) *Entrepreneurship: A Contemporary Approach* (3rd edn). Fort Worth, TX: Dryden Press.

Kuratko, D.F. and Hodgetts, R.M. (1998) *Entrepreneurship: A Contemporary Approach* (4th edn). Fort Worth, TX: Dryden Press.

Land Use Coordination Office (LUCO) (2001) About LUCO: Background. http://www.luco.gov.bc.ca/lucoinfo

La Page, W.F. (1994) Using panels for travel and tourism research. In B. Ritchie and C.R. Goeldner (eds) *Travel, Tourism, and Hospitality Research: A Handbook for Managers and Researchers* (2nd edn) (pp. 481–92). Toronto: John Wiley.

Langdon, P. (December, 2001) The long road to rebuilding Lower Manhattan. *Planning – American Planning Association* 67 (12), 12–15.

Langlois, T. (1979) The practice of local government planning. In American Planning Association (APA) (1999) *Study Guide for the Comprehensive AICP Exam* (pp. 132–9). Memphis, TN: University of Memphis.

Lankford, S.V. (1994) Attitudes and perceptions toward tourism and rural regional development. *Journal of Travel Research* 32 (3), 35–43.

Lankford, S.V. and Howard, D.R. (1994) Developing a tourism impact scale. *Annals of Tourism Research* 21 (1), 121–39.

Lawrence, T.B., Wickens, D. and Phillips, N. (1997) Managing legitimacy in ecotourism. *Tourism Management* 18 (5), 307–16.

Laws, E. and Le Pelley, B. (2000) Managing complexity and change in tourism: The case of a historic city. *International Journal of Tourism Research* 2 (4), 229–46.

Laycock, G. (1991) 'Good times' are killing the Keys. *Audubon.* Sept/Oct, 38–49.

Le Blanc, G. (1992) Factors affecting customer evaluations of service quality in travel agencies: An investigation of customer perceptions. *Journal of Travel Research* 30 (4), 11–16.

Leeworthy, V.R. and Wiley P.C. (1996) Visitor profiles: Florida Keys. Key West: Consulting Report.

Legislative Committee on Intergovernmental Relations, Florida Legislature, February 2001. Overview of Municipal Incorporations in Florida, Tallahassee, FL.

Leheny, D. (1995) A political economy of Asian sex tourism. *Annals of Tourism Research* 22 (2), 367–84.

Leiper, N. (1979) The framework of tourism: towards a definition of tourism and the tourist industry. *Annals of Tourism Research* 6 (4), 380–407.

Leithwood, K., Jantzi, D. and Steinbach, R. (1999) *Changing Leadership for Changing Times.* Buckingham/Philadelphia: Open University Press.

Lennon, J.J. (2001) Towards a better understanding of visitor attractions in Scotland: The case of the Scottish Visitor Attraction Monitor. In J.J. Lennon (ed.) *Tourism Statistics: International Perspectives and Current Issues* (pp. 142–59). London: Continuum.

Levi-Strauss, C. (1969) *The Elementary Structures of Kinship*. Boston: Beacon Press.

Levine, S. and White, P.E. (1961) Exchange as a conceptual framework for the study of interorganizational relations. *Administrative Science Quarterly* 5, 583–601.

Lewicki, R. and Litterer, J. (1985) *Negotiation*. Homewood, IL: Richard D. Irwin, Inc.

Lewis, J.B. (1998) A rural tourism development model. *Tourism Analysis* 2, 91–105.

Lewis, M. (2000) The soul of St. Louis. The community's gathering place. Our regional backyard. *Planning* (American Planning Association). April, 10–11.

Lindberg, K. and Johnson, R.L. (1997) Modeling resident attitudes towards tourism. *Annals of Tourism Research* 24 (2), 402–24.

Lindberg, K., McCool, S. and Stankey, G. (1997) Rethinking carrying capacity. *Annals of Tourism Research* 24 (2), 461–65.

Little, R.L. and Krannich, R.D. (1982) Organizing for local control in rapid growth communities. In B.A. Weber and R.E. Howell (eds) *Coping with Rapid Growth in Rural Communities* (pp. 73–81). Boulder, CO: Westview Press.

Logan, J. and Molotch, H.L. (1987) *Urban Fortunes: The Political Economy of Place*. Berkley: University of California Press.

Loftman, P. and Nevin, B. (1998) Pro-growth local economic development strategies: Civic promotion and local needs in Britain's second city. In T. Hall and P. Hubbard (eds) *The Entrepreneurial City: Geographies of Politics, Regime and Representation* (pp. 129–48). Chichester, UK: John Wiley.

Longenecker, J.G., Moore, C.W. and Petty, J.W. (1994) *Small Business Management: An Entrepreneurial Emphasis* (9th edn). Cincinnati, OH: South Western Publishing.

Loomis, L. and Graefe, A.R. (1992) Overview of NPCA's visitor impact management process. Paper presented at the IVth World Congress on Parks and Protected Areas, Caracas, Venezuela.

Love, J.F. (1995) *McDonald's: Behind the Arches*. New York: Bantam Books.

Lovelock, C.H. (1992) The search for synergy: What marketers need to know about service operations. In C.H. Lovelock (ed.) *Managing Services* (2nd edn) (pp. 392–408). Englewood Cliffs, NJ: Prentice Hall.

Lucero, L. and Soule, J. (2002) A win for Lake Tahoe: The Supreme Court validates moratoriums in a path-breaking decision. *Planning – American Planning Association* 68 (6), 4–7.

Luehrman, T.A. (1998) Strategy as a portfolio of real options. *Harvard Business Review* 76 (5), 89–99.

Lundgren, J.O. (1972) The development of tourist travel systems – a metropolitan economic hegemony par excellence. *Jarbuch für Fredenverkehr*, 20, 86–120.

Lundgren, J.O. (1973) Agricultural marketing and distribution arrangements with respect to the resort hotel in the Caribbean. In *Proceedings of the Sixth West Indian Agricultural Economics Conference,* University of the West Indies.

Lundtorp, S. and Wanhill, S. (2001) The resort lifecycle theory: Generating processes and estimation. *Annals of Tourism Research* 28 (4), 947–64.

Lynn, F.M. and Kartez, J.D. (1995) The redemption of citizen advisory committees: A perspective from critical theory. In O.Renn, T. Webler and P. Wiedemann (eds) *Fairness and Competence in Citizen Participation: Evaluating Models for Environmental Discourse* (pp. 87–101). The Netherlands: Kluwer Academic Press.

MacArthur, B. (1999) *Twentieth Century Protest*. London: Penguin Books.

MacCannell, D. (1973) Staged authenticity: arrangements of social space in tourist settings. *American Journal of Sociology* 79, 583–603.

MacEochaidh, G. (1994) Tourism development at the community level in disadvantaged areas. In U. Kockel (ed.) *Travel, Culture, Tourism and Development: The Case of Ireland* (pp. 183–8). Liverpool: Liverpool University Press.

MacIntyre, D. (2000) This is only the beginning of the tourism revolution. *THESCOTSMAN.CO.UK..*scotsman.com. Accessed on 12 January 2000.

McBoyle, G. (1996) Green tourism and Scottish distilleries. *Tourism Management* 17 (4), 255–63.

McCarthy, E.J. and Perreault, W.D. (1984) *Basic Marketing* (8th edn). Homewood, IL: Irwin.

McDonnell, I., Allen, J. and O'Toole, W. (1999) *Festival and Special Event Management*. Milton, Queensland: Jacaranda Wiley.

McGibbon, J. (2000) *The Business of Alpine Tourism in a Globalising World* (p. 203). Rosenheim, Germany: Vetterling Druick.

McGinnes, J. (2001) Eden asks visitors to choose their days as popularity soars. *Western Morning News*, 28 July, 4.

McGinnes, S. (2000) Symphony spectacle. *Times Colonist*. Victoria, British Columbia, 8 August: A1–2.

McIntyre, G. (1993) *Sustainable Tourism Development: Guide for Local Planners*. Madrid: World Tourism Organization.

Madrigal, R. (1995) Residents' perceptions and the role of government. *Annals of Tourism Research* 22 (1), 86–102.

Mann, M. (2000) *The Community Tourism Guide: Exciting Holidays for Responsible Travellers*. London: Earthscan Publications Ltd.

Mazanec, J.A. (ed.) (1997) *International City Tourism*. London: Pinter.

Martin, B., McGuire, F. and Allen, L. (1998) Retirees' attitudes towards tourism: Implications for sustainable development. *Tourism Analysis* 3, 43–51.

Masberg, B. (1998) Defining the tourist: Is it possible? A view from the convention and visitors bureau. *Journal of Travel Research* 37 (1), 67–70.

Mason, P. and Cheyne, J. (2000) Residents' attitudes to proposed tourism development. *Annals of Tourism Research* 27 (2), 391–411.

Masten, S. (2000) *Testimony on S. 2899 and H.R. 4909 Native Hawaiian Recognition Before the Senate Committee on Indian Affairs and House Committee on Resources.* *www.ncai.org/main/pages/issu . . . sues/documents/presmastestS2889.htm:* Accessed on 30 August 2000.

Masters, J., Buris, T., Hollon, S. and Rimm, D. (1987) *Behavior Therapy: Techniques and Empirical Findings* (3rd edn). Toronto: Harcourt Brace Jovanovich College Publishers.

Mathieson, A. and Wall, G. (1982) *Tourism Economic, Physical and Social Impacts*. London: Longman.

Mayo, E.J. and Jarvis, L.P. (1981) *The Psychology of Leisure Travel*. Boston, MA: CBI.

Meade II, W.K. and Nason, R.W. (1991) Toward a unified theory of macromarketing: A systems theoretic approach. *Journal of Macromarketing* Fall, 72–82.

Mei, A., Dean, A. and Whit, C. (1999) Analysing service quality in the hospitality industry. *Managing Service Quality* 9 (2), 136–43.

Meis, S. (2001) Towards comparative studies in tourism satellite accounts. In J.J. Lennon (ed.) *Tourism Statistics* (pp. 14–23). London: Continuum.

Meisch, L. (1995) Gringas and Otavalenos: changing tourist relations. *Annals of Tourism Research* 22 (2), 441–62.

Metelka, C.J. (1977) Tourism and development: With friends like these who needs enemies? Paper presented at the Fifth Pacific Regional Science Conference, Vancouver, August.

Michael, E. and Plowman, G. (2002) Mount Stirling: The politics of process failure. _Journal of Sustainable Tourism_ 10 (2),154–69.

Michaud, J.L. _et al._ (1991) Tourisme qualitatif – ses conditions et ses chances futures sur le plan economique, social et ecologique. _Tourisme Qualitatif,_ AIEST Publication, 33, 63–78.

Middleton, V.T.C. (1988) _Marketing in Travel and Tourism._ Oxford: Butterworth-Heinemann.

Midwest Treaty Network (1997) _Midwest Treaty Network Calls for Governor to Drop Gaming Threat._ December. www.alphacdc.com/treaty/gaming.html Accessed on 30 August 2000.

Miles, R.E. and Snow, C.C. (1978) _Organizational Strategy, Structure, and Process._ New York: McGraw-Hill.

Mill, R.C. and Morrison, A.M. (1992) _The Tourism System: An Introductory Text_ (2nd edn). Englewood Cliffs, NJ: Prentice-Hall.

Miller Consulting, Inc. (2001) Florida Keys Hurricane Evacuation Study: Final Report. Contract No. C7391. Tallahassee, FL: Florida Department of Transportation.

Miller, P. (1998) Email from Paul Miller to Peter Murphy, 9/9/98.

Milman, A. and Pizam, A. (1988) Social impacts of tourism on Central Florida. _Annals of Tourism Research_ 15 (2), 191–204.

Ministry of Tourism (1992) _A Vision for Tourism._ Victoria, British Columbia: Ministry of Tourism.

Minnesota Indian Gaming Association (MIGA) (2002) _The Principle of Indian Sovereignty._ www.minnesotagaming.com/migasix.html.: Accessed on 12 December 2002.

Mintzberg, H. (1979) _The Structuring of Organizations._ Englewood Cliffs, NJ: Prentice-Hall.

Mitchell, R.E. (1997) Entrepreneurship and economic security: Enemies or allies. Unpublished paper. Faculty of Business, University of Victoria, Canada.

Mitchell, R.E. and Reid, D.G. (2001) Community integration: island tourism in Peru. _Annals of Tourism Research_ 28 (1), 113–39.

Moeller, G.H. and Shafer, E.L. (1994) The Delphi technique: A tool for long-range travel and tourism planning. In B. Ritchie and C.R. Goeldner (eds) _Travel, Tourism, and Hospitality Research: A Handbook for Managers and Researchers_ (2nd edn) (pp. 473–80). Toronto: John Wiley.

Molotch, H.L. (1976) The city as a growth machine: toward a political economy of place. _American Journal of Sociology_ 82 (2), 309–22.

Monroe County Growth Management Division (1992) Monroe County Year 2010 Comprehensive Plan. Marathon, FL: Monroe County.

Monroe County Growth Management Division (1992) Ordinance No. 16 – 1992 – Rate of Growth Ordinance. Marathon, FL: Monroe County.

Monroe County Growth Management Division (1998–2002). Monroe County Public Facilities Capacity Assessments. Marathon, FL: Monroe County.

Monroe County, Florida (1999) _1999 Annual Report._ Key West, FL: Office of Management and Budget Staff.

Monroe County Growth Management Division (1999) Liveable Community Keys Work Program: An Initiative of the Monroe County Planning Department. Marathon, FL: Monroe County.

Monroe County Board of County Commissioners (MCBOCC) (2002) *Fiscal Year 2002 Adopted Annual Operating and Capital Budget*. Key West, FL: Office of Management and Budget Staff.

Monroe County. Monroe County Code of Ordinances. Chapter 9.5 Land Development Regulations.

Montgomery, B. (1986) *Working Together: A Practical Guide to Collaborative Decision Making*. Melbourne: Nelson.

Moore, K. (1992) Greening corporate strategy – extending the firm's value chain. Paper presented at the Administrative Sciences Association of Canada, Quebec City.

Morgan, N. and Pritchard, A. (1998) *Tourism Promotion and Power: Creating Images, Creating Identities*. Chichester, NY: Wiley.

Mormont, M. (1987) Tourism and rural change: the symbolic impact. In M. Bouquet and M. Winter (eds) *Who from their Labours Rest? Conflict and Practice in Rural Tourism* (pp. 35–43). Aldershot: Avebury.

Morrison, A.M. (1989) *Hospitality and Travel Marketing*. Albany, NY: Delmar.

Morrison, A.M., Braunlich, C.G., Kamaruddin, N. and Cai, L.A. (1995) National tourist offices in North America: An analysis. *Tourism Management* 16 (8), 605–17.

Morrison, A.M., Bruen, S.M. and Anderson, D.J. (1998) Convention and visitor bureaus in the U.S.A.: A profile of bureaus, bureau executives, and budgets. *Journal of Travel and Tourism Marketing* 7 (1), 1–19.

Morrison, A., Rimmington, M. and Williams, C. (1999) *Entrepreneurship in the Hospitality, Tourism and Leisure Industries*. Oxford: Butterworth-Heinemann.

Moser, P. and Moser, W. (1986) Reflections on the MAB–6 Obergurgl project and tourism in an alpine environment. *Mountain Research and Development* 6 (2), 101–18.

Moser, W. and Peterson, J. (1981) Limits to Obergurgl's growth. *Ambio*, 10 (2–3): 68–72).

Moscovici, S. (1984) The phenomenon of social representations. In R.M. Farr and S. Moscovici (eds) *Social Representations* (pp. 3–69). Cambridge: University of Cambridge Press.

Moutinho. L. (1999) Segmentation, targeting, positioning and strategic marketing. In L. Moutinho (ed.) *Strategic Management in Tourism* (pp. 121–66). Wallingford, Oxon: CABI Publishing.

Murphy, A.E. (2003) Illustrating the utility of a modified gap analysis as a regional tourism planning tool: Case study of potential Japanese and German travellers to the Cowichan Region. *Journal of Travel Research* 41 (4), 400–9.

Murphy, A.E. and Williams, P.W. (1999) Attracting Japanese tourists into the rural hinterland: implications for rural development and planning. *Tourism Management* 20, 487–99.

Murphy, P.E. (1980a) Tourism management in host communities. *The Canadian Geographer* 24 (1), 1–2.

Murphy, P.E. (1980b) Tourism management using land use planning and landscape design: the Victoria experience. *The Canadian Geographer* 24 (1), 60–71.

Murphy, P.E. (1982) Tourism planning in London: An exercise in spatial and seasonal management. *The Tourist Review* 1, 19–23.

Murphy, P.E. (1983a) Perceptions and attitudes of decision-making groups in tourism centers. *Journal of Travel Research* 21 (3), 8–12.

Murphy, P.E. (1983b) Tourism as a community industry – an ecological model of tourism. *Tourism Management* 4 (3), 180–93.

Murphy, P.E. (1985) *Tourism: A Community Approach*. London: Methuen.

Murphy, P.E. (1988) Community driven tourism planning. *Tourism Management* 9 (2) 96–104.

Murphy, P.E. (1991a) Community partnerships: The need for mutual education. In R.D. Bratton, F.M. Go and J.R.B. Ritchie (eds) *New Horizons in Tourism and Hospitality Education, Training and Research* (pp. 7–16). Conference Proceedings, Calgary, Alberta: University of Calgary.

Murphy, P.E. (1991b) Getting the most from hallmark events. In P.E. Murphy (ed.) *Tourism Research: Meeting the Needs of Industry* (pp. 85–90). Annual Conference Proceedings of the Travel and Tourism Research Association (Canada), Victoria, BC, Canada.

Murphy, P.E. (1997) Attraction land use management in Disney theme parks. In P.E. Murphy (ed.) *Quality Management in Urban Tourism* (pp. 221–33). Chichester: John Wiley.

Murphy, P.E. and Andressen, B. (1988) Tourism development on Vancouver Island. *Professional Geographer* 40 (1), 32–42.

Murphy, P.E. and Bayley, R. (1989) Tourism and disaster planning. *Geographical Review* 79 (1), 34–42.

Murphy, P.E. and Pritchard, M. (1997) Destination price-value perceptions: An examination of origin and seasonal influences. *Journal of Travel Research* 35 (3), 16–22.

Murphy, P.E., Pritchard, M. and Smith, B. (2000) The destination product and its impact on traveller perceptions. *Tourism Management* 21 (1), 43–52.

Murphy, P.E., Andressen, B., Duffus, D., Hays, W., Newcomb, J., Nowell, D. and Searle, R. (1985) Geographers as assistants in a community decision-making process. *The Operational Geographer* 8, 55–7.

Mutch, A. (1996) The English tourist network automation project: A case study in interorganizational system failure. *Tourism Management* 17 (8), 603–9.

Nagel, T. (1987) *The Strategy and Tactics of Pricing.* Englewood Cliffs: Prentice-Hall.

Naisbitt, J. (1984) *Megatrends: Ten New Directions Transforming our Lives.* New York: Warner Books.

National Academy of Sciences, Oceans Study Board, Water Science and Technology Board, Division on Earth and Life Studies (2002). A Review of the Florida Keys Carrying Capacity Study. Washington, DC: National Academy Press.

National Native Title Tribunal (2003) Home Page. *NNTT. www.nntt.gov.au/* Accessed on 29 January 2003.

National Office for the Information Economy (2000) *Take the Plunge 2000: Sink or Swim?* Canberra, Australia: National Office for the Information Economy.

National Task Force on Tourism Data (1985) *Final Joint Report of the Working Groups on User Needs and Current Data Issues.* Ottawa: Statistics Canada.

Netter, E. (ed.) (1981) Land use law issues for the eighties. *Land Use Law and Zoning Digest.* Washington, DC: Planners Press, American Planning Association.

New Oregon Meridian (2001) *We Have Met the Enemy and he is us.* www.planneronline.homestead.com/files/pororeport.htm. Accessed on 5 December 2001.

Newsweek (1986) The fall of the wild. *Newsweek* 28 July, 52–4.

Newsweek (1988) Fighting for Yellowstone. *Newsweek*, 19 September, 18–20.

Newsweek (1994) Of mice and men. *Newsweek*, 5 September, 41–7.

Nickson, D. (2000) Human resource issues in travel and tourism. In Moutinho, L. (ed). *Strategic Management in Tourism* (pp. 169–85). Wallingford, Oxon: CABI Publishing.

Normann, R. (1991) *Service Management.* Chichester: John Wiley.

Normann, R. and Ramirez, R. (1993) From value chain to value constellation: designing interactive strategy. *Harvard Business Review* 71, 65–77.

Nozick, M. (1993) Five principles of sustainable community development. In E. Shragge (ed.) *Community Economic Development: In Search of Empowerment and Alternatives* (pp. 18–43). Montreal: Black Rose Books.

Oakes, T.S. (1997) Ethnic tourism in rural Guizhou: Sense of place and the commerce of authenticity. In M. Picard and R.E. Wood (eds) *Tourism, Ethnicity, and the State in Asian and Pacific Societies* (pp. 35–70). Honolulu: University of Hawaii Press.

O'Connor, N. and Flanagan, S. (2002) The sociological impacts of *Ballykissangel* on the village of Avoca, County Wicklow. In N. Andrews, F. Convery, S. Flanagan and J. Ruddy (eds) *Tourism and the Environment: Sustainability in Tourism Development* (pp. 255–65). Dublin: Dublin Institute of Technology.

Odum, E.P. (1970) The strategy of ecosystem development, *Science* 164, 262–70.

One Thousand Friends of Florida (2002) Building better communities. *1000 Friends of Florida*. http://www.1000fof.org/. Accessed on 18 December 2002.

Open Group (2002) Conduct a gap analysis. *Open Group*. http://www.opengroup.org/togaf/p2/ta/ta_gapan.htm. Accessed on 19 December 2002.

Oppermann, M. (1995) Holidays on the farm: A case study of German hosts and guests. *Journal of Travel Research* 34 (1), 63–72.

Organ, D.W. (1988) *Organizational Citizenship Behavior: The Good Soldier Syndrome.* Lexington, MA: Lexington Books.

O'Neill, T. (2002) Saving places. *National Geographic* 202 (4), 58–73.

O'Toole, T. with Tarling, L. (2000) *Bread Winner: A Fresh Approach to Rising to the Top.* Melbourne, Victoria: Information Australia.

Page, S.J., Farer, P. and Lawton, G.R. (1999) Small business development and tourism: *terra incognita*? *Tourism Management* 20 (4), 435–59.

Palmer, A. (1998) Evaluating the governance style of marketing groups. *Annals of Tourism Research* 25 (1) 185–201.

Palmer, A. and Bejou, D. (1995) Tourism destination marketing alliances. *Annals of Tourism Research* 22 (3), 616–29.

Parasuraman, A., Zeithaml, V.A. and Berry, L.L. (1985) A conceptual model of service quality and implications for future research. *Journal of Marketing* 49 (Fall), 41–50.

Parasuraman, A., Zeithaml, V.A. and Berry, L.L. (1988) SERVQUAL: A multiple item scale for measuring consumer perceptions of service quality. *Journal of Retailing* 64 (1),12–40.

Parasuraman, A., Zeithaml, V.A. and Berry, L.L. (1990) *Delivering Quality Service.* New York: Free Press.

Parasuraman, A., Zeithaml, V.A. and Berry, L.L. (1991) Refinement and reassessment of the SERVQUAL scale. *Journal of Retailing* 67 (4), 420–50.

Parker, S. (2000) Collaboration on tourism policy making: Environmental and commercial sustainability on Bonarie, NA. In B. Bramwell and B. Lane (eds) *Tourism Collaboration and Partnerships: Politics, Practice and Sustainability* (pp. 78–97). Clevedon, UK: Channel View Publications.

Patterson, L. (2003) State planning authority stumbles at first hurdle. *Echo* (Byron Shire). Thursday, 14 January, 17 (33), 1–2.

Pearce, D. (1989) *Tourist Development* (2nd edn). Harlow, UK: Longman.

Pearce, D. (1992) *Tourist Organizations.* Harlow, UK: Longman.

Pearce, P.L. (1982) *The Social Psychology of Tourist Behaviour.* Oxford: Pergamon.

Pearce, P.L. and Stringer, P.F. (1991) Psychology and tourism. *Annals of Tourism Research* 18 (1), 136–54.

Pearce, P.L., Moscardo, G. and Ross, G.F. (1996) *Tourism Community Relationships*. Oxford: Pergamon – Elsevier Science.

Pearce, P.L., Morrison, A.M. and Rutledge, J.L. (1998) *Tourism: Bridges Across Continents*. Sydney: McGraw-Hill.

Pearce, P.L. and Moscardo, G. (1999) Tourism community analysis: asking the right questions. In D.G. Pearce and R.W. Butler (eds) *Contemporary Issues in Tourism Development* (pp. 31–51). London and New York: Routledge.

Pedersen, K. and Viken, A. (1996) From Sami nomadism to global tourism. In M.F. Price (ed.) *People and Tourism in Fragile Environments* (pp. 69–88). Chichester, UK: John Wiley.

Perdue, R., Long, P. and Allen, L. (1987) Rural resident tourism perceptions and attitudes. *Annals of Tourism Research* 14 (3), 420–9.

Perdue, R., Long, P. and Allen, L. (1990) Resident support for tourism development. *Annals of Tourism Research* 17 (4), 586–99.

Peters, T.J. and Austin, N. (1985) *A Passion for Excellence*. New York: Random House.

Peters, T.J. and Waterman, R.H. (1984). *In Search of Excellence*. New York: Warner Books.

Peterson, D. (2002) *Florida Keys Carrying Capacity Study*. Department of the Army, Jacksonville District, 6 September 2002. Personal communication.

Phillips, P.A. and Moutinho, L. (2000) The strategic planning index: a tool for measuring strategic planning effectiveness. *Journal of Travel Research* 38 (4), 369–79.

Pine II, J.B. and Gilmore, J.H. (1999) *The Experience Economy*. Boston: MA: Harvard Business School Press.

Pizam, A., Tarlow, P.E. and Bloom, J. (1997) Making tourists feel safe: whose responsibility is it? *Journal of Travel Research* 36 (1), 23–8.

Plog, S.C. (1973) Why destination areas rise and fall in popularity. *Cornell Hotel and Restaurant Administration Quarterly*, November, 13–16.

Plog, S.C. (1998) Why destination preservation makes economic sense. In W.F. Theobald (ed.) *Global Tourism* (2nd edn) (pp. 251–66). Oxford: Butterworth-Heinemann.

Poon, A. (1993) *Tourism, Technology and Competitive Strategies*. Wallingford, Oxon: CAB International.

Porteous, J.D. (1973) The Burnside gang: territoriality, social space, and community planning. In C.N. Forward (ed.) *Residential and Neighbourhood Studies in Victoria* (pp. 130–48). Western Geographical Series, Vol. 5. Victoria, BC: University of Victoria.

Porter, M.E. (1980) *Competitive Strategy*. New York: Free Press.

Porter, M.E. (1990) *The Competitive Advantage of Nations*, New York: Free Press.

Porter, M.E. (1998) *On Competition*. Cambridge, MA: Harvard University Press.

Potts, F.C., Goodwin, H. and Walpole, M.J. (1996) People, wildlife and tourism in and around Hwange National Park, Zimbabwe. In M.F. Price (ed.) *People and Tourism in Fragile Environments* (pp. 199–220). Chichester, UK: John Wiley.

Potts, T.D. and Harrill, R. (1998) Enhancing communities for sustainability: A travel ecology approach. *Tourism Analysis* 3, 133–42.

Prentice, R. (1993) Community-driven tourism planning and residents' preferences. *Tourism Management* 14 (3), 218–27.

Price, G.C. (2003) Ecotourism and environmental learning: Opportunities and obstacles in the Australian milieu. Paper presented at Annual Council of Australian University Tourism and Hospitality Education (CAUTHE) Conference, Coffs Harbour, NSW, Australia.

Pritchard, M. and Swanson, W. (1993) *B.C. Tourism: 1993 Advertising Effectiveness Study*. Victoria, BC: Faculty of Business, University of Victoria.

Public Roads On-Line (Summer 1996) *Creating the Interstate System.* www.tfhrc. gov/pubrds/summer96/p96su10.htm. Accessed on 3 June 2001.

Putnam, R.D. (1993) *Making Democracy Work: Civic Traditions in Modern Italy,* Princeton, NJ: Princeton University Press.

Putnam, R.D. (2000) *Bowling Alone: The Collapse and Revival of American Community.* New York: Simon & Schuster.

Queen Charlotte Islands Information (2002) Welcome to the Queen Charlotte Islands/Haida Gwaii. *General Island Information.* www.qcinfo.com. Accessed on 1 January 2002.

Raiffa, H. (1982) *The Art and Science of Negotiation.* Cambridge, MA: Harvard University Press.

Randhawa, H. (1990) Out of the ashes: Rediscovering Yellowstone National Park. *Westworld,* September: 7–8.

Reed, M.G. (1996) Co-operative management of environmental resources: A case study from Northern Ontario, Canada. *Economic Geography,* 71, 132–49.

Reed, M.G. (1997) Power relations and community-based tourism planning. *Annals of Tourism Research* 24 (3), 556–91.

Reed, M.G. (2000) Collaborative tourism planning an adaptive experiment in emergent tourism settings, In B. Bramwell and B. Lane (eds) *Tourism Collaboration and Partnerships: Politics, Practice and Sustainability* (pp. 247–71). Clevedon, UK: Channel View Publications.

Richardson, J.T. (1996) *Marketing Australian Travel and Tourism,* Melbourne: Hospitality Press.

Richardson, J.L. (1997) Economics: Hegemonic Discourse, *Quadrant,* March, 52–60.

Richardson, J.L. (1999) *A History of Australian Travel and Tourism.* Melbourne: Hospitality Press.

Richins, H. (1997/98) Community tourism development scenarios and their use in tourism research. *Asia Pacific Journal of Tourism Research* 2 (1), 31–42.

Riley, M. (1995) Tourism development under close control: The case of the Falkland Islands. *Tourism Management* 16 (6), 471–74.

Ritchie, J.R.B. (1988) Consensus policy formation in tourism. Measuring resident views via survey research. *Tourism Management* 9, 199–212.

Ritchie, J.R.B. (1994) The nominal group technique – applications in tourism research. In J.R.B. Ritchie and C.R. Goeldner (eds) *Travel, Tourism, and Hospitality Research* (2nd edn) (pp. 493–501). New York: John Wiley.

Ritchie, J.R.B. (1999) Crafting a value-driven vision for a national tourism treasure. *Tourism Management* 20 (3), 273–82.

Ritchie, J.R.B. (2000) Interest based formulation of tourism policy for environmentally sensitive destinations. In B. Bramwell and B. Lane (eds) *Tourism Collaboration and Partnerships: Politics, Practice and Sustainability* (pp. 44–77). Clevedon, UK: Channel View Publications.

Ritchie, M. (2001) An assessment of the role and effectiveness of local government in tourism destination development: Case study of Nillumbik. Unpublished MA thesis. La Trobe University, Melbourne, Australia.

Robson, J. and Robson, I. (1996) From shareholders to stakeholders: Critical issues for tourism marketers. *Tourism Management* 17 (7), 533–40.

Rock, A. (1999) Strategy vs. tactics from a venture capitalist. In the *Harvard Business Review on Entrepreneurship.* Boston, MA: Harvard Business School Press, 135–47.

Roddick, A. (2000) *Business as Unusual.* London: Thorsons.

Roehl, W.S., Ditton, R.B. and Fesenmaier, D.R. (1989) Community-tourism ties. *Annals of Tourism Research* 16 (4), 504–13.

Rogers, M. (2001) Triple bottom line audit: A framework for community based action. In M.F. Rogers and Y.M.J. Collins (eds) *The Future of Australia's Country Towns* (pp. 135–45). Centre for Sustainable Regional Communities, La Trobe University, Bendigo, Victoria, Australia.

Rosenow, J.E. and Pulsipher, G.L. (1979) *Tourism: The Good, The Bad, and The Ugly.* Lincoln, NE: Century Three Press.

Ross, G.F. (1993) Ideal and actual images of backpacker visitors in northern Australia. *Journal of Travel Research.* Fall, 32 (2), 54–7.

Ross, G.F. (1994) *The Psychology of Tourism.* Melbourne: Hospitality Press.

Rothman, H.K. (1998) *Devil's Bargains.* Lawrence, KS: University Press of Kansas.

Runyan, D. (1977) Tools for community managed impact assessment. *AIP Journal – American Institute of Planners* 43 (2), 125–35.

Russell, R. and Faulkner, B. (1999) Movers and shakers: chaos makers in tourism development. *Tourism Management* 20 (4), 411–23.

Ryan, C. and Montgomery D. (1994) The attitudes of Bakewell residents to tourism and numbers in community responsive tourism. *Tourism Management* 15 (5), 358–69.

Sakal, M., Brown, J. and Mak, J. (2000) Population aging and Japanese international travel in the 21st century. *Journal of Travel Research* 38 (3), 212–30.

Saunders, R. (1995) *Conflict Resolution through Environmental Impact Assessment.* International Association of Impact Assessment Conference, Durban, South Africa. A version of this paper was also presented to the Environmental Defender's Office Conference on Commonwealth EIA in Sydney, October 1995, and was reprinted in 'Significant Environmental Speeches' Summer 1995/96.

Saunders, R. and Stephens, A. (1998). *Mount Stirling: political and environmental convergence for sustainable development.* Conference Paper, University of Manchester, October 1998 (subsequently reprinted with some editing in *Environmental Impact Assessment Review* 19 (3), 319–32.

Saporito, B. (2003) Can Wal-Mart get any bigger? *Time International,* 13 January 40–5.

Scace, R.C., Grifone, E. and Usher, R. (1992) *Ecotourism in Canada.* Canadian Environmental Advisory Council. Ottawa: Environment Canada.

Schein, E. (1992) *Organisational Culture and Leadership* (2nd edn). San Francisco: Jossey-Bass.

Schermerhorn, Jr, J.R., Hunt, J.G. and Osborn, R.N. (1995) *Basic Organizational Behavior.* New York: John Wiley.

Schonland, A. and Williams, P.W. (1996) Using the internet for travel and tourism survey research: experiences from the net traveller survey. *Journal of Travel Research* 35 (2), 81–7.

Schul, P. and Crompton, J.L. (1983) Search behaviour of international vacationers: travel-specific lifestyles and sociodemographic variables. *Journal of Travel Research* 22 (2), 25–30.

Schumpeter, J. (1934) *The Theory of Economic Development.* Cambridge, MA: Harvard University Press.

Schumpeter, J.A. (1951) Change and the entrepreneur. In R.V. Clemence (ed.) *Essays of J.A. Schumpeter.* Reading, MA: Addison-Wesley.

Schwilgin, F.A. (1973) *Town Planning Guidelines.* Ottawa: Department of Public Works.

Scottish Tourism Board (ND) *Tourism Framework for Action 2002–2005.* Scottish Executive.

Selin, S.W. (1993) Collaborative alliances: new interorganizational forms in tourism. *Journal of Travel and Tourism Marketing* 2 (2), 217–27.

Selin, S.W. and Beason, K. (1991a) Conditions facilitating collaborative tourism planning: a qualitative perspective. *Tourism: Building Credibility for a Credible Industry* (pp. 203–9). Proceedings of the Twenty Second Travel and Tourism Research Association, Long Beach, California.

Selin, S.W. and Beason, K. (1991b) Interorganizational relations in tourism. *Annals of Tourism Research* 18 (4), 639–52.

Selin, S.W. and Myers, N.A. (1998) Tourism marketing alliances: Member satisfaction and effectiveness attributes of a regional initiative. *Journal of Travel and Tourism Marketing* 7 (3), 79–94.

Service General Technical Report INT–176, Intermountain Forest and Range Experiment Station, Ogden, UT.

Shackelton, V. (1995) *Business Leadership*. London: Routledge.

Shapero, A. (1975) *Entrepreneurship and Economic Development*. Project ISEED, Ltd. Milwaukee, WI: Center for Venture Management.

Sharpley, R. and Sharpley, J. (1997) *Rural Tourism: An Introduction*. Oxford: Alden Press (International Thomson Business Press).

Shaw, G. and Williams, A.M. (1994) Tourism and entrepreneurship. In G. Shaw and A.M. Williams, *Critical Issues in Tourism: A Geographical Perspective* (pp. 120–37). Oxford: Blackwell.

Shaw, G. and Williams, A.M. (1994) *Critical Issues in Tourism: A Geographical Perspective*. Oxford: Blackwell.

Shaw, G. and Williams, A.M. (1997) The private sector: tourism entrepreneurship – a constraint or resource? In G. Shaw and A. Williams (eds) *The Rise and Fall of British Coastal Resorts: Cultural and Economic Perspectives*. London: Mansell.

Shaw, G. and Williams, A.M. (1998) Entrepreneurship, small business culture and tourism development. In D. Ioannides and K.G. Debbage (eds) *The Economic Geography of the Tourist Industry* (pp. 235–55). London: Routledge.

Sheldon, P.J. and Var, T. (1984) Resident attitudes to tourism in North Wales. *Tourism Management* 5 (1), 40–7.

Shivlani, M. (2000) *Monroe County's Registered Voters' Views on Tourism and Related Issues*. Marathon, FL: Growth Management Division, Monroe County.

Shostack, G.L. (1977) Breaking free for product marketing. *Journal of Marketing*, 41 (April), 73–8.

Simmons, D.G. (1994) Community participation in tourism planning. *Tourism Management* 15 (2), 98–108.

Smith, C. and Jenner, P. (1998) Tourism and the internet. *Travel and Tourism Analyst* 1, 62–81.

Smith, F.J. and Hester, R.T. (1982) *Community Goal Setting*. Stroudsburg, PA: Hutchinson Press.

Smith, S.L.J. (1995) *Tourism Analysis: A Handbook* (2nd edn). Harlow, Essex: Longman.

Smith, S.L.J. (2003a) A vision for the Canadian tourism industry. *Tourism Management* 24 (2), 123–34.

Smith, S.L.J. (2003b) The geographical structure of Canadian tourism. In J. Aramberri and R. Butler (eds) *Tourism Development: Issues for a Vulnerable Industry*. Clevedon, UK: Channel View Publications (forthcoming).

Smith, V.L. (ed.) (1989) *Hosts and Guests: The Anthropology of Tourism* (2nd edn). Philadelphia: University of Pennsylvania Press.

Smith, V.L. (1996) The Inuit as hosts: Heritage and wilderness tourism in Nunavut. In M.F. Price (ed.) *People and Tourism in Fragile Environments* (pp. 33–50). Chichester, UK: John Wiley.

Smith, V.L. and Brent, M. (eds) (2001) *Hosts and Guests Revisited: Tourism Issues of the 21st Century*. New York: Cognizant Communication Corp.

Spears, M.C. (1995) *Foodservice Organisations: A Managerial and Systems Approach* (3rd edn). Columbus, OH: Merrill.

Special Hilo/East Hawaii Tourism Group (1998) *Opportunities at Hand*. Hilo, HI: Office of the Governor.

Stahl, M.J. and Grigsby, D.W. (1992) *Strategic Management for Decision Making*. Boston: PWS-Kent.

Stankey, G.H., Cole, D.N., Lucas, R.C., Peterson, M.E., and Frissell, S.S. (1985) *The Limits of Acceptable Change (LAC) System for Wilderness Planning*. USDA Forest.

State of Alaska Division of Community and Economic Development (ND). *Alaska Community Tourism Handbook: How to Develop Tourism in Your Community*. Department of Community and Economic Development.

Stitt, A.J. (1998) *Alternative Dispute Resolution For Organizations: How to design a system for effective conflict resolution*. Toronto: John Wiley and Sons, Canada Ltd.

Stoner, J.A.F., Freeman, R.E. and Gilbert, Jr, D.R. (1995) *Management* (6th edn). Englewood Cliffs, NJ: Prentice-Hall.

Storey, D.J. (1994) *Understanding the Small Business Sector*. Routledge: London.

Strong, G. (2002) Struggling country towns use the toilet to make tourists spend a penny. *The Age* (Melbourne), 23 September, 6.

Suchman, M.C. (1994) Managing legitimacy: Strategic and institutional approaches. *Academy of Management Review* 20 (3), 571–610.

Sullivan, T. (1984) *Resolving Development Disputes Through Negotiation*. New York: Plenum Press.

Susskind, L. (2001) *Mediating Public Disputes Seminar*. RMIT University, Melbourne, Australia. Thursday, 15 March.

Susskind, L. and Cruikshank, J. (1987) *Breaking the Impasse: Consensual Approaches to Resolving Public Disputes*. New York: Basic Books.

Susskind, L. and Field, P. (1996) *Dealing with An Angry Public: The Mutual Gains Approach to Resolving Disputes*. New York: The Free Press.

Susskind, L., Amundsen, O., Matsuura, M., Kaplan, M. and Lampe, D. (1999) *Using Assisted Negotiation to Settle Land Use Disputes: A Guidebook for Public Officials Public Disputes*. Cambridge, MA: Lincoln Institute of Land Policy.

Susskind, L., McKearnan, S. and Thomas-Larmer, J. (1999) *The Consensus Building Handbook: A Comprehensive Guide to Reaching Agreement*. Thousand Oaks, CA: Sage Publications.

Suttles, G.D. (1970) *The Social Construction of Communities*. Chicago: University of Chicago Press.

Swarbrooke, J. (1999) *Sustainable Tourism Management*. New York: CABI Publishers.

Takeuchi, H. and Quelch, J. (1983) Quality is more than making a good product. *Harvard Business Review*, 61 (July-August), 139–45.

Tannenbaum, R., Weschler, L.R. and Massarik, F. (1961) *Leadership and Organization*. New York: McGraw-Hill.

Task Force on Regional Development (TFRD) (1993) *Developing Australia: A Regional Perspective*. Canberra: Australian Government Printing Office.

Taylor, G. (1995) The community approach: Does it really work? *Tourism Management* 16 (7), 487–9.

Taylor, G., Rogers, J. and Stanton, B. (1994) Bridging the research gap between industry and researchers. *Journal of Travel Research* 32 (4), 9–11.

Taylor, P. (1999) Business urged to get a connection as web turns out to be more than a fad. *The Financial Times*, 6 July, 14.

Teas, K. (1993) Expectations, performance evaluation and consumer perceptions of quality. *Journal of Marketing* 57 (4), 18–34.

Telfer, D.J. (2000) Tastes of Niagara: building strategic alliances between tourism and agriculture. *International Journal of Hospitality and Tourism Administration* 1 (1), 71–88.

Telfer, D.J. (2001) Strategic alliances along the Niagara Wine Route. *Tourism Management* 22 (1), 21–30.

The Age (2000) Reconciliation report urges treaty talks. *The Age* 7 December, 1.

The Economist (1988) National parks: Live and let die. *The Economist* 17 September, 34.

The Economist (1999) The Florida Keys: Death in the Afternoon. *The Economist* 11 September, 35–6.

The Economist (2000a) What price coral? *The Economist* 4–10 November, 103–6.

The Economist (2000b) Blackpool as Las Vegas. *The Economist* 26 August–1 September, 50.

The Economist (2000c) Tourism in South Africa: Image problem. *The Economist* 16–22 December, 75.

The Economist (2001a) Survey the Young: The kids are all right. *The Economist* 23–5 December, 4–6.

The Economist (2001b) Keeping the customer satisfied. *The Economist* 14 July, 9.

The Economist (2001c) A long march: Special report on mass customisation. *The Economist* 14 July, 63–5.

The Economist (2001d) Airlines: Flying blind. *The Economist* 13 October, 16–7.

The Economist (2001e) When Hawaii's loss is Tokyo's gain. *The Economist* 22 December, 79.

The Economist (2003a) Fear and management: When to terrorise the talent. *The Economist* 22 February, 59–60.

The Economist (2003b) SARS: A plague on all our businesses. *The Economist* 19 April, 51.

The Weekend Australian (2001) The green dream. *The Weekend Australian* August 18–19, R4-R5.

Thomas, R. (1998) Introduction. In R. Thomas (ed.) *The Management of Small Tourism and Hospitality Firms* (pp. 1–16). London: Cassell.

Thomas, R. (2000) Small firms in the tourism industry: Some conceptual issues. *International Journal of Tourism Research* 2 (5), 307–82.

Thompson, J.R. and Cooper, R.D. (1979) Additional evidence on the limited size of evoked and inept sets of travel destinations. *Journal of Travel Research* 18, 23–5.

Thompson, L. (2001) The long good buy: How to plan, fund, and complete a multijurisdictional recreation corridor. *Planning – American Planning Association* 67 (5), 4–9.

Thompson, W.N. (2003) History, development and legislation of Native American Casino Gaming. In C.H.C. Hsu (ed.) *Legalized Casino Gaming in the United States* (pp. 41–61). New York: Haworth Hospitality Press.

Tiegerman-Farber, E. and Radziewicz, C. (1998) *Collaborative Decision-making: The Pathway to Inclusion.* Upper Saddle River, NJ: Prentice-Hall.

Tierney, P. (2000) Internet based evaluation of tourism web site effectiveness: methodological issues and survey results. *Journal of Travel Research* 39 (2) 212–19.

Timmons, J. (1994) *New Venture Creation.* Boston, MA: Irwin.

Timothy, D.J. (1998) Cooperative tourism planning in a developing destination. *Journal of Sustainable Tourism* 6 (1), 52–68.

Timothy, D.J. (1999) Participatory planning: A view of tourism in Indonesia. *Annals of Tourism Research* 26 (2), 371–91.

Timothy, D.J. (2000) Cross-border partnership in tourism resource management: International parks along the U.S. Canada border. In B. Bramwell and B. Lane (eds) *Tourism Collaboration and Partnerships: Politics, Practice and Sustainability* (pp. 20–43). Clevedon, UK: Channel View Publications.

Tisdell, C.A. and Roy, K.C. (eds) (1998) *Tourism and Development: Economic, Social, Political and Environmental Issues*. Commack, New York: Nova Science Publishers.

Tonge, R. and Myott, D. (1993) *How to Plan, Develop and Market Local and Regional Tourism*. Coolum Beach, Queensland: Gull Publishing Pty Ltd.

Tosun, C. (2000) Limits to community participation in the tourism development process in developing countries. *Tourism Management* 21 (6), 613–33.

Tosun, C. and Jenkins, C.L. (1996) Regional planning approaches to tourism development: The case of Turkey. *Tourism Management* 17 (7), 519–31.

Tosun, C. and Jenkins, C.L. (1998) The evolution of tourism planning in third-world countries: A critique. *Progress in Tourism and Hospitality Research* 4, 101–14.

Tourism British Columbia (1995) *Towards a Tourism Growth Management Strategy*. Victoria, British Columbia: Ministry of Small Business, Tourism and Culture.

Tourism Concern (2000) *The Community Tourism Guide*. London: Earthscan.

Tourist Development Council (1999) *Approved Resident Survey*. Marathon, FL: Monroe County.

Tourism Forum (UK) ND. *Tomorrow's Tourism: A Growth Industry for the New Millennium*. Department for Culture, Media and Sport.

Tourism Queensland (2000) *Tourism Queensland 2000–2001 Annual Report*. Brisbane, Queensland: Tourism Queensland.

Tourism Tasmania (2002) Tourism Tasmania Board of Directors. *Tourism Tasmania Corporate*. http://www.tourismtasmania.com.au/org/board/index.html. Accessed on 18 December 2002.

Tourism Victoria (2002) *Victoria's Tourism Industry Strategic Plan, 2002–2006*, Melbourne, Australia: Tourism Victoria.

Tourism Victoria (1995) *Five Year Business Plan (1996–2000)*. Victoria, British Columbia, Canada: Tourism Victoria.

Tribe, J. (1997) The indiscipline of tourism. *Annals of Tourism Research* 24 (3), 638–57.

Trist, E.L. (1977) Collaboration in work settings: A personal perspective. *The Journal of Applied Behavioral Sciences* 13, 268–78.

Trist, E.L. (1988) Referent organizations and the development of interorganizational domains. *Human Relations* 36, 247–68.

Tyler, D. (1998) Getting tourism on the agenda: policy development in the London borough of Southwark. In Tyler, D., Guerrier, Y. and Robertson, M. (eds) *Managing Tourism in Cities* (pp. 45–64). Chichester: John Wiley.

Tyrangiel, J. and Nugent, B. (2002) 'Bono: The world's biggest rock star is also Africa's biggest advocate. But Bono knows he has to make the case for aid with his head, not his heart.' *Time International*. 4 March, 54–60.

UNESCO (1993). *World Heritage Newsletter*. No. 2. http://whc.unesco.org/news/2newsen.htm. Accessed on 15 November 2002.

US Army Corps of Engineers Jacksonville District. Florida Keys Carrying Capacity Study. [Online], Available: http://www.saj.usace.army.mil/projects/proj4.htm [August, 2002].

US Code (2001a) Title 22, Foreign Relations and Intercourse, Chapter 31, International Travel, Subchapter III, Administration, Section 2.124. Tourism Policy Council. *U.S. Code Online via GPO Access*. [cite: 22USC2124] www.wais.access.gpo.gov. Accessed on 25 September 2002.

US Code (2001b) Title 22, Foreign Relations and Intercourse, Chapter 31, International Travel, Subchapter III, Administration, Section 2.124c. Rural Tourism Development Foundation. *U.S. Code Online via GPO Access.* [cite: 22USC2124] www.wais.access.gpo.gov. Accessed on 25 September 2002.

US Code (2001c) Title 36, Parks, Forests and Public Property, Chapter 1, National Park Service Department of the Interior, Part 2, Resource Protection, Public Use and Recreation. *U.S. Code Online via GPO Access.* [cite: 36CFR2] www.wais. access.gpo.gov. Accessed on 25 September 2002.

US Senate (2001) *Travel America Now Act of 2001.* 107th Congress, 1st Session [cite: S1500IS] www.//thomas.loc.gov/cgi-bin/query . . . Accessed January 2002.

Urban Land Institute with Program for Community Problem Solving (1994). *Planning and Development Consensus – Building Manual.* Washington, DC: ULI.

Ury, W.L. and Smoke, R. (1985). Anatomy of a crisis. *Negotiation Journal* 1, 1.

Urry, J. (1990) *The Tourist Gaze,* London: Sage.

URS Greiner, Inc., 1999–2002. US 1 Travel Time and Delay Studies for Monroe County. Marathon, FL: Monroe County.

Van der Wagen, L. and Davies, C. (1998) *Supervision and Leadership.* Melbourne: Hospitality Press.

Vanhaverbeke, W. (2001) Realizing new regional core competencies: establishing a customer-oriented SME network. *Entrepreneurship and Regional Development* 13 (2), 97–116.

Van Tiggelen, J. (2001) Beyond the Big Koala: Teaching small towns how to cheat death (Lesson One: Turn the toilet block into a tourist attraction). *The Age – Good Weekend Magazine* (Melbourne). 5 May, 18–23.

Vesper, K.H. (1996) *New Venture Experience.* Seattle: Vector Books.

Waddock, S.A. and Bannister, B.D. (1991) Correlates of effectiveness and partner satisfaction in social partnerships. *Journal of Organizational Change Management* 4 (2), 74–89.

Wahab, S. (1975) *Tourism Management.* London: Tourism International Press.

Wahab, S. and Pigram, J.J. (eds) (1997) *Tourism, Development and Growth: The Challenge of Sustainability.* London: Routledge.

Wall, G. (1996) Perspectives on tourism in selected Balinese villages. *Annals of Tourism Research* 23 (1), 123–37.

Wall, G. and Dibnah, S. (1992) The changing status of tourism in Bali, Indonesia. *Progress in Tourism, Recreation and Hospitality Management* 4, 120–30.

Walle, A.H. (1995) Business ethics and tourism: from micro to macro perspectives. *Tourism Management* 16 (4), 263–8.

Walsh-Martin, M. (1998) *Making it Happen.* Melbourne: Scribe Publications.

Walz, S.M. and Niehoff, B.P. (2000) Organizational citizenship behaviors: their relationship to organizational effectiveness. *Journal of Hospitality and Tourism Research* 24 (3), 301–19.

Wanhill, S.R.C. (1996) Local enterprise development in tourism. *Tourism Management* 17 (1), 35–42.

Ward, S. (1998) Place marketing: A historical comparison of Britain and North America. In T. Hall and P. Hubbard (eds) *The Entrepreneurial City: Geographies of Politics, Regime and Representation* (pp. 31–53). New York, NY: John Wiley.

Warnken, J. and Buckley, R. (1996) Coastal tourism development as a test-bed for EIA triggers: Outcomes under mandatory and discretionary EIA frameworks. *Environment and Planning Law Journal* 13 (4), 239–45.

Warren, R.L. (1977) *Social Change and Human Purpose.* Chicago: Rand McNally.

Watkins, L. (1987) *Billion Dollar Miracle.* Auckland: Traveldigest.

Wearing, S. and McLean, J. (1998) *Developing Ecotourism: A Community Based Approach*. Williamstown, Victoria: HM Leisure Planning.

Wearing, S. and Neil, J. (1999) *Ecotourism: Impacts, Potentials and Possibilities*. Oxford: Butterworth-Heinemann.

Weaver, D.B. (2000) A broad context model of destination development scenarios. *Tourism Management* 21 (3), 217–24.

Weaver, D. and Opperman, M. (2000) *Tourism Management*. Milton Keys, Essex: John Wiley.

Weaver, G.D. (1986) *Tourism USA: Guidelines for Tourism Development*. Columbia, Missouri: University of Missouri-Columbia, Department of Recreation and Park Administration/Washington, DC: United States Travel and Tourism Administration.

Webler, T. (1995) Right discourse in citizen participation: An evaluative yardstick. In O. Renn, T. Webler and P. Wiedemann (eds) *Fairness and Competence in Citizen Participation: Evaluating Models for Environmental Discourse* (pp. 35–86). The Netherlands: Kluwer Academic Press.

Webster, M. (1998) Strategies for growth. In R. Thomas (ed.) *The Management of Small Tourism and Hospitality Firms* (pp. 208–18). London: Cassell.

Weiermair K. (1997) Service quality and its management in tourism enterprises. (Calidad de servicios y su gestion en las empresas turisticas). In Papers de Turisme, Fundacion de Cavanilles de Altos Estudios Turisticos (pp. 54–68). University of Alicante, Spain. No. 20.

West Central Community Futures Development Corporation (WCCFDC) (2002) *West Coast Community Futures Development Corporation* (pp. 1–2). www.agt.net/public/westcent. Accessed on 1 February.

Western Morning News (2001) *Welcome to Eden*. Plymouth: Western Morning News Company.

Wheatcroft, S. (1994) *Aviation and Tourism Policies: Balancing the Benefits: A World Tourism Organisation Publication*. London & New York: Routledge.

Wheeler, B. (1994) Egotourism, sustainable tourism and the environment – a symbiotic, symbolic or shambolic relationship. In A.V. Seaton (ed.) *Tourism: The State of the Art* (pp. 647–54). Chichester: John Wiley.

Wight, P. (1996) North American ecotourism markets: motivations, preferences and destinations. *Journal of Travel Research* 35 (1), 3–10.

Williams, A.M., Shaw, G. and Greenwood, J. (1989) From tourist to tourism entrepreneur, from consumption to production: evidence from Cornwall, England. *Environment and Planning A* 21, 1639–53.

Williams, J. and Lawson, R. (2001) Community issues and resident opinions of tourism. *Annals of Tourism Research* 28 (2), 269–90.

Williams, P.W. (1994) Frameworks for assessing tourism's environmental impacts. In J.R.B. Ritchie and C.R. Goeldner (eds) *Travel, Tourism, and Hospitality Research* (2nd edn) (pp. 425–36). New York: John Wiley.

Williams, P.W. and Gill, A. (1991) *Carrying Capacity Management in Tourism Settings: A Tourism Growth Management Process*, Centre for Tourism Policy and Research, Simon Fraser University, Vancouver, BC, Canada.

Williams, P.W. and Gill, A. (1998) Tourism carrying capacity management issues. In W. Theobald (ed.) *Global Tourism: The Next Decade* (2nd edn) (pp. 231–46). Oxford: Butterworth-Heinemann.

Winkle, G., Olson, R., Wheeler, F. and Cohen, M. (1976) *The Museum Visitor and Orientation Media: An Experimental Comparison of Different Approaches in the Smithsonian Institute and National Museum of History and Technology*. New York: City University of New York, Center for Environment and Behavior.

Wober, K. (1997) Local tourism organizations in European cities. In J.A. Mazanec (ed.) *International City Tourism* (pp. 3–12). London: Pinter.

Wober, K. (1997) Introducing a harmonization procedure for European City tourism statistics. In J.A. Mazanec (ed.) *International City Tourism* (pp. 26–38). London: Pinter.

Wood, W.A. (1991) Partnership in action – the Cowichan and Chemainus Valleys ecomuseum heritage region project. In R.S. Tabata, J. Yamashiro and G. Cherem (eds) *Joining Hands for Quality Tourism* (pp. 447–50). Proceedings of the Heritage Interpretation International Third Global Congress, Honolulu, Hawaii.

Wood, W. (1993) *The Making of a Heritage Region Ecomuseum.* Duncan, BC: The Cowichan and Chemainus Valleys Ecomuseum Society.

Woodley, A. (1992) Tourism and sustainable development: The community perspective. In J.G. Nelson, R. Butler and G. Wall (eds) *Tourism and Sustainable Development: Monitoring, Planning and Managing* (pp. 135–47). Waterloo, Ontario: Heritage Resources Centre, University of Waterloo.

Woodside, A.G. and Wilson, E.J. (1985) Effects of consumer awareness of brand advertising on preference. *Journal of Advertising Research*, 25, 44–53.

Woodside, A.G. and Carr, J.A. (1988) Consumer decision making and competitive marketing strategies: applications for tourism planning. *Journal of Travel Research* 26 (3) 2–7.

Woodside, A.G. and Lysonski, S. (1989) A general model of traveler destination choice. *Journal of Travel Research* 17 (Spring) 8–14.

World Tourism Organisation (1991) *Resolutions of International Conference on Travel and Tourism* (Recommendation No. 29). Ottawa, Canada.

World Tourism Organisation (1993) *Indicators for the Sustainable Management of Tourism.* Winnipeg: International Institute for Sustainable Development.

World Tourism Organisation (1999) *Global Code of Ethics for Tourism.* www.world-tourism.org/projects/ethics/ethics.htm. Accessed on 23 April 2003.

World Tourism Organisation (2002) Tourism stalls in 2001. *News Releases. www.world-tourism.org/market_research/recovery/background.htm.* Accessed on 8 August 2002.

World Travel and Tourism Council (1999) www.wttc.org/economic_research/keystats.htm. Accessed on 31 July 2000.

Yip, G.S. (1985) Who needs strategic planning? *The Journal of Business Strategy* 6 (Fall) 30–41.

Yoon, T. and Ekinci, Y. (2001) An examination of the SERVQUAL scale using the Guttman scaling procedure. In *2001 – A Tourism Odyssey: 32nd Annual Conference Proceedings Travel and Tourism Research Association Annual* (pp. 399–406). 10–13 June 2001, Fort Myers, FL.

Zeithaml, V., Parasuraman, A. and Berry, L.L. (1990) *Delivering Quality Service: Balancing Customer Perceptions and Expectations.* New York: Free Press.

Zenzen, J.M. (1998) *Battling for Manassas: The Fifty-Year Preservation Struggle at Manassas National Battlefield Park.* University Park Pennsylvania: The Pennsylvania State University Press.

Zhang, Y. (2001) A comparative examination of the diffusion of international tourism in Yunnan (PRC) and Victoria (Australia). Unpublished MA thesis, School of Tourism and Hospitality, La Trobe University, Australia.

Index

NB. Page numbers in italic refer to illustrations.